GO!

Learn | Practice | Succeed

Microsoft®
Office 365®

2019 Edition

Shelley
Gaskin | Alicia
Vargas | Debra
Geoghan | Nancy
Graviett

Series Editor: Shelley Gaskin

Pearson

VP Courseware Portfolio Management: Andrew Gilfillan
Executive Portfolio Manager: Jenifer Niles
Team Lead, Content Production: Laura Burgess
Content Producer: Shannon LeMay-Finn
Development Editor: Ginny Munroe
Portfolio Management Assistant: Bridget Daly
Director of Product Marketing: Brad Parkins
Director of Field Marketing: Jonathan Cottrell
Product Marketing Manager: Heather Taylor
Field Marketing Manager: Bob Nisbet
Product Marketing Assistant: Liz Bennett
Field Marketing Assistant: Derrica Moser
Senior Operations Specialist: Diane Peirano

Senior Art Director: Mary Seiner
Interior and Cover Design: Pearson CSC
Cover Photo: Jag_cz/Shutterstock, everything possible/Shutterstock
Senior Product Model Manager: Eric Hakanson
Manager, Digital Studio: Heather Darby
Digital Content Producer, MyLab IT: Becca Golden
Course Producer, MyLab IT: Amanda Losonsky
Digital Studio Producer: Tanika Henderson
Full-Service Project Management: Pearson CSC, Katie Ostler
Composition: Pearson CSC
Printer/Binder: LSC Communications, Inc.
Cover Printer: LSC Comunications, Inc.

Credits and acknowledgments borrowed from other sources and reproduced, with permission, in this textbook appear on appropriate page within text.

Google and the Google logo are registered trademarks of Google LLC, used with permission. Found on pages: 124, 147, 220, 270, 279, 293, 347, 368.

Microsoft and/or its respective suppliers make no representations about the suitability of the information contained in the documents and related graphics published as part of the services for any purpose. all such documents and related graphics are provided "as is" without warranty of any kind. microsoft and/or its respective suppliers hereby disclaim all warranties and conditions with regard to this information, including all warranties and conditions of merchantability, whether express, implied or statutory, fitness for a particular purpose, title and non-infringement. in no event shall Microsoft and/or its respective suppliers be liable for any special, indirect or consequential damages or any damages whatsoever resulting from loss of use, data or profits, whether in an action of contract, negligence or other tortious action, arising out of or in connection with the use or performance of information available from the services.

The documents and related graphics contained herein could include technical inaccuracies or typographical errors. changes are periodically added to the information herein. microsoft and/or its respective suppliers may make improvements and/or changes in the product(s) and/or the program(s) described herein at any time. partial screen shots may be viewed in full within the software version specified.

Microsoft® and Windows® are registered trademarks of the Microsoft Corporation in the U.S.A. and other countries. Screenshots and icons reprinted with permission from the Microsoft Corporation. This book is not sponsored or endorsed by or affiliated with the Microsoft Corporation.

Library of Congress Cataloging-in-Publication Data

On file with the Library of Congress.

2 2019

 **Pearson**

ISBN-10: 0-13-567279-1
ISBN-13: 978-0-13-567279-2

Brief Contents

Table of Contents

INTRODUCTION TO
Microsoft Word 2019   101

INTRODUCTION TO
Microsoft Excel 2019   169

INTRODUCTION TO

Microsoft Access 2019   241

Chapter 1   Getting Started with Microsoft Access 2019   243

INTRODUCTION TO

Microsoft PowerPoint 2019   319

Chapter 1 Getting Started with Microsoft PowerPoint 321

About the Authors

Shelley Gaskin, Series Editor, is a professor in the Business and Computer Technology Division at Pasadena City College in Pasadena, California. She holds a bachelor's degree in Business Administration from Robert Morris College (Pennsylvania), a master's degree in Business from Northern Illinois University, and a doctorate in Adult and Community Education from Ball State University (Indiana). Before joining Pasadena City College, she spent 12 years in the computer industry, where she was a systems analyst, sales representative, and director of Customer Education with Unisys Corporation. She also worked for Ernst & Young on the development of large systems applications for their clients. She has written and developed training materials for custom systems applications in both the public and private sector, and has also written and edited numerous computer application textbooks.

This book is dedicated to my husband Fred, and to my students, who inspire me every day.

Alicia Vargas is a faculty member in Business Information Technology at Pasadena City College. She holds a master's and a bachelor's degree in business education from California State University, Los Angeles, and has authored several textbooks and training manuals on Microsoft Word, Microsoft Excel, and Microsoft PowerPoint.

This book is dedicated with all my love to my husband Vic, who makes everything possible; and to my children Victor, Phil, and Emmy, who are an unending source of inspiration and who make everything worthwhile.

Debra Geoghan is a Professor of Computer Science in the STEM department at Bucks County Community College, teaching computer classes ranging from basic computer literacy to cybercrime, computer forensics, and networking. She has certifications from Microsoft, CompTIA, and Apple. Deb has taught at the college level since 1996 and also spent 11 years in the high school classroom. She holds a B.S. in Secondary Science Education from Temple University and an M.A. in Computer Science Education from Arcadia University.

Throughout her teaching career Deb has worked with educators to integrate technology across the curriculum. At BCCC she serves on many technology committees, presents technology workshops for BCCC faculty, and heads the Computer Science Area. Deb is an avid user of technology, which has earned her the nickname "gadget lady."

This book is dedicated to my colleagues and students at Bucks County Community College: for your suggestions and encouragement throughout this process. You inspire me every day. And most importantly—my family. My husband and sons for your patience, help, and love— I couldn't have done this without your love and support.

Nancy Graviett is a professor and department chair in Business Technology at St. Charles Community College in Cottleville, Missouri. She holds a bachelor's degree in marketing and a master's degree in business education from the University of Missouri and has completed a certificate in online education. Nancy has authored textbooks on WordPerfect, Google, Microsoft Outlook, and Microsoft Access.

This book is dedicated to my husband, Dave, and my children, Matthew and Andrea. I cannot thank my family enough for the love and support they share everyday.

Introducing seamless digital instruction, practice, and assessment

Using GO! with MyLab IT has never been better! With the integrated etext and pre-built learning modules, instructors can assign learning easily and students can get started quickly.

▶ **Proven content and pedagogical approach of *guided instruction, guided practice, and mastery*** is effective for all types of learners and all types of course delivery—face-to-face in the classroom, online, and hybrid.

▶ **Students learn Microsoft Office skills by creating practical projects** they will see in their academic and professional lives.

▶ **With GO! MyLab IT students can learn, practice, and assess live or in authentic simulations of Microsoft Office.**

- **Microsoft Office autograded Grader** projects for the instructional, mastery, and assessment projects allow students to work live in Excel, Word, Access, or PPT so that during each step of the learning process, they can receive immediate, autograded feedback!
- **Microsoft Office authentic simulations** allow students to practice what they are learning in a safe environment with learning aids for instant help—*Read*, *Watch*, or *Practice*. Authentic simulations can also be used for assessment without learning aids.

What's New?

- The **book (print or etext) is the student's guide** to completing all autograded Grader projects for instruction, practice, and assessment.
- The **GO! *Learn How* videos**, integrated in the etext, give students an instructor-led, step-by-step guide through the A & B projects.
- **Improved business case connection** throughout the instruction so students always understand the *what* and *why*.
- **Mac tips** are woven into the instruction for each project so Mac students can proceed successfully.
  - All text and Grader projects created and tested by the authors on both a Mac and a PC.
  - Content not limited by Mac compatibility! Everything students need to know for MOS exams, Excel, and Access that are not possible on the Mac are still covered!
- **MyLab IT Prebuilt Learning modules** make course setup a snap. The modules are based on research and customer use, and can be easily customized to meet your course requirements.
- **Critical Thinking assessments and badges** expand coverage of Employability Skills.
- **New combined Office Features and Windows chapter** with Grader projects and auto-graded Windows projects for a fast and concise overview of these important features. Shorter and easier to assign.

- **Regular content updates to stay current with Office 365** updates and new features:
  - New *Semester Updates* for the etext and Grader projects through MyLab IT
  - New *Lessons on the GO!* to help you teach new features

What's New for Grader Projects

- **Autograded *Integrated Projects*** covering Word, Excel, Access, and PPT.
- Projects **A & B Grader reports now include *Learning Aids*** for immediate remediation.
- Autograded Critical Thinking Quizzes and Badges
  - Critical Thinking Modules include a Capstone and Quiz that enable students to earn a Critical Thinking Badge
  - Critical Thinking quizzes for the A & B instructional projects
- A **final output image** is provided so students can visualize what their solution should look like.
- **Mac Compatibility:** All Grader projects are built for PC and Mac users, excluding Access. Only projects that have features not supported on the Mac are not 100% compatible.

What's New for Simulations

- Simulations are updated by the authors for improved reinforcement of the software navigation in each instructional project—as always, they are matched one-to-one with the text Activities.
- *Student Action Visualization* provides an immediate playback for review by students and instructors when there's a question about why an action is marked as incorrect.

The Program

The GO! series has been used for over 17 years to teach students Microsoft Office successfully because of the *Quality of Instruction, Ease of Implementation*, and *Excellence in Assessment*. Using the hallmark Microsoft Procedural Syntax and Teachable Moment approach, students understand how to navigate the Microsoft Office ribbon so they don't get lost, and they get additional instruction and tips *when* they need them. Learning by doing is a great approach for skill-based learning, and creating a real-world document, spreadsheet, presentation, or database puts the skills in context for effective learning!

To improve student results, we recommend pairing the text content with **MyLab IT,** which is the teaching and learning platform that empowers you to reach every student. By combining trusted author content with digital tools and a flexible platform, MyLab personalizes the learning experience and will help your students learn and retain key course concepts while developing skills that future employers are seeking in their candidates.

Solving Teaching and Learning Challenges

The GO! series continues to evolve based on author interaction and experience with real students. GO! is written to ensure students know where they are going, how to get there, and why. Today's software is cloud based and changes frequently, so students need to know how the software functions so they can adapt quickly.

Each chapter is written with two instructional projects organized around **student learning outcomes** and **numbered objectives,** so that students understand what they will learn and be able to do when they finish the chapter. The **project approach** clusters the learning objectives around the projects rather than around the software features. This tested pedagogical approach teaches students to solve real problems as they practice and learn the software features. By using the textbook (print or digital), students can complete the A & B instructional projects as autograded Grader projects in MyLab IT. The *Learn How* videos, integrated in the etext or learning modules, give students an instructor-led, step-by-step guide through the project. This unique approach enhances learning and engages students because they receive immediate feedback. Additionally, students can practice the skills they are learning in the MyLab IT simulations, where they also get immediate feedback and help when needed! Both *Graders* and *Simulations* are available in assessment form so that students can demonstrate mastery.

The **Clear Instruction** in the project steps is written following *Microsoft Procedural Syntax* to guide students where to go and *then* what to do, so they never get lost! With the **Teachable Moment** approach, students learn important concepts when they need to as they work through the instructional projects. No long paragraphs of text. And with the integrated etext in MyLab IT, students can access their book anywhere, anytime.

The page design drives effective learning; textbook pages are clean and uncluttered, with screenshots that validate the student's actions and engage visual learners. Important information is boxed within the text so that students won't miss or skip the *Mac Tips, Another Way, By Touch, Note, Alert,* or *More Knowledge* details. **Color-Coded Steps** guide students through the projects with colors coded by project and the **End-of-Project Icon** helps students know when they have completed the project, which is especially useful in self-paced or online environments.

Students can engage in a wide variety of end-of-chapter projects where they apply what they learned in outcomes-based, problem-solving, and critical thinking projects—many of which require students to create a complete project from scratch.

Within the GO! etext and MyLab IT, students also have access to the *GO! Learn How* training videos, the *GO! to Work* videos (which demonstrate how Microsoft Office is used in a variety of jobs), the GO! for Job Success videos (which teach essential employability skills), and the *Where We're Going* videos, which provide a clear and concise overview of the instructional projects to ensure student success!

This complete, highly effective offering ensures students can learn the skills they need to succeed!

Developing Employability Skills

For students to succeed in a rapidly changing job market, they should be aware of their career options and how to go about developing a variety of skills. With MyLab IT and GO! we focus on developing these skills in the following ways:

High-Demand Office Skills are taught to help students gain these skills and prepare for the Microsoft Office Specialist (MOS) certification exams. The MOS objectives are covered throughout the content and highlighted with the MOS icons.

Essential Employability Skills are taught throughout the chapters using GO! for Job Success Videos and discussions, along with the new Critical Thinking badge students can earn by successfully completing the Critical Thinking Modules.

Employability Skills Matrix (ESM)							
	Grader Projects	Project K	Project M	Project O Group Project	Critical Thinking Projects and Badge	GO! To Work and Job Success Videos	MOS Practice Exams	MOS Badges
Critical Thinking	x	x	x		x		x	x
Communication	x			x		x		
Collaboration				x		x		
Knowledge Application and Analysis	x	x	x		x		x	x
Social Responsibility						x		

Real-World Projects and GO! To Work Videos

The projects in GO! help you learn skills you'll need in the work-force and everyday life. And the GO! to Work videos give you insight into how people in a variety of jobs put Microsoft Office into action every day.

Projects in GO! are real-world projects you create from start to fin-ish, so that you are using the software features and skills as you will on the job and in everyday life.

GO! to Work videos feature people from a variety of real jobs explaining how they use Microsoft Office every day to help you see the relevance of learning these programs.

GO! for Job Success Videos and Discussions

Important professional skills you need to succeed in a work environment, such as Accepting Criticism, Customer Service, and Interview Skills, are covered in a video with discussion questions or an overall discussion topic. These are must-have skills.

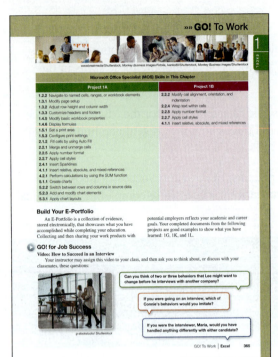

Skills Badging

Within MyLab IT 2019, you can earn digital badges that demonstrate mastery of specific skills related to Office 2019 or Critical Thinking. These badges can be easily shared across social networks, such as LinkedIn, leading to real opportunities to connect with potential employers.

Applied Learning Opportunities

Throughout the chapters there are two projects for instruction, two for review, and a variety of outcomes-based projects to demonstrate mastery, critical thinking, and problem solving. In addition, within MyLab IT, GO! Learn How videos walk students through the A & B instructional project objectives. Grader projects and simulations provide hands-on instruction, training, and assessment.

▼ Live-in-the-Application Grader Projects

The MyLab IT Grader projects are autograded so students receive immediate feedback on their work. By completing these projects, students gain real-world context as they work live in the application, to learn and demonstrate an understanding of how to perform specific skills to complete a project.

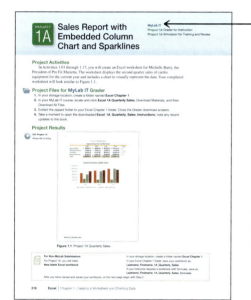

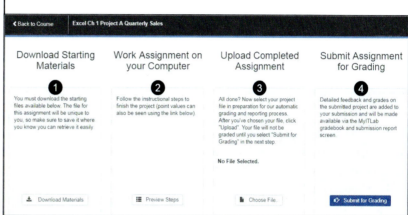

▼ Microsoft Office Simulations

The realistic and hi-fidelity simulations help students feel like they are working in the real Microsoft applications and enable them to explore, use 96% of Microsoft methods, and do so without penalty.

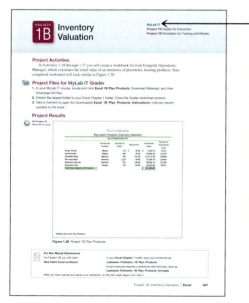

Instructor Teaching Resources

This program comes with the following teaching resources.

Resources available to instructors at www.pearsonhighered.com/go	Features of the Resources
Annotated Instructor Edition Tabs	Available for each chapter and include: • Suggested course implementation strategies and resources for the instructional portion of the chapter • Suggested strategies and resources for the Review, Practice, and Assessment portion of the chapter • Teaching tips
Annotated Solution Files	Annotated solution files in PDF feature callouts to enable easy grading.
Answer Keys for Chapter, MOS, and Critical Thinking Quizzes	Answer keys for each matching and multiple choice question in the chapter.
Application Capstones	Capstone projects for Word, Excel, Access, and PowerPoint that cover the objectives from all three chapters of each application. These are available as autograded Grader projects in MyLab IT, where students can also earn a proficiency badge if they score 90% or higher.
Collaborative Team Project	An optional exercise to assign to students to learn to work in groups.
Content Updates	A living document that features any changes in content based on Microsoft Office 365 changes as well as any errata.
Critical Thinking Quiz and Answers	Additional quiz and answers.
End-of-Chapter Online Projects H-J and M-O	Additional projects that can be assigned at instructor discretion.
Image Library	Every image in the book.
Instructor Manual	Available for each chapter and includes: • Suggested course implementation strategies and resources for the instructional portion of the chapter • Suggested strategies and resources for the Review, Practice, and Assessment portion of the chapter • Objectives • Teaching notes • Discussion questions
List of Objectives and Outcomes	Available for each chapter to help you determine what to assign • Includes every project and identifies which outcomes, objectives, and skills are included from the chapter
Lessons on the GO!	Projects created to teach new features added to Office 365. Available online only.
MOS Mapping and Additional Content	Based on the Office 2019 MOS Objectives • Includes a full guide of where each objective is covered in the textbook. • For any content not covered in the textbook, additional material is available in the Online Appendix document.
PowerPoint Presentations	PowerPoints for each chapter cover key topics, feature key images from the text, and include detailed speaker notes in addition to the slide content. PowerPoints meet accessibility standards for students with disabilities. Features include, but are not limited to: • Keyboard and screen reader access • Alternative text for images • High color contrast between background and foreground colors Audio PPTs contain spoken audio within traditional PowerPoint presentations.
Prepared Exams by Project, Chapter, and Application	An optional exercise that can be used to assess students' ability to perform the skills from each project, chapter, or across all chapters in an application • Each Prepared Exam folder includes the needed data files, instruction file, solution, annotated solution, and scorecard.

Resources available to instructors at www.pearsonhighered.com/go	Features of the Resources
Scorecards and Rubrics	Scorecards allow for easy scoring when hand-grading projects with definitive solutions. Rubrics are for projects without a definitive solution. These are available in Microsoft Word format, enabling instructors to customize the assignments for their classes.
Scripted Lectures	A lecture guide that provides the actions and language to help instructors demonstrate skills from the chapter.
Skills and Procedures Summary Charts	Concise list of key skills, including software icon and keyboard shortcut.
Solution Files, Solution File PDFs, and Solution Files with Formulas (Excel only)	Available for all exercises with definitive solutions.
Student Assignment Trackers	Document with a grid of suggested student deliverables per chapter that can be provided to students with columns for Due Date, Possible Points, and Actual Points.
Student Data Files	Files that students need to complete projects that are not delivered as Grader projects in MyLab IT.
Syllabus Template	Syllabus templates set up for 8-week, 12-week, and 16-week courses.
TestGen and Test Bank	TestGen enables instructors to: • Customize, save, and generate classroom tests • Edit, add, or delete questions from the Test Item Files • Analyze test results • Organize a database of tests and student results. The Test Gen contains approximately 75–100 total questions per chapter, made up of multiple-choice, fill-in-the blank, true/false, and matching. Questions include these annotations: • Correct answer • Difficulty level • Learning objective Alternative versions of the Test Bank are available for the following LMS: Blackboard CE/Vista, Blackboard, Desire2Learn, Moodle, Sakai, and Canvas.
Transition Guide	A detailed spreadsheet that provides a clear mapping of content from GO! Microsoft Office 2016 to GO! Microsoft Office 365, 2019 Edition.

Reviewers of the GO! Series

Carmen Montanez	Allan Hancock College	Therese ONeil	Indiana University of Pennsylvania
Jody Derry	Allan Hancock College	Bradley Howard	Itawamba Community College
Roberta McDonald	Anoka-Ramsey Community College	Edna Tull	Itawamba Community College
Paula Ruby	Arkansas State University	Pamela Larkin	Jefferson Community and Technical College
Buffie Schmidt	Augusta University	Sonya Shockley	Madisonville Community College
Julie Lewis	Baker College	Jeanne Canale	Middlesex Community College
Melanie Israel	Beal College	John Meir	Midlands Technical College
Suzanne Marks	Bellevue College	Robert Huyck	Mohawk Valley Community College
Ellen Glazer	Broward College	Mike Maesar	Montana Tech
Charline Nixon	Calhoun Community College	Julio Cuz	Moreno Valley College
Joseph Cash	California State University, Stanislaus	Lynn Wermers	North Shore Community College
Shaun Sides	Catawba Valley Community College	Angela Mott	Northeast Mississippi Community College
Linda Friedel	Central Arizona College	Connie Johnson	Owensboro Community & Technical College
Vicky Semple	Central Piedmont Community College	Kungwen Chu	Purdue University Northwest
Amanda Davis	Chattanooga State Community College	Kuan Chen	Purdue University Northwest
Randall George	Clarion University of Pennsylvania	Janette Nichols	Randolph Community College
Beth Zboran	Clarion University of Pennsylvania	Steven Zhang	Roane State Community College
Lee Southard	College of Coastal Georgia	Elizabeth Drake	Santa Fe College
Susan Mazzola	College of the Sequoias	Sandy Keeter	Seminole State
Vicki Brooks	Columbia College	Pat Dennis	South Plains College
Leasa Richards-Mealy	Columbia College	Tamara Dawson	Southern Nazarene University
Heidi Eaton	Elgin Community College	Richard Celli	SUNY Delhi
Ed Pearson	Friends University	Lois Blais	Walters State Community College
Nancy Woolridge	Fullerton College	Frederick MacCormack	Wilmington University
Wayne Way	Galveston College	Jessica Brown	Wilmington University
Leslie Martin	Gaston College	Doreen Palucci	Wilmington University
Don VanOeveren	Grand Rapids Community College	Rebecca Anderson	Zane State College

Microsoft Office Features and Windows 10 File Management

1

OFFICE AND WINDOWS

PROJECT 1A

Outcomes
Use the features common across all Microsoft Office applications to create and save a Microsoft Word document.

Objectives
1. Explore Microsoft Office
2. Create a Folder for File Storage
3. Download and Extract Zipped Files, Enter and Edit Text in an Office Application, and use Editor to Check Documents
4. Perform Office Commands and Apply Office Formatting
5. Finalize an Office Document
6. Use the Office Help Features

PROJECT 1B

Outcomes
Use Windows 10 features and the File Explorer program to manage files and folders.

Objectives
7. Explore Windows 10
8. Prepare to Work with Folders and Files
9. Use File Explorer to Extract Zipped Files and to Display Locations, Folders, and Files
10. Start Programs and Open Data Files
11. Create, Rename, and Copy Files and Folders

Petar Djordjevic/Shutterstock

In This Chapter

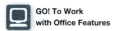

GO! To Work
with Office Features

In this chapter, you will practice using the features of Microsoft Office that work similarly across Word, Excel, Access, and PowerPoint. These features include performing commands, adding document properties, applying formatting to text, and searching for Office commands quickly. You will also practice using the file management features of Windows 10 so that you can create folders, save files, and find your documents easily.

The projects in this chapter relate to the **Bell Orchid Hotels**, headquartered in Boston, and which own and operate restaurants, resorts, and business-oriented hotels. Resort property locations are in popular destinations, including Honolulu, Orlando, San Diego, and Santa Barbara. The resorts offer deluxe accommodations and a wide array of dining options. Other Bell Orchid hotels are located in major business centers and offer the latest technology in their meeting facilities. Bell Orchid offers extensive educational opportunities for employees. The company plans to open new properties and update existing properties over the next decade.

Chef Notes

Project Activities

In Activities 1.01 through 1.19, you will create a handout for the Executive Chef at Skyline Metro Grill to give to her staff at a meeting where they will develop new menu ideas for wedding rehearsal dinners. The restaurant is located within Bell Orchid's San Diego resort hotel. Your completed notes will look similar to Figure 1.1.

Project Files for **MyLab IT Grader**

1. For Project 1A, you will start with a blank Word document, and then you will learn how to create a folder for your MyLab IT files as you work through the Project instruction. At the appropriate point in the Project, you will be instructed to download your files from your MyLab IT course.

Project Results

GO! Project 1A

Where We're Going

Figure 1.1 (Wavebreakmedia/Shutterstock)

For Non-MyLab Submissions　　　　　　**Start with a blank Word document**

For Project 1A, you will begin with a blank Word document and then learn how to create a folder and save a Word document as you work through the Project instruction.

N O T E   If You Are Using a Touch Screen

Tap an item to click it.

Press and hold for a few seconds to right-click; release when the information or commands display.

Touch the screen with two or more fingers and then pinch together to zoom out or stretch your fingers apart to zoom in.

Slide your finger on the screen to scroll—slide left to scroll right and slide right to scroll left.

Slide to rearrange—similar to dragging with a mouse.

Swipe to select—slide an item a short distance with a quick movement—to select an item and bring up commands, if any.

Objective 1   Explore Microsoft Office

ALERT   Because Office 365 is a cloud-based subscription service that receives continuous updates, you may encounter some variations in what appears on your screen and what is shown in this instruction. Microsoft Office 365 is fully installed on your PC or Mac; no internet access is necessary to create or edit documents. When you *are* connected to the internet, you will receive monthly upgrades and new features, so you always have the latest versions of Office apps as soon as they are available. Your subscription gives you continuous free access to the latest innovations and refinements.

ALERT   Is Your Screen More Colorful and a Different Size Than the Figures in This Textbook?

Your installation of Microsoft Office may use the default Colorful theme, where the ribbon in each application is a vibrant color and the title bar displays with white text. In this textbook, figures shown use the White theme, but you can be assured that all the commands are the same. You can keep your Colorful theme, or if you prefer, you can change your theme to White to match the figures here. To do so, open any application and display a new document. On the ribbon, click the File tab, and then on the left, click Options. With General selected on the left, under Personalize your copy of Microsoft Office, click the Office Theme arrow, and then click White. Change the Office Background to No Background. (In macOS, display the menu bar, click the application name—Word, Excel, and so on—click Preferences, and then click General. Under Personalize, click the Office Theme arrow to select either Colorful or Classic.)

Additionally, the figures in this book were captured using a screen resolution of 1280 x 768. If that is not your screen resolution, your screen will closely resemble, but not match, the figures shown. To view or change your screen's resolution, on the desktop, right-click in a blank area, click Display settings, click the Resolution arrow, and then select the resolution you want.

GO! Learn How
Video OF1-1

The term *desktop application* or *desktop app* refers to a computer program that is installed on your PC and that requires a computer operating system such as Microsoft Windows to run. The programs in Office 365 and in Microsoft Office 2019 are considered to be desktop apps. A desktop app typically has hundreds of features and takes time to learn.

Activity 1.01 | Exploring Microsoft Office

1 On the computer you are using, start Microsoft Word, and then compare your screen with Figure 1.2.

Depending on which operating system you are using and how your computer is set up, you might start Word from the taskbar or from the Start menu. On an Apple Mac computer, you might start the program from the Dock.

On the left, the Home tab is active in this view, referred to as *Backstage view*, which is a centralized space for all your file management tasks such as opening, saving, printing, publishing, or sharing a file—all the things you can do *with* a file. In macOS the File tab is on the menu bar.

Documents that you have recently opened, if any, display under the Recent tab. You can also click the Pinned tab to see documents you have pinned there, or you can click the Shared with Me tab to see documents that have been shared with you by others.

On the left, you can click New to find a *template*—a preformatted document that you can use as a starting point and then change to suit your needs. Or you can click Open to navigate to your files and folders. You can also look at Account information, give feedback to Microsoft, or look at the Word Options dialog box.

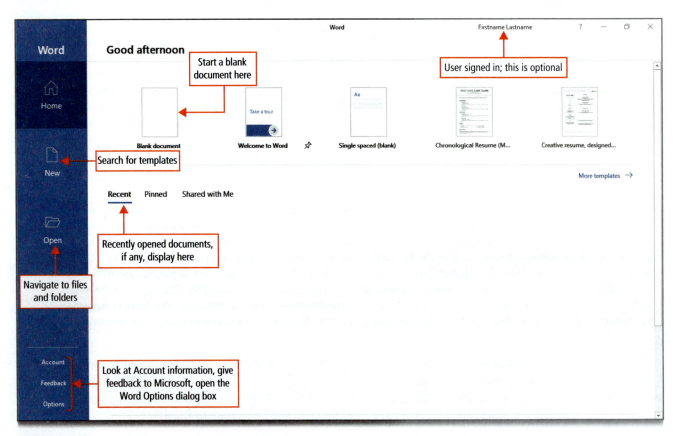

Figure 1.2

2 Click **Blank document**. Compare your screen with Figure 1.3, and then take a moment to study the description of the screen elements in the table in Figure 1.4.

> **NOTE** **Displaying the Full Ribbon**
>
> If your full ribbon does not display, click any tab, and then at the right end of the ribbon, click ⊞ to pin the ribbon to keep it open while you work.

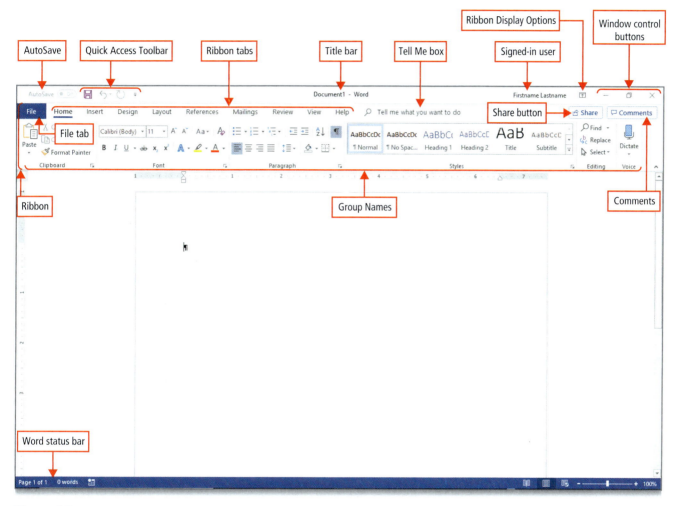

Figure 1.3

Screen Element	Description
AutoSave (off unless your document is saved to OneDrive using an Office 365 subscription)	Saves your document every few seconds so you don't have to. On a Windows system, AutoSave is available in Word, Excel, and PowerPoint for Office 365 subscribers. AutoSave is enabled only when a file is stored on OneDrive, OneDrive for Business, or SharePoint Online. Changes to your document are saved to the cloud as you are working, and if other people are working on the same file, AutoSave lets them see your changes in a matter of seconds.
Comments	Displays a short menu from which you can add a comment to your document or view other comments already in the document.
File tab	Displays Microsoft Office Backstage view, which is a centralized space for all your file management tasks such as opening, saving, printing, publishing, or sharing a file—all the things you can do *with* a file. (In macOS the File tab is on the menu bar.)
Group names	Indicate the name of the groups of related commands on the displayed ribbon tab.
Quick Access Toolbar	Displays buttons to perform frequently used commands and resources with a single click. The default commands include Save, Undo, and Redo. You can add and delete buttons to customize the Quick Access Toolbar for your convenience.
Ribbon	Displays a group of task-oriented tabs that contain the commands, styles, and resources you need to work in Microsoft Office desktop apps. The look of your ribbon depends on your screen resolution. A high resolution will display more individual items and button names on the ribbon.
Ribbon Display Options	Displays three ways you can display the ribbon: Auto-hide Ribbon, Show Tabs, or Show Tabs and Commands; typically, you will want to use Show Tabs and Commands, especially while you are learning Office.
Ribbon tabs	Display the names of the task-oriented tabs relevant to the open document.
Share	Opens the Share dialog box from which you can save your file to the cloud—your OneDrive—and then share it with others so you can collaborate. Here you can also email the Office file or a PDF of the file directly from Outlook if you are using Outlook to view and send email. A *dialog box* enables you to make decisions about an individual object or topic.
Signed-in user	Identifies the user who is signed in to Office.
Status bar	Displays file information on the left; on the right displays buttons for Read Mode, Print Layout, and Web Layout views; on the far right edge, displays Zoom controls.
Tell me what you want to do	Provides a search feature for Microsoft Office commands that you activate by typing what you are looking for in the *Tell me what you want to do* area. As you type, every keystroke refines the results so that you can click the command as soon as it displays.
Title bar	Displays the name of the file and the name of the program; the window control buttons are grouped on the right side of the title bar.
Window control buttons	Displays buttons for commands to Minimize, Restore Down, or Close the window.

Figure 1.4

GO! Learn How

Video OF1-2

Objective 2 Create a Folder for File Storage

A *location* is any disk drive, folder, or other place in which you can store files and folders. A *file* is information stored on a computer under a single name. A *folder* is a container in which you store files. Where you store your files depends on how and where you use your data. For example, for your college classes, you might decide to store your work on a removable USB flash drive so that you can carry your files to different locations and access your files on different computers.

If you do most of your work on a single computer, for example your home desktop system or your laptop computer that you take with you to school or work, then you can store your files in one of the folders on your hard drive provided by your Windows operating system—Documents, Music, Pictures, or Videos.

The best place to store files if you want them to be available anytime, anywhere, from almost any device is on your *OneDrive*, which is Microsoft's free *cloud storage* for anyone with a free Microsoft account. Cloud storage refers to online storage of data so that you can access your data from different places and devices. *Cloud computing* refers to applications and services that are accessed over the internet, rather than to applications that are installed on your local computer.

Besides being able to access your documents from any device or location, OneDrive also offers *AutoSave*, which saves your document every few seconds, so you don't have to. On a Windows system, AutoSave is available in Word, Excel, and PowerPoint for Office 365 subscribers. Changes to your document are saved to the cloud as you are working, and if other people are working on the same file—referred to as *real-time co-authoring*—AutoSave lets them see your changes in a matter of seconds.

If you have an *Office 365* subscription—one of the versions of Microsoft Office to which you subscribe for an annual fee or download for free with your college *.edu* address—your storage capacity on OneDrive is a terabyte or more, which is more than most individuals would ever require. Many colleges provide students with free Office 365 subscriptions. The advantage of subscribing to Office 365 is that you receive monthly updates with new features.

Because many people now have multiple computing devices—desktop, laptop, tablet, smartphone—it is common to store data *in the cloud* so that it is always available. *Synchronization*, also called *syncing*—pronounced SINK-ing—is the process of updating computer files that are in two or more locations according to specific rules. So, if you create and save a Word document on your OneDrive using your laptop, you can open and edit that document on your tablet in OneDrive. When you close the document again, the file is properly updated to reflect your changes. Your OneDrive account will guide you in setting options for syncing files to your specifications. You can open and edit Office files by using Office apps available on a variety of device platforms, including iOS, Android, in a web browser, and in Windows.

MORE KNOWLEDGE | **Creating a Microsoft Account**

Use a free Microsoft account to sign in to Microsoft Office so that you can work on different PCs and use your free OneDrive cloud storage. If you already sign in to a Windows PC or tablet, or you sign in to Xbox Live, Outlook.com, or OneDrive, use that account to sign in to Office. To create a new Microsoft account, in your browser, search for *sign up for a Microsoft account*. You can use any email address as the user name for your new Microsoft account—including addresses from Outlook.com or Gmail.

Activity 1.02 | Creating a Folder for File Storage

Your computer's operating system, either Windows or macOS, helps you to create and maintain a logical folder structure, so always take the time to name your files and folders consistently.

NOTE **This Activity is for Windows PC users. Mac users refer to the document *Creating a Folder for File Storage on a Mac*.**

Mac users can refer to the document Creating a Folder for File Storage on a Mac available within MyLab IT or, for non-MyLab users, your instructor can provide this document to you from the Instructor Resource Center.

In this Activity, you will create a folder in the storage location you have chosen to use for your files, and then you will save your file. This example will use the Documents folder on the PC at which you are working. If you prefer to store on your OneDrive or on a USB flash drive, you can use similar steps.

1 ▶ Decide where you are going to store your files for this Project.

As the first step in saving a file, determine where you want to save the file, and if necessary, insert a storage device.

2 At the top of your screen, in the title bar, notice that *Document1 – Word* displays.

The Blank option on the opening screen of an Office program displays a new unsaved file with a default name—*Document1, Presentation1*, and so on. As you create your file, your work is temporarily stored in the computer's memory until you initiate a Save command, at which time you must choose a file name and a location in which to save your file.

3 In the upper left corner of your screen, click the **File tab** to display **Backstage** view, and then on the left, if necessary, click **Info**. Compare your screen with Figure 1.5.

Recall that Backstage view is a centralized space that groups commands related to *file* management; that is why the tab is labeled *File*. File management commands include opening, saving, printing, or sharing a file. The *Backstage tabs*—*Info, New, Open, Save, Save As, Print, Share, Export,* and *Close*—display along the left side. The tabs group file-related tasks together.

Here, the *Info tab* displays information—*info*—about the current file, and file management commands display under Info. For example, if you click the Protect Document button, a list of options that you can set for this file that relate to who can open or edit the document displays.

On the right, you can also examine the *document properties*. Document properties, also known as *metadata*, are details about a file that describe or identify it, such as the title, author name, subject, and keywords that identify the document's topic or contents.

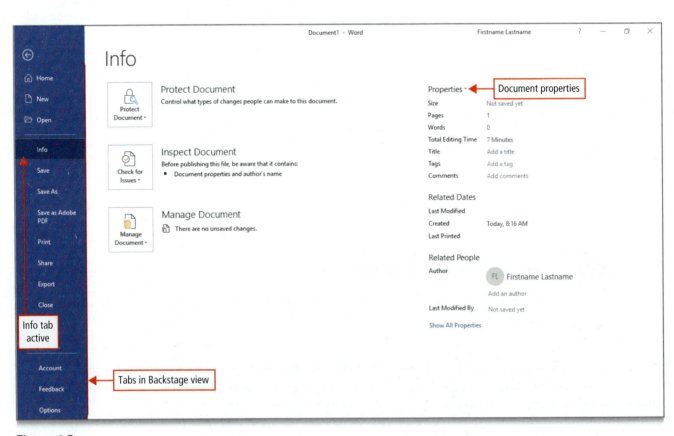

Figure 1.5

4 On the left, click **Save As**, and notice that, if you are signed into Office with a Microsoft account, one option for storing your files is your **OneDrive**. Compare your screen with Figure 1.6.

When you are saving something for the first time, for example a new Word document, the Save and Save As commands are identical. That is, the Save As commands will display if you click Save or if you click Save As.

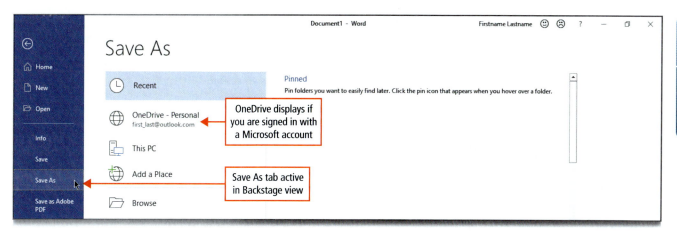

Figure 1.6

> **NOTE**   **Saving After Your File Is Named**
>
> After you name and save a file, the Save command on the Quick Access Toolbar saves any changes you make to the file without displaying Backstage view. The Save As command enables you to name and save a *new* file based on the current one—in a location that you choose. After you name and save the new document, the original document closes, and the new document—based on the original one—displays.

5 To store your Word file in the **Documents** folder on your PC, click **Browse** to display the **Save As** dialog box. On the left, in the **navigation pane**, scroll down; if necessary click > to expand This PC, and then click **Documents**. Compare your screen with Figure 1.7.

In the Save As dialog box, you must indicate the name you want for the file and the location where you want to save the file. When working with your own data, it is good practice to pause at this point and determine the logical name and location for your file.

In the Save As dialog box, a *toolbar* displays, which is a row, column, or block of buttons or icons, that displays across the top of a window and that contains commands for tasks you perform with a single click.

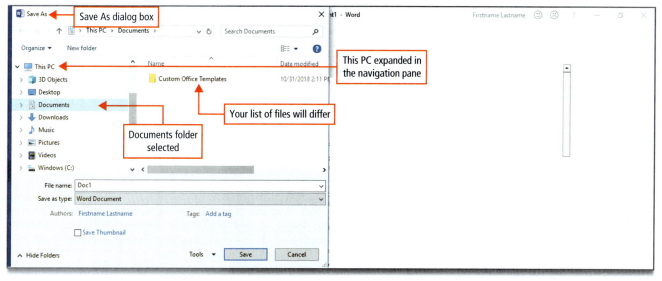

Figure 1.7

6 On the toolbar, click **New folder**.

In the file list, Windows creates a new folder, and the text *New folder* is selected.

7 Type **Office Features Chapter 1** and press [Enter]. In the **file list**, double-click the name of your new folder to open it and display its name in the **address bar**. Compare your screen with Figure 1.8.

In Windows-based programs, the [Enter] key confirms an action.

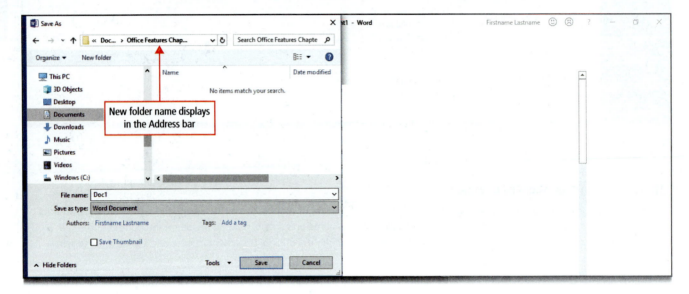

Figure 1.8

8 In the lower right corner of the **Save As** dialog box, click **Cancel**. In the upper left corner of Backstage view, click the **Back** arrow ⬅.

9 In the upper right corner of the Word window, click **Close** ☒. If prompted to save your changes, click Don't Save. Close any other open windows or programs.

| Objective 3 | Download and Extract Zipped Files, Enter and Edit Text in an Office Application, and Use Editor to Check Documents |

GO! Learn How
Video OF1-3

Download refers to the action of transferring or copying a file from another location—such as a cloud storage location, your college's Learning Management System, or from an internet site like MyLab IT—to your computer. Files that you download are frequently *compressed files*, which are files that have been reduced in size, take up less storage space, and can be transferred to other computers faster than uncompressed files.

A compressed folder might contain a group of files that were combined into one compressed folder, which makes it easier to share a group of files. To *extract* means to decompress, or pull out, files from a compressed form. The terms *zip* and *unzip* refer to the process of compressing (zipping) and extracting (unzipping). Windows 10 includes *Compressed Folder Tools*, available on the ribbon, to assist you in extracting compressed files. Similar tools are available in macOS. You do not need to install a separate program to zip or unzip files; modern operating systems like Windows and macOS provide sophisticated tools for these tasks.

All programs in Microsoft Office require some typed text. Your keyboard is still the primary method of entering information into your computer. Techniques to enter text and to *edit*—make changes to—text are similar across all Microsoft Office programs.

For Non-MyLab Submissions

Start Word and click Blank document. Click the File tab, on the left click Save As, click Browse, and then navigate to your **Office Features Chapter 1 folder.** At the bottom of the **Save As** dialog box, in the **File name** box, using your own name, name the file **Lastname_Firstname_Office_Features_1A_Chef_Notes** and then click Save. Then, move to Step 3 in Activity 1.03.

Activity 1.03 | **Downloading and Extracting Zipped Files from MyLab IT and Entering and Editing Text in an Office Program**

1 ► Sign in to your MyLab IT course. Locate and click the Grader project **Office Features 1A Chef Notes**, click **Download Materials**, and then click **Download All Files**. Using the Chrome browser (if you are using a different browser see notes below), extract the zipped folder to your **Office Features Chapter 1 folder** as follows (or use your favorite method to download and extract files):

- In the lower left, next to the downloaded zipped folder, click the small **arrow**, and then click **Show in folder**. The zipped folder displays in *File Explorer*—the Windows program that displays the contents of locations, folders, and files on your computer—in the Downloads folder. (Unless you have changed default settings, downloaded files go to the Downloads folder on your computer.)
- With the zipped folder selected, on the ribbon, under **Compressed Folder Tools**, click the **Extract tab**, and then at the right end of the ribbon, click **Extract all** (you may have to wait a few seconds for the command to become active).
- In the displayed **Extract Compressed (Zipped) Folders** dialog box, click **Browse**. In the **Select a destination** dialog box, use the navigation pane on the left to navigate to your **Office Features Chapter 1 folder**, and double-click its name to open the folder and display its name in the **Address bar**.
- In the lower right, click **Select Folder**, and then in the lower right, click **Extract**; when complete, a new File Explorer window displays showing the extracted files in your chapter folder. Take a moment to open **Office_Features_1A_Chef_Notes_Instructions**; note any recent updates to the book.
- **Close** ☒ both File Explorer windows, close any open documents, and then close the Grader download screens. You can also close MyLab IT and, if open, your Learning Management system.

NOTE   Using the Edge Browser or Firefox Browser to Extract Files

Microsoft Edge: At the bottom, click Open, click Extract all, click Browse, navigate to and open your Chapter folder, click Select Folder, click Extract.
Firefox: In the displayed dialog box, click OK, click Extract all, click Browse, navigate to and open your Chapter folder, click Select Folder, and then click Extract.

MAC TIP   Using the Chrome browser, in MyLab IT, after you click Download Materials, in the lower left, to the right of the zipped folder, click the arrow. Click Open. Click the blue folder containing the unzipped files. Use Finder commands to move or copy the files to your Office Features Chapter 1 folder.

2 ► On the Windows taskbar, click **File Explorer** 📁. Navigate to your **Office Features Chapter 1 folder**, and then double-click the Word file you downloaded from MyLab IT that displays your name—**Student_Office_Features_1A_Chef_Notes**. In this empty Word document, if necessary, at the top, click **Enable Editing**.

MAC TIP   When the Word application is not open, on the Dock, use the macOS Finder commands to locate your Word document. When the Word application is open, use the File tab on the menu bar.

3 ► On the ribbon, on the **Home tab**, in the **Paragraph group**, if necessary, click **Show/Hide** ¶ so that it is active—shaded. On the **View tab**, if necessary, in the **Show group**, select the **Ruler** check box so that rulers display below the ribbon and on the left side of your window, and then redisplay the **Home tab**.

The *insertion point*—a blinking vertical line that indicates where text or graphics will be inserted—displays. In Office programs, the mouse *pointer*—any symbol that displays on your screen in response to moving your mouse device—displays in different shapes depending on the task you are performing and the area of the screen to which you are pointing.

When you press Enter, Spacebar, or Tab on your keyboard, characters display to represent these keystrokes. These screen characters do not print and are referred to as *formatting marks* or *nonprinting characters*.

When working in Word, display the rulers so that you can see how margin settings affect your document and how text and objects align. Additionally, if you set a tab stop or an indent, its location is visible on the ruler.

MAC TIP To display group names on the ribbon, display the menu bar, click Word, click Preferences, click View, under Ribbon, select the Show group titles check box.

NOTE   Activating Show/Hide in Word Documents

When Show/Hide is active—the button is shaded—formatting marks display. Because formatting marks guide your eye in a document—like a map and road signs guide you along a highway—these marks will display throughout this instruction. Expert Word users keep these marks displayed while creating documents.

4 ▶ Type **Skyline Grille Info** and notice how the insertion point moves to the right as you type. Point slightly to the right of the letter *e* in *Grille* and click to place the insertion point there. Compare your screen with Figure 1.9.

A *paragraph symbol* (¶) indicates the end of a paragraph and displays each time you press Enter. This is a type of formatting mark and does not print.

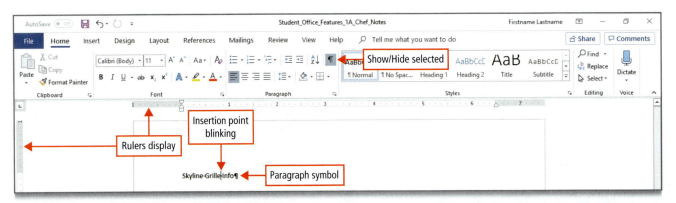

Figure 1.9

5 ▶ On your keyboard, locate and then press the Backspace key one time to delete the letter *e*.

Pressing Backspace removes a character to the left of the insertion point.

MAC TIP   Press delete.

6 ▶ Press → one time to place the insertion point to the left of the *I* in *Info*. Type **Chef** and then press Spacebar one time.

By *default*, when you type text in an Office program, existing text moves to the right to make space for new typing. Default refers to the current selection or setting that is automatically used by a program unless you specify otherwise.

7 ▶ Press Del four times to delete *Info* and then type **Notes**

Pressing Del removes a character to the right of the insertion point.

MAC TIP   Press fn + delete to delete characters to the right of the insertion point.

8 With your insertion point blinking after the word *Notes*, on your keyboard, hold down the Ctrl key. While holding down Ctrl, press ← three times to move the insertion point to the beginning of the word *Grill*.

> This is a **keyboard shortcut**—a key or combination of keys that performs a task that would otherwise require a mouse. This keyboard shortcut moves the insertion point to the beginning of the previous word.

> A keyboard shortcut is indicated as Ctrl + ← (or some other combination of keys) to indicate that you hold down the first key while pressing the second key. A keyboard shortcut can also include three keys, in which case you hold down the first two and then press the third. For example, Ctrl + Shift + ← selects one word to the left.

 **MAC TIP**   Press option + ←.

9 With the insertion point blinking at the beginning of the word *Grill*, type **Metro** and press Spacebar one time.

10 Click to place the insertion point after the letter *s* in *Notes* and then press Enter one time. With the insertion point blinking, type the following and include the spelling error: **Exective Chef, Madison Dunham** (If Word autocorrects *Exective* to *Executive*, delete *u* in the word.)

11 With your mouse, point slightly to the left of the *M* in *Madison*, hold down the left mouse button, and then **drag**—hold down the left mouse button while moving your mouse—to the right to select the text *Madison Dunham* but not the paragraph mark following it, and then release the mouse button. Compare your screen with Figure 1.10.

> The **mini toolbar** displays commands that are commonly used with the selected object, which places common commands close to your pointer. When you move the pointer away from the mini toolbar, it fades from view.

> **Selecting** refers to highlighting—by dragging or clicking with your mouse—areas of text or data or graphics so that the selection can be edited, formatted, copied, or moved. The action of dragging includes releasing the left mouse button at the end of the area you want to select.

> The Office programs recognize a selected area as one unit to which you can make changes. Selecting text may require some practice. If you are not satisfied with your result, click anywhere outside of the selection, and then begin again.

MAC TIP   The mini toolbar may not display; use ribbon commands.

BY TOUCH   Tap once on *Madison* to display the gripper—a small circle that acts as a handle—directly below the word. This establishes the start gripper. If necessary, with your finger, drag the gripper to the beginning of the word. Then drag the gripper to the end of *Dunham* to select the text and display the end gripper.

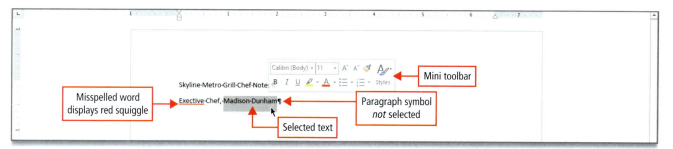

Figure 1.10

12 With the text *Madison Dunham* selected, type **Sarah Jackson**

In any Windows-based program, such as the Microsoft Office programs, selected text is deleted and then replaced when you begin to type new text. You will save time by developing good techniques for selecting and then editing or replacing selected text, which is easier than pressing Backspace or Del numerous times to delete text.

Activity 1.04 | Checking Spelling

> **ALERT** **The Display of Spelling Suggestions Varies Among Office Versions**
>
> Depending on your version of Office (Office 365 or Office 2019), you may see variations in how the spelling checking displays suggestions for corrections. You will still be able to follow the screen prompts to select the correct spelling.

Microsoft Office has a dictionary of words against which all entered text is checked. In Word and PowerPoint, words that are not in the dictionary display a red squiggle, indicating a possible misspelled word, a proper name, or an unusual word—none of which are in the Office dictionary. In Excel and Access, you can initiate a check of the spelling, but red squiggles do not display.

1 Notice that the misspelled word *Exective* displays with a red squiggle.

2 Point to *Exective* and then *right-click*—click your right mouse button one time.

A *shortcut menu* displays, which displays commands and options relevant to the selected text or object. These are *context-sensitive commands* because they relate to the item you right-clicked. These are also referred to as *context menus*. Here, the shortcut menu displays commands related to the misspelled word.

> **BY TOUCH** Tap and hold a moment—when a square displays around the misspelled word, release your finger to display the shortcut menu.

3 Press Esc two times to cancel the shortcut menus, and then in the lower left corner of your screen, on the status bar, click the **Proofing** icon, which displays an *X* because some errors are detected. In the **Editor** pane that displays on the right, if necessary, click the Results button, and then under **Suggestions**, to the right of *Executive*, click, and then compare your screen with Figure 1.11.

The Editor pane displays on the right. *Editor*, according to Microsoft, is your digital writing assistant in Word and also in Outlook. Editor displays misspellings, grammatical mistakes, and writing style issues as you type by marking red squiggles for spelling, blue double underlines for grammar, and dotted underlines for writing style issues.

Here you have many more options for checking spelling than you have on the shortcut menu. The suggested correct word, *Executive*, displays under Suggestions. The displayed menu provides additional options for the suggestion. For example, you can have the word read aloud, hear it spelled out, change all occurrences in the document, or add to AutoCorrect options.

In the Editor pane, you can ignore the word one time or in all occurrences, change the word to the suggested word, select a different suggestion, or add a word to the dictionary against which Word checks.

> **MAC TIP** In the Spelling and Grammar dialog box, click Executive, and then click Change. The Editor pane is not available on a Mac.

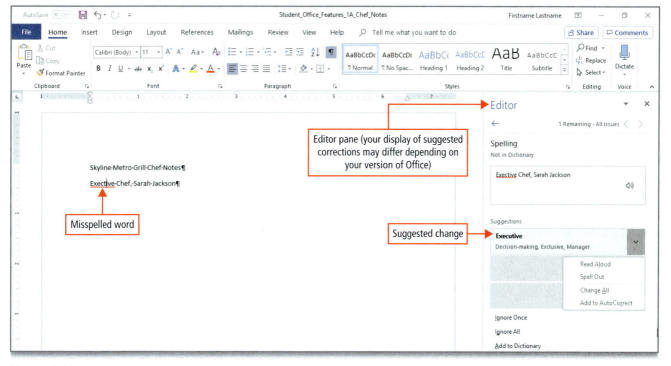

Figure 1.11

🔄 **ANOTHER WAY** Press [F7] to display the Editor pane; or, on the Review tab, in the Proofing group, you can check your document for Spelling.

 4 In the **Editor** pane, under **Suggestions**, click *Executive* to correct the spelling. In the message box that displays, click **OK**.

5 If necessary **Close** the **Editor** pane by clicking ⊠ in the upper right corner.

Objective 4 Perform Office Commands and Apply Office Formatting

GO! Learn How
Video OF1-4

Formatting refers to applying Office commands to make your document easy to read and to add visual touches and design elements to make your document inviting to the reader. This process establishes the overall appearance of text, graphics, and pages in your document.

Activity 1.05 | Performing Commands from a Dialog Box

MOS
1.2.4

In a dialog box, you make decisions about an individual object or topic. In some dialog boxes, you can make multiple decisions in one place.

1 On the ribbon, click the **Design tab**, and then in the **Page Background group**, click **Page Color**.

2 At the bottom of the menu, notice the command **Fill Effects** followed by an **ellipsis** (. . .). Compare your screen with Figure 1.12.

An *ellipsis* is a set of three dots indicating incompleteness. An ellipsis following a command name indicates that a dialog box will display when you click the command.

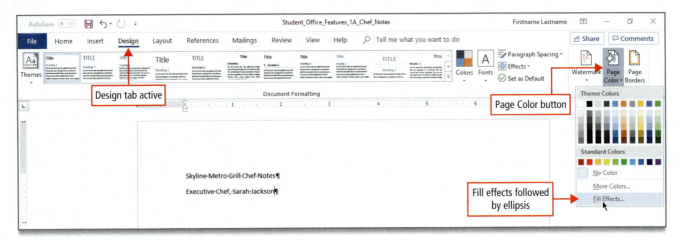

Figure 1.12

3 Click **Fill Effects** to display the **Fill Effects** dialog box. Compare your screen with Figure 1.13.

Fill is the inside color of a page or object. Here, the dialog box displays a set of tabs across the top from which you can display different sets of options. Some dialog boxes display the option group names on the left. The Gradient tab is active. In a *gradient fill*, one color fades into another.

🖥️ **MAC TIP** Click More Colors to display the Colors dialog box.

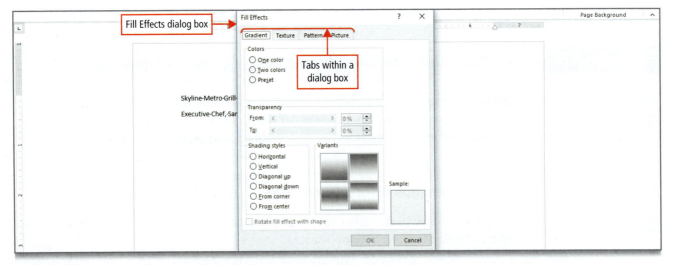

Figure 1.13

4 ▶ Under **Colors**, click the **One color** option button.

The dialog box displays settings related to the *One color* option. An ***option button*** is a round button that enables you to make one choice among two or more options.

5 ▶ Click the **Color 1 arrow**—the arrow under the text *Color 1*—and then in the eighth column, point to the second color to display a ScreenTip with the name of the color.

When you click an arrow in a dialog box, additional options display. A ***ScreenTip*** displays useful information about mouse actions, such as pointing to screen elements or dragging.

6 ▶ Click the color, and then notice that the fill color displays in the **Color 1** box. In the **Dark Light** bar, click the **Light arrow** as many times as necessary until the scroll box is all the way to the right—or drag the scroll box all the way to the right. Under **Shading styles**, click the **From corner** option button. Under **Variants**, click the **upper right variant**. Compare your screen with Figure 1.14.

This dialog box is a good example of the many different elements you may encounter in a dialog box. Here you have option buttons, an arrow that displays a menu, a slider bar, and graphic options that you can select.

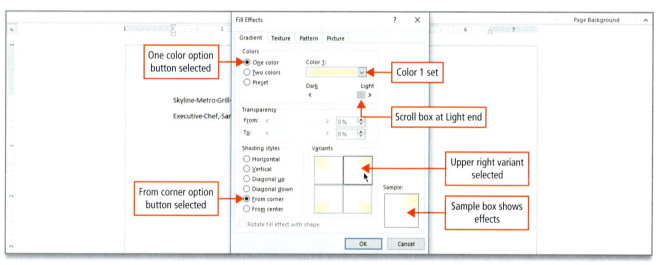

Figure 1.14

7 ▶ At the bottom of the dialog box, click **OK**, and notice the subtle page color.

In Word, the gold shading page color will not print—even on a color printer—unless you set specific options to do so. However, a subtle background page color is effective if people will be reading the document on a screen. Microsoft's research indicates that two-thirds of people who open Word documents on a screen never print or edit them; they only read them.

Activity 1.06 | Using Undo and Applying Text Effects

1 Point to the *S* in *Skyline*, and then drag down and to the right to select both paragraphs of text and include the paragraph marks. On the mini toolbar, click **Styles**, and then *point to* but do not click **Title**. Compare your screen with Figure 1.15.

> A *style* is a group of formatting commands, such as font, font size, font color, paragraph alignment, and line spacing that can be applied to a paragraph with one command.
>
> *Live Preview* is a technology that shows the result of applying an editing or formatting change as you point to possible results—before you actually apply it.

MAC TIP The mini toolbar and Live Preview are not available; use ribbon commands.

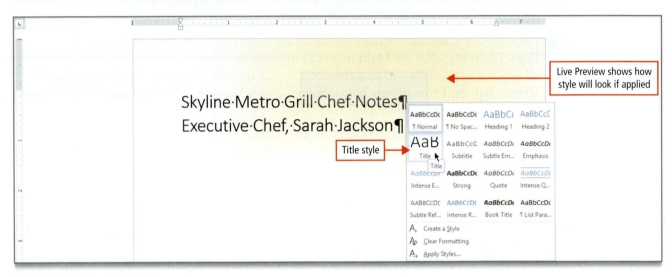

Live Preview shows how style will look if applied

Title style

Figure 1.15

2 In the **Styles** gallery, click **Title**.

> A *gallery* is an Office feature that displays a list of potential results.

MAC TIP On the Home tab, in the Styles gallery, click Title.

3 On the ribbon, on the **Home tab**, in the **Paragraph group**, click **Center** ☰ to center the two paragraphs.

> *Alignment* refers to the placement of paragraph text relative to the left and right margins. *Center alignment* refers to text that is centered horizontally between the left and right margins. You can also align text at the left margin, which is the default alignment for text in Word, or at the right.

ANOTHER WAY Press Ctrl + E to use the Center command.

MAC TIP Press command ⌘ + E to use the Center command.

4 With the two paragraphs still selected, on the **Home tab**, in the **Font Group**, click **Text Effects and Typography** A ▾ to display a gallery.

5 In the second row, click the first effect. Click anywhere to *deselect*—cancel the selection— the text and notice the text effect.

6 Because this effect might be difficult to read, in the upper left corner of your screen, on the **Quick Access Toolbar**, click **Undo** ↶.

The *Undo* command reverses your last action.

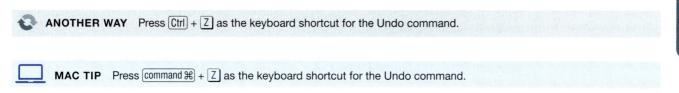

ANOTHER WAY Press ⌈Ctrl⌉ + ⌈Z⌉ as the keyboard shortcut for the Undo command.

MAC TIP Press ⌈command ⌘⌉ + ⌈Z⌉ as the keyboard shortcut for the Undo command.

7 With all of the text still selected, display the **Text Effects and Typography** gallery again, and then in the first row, click the fifth effect. Click anywhere to deselect the text and notice the text effect. Compare your screen with Figure 1.16.

As you progress in your study of Microsoft Office, you will practice using many dialog boxes and commands to apply interesting effects such as this to your Word documents, Excel worksheets, Access database objects, and PowerPoint slides.

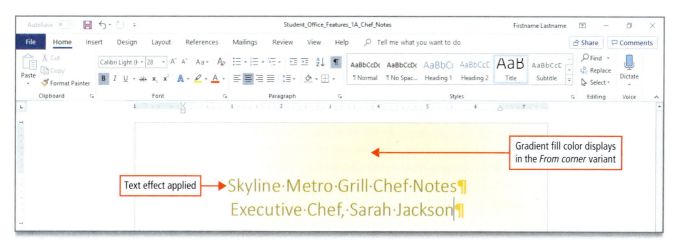

Figure 1.16

Activity 1.07 | Performing Commands from and Customizing the Quick Access Toolbar

The ribbon that displays across the top of the program window groups commands in the way that you would most logically use them. The ribbon in each Office program is slightly different, but all contain the same three elements: *tabs*, *groups*, and *commands*.

Tabs display across the top of the ribbon, and each tab relates to a type of activity; for example, laying out a page. Groups are sets of related commands for specific tasks. Commands— instructions to computer programs—are arranged in groups and might display as a button, a menu, or a box in which you type information.

You can also minimize the ribbon so only the tab names display, which is useful when working on a smaller screen such as a tablet computer where you want to maximize your screen viewing area.

1 In the upper left corner of your screen, above the ribbon, locate the **Quick Access Toolbar**.

Recall that the Quick Access Toolbar contains commands that you use frequently. By default, only the commands Save, Undo, and Redo display, but you can add and delete commands to suit your needs. Possibly the computer at which you are working already has additional commands added to the Quick Access Toolbar.

2 At the end of the **Quick Access Toolbar**, click the **Customize Quick Access Toolbar** button ⏷, and then compare your screen with Figure 1.17.

A list of commands that Office users commonly add to their Quick Access Toolbar displays, including New, Open, Email, Quick Print, and Print Preview and Print. Commands already on the Quick Access Toolbar display a check mark. Commands that you add to the Quick Access Toolbar are always just one click away.

Here you can also display the More Commands dialog box, from which you can select any command from any tab to add to the Quick Access Toolbar.

👉 **BY TOUCH** Tap once on Quick Access Toolbar commands.

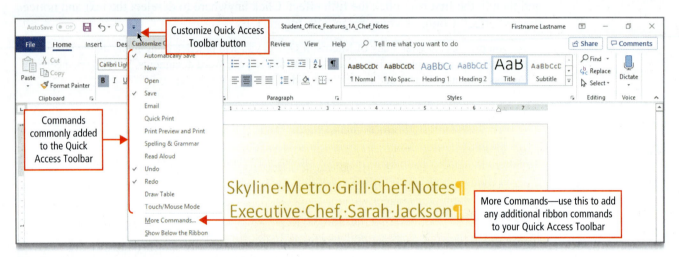

Figure 1.17

3 On the list, click **Print Preview and Print**, and then notice that the icon is added to the **Quick Access Toolbar**. Compare your screen with Figure 1.18.

The icon that represents the Print Preview command displays on the Quick Access Toolbar. Because this is a command that you will use frequently while building Office documents, you might decide to have this command remain on your Quick Access Toolbar.

🔄 **ANOTHER WAY** Right-click any command on the ribbon, and then on the shortcut menu, click Add to Quick Access Toolbar.

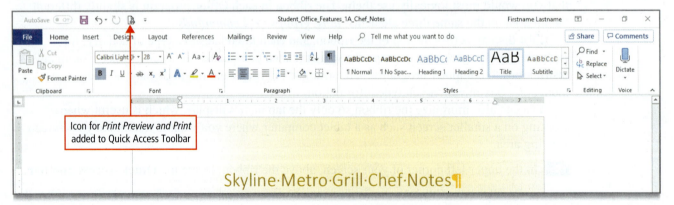

Figure 1.18

Activity 1.08 | Performing Commands from the Ribbon

1 In the second line of text, click to place the insertion point to the right of the letter *n* in *Jackson*. Press [Enter] three times. Compare your screen with Figure 1.19.

Word creates three new blank paragraphs, and no Text Effect is applied.

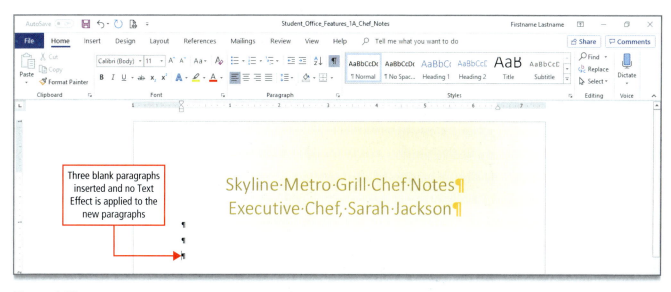

Figure 1.19

2 Click to position the insertion point to the left of the **second blank paragraph** that you just inserted. On the ribbon, click the **Insert tab**. In the **Illustrations group**, *point* to **Pictures** to display its ScreenTip.

Many buttons on the ribbon have this type of *enhanced ScreenTip*, which displays useful descriptive information about the command.

3 Click **Pictures**. In the **Insert Picture** dialog box, navigate to your **Office Features Chapter 1 folder**, double-click the **of01A_Chefs** picture, and then compare your screen with Figure 1.20.

The picture displays in your Word document.

 MAC TIP Click Picture from File, then navigate to your Office Features Chapter 1 folder.

 For Non-MyLab Submissions
The of01A_Chefs picture is included with this chapter's Student Data Files, which you can obtain from your instructor or by downloading the files from www.pearsonhighered.com/go

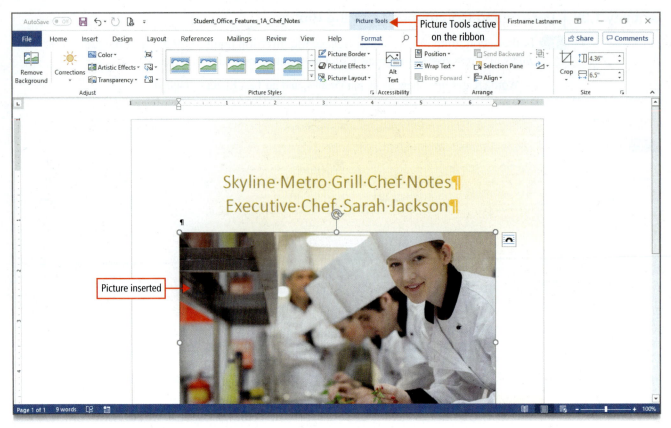

Figure 1.20

4 ▶ In the upper right corner of the picture, point to the **Layout Options** button to display its ScreenTip, and then compare your screen with Figure 1.21.

> *Layout Options* enable you to choose how the *object*—in this instance an inserted picture—interacts with the surrounding text. An object is a picture or other graphic such as a chart or table that you can select and then move and resize.
>
> When a picture is selected, the Picture Tools become available on the ribbon. Additionally, *sizing handles*—small circles or squares that indicate an object is selected—surround the selected picture.

Figure 1.21

5 ▶ With the image selected, click **Layout Options**, and then under **With Text Wrapping**, in the second row, click the first layout—**Top and Bottom**. In the upper right corner of the **Layout Options** dialog box, click **Close**.

6 ▶ On the ribbon, with the **Picture Tools Format tab** active, at the right, in the **Size group**, click in the **Shape Height** box ⬚ 0.29" ⬚ to select the existing text. Type **2** and press Enter.

7 ▶ On the **Picture Tools Format tab**, in the **Arrange group**, click **Align**, and then at the bottom of the list, locate **Use Alignment Guides**. If you do not see a checkmark to the left of **Use Alignment Guides**, click the command to enable the guides.

8 ▶ If necessary, click the image again to select it. Point to the image to display the 🔖 pointer, hold down the left mouse button and move your mouse slightly to display a green line at the left margin, and then drag the image to the right and down slightly until a green line displays in the center of the image as shown in Figure 1.22, and then release the left mouse button.

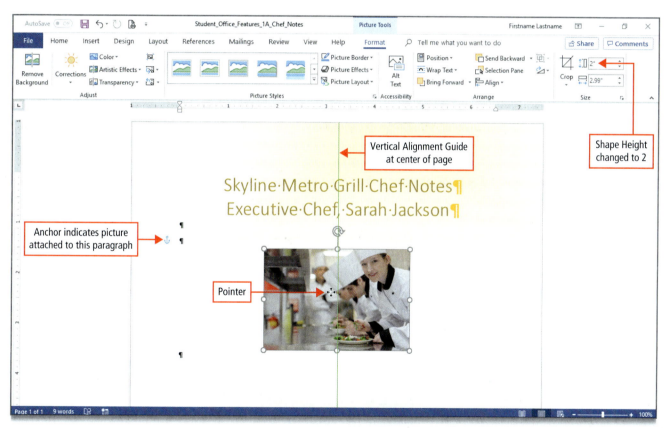

Figure 1.22

9 ▶ Be sure that there are two blank paragraphs above the image and that the anchor symbol is attached to the second blank paragraph mark—if necessary, drag the picture up slightly or down slightly. If you are not satisfied with your result, on the Quick Access Toolbar, click Undo ↺ and begin again.

> *Alignment guides* are green lines that display to help you align objects with margins or at the center of a page.

> Inserted pictures anchor—attach to—the paragraph at the insertion point location—as indicated by an anchor symbol.

10 On the ribbon, on the **Picture Tools Format tab**, in the **Picture Styles group**, point to the first style to display the ScreenTip *Simple Frame, White*, and notice that the image displays with a white frame.

NOTE   The Size of Groups on the Ribbon Varies with Screen Resolution

Your monitor's screen resolution might be set higher than the resolution used to capture the figures in this book. At a higher resolution, the ribbon expands some groups to show more commands that are available with a single click, such as those in the Picture Styles group. Or, the group expands to add descriptive text to some buttons, such as those in the Arrange group. Regardless of your screen resolution, all Office commands are available to you. In higher resolutions, you will have a more robust view of the ribbon commands.

11 Watch the image as you point to the second picture style, and then to the third, and then to the fourth.

Recall that Live Preview shows the result of applying an editing or formatting change as you point to possible results—*before* you actually apply it.

12 In the **Picture Styles group**, click the fourth style—**Drop Shadow Rectangle**. Reposition the picture up or down so that it is anchored to the second blank paragraph above the image, and then click anywhere outside of the image to deselect it. Notice that the Picture Tools no longer display on the ribbon. Compare your screen with Figure 1.23.

Contextual tabs on the ribbon display only when you need them.

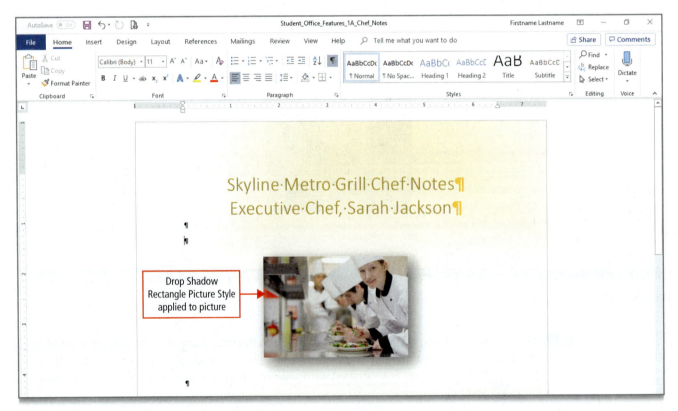

Figure 1.23

13 On the **Quick Access Toolbar**, click **Save** 🖫 to save the changes you have made.

Activity 1.09 | Minimizing the Ribbon

1 ▶ Point to any tab on the ribbon and right-click to display a shortcut menu.

Here you can choose to display the Quick Access Toolbar below the ribbon or collapse the ribbon to maximize screen space. You can also customize the ribbon by adding, removing, renaming, or reordering tabs, groups, and commands, although this is not recommended until you become an expert Word user.

2 ▶ Click **Collapse the Ribbon** and notice that only the ribbon tabs display. Click the **Home tab** to display the commands. Click in the last blank paragraph—or anywhere in the document— and notice that the ribbon goes back to the collapsed display.

MAC TIP To minimize the ribbon, click the up arrow on the top right of the screen.

3 ▶ Right-click any ribbon tab, and then click **Collapse the Ribbon** again to remove the check mark from this command.

Most expert Office users prefer the full ribbon display.

4 ▶ Point to any tab on the ribbon, and then on your mouse device, roll the mouse wheel. Notice that different tabs become active as you roll the mouse wheel.

You can make a tab active by using this technique, instead of clicking the tab.

MORE KNOWLEDGE **Displaying KeyTips**

Instead of a mouse, some individuals prefer to navigate the ribbon by using keys on the keyboard. You can do this by activating the *KeyTip* feature where small labels display on the ribbon tabs and also on the individual ribbon commands. Press [Alt] to display the KeyTips on the ribbon tabs, and then press [N] to display KeyTips on the ribbon commands. Press [Esc] to turn the feature off. NOTE: This feature is not yet available on a Mac.

Activity 1.10 | Changing Page Orientation and Zoom Level

1.2.1

1 ▶ On the ribbon, click the **Layout tab**. In the **Page Setup group**, click **Orientation**, and notice that two orientations display—*Portrait* and *Landscape*. Click **Landscape**.

In **portrait orientation**, the paper is taller than it is wide. In **landscape orientation**, the paper is wider than it is tall.

2 ▶ In the lower right corner of the screen, locate the **Zoom slider** .

Recall that to zoom means to increase or decrease the viewing area. You can zoom in to look closely at a section of a document, and then zoom out to see an entire page on the screen. You can also zoom to view multiple pages on the screen.

3 Drag the **Zoom slider** ◖――――▮――――⊞ to the left until you have zoomed to approximately *60%*. Compare your screen with Figure 1.24.

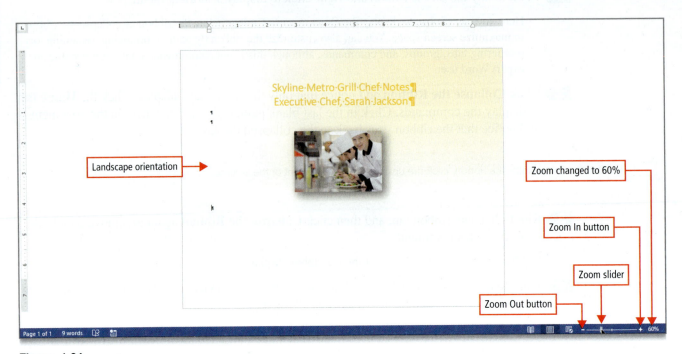

Figure 1.24

🔲 **BY TOUCH** Drag the Zoom slider with your finger.

---

4 Use the technique you just practiced to change the **Orientation** back to **Portrait**.

The default orientation in Word is Portrait, which is commonly used for business documents such as letters, reports, and memos.

5 In the lower right corner, click the **Zoom In** button ⊞ as many times as necessary to return to the **100%** zoom setting.

Use the zoom feature to adjust the view of your document for editing and for your viewing comfort.

🔄 **ANOTHER WAY** You can also control Zoom from the ribbon. On the View tab, in the Zoom group, you can control the Zoom level and also zoom to view multiple pages.

---

6 On the **Quick Access Toolbar**, click **Save** 🔲.

MORE KNOWLEDGE **Zooming to Page Width**

Some Office users prefer *Page Width*, which zooms the document so that the width of the page matches the width of the window. Find this command on the View tab, in the Zoom group.

Activity 1.11 | Formatting Text by Using Fonts, Alignment, Font Colors, and Font Styles

MOS
2.2.5

1 If necessary, on the right edge of your screen, drag the vertical scroll box to the top of the scroll bar. To the left of *Executive Chef, Sarah Jackson*, point in the margin area to display the ⬦ pointer and click one time to select the entire paragraph. Compare your screen with Figure 1.25.

Use this technique to select complete paragraphs from the margin area—drag downward to select multiple-line paragraphs—which is faster and more efficient than dragging through text.

Figure 1.25

2 On the **Home tab**, in the **Font Group**, click **Clear All Formatting** ⬦. Compare your screen with Figure 1.26.

This command removes all formatting from the selection, leaving only the normal, unformatted text.

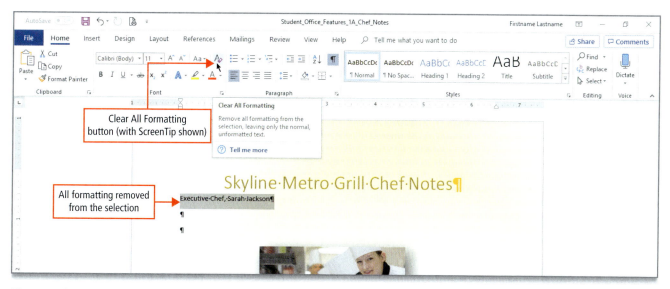

Figure 1.26

3 With the text still selected, on the **Home tab**, in the **Paragraph group**, click **Center** ▤.

4 With the text still selected, on the **Home tab**, in the **Font group**, click the **Font button arrow** [Calibri (Body) ▾]. On the alphabetical list of font names, scroll down and then locate and *point to* **Cambria**.

A *font* is a set of characters with the same design and shape. The default font in a Word document is Calibri, which is a *sans serif font*—a font design with no lines or extensions on the ends of characters.

The Cambria font is a *serif font*—a font design that includes small line extensions on the ends of the letters to guide the eye in reading from left to right.

The list of fonts displays as a gallery showing potential results. For example, in the Font gallery, you can point to see the actual design and format of each font as it would look if applied to text.

5 ▶ Point to several other fonts and observe the effect on the selected text. Then, scroll back to the top of the **Font** gallery. Under **Theme Fonts**, click **Calibri Light**.

A *theme* is a predesigned combination of colors, fonts, line, and fill effects that look good together and is applied to an entire document by a single selection. A theme combines two sets of fonts—one for text and one for headings. In the default Office theme, Calibri Light is the suggested font for headings.

6 ▶ With the paragraph *Executive Chef, Sarah Jackson* still selected, on the **Home tab**, in the **Font group**, click the **Font Size button arrow** 11 ⌄, point to **20**, and then notice how Live Preview displays the text in the font size to which you are pointing. Compare your screen with Figure 1.27.

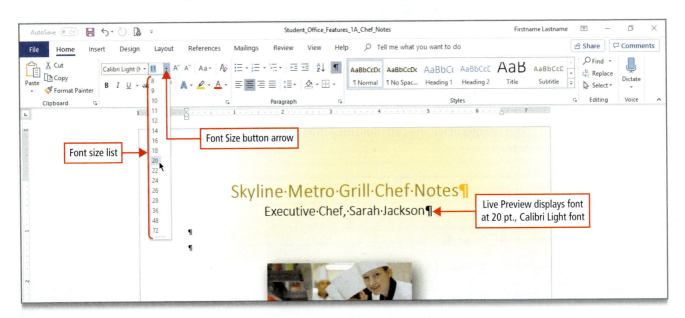

Figure 1.27

7 ▶ On the list of font sizes, click **20**.

Fonts are measured in *points*, with one point equal to 1/72 of an inch. A higher point size indicates a larger font size. Headings and titles are often formatted by using a larger font size. The word *point* is abbreviated as *pt*.

8 ▶ With *Executive Chef, Sarah Jackson* still selected, on the **Home tab**, in the **Font group**, click the **Font Color button arrow** A ⌄. Under **Theme Colors**, in the sixth column, click the fifth (next to last) color, and then click in the last blank paragraph to deselect the text.

9 ▶ With your insertion point in the blank paragraph below the picture, type **Rehearsal Dinner Menu Ideas** and then press Enter two times.

10 Type **Appetizers** and press [Enter] two times. Type **Salads** and press [Enter] two times. Type **Main Dishes** and press [Enter] two times.

11 Type **Desserts** and press [Enter] four times. Compare your screen with Figure 1.28.

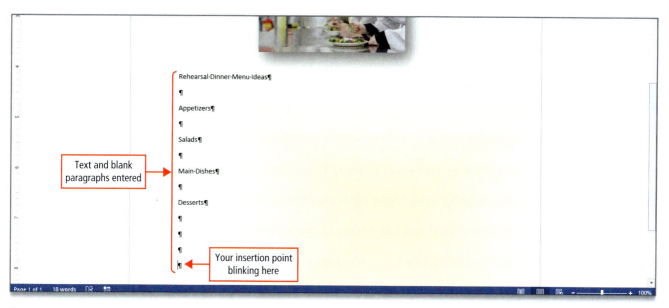

Text and blank
paragraphs entered

Rehearsal·Dinner·Menu·Ideas¶

¶

Appetizers¶

¶

Salads¶

¶

Main·Dishes¶

¶

Desserts¶

¶

¶

¶

¶

Your insertion point
blinking here

Page 1 of 1   18 words

Figure 1.28

12 Click anywhere in the word *Dinner* and then **triple-click**—click the left mouse button three times—to select the entire paragraph. If the entire paragraph is not selected, click in the paragraph and begin again.

13 With the paragraph selected, on the mini toolbar, click the **Font Color** button [A ▾], and notice that the text color of the selected paragraph changes.

The font color button retains its most recently used color—the color you used to format *Executive Chef, Sarah Jackson* above. As you progress in your study of Microsoft Office, you will use other commands that behave in this manner; that is, they retain their most recently used format. This is commonly referred to as *MRU*—most recently used.

Recall that the mini toolbar places commands that are commonly used for the selected text or object close by so that you reduce the distance you must move your mouse to access a command. If you are using a touch screen device, most commands that you need are close and easy to touch.

🖥 **MAC TIP**   Use commands on the ribbon, on the Home tab.

14 With the paragraph *Rehearsal Dinner Menu Ideas* still selected and the mini toolbar displayed, on the mini toolbar, click **Bold** [B] and **Italic** [I].

Font styles include bold, italic, and underline. Font styles emphasize text and are a visual cue to draw the reader's eye to important text.

15 On the mini toolbar, click **Italic** I again to turn off the Italic formatting. Click anywhere to deselect, and then compare your screen with Figure 1.29.

> A *toggle button* is a button that can be turned on by clicking it once, and then turned off by clicking it again.

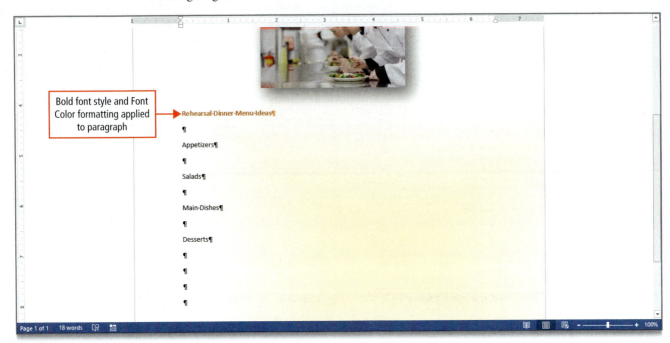

Figure 1.29

Activity 1.12 | Using Format Painter

Use the ***Format Painter*** to copy the formatting of specific text or copy the formatting of a paragraph and then apply it in other locations in your document.

1 To the left of *Rehearsal Dinner Menu Ideas*, point in the left margin to display the ▷ pointer, and then click one time to select the entire paragraph. Compare your screen with Figure 1.30.

> Use this technique to select complete paragraphs from the margin area. This is particularly useful if there are many lines of text in the paragraph. You can hold down the left mouse button and drag downward instead of trying to drag through the text.

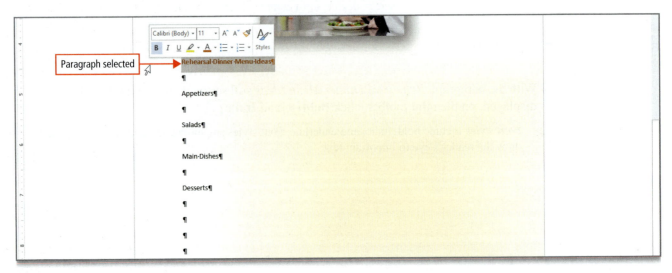

Figure 1.30

2 With *Rehearsal Dinner Menu Ideas* still selected, on the mini toolbar, click **Format Painter** 🖌. Then, move your mouse to the right of the word *Appetizers*, and notice the ⎯⎯ mouse pointer. Compare your screen with Figure 1.31.

The pointer takes the shape of a paintbrush and contains the formatting information from the paragraph where the insertion point is positioned or from what is selected. Information about the Format Painter and how to turn it off displays in the status bar.

MAC TIP   On the Home tab, in the Clipboard group, click Format Painter.

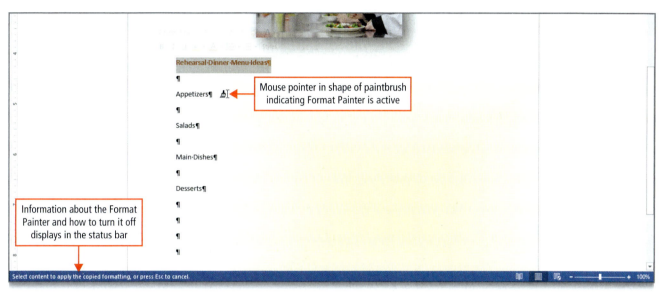

Figure 1.31

3 With the ⎯⎯ pointer, drag to select the paragraph *Appetizers* and notice that the font color and Bold formatting is applied. Then, click anywhere in the word *Appetizers*, right-click to display the mini toolbar, and on the mini toolbar, *double-click* **Format Painter** 🖌.

4 Select the paragraph *Salads* to copy the font color and Bold formatting, and notice that the pointer retains the ⎯⎯ shape. You might have to move the mouse slightly to see the paintbrush shape.

When you *double-click* the Format Painter button, the Format Painter feature remains active until you either click the Format Painter button again, or press ⎡Esc⎤ to cancel it—as indicated on the status bar.

5 With Format Painter still active, drag to select the paragraph *Main Dishes*, and then on the ribbon, on the **Home tab**, in the **Clipboard group**, notice that **Format Painter** is selected, indicating that it is active. Compare your screen with Figure 1.32.

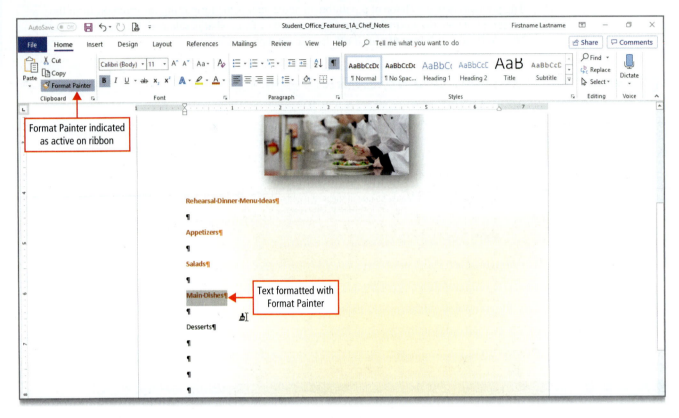

Figure 1.32

6 Select the paragraph *Desserts* to copy the format, and then on the ribbon, click **Format Painter** to turn the command off.

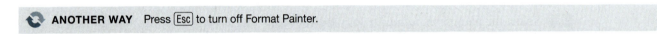
ANOTHER WAY Press Esc to turn off Format Painter.

7 On the **Quick Access Toolbar**, click **Save** to save the changes you have made to your document.

Activity 1.13 | Using Keyboard Shortcuts and Using the Clipboard to Copy, Cut, and Paste

The *Clipboard* is a temporary storage area that holds text or graphics that you select and then cut or copy. When you *copy* text or graphics, a copy is placed on the Clipboard and the original text or graphic remains in place. When you *cut* text or graphics, a copy is placed on the Clipboard, and the original text or graphic is removed—cut—from the document.

After copying or cutting, the contents of the Clipboard are available for you to *paste*—insert—in a new location in the current document, or into another Office file.

1 On your keyboard, hold down ⌈Ctrl⌉ and press ⌈Home⌉ to move to the beginning of your document, and then take a moment to study the table in Figure 1.33, which describes similar keyboard shortcuts with which you can navigate quickly in a document.

MAC TIP Press ⌈command ⌘⌉ + ⌈fn⌉ + to move to the top of a document.

To Move	On a Windows PC press:	On a Mac press:
To the beginning of a document	⌈Ctrl⌉ + ⌈Home⌉	⌈command ⌘⌉ + ⌈fn⌉ + ⌈←⌉
To the end of a document	⌈Ctrl⌉ + ⌈End⌉	⌈command ⌘⌉ + ⌈fn⌉ + ⌈→⌉
To the beginning of a line	⌈Home⌉	⌈command ⌘⌉ + ⌈←⌉
To the end of a line	⌈End⌉	⌈command ⌘⌉ + ⌈→⌉
To the beginning of the previous word	⌈Ctrl⌉ + ⌈←⌉	⌈option⌉ + ⌈←⌉
To the beginning of the next word	⌈Ctrl⌉ + ⌈→⌉	⌈option⌉ + ⌈→⌉
To the beginning of the current word (if insertion point is in the middle of a word)	⌈Ctrl⌉ + ⌈←⌉	⌈option⌉ + ⌈←⌉
To the beginning of the previous paragraph	⌈Ctrl⌉ + ⌈↑⌉	⌈command ⌘⌉ + ⌈↑⌉
To the beginning of the next paragraph	⌈Ctrl⌉ + ⌈↓⌉	⌈command ⌘⌉ + ⌈↓⌉
To the beginning of the current paragraph (if insertion point is in the middle of a paragraph)	⌈Ctrl⌉ + ⌈↑⌉	⌈command ⌘⌉ + ⌈↑⌉
Up one screen	⌈PgUp⌉	⌈fn⌉ + ⌈↑⌉
Down one screen	⌈PgDn⌉	⌈fn⌉ + ⌈↓⌉

Figure 1.33

2 To the left of *Skyline Metro Grill Chef Notes*, point in the left margin area to display the pointer, and then click one time to select the entire paragraph. On the **Home tab**, in the **Clipboard group**, click **Copy**.

Because anything that you select and then copy—or cut—is placed on the Clipboard, the Copy command and the Cut command display in the Clipboard group of commands on the ribbon. There is no visible indication that your copied selection has been placed on the Clipboard.

ANOTHER WAY Right-click the selection, and then click Copy on the shortcut menu; or, use the keyboard shortcut ⌈Ctrl⌉ + ⌈C⌉.

MAC TIP Press ⌈command ⌘⌉ + ⌈C⌉ as a keyboard shortcut for the Copy command.

3 On the **Home tab**, in the **Clipboard group**, to the right of the group name *Clipboard*, click the **Dialog Box Launcher** button 🔳, and then compare your screen with Figure 1.34.

The Clipboard pane displays with your copied text. In any ribbon group, the ***Dialog Box Launcher*** displays either a dialog box or a pane related to the group of commands. It is not necessary to display the Clipboard in this manner, although sometimes it is useful to do so.

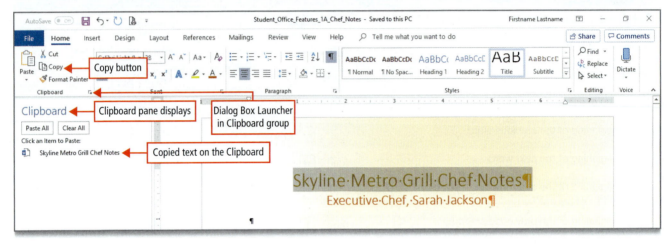

Figure 1.34

4 In the upper right corner of the **Clipboard** pane, click **Close** ✕.

5 Press Ctrl + End to move to the end of your document. On the **Home tab**, in the **Clipboard group**, point to **Paste**, and then click the *upper* portion of this split button.

The Paste command pastes the most recently copied item on the Clipboard at the insertion point location. If you click the lower portion of the Paste button, a gallery of Paste Options displays. A ***split button*** is divided into two parts; clicking the main part of the button performs a command, and clicking the arrow displays a list or gallery with choices.

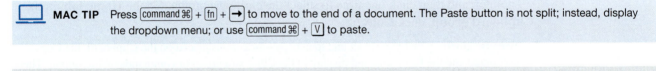

🔄 **ANOTHER WAY**   Right-click, on the shortcut menu under Paste Options, click the desired option button; or, press Control + V.

6 Below the pasted text, click **Paste Options** 📋 as shown in Figure 1.35.

Here you can view and apply various formatting options for pasting your copied or cut text. Typically, you will click Paste on the ribbon and paste the item in its original format. If you want some other format for the pasted item, you can choose another format from the ***Paste Options gallery***, which provides a Live Preview of the various options for changing the format of the pasted item with a single click. The Paste Options gallery is available in three places: on the ribbon by clicking the lower portion of the Paste button—the Paste button arrow; from the Paste Options button that displays below the pasted item following the paste operation; or on the shortcut menu if you right-click the pasted item.

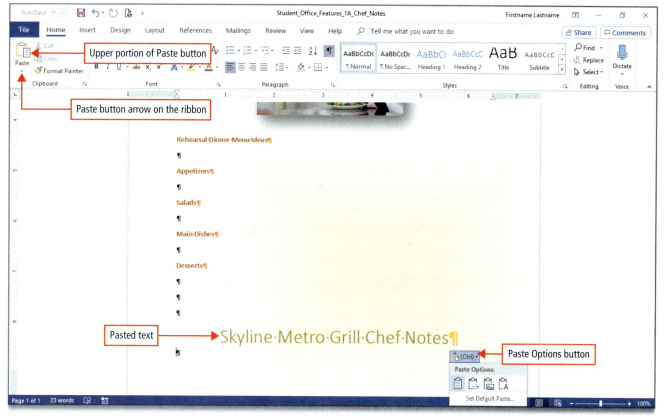

Figure 1.35

> **7** In the **Paste Options** gallery, *point* to each option to see the Live Preview of the format that would be applied if you clicked the button.

>> The contents of the Paste Options gallery are contextual; that is, they change based on what you copied and where you are pasting.

> **8** Press Esc to close the gallery; the button will remain displayed until you take some other screen action.

> **9** On your keyboard, press Ctrl + Home to move to the top of the document, and then click the **chefs image** one time to select it. While pointing to the selected image, right-click, and then on the shortcut menu, click **Cut**.

>> Recall that the Cut command cuts—removes—the selection from the document and places it on the Clipboard.

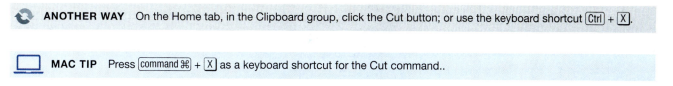

ANOTHER WAY On the Home tab, in the Clipboard group, click the Cut button; or use the keyboard shortcut Ctrl + X.

MAC TIP Press command ⌘ + X as a keyboard shortcut for the Cut command..

> **10** Press Ctrl + End to move to the end of the document.

11 With the insertion point blinking in the blank paragraph at the end of the document, right-click, and notice that the **Paste Options** gallery displays on the shortcut menu. Compare your screen with Figure 1.36.

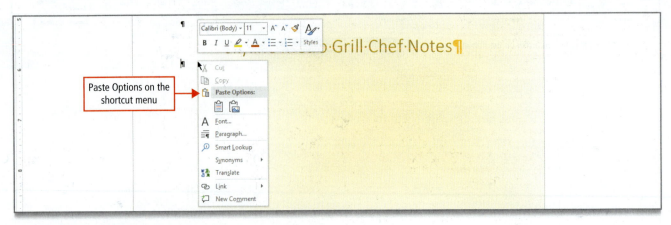

Figure 1.36

12 On the shortcut menu, under **Paste Options**, click the first button—**Keep Source Formatting**.

🖥 **MAC TIP** On the shortcut menu, click Paste, click the Paste Options button, and then click Keep Source Formatting.

13 Point to the picture to display the ⬚ pointer, and then drag to the right until the center green **Alignment Guide** displays and the blank paragraph is above the picture. Release the left mouse button.

🖥 **MAC TIP** In the Arrange group, on the Picture Format tab, click Align, click Align Center.

14 Above the picture, select the text *Chef Notes*, type **Festive Salad** and then compare your screen with Figure 1.37.

Figure 1.37

15 Click **Save** 💾.

Activity 1.14 | Adding Alternative Text for Accessibility

5.4.3

1 Point to the **chefs picture** and right-click. On the shortcut menu, click **Edit Alt Text** to display the **Alt Text** pane.

Alternative text helps people using a *screen reader*, which is software that enables visually impaired users to read text on a computer screen to understand the content of pictures. *Alt text* is the term commonly used for this feature.

2 ▶ In the **Alt Text** pane, notice that Word generates a suggested description of the picture. Click in the box, select the existing text, and then type **Young chefs making salads in a restaurant kitchen** and then compare your screen with Figure 1.38.

Anyone viewing the document with a screen reader will see the alternative text displayed instead of the picture.

Figure 1.38

3 ▶ **Close** ⊠ the **Alt Text** pane. Press Ctrl + Home to move to the top of your document. On the Quick Access Toolbar, click **Save** 🖫 to the changes you have made to your document.

GO! Learn How
Video OF1-5

Objective 5 | Finalize an Office Document

There are steps you will want to take to finalize your documents. This typically includes inserting a footer for identifying information and adding Document Properties to facilitate searching. Recall that Document Properties—also known as metadata—are details about a file that describe or identify it, such as the title, author name, subject, and keywords that identify the document's topic or contents. You might also want to take some security measures or mark information to find later.

Activity 1.15 | Inserting a Footer, Inserting Document Info, and Adding Document Properties

MOS
1.3.2

1 ▶ On the **Insert tab**, in the **Header & Footer group**, click **Footer**. At the bottom of the list, click **Edit Footer**, and then with the **Header & Footer Tools Design tab** active, in the **Insert group**, click **Document Info**. Click **File Name** to add the file name to the footer.

A *footer* is a reserved area for text and graphics that displays at the bottom of each page in a document. It is common in organizations to add the file name to the footer of documents so that documents are easily identified.

MAC TIP   In the Insert group, click Field. In the dialog box, under Categories, click Document Information. Then under Field names, click FileName. Click OK.

2 ▶ On the right end of the ribbon, click **Close Header and Footer**

3 ▶ On the **Quick Access Toolbar**, point to the **Print Preview and Print** button you placed there, right-click, and then click **Remove from Quick Access Toolbar**.

> If you are working on your own computer and you want to do so, you can leave the icon on the toolbar; in a college lab, you should return the software to its original settings.

4 ▶ Click the **File tab** to display **Backstage** view. With the **Info tab** active, in the lower right corner, click **Show All Properties**. Click in the **Tags** box, and then type **rehearsal dinners, menus**

> *Tags*—also referred to as *keywords*—are custom file properties in the form of words that you associate with a document to give an indication of the document's content. Use tags to assist in searching for and organizing files.

5 ▶ Click in the **Subject** box, and then type your course name and number—for example, *CIS 10, #5543*. Under **Related People**, be sure your name displays as the author. (To edit the Author, right-click the name, click Edit Property, type the new name, click in a white area to close the list, and then click OK.)

6 ▶ On the left, click **Save** to save your document and return to the Word window.

Activity 1.16 │ Inspecting a Document

Word, Excel, and PowerPoint all have the same commands to inspect a file before sharing it.

1.4.1, 1.4.2, 1.4.3

1 ▶ With your document displayed, click the **File tab**, on the left, if necessary, click **Info**, and then on the right, click **Check for Issues**.

2 ▶ On the list, click **Inspect Document**.

> The *Inspect Document* command searches your document for hidden data or personal information that you might not want to share publicly. This information could reveal company details that should not be shared.

3 ▶ In the lower right corner of the **Document Inspector** dialog box, click **Inspect**.

> The Document Inspector runs and lists information that was found and that you could choose to remove.

4 ▶ In the lower right corner of the dialog box, click **Close**, and then click **Check for Issues** again. On the list, click **Check Accessibility**.

> The *Check Accessibility* command checks the document for content that people with disabilities might find difficult to read. The Accessibility Checker pane displays on the right and lists objects that might require attention.

5 ▶ Close ☒ the **Accessibility Checker** pane, and then click the **File tab**.

6 ▶ Click **Check for Issues**, and then click **Check Compatibility**.

> The *Check Compatibility* command checks for features in your document that may not be supported by earlier versions of the Office program. This is only a concern if you are sharing documents with individuals with older software.

7 ▶ Click **OK**. Leave your Word document displayed for the next Activity.

Activity 1.17 | Inserting a Bookmark and a 3D Model

1.1.2, 5.2.6

A *bookmark* identifies a word, section, or place in your document so that you can find it quickly without scrolling. This is especially useful in a long document.

3D models are a new kind of shape that you can insert from an online library of ready-to-use three-dimensional graphics. A 3D model is most powerful in a PowerPoint presentation where you can add transitions and animations during your presentation, but you can also insert a 3D model into a Word document for an impactful image that you can position in various ways.

1 ▶ In the paragraph *Rehearsal Dinner Menu Items*, select the word *Menu*.

2 ▶ On the **Insert tab**, in the **Links group**, click **Bookmark**.

3 ▶ In the **Bookmark** name box, type **menu** and then click **Add**.

4 ▶ Press [Ctrl] + [Home] to move to the top of your document.

5 ▶ On the **Home tab**, at the right end of the ribbon, in the **Editing group**, click the **Find button arrow**, and then click **Go To**.

ANOTHER WAY Press [Ctrl] + [G], which is the keyboard shortcut for the Go To command.

MAC TIP On the menu bar, click Edit, point to Find, click Go To. In the dialog box, click Bookmark.

6 ▶ Under **Go to what**, click **Bookmark**, and then with *menu* indicated as the bookmark name, click **Go To**. **Close** the **Find and Replace** dialog box, and notice that your bookmarked text is selected for you.

7 ▶ Click to position your insertion point at the end of the word *Desserts*. On the **Insert tab**, in the **Illustrations group**, click **3D Models** to open the **Online 3D Models** dialog box.

NOTE   3D Models Not Available?

If the 3D Models command is not available on your system, in the **Illustrations group**, click **Pictures**, and then from the files downloaded with this project, click of01A_Cupcake. Change the Height to .75" and then move to Step 12.

8 ▶ In the search box, type **cupcake** and then press [Enter].

9 ▶ Click the image of the **cupcake in a pink and white striped wrapper**—or select any other cupcake image. At the bottom, click **Insert**.

10 ▶ Point to the **3D control** in the center of the image, hold down the left mouse button, and then rotate the image so the top of the cupcake is pointing toward the upper right corner of the page—your rotation need not be exact. Alternatively, in the 3D Model Views group, click the More button [▾], and then locate and click Above Front Left.

11 ▶ With the cupcake image selected, on the **3D Model Tools Format tab**, in the **Size group**, click in the **Height** box, type **.75"** and press [Enter].

12 ▶ In the **Arrange group**, click **Wrap Text**, and then click **In Front of Text**. Then, in the **Arrange group**, click **Align**, and click **Align Right** to position the cupcake at the right margin.

13 ▶ Press [Ctrl] + [Home] to move to the top of your document. On the **Quick Access Toolbar**, click **Save** [💾].

Activity 1.18 | Printing a File and Closing a Desktop App

1 Click the **File tab** to return to **Backstage** view, on the left click **Print**, and then compare your screen with Figure 1.39.

> Here you can select any printer connected to your system and adjust the settings related to how you want to print. On the right, the ***Print Preview*** displays, which is a view of a document as it will appear on paper when you print it. Your page color effect will not display in Print Preview nor will the shading print. This effect appears only to anyone viewing the document on a screen.

> At the bottom of the Print Preview area, in the center, the number of pages and page navigation arrows with which you can move among the pages in Print Preview display. On the right, the Zoom slider enables you to shrink or enlarge the Print Preview. ***Zoom*** is the action of increasing or decreasing the viewing area of the screen.

ANOTHER WAY   From the document screen, press [Ctrl] + [P] or [Ctrl] + [F2] to display Print in Backstage view.

MAC TIP   Press [command ⌘] + [P].

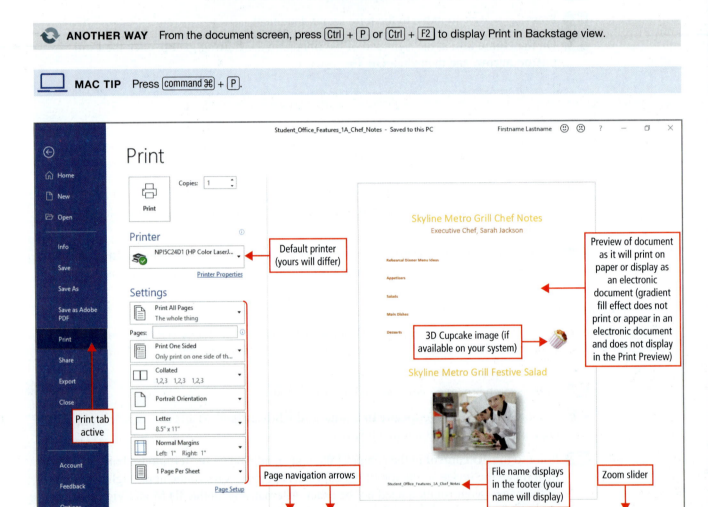

Figure 1.39

2 On the left, click **Save**. In the upper right corner of your screen, click **Close** ⊠ to close Word.

MAC TIP   On the menu bar, click File, click Close.

> **For Non-MyLab Submissions: Determine What Your Instructor Requires as Your Submission**
> As directed by your instructor, submit your completed Word document.

3 In **MyLab IT**, locate and click the Grader Project **Office Features 1A Chef Notes**. In **step 3**, under **Upload Completed Assignment**, click **Choose File**. In the **Open** dialog box, navigate to your **Office Features Chapter 1 folder**, and then click your **Student_Office_Features_1A_ Chef_Notes** file one time to select it. In the lower right corner of the **Open** dialog box, click **Open**.

> The name of your selected file displays above the Upload button.

4 To submit your file to MyLab IT for grading, click **Upload**, wait a moment for a green **Success!** message, and then in **step 4**, click the blue **Submit for Grading** button. Click **Close Assignment** to return to your list of **Course Materials**.

MORE KNOWLEDGE   **Creating an Electronic Image of Your Document**

You can create an electronic image of your document that looks like a printed document. To do so, in Backstage view, on the left click Export. On the right, click Create PDF/XPS, and then click the Create PDF/XPS button to display the Publish as PDF or XPS dialog box.

PDF stands for *Portable Document Format*, which is a technology that creates an image that preserves the look of your file. This is a popular format for sending documents electronically, because the document will display on most computers. *XPS* stands for *XML Paper Specification*—a Microsoft file format that also creates an image of your document and that opens in the XPS viewer.

ALERT   **The Remaining Activities in This Chapter Are Optional**

The following Activities describing the Office Help features are recommend but are optional to complete.

Objective 6   Use the Office Help Features

GO! Learn How
Video OF1-6

Within each Office program, you will see the ***Tell Me*** feature at the right end of the ribbon—to the right of the Help tab. This is a search feature for Microsoft Office commands that you activate by typing in the *Tell me what you want to do* box. Another way to use this feature is to point to a command on the ribbon, and then at the bottom of the displayed ScreenTip, click *Tell me more*.

Activity 1.19 │ Using Microsoft Office Tell Me, Tell Me More, the Help Tab, and Adding Alt Text to an Excel Chart

MOS
5.3.3

1 Start Excel and open a **Blank workbook**. With cell **A1** active, type **456789** and press Enter. Click cell **A1** again to make it the active cell.

2 At the top of the screen, click in the *Tell me what you want to do* box, and then type **format as currency** In the displayed list, to the right of **Accounting Number Format**, click the ▶ arrow. Compare your screen with Figure 1.40.

> As you type, every keystroke refines the results so that you can click the command as soon as it displays. This feature helps you apply the command immediately; it does not explain how to locate the command.

💻 **MAC TIP**   Click the Help tab on the menu bar.

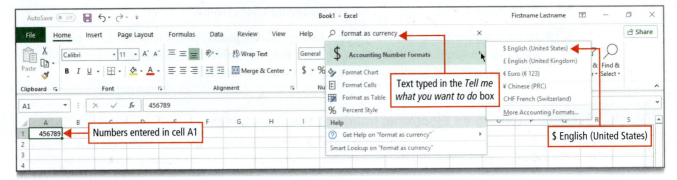

Figure 1.40

3 Click **$ English (United States)**.

4 On the **Home tab**, in the **Font group**, *point* to the **Font Color** button 🅰▾ to display its ScreenTip, and then click **Tell me more**.

> ***Tell me more*** is a prompt within a ScreenTip that opens the Office online Help system with explanations about how to perform the command referenced in the ScreenTip.

5 In the **Help** pane that displays on the right, if necessary, click **Change the color of text**. Compare your screen with Figure 1.41.

> As you scroll down, you will notice that the Help pane displays extensive information about the topic of changing the color of text, including how to apply a custom color.

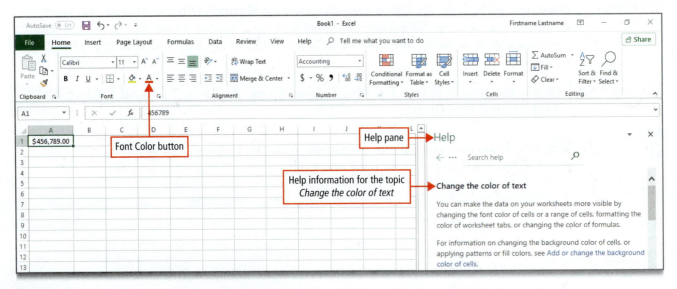

Figure 1.41

6 **Close** ✕ the **Help** pane.

7 On the ribbon, click the **Help tab**. In the **Help** group, click **Help**. In the **Help** pane, type **3D models** and then click the **Search** button 🔍. Click **Get creative with 3D models**, and then compare your screen with Figure 1.42.

> Some Help topics include videos like this one to demonstrate and explain the topic.

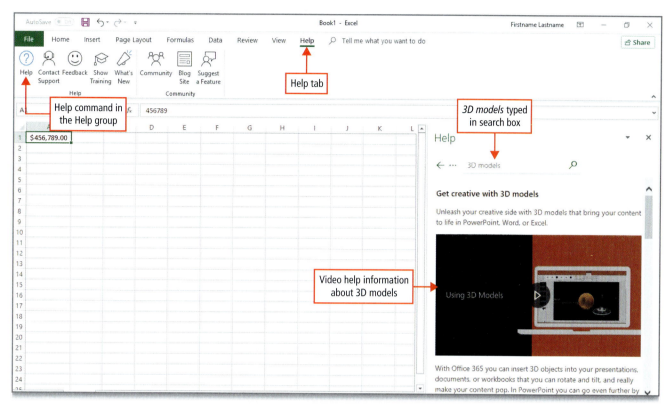

Figure 1.42

8 In the **Help** group and the **Community** group, look at the buttons.

> Here you can Contact Support, send Feedback, Show Training developed by Microsoft, and see new features. In the Community group, you can visit the Excel Community, read the Excel Blog, and suggest new features.

9 ▶ Click **Show Training**, and then compare your screen with Figure 1.43.

Here you can view training videos developed by Microsoft.

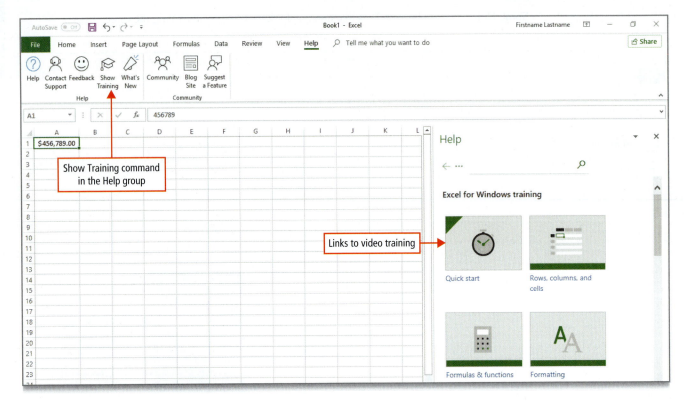

Figure 1.43

10 ▶ Click cell **A1**, and then click the **Insert tab**. In the **Charts group**, click **Recommended Charts**, and then in the **Insert Chart** dialog box, with the first chart selected, click **OK**.

11 ▶ Click the **Chart Tools Format tab**, and then in the **Accessibility group**, click **Alt Text**.

Here you can add text to describe the chart, similar to the Alt Text you added for the chef's image.

12 ▶ Close ☒ the **Help** pane, **Close** ☒ the **Alt Text** pane, and then in the upper right corner of the Excel window, click **Close** ☒. Click **Don't Save**.

MORE KNOWLEDGE **Don't Type, Talk! With the New Dictate Feature**

Office 365 subscribers will see the *Dictate* feature in Word, PowerPoint, Outlook, and OneNote for Windows 10. When you enable Dictate, you start talking and as you talk, text appears in your document or slide. Dictate is one of Microsoft's Office Intelligent Services, which adds new cloud-enhanced features to Office. Dictate is especially useful in Outlook when you must write lengthy emails. The Dictate command is on the Home tab in Word and PowerPoint and on the Message tab in Outlook.

You have completed Project 1A **END**

Hotel Files

Project Activities

In Activities 1.20 through 1.38, you will assist Barbara Hewitt and Steven Ramos, who work for the Information Technology Department at the Boston headquarters office of the Bell Orchid Hotels. Barbara and Steven must organize some of the files and folders that comprise the corporation's computer data. As you progress through the project, you will insert screenshots of windows that you create into a PowerPoint presentation with five slides that will look similar to Figure 1.44.

Project Files for **MyLab IT** Grader

For Project 1B, you will start with the Windows 10 desktop displayed, and then learn how to create a folder for your MyLab IT files as you work through the project instruction. At the appropriate point in the project, you will be instructed to download your files from your MyLab IT course.

Project Results

GO! Project 1B
Where We're Going

Figure 1.44

For Non-MyLab Submissions Start with the Windows 10 Desktop Displayed

For Project 1B, you will start with the Windows 10 desktop displayed and learn how to create a folder and save a new PowerPoint presentation as you work through the project instruction. Additionally, you will need the Student Data Files **win01_1B_Bell_Orchid** from your instructor or from www.pearsonhighered.com/go.

Objective 7 | Explore Windows 10

A *program* is a set of instructions that a computer uses to accomplish a task. A computer program that helps you perform a task for a specific purpose is referred to as an *application*. As an example, there are applications to create a document using word processing software, to play a game, to view the latest weather report, to edit photos or videos, or to manage financial information.

An *operating system* is a specific type of computer program that manages the other programs on a computing device such as a desktop computer, a laptop computer, a smartphone, a tablet computer, or a game console. You need an operating system to:

- Use application programs.
- Coordinate the use of your computer hardware such as a keyboard, mouse, touchpad, touchscreen, game controller, or printer.
- Organize data that you store on your computer and access data that you store on your own computer and in other locations.

Windows 10 is an operating system developed by Microsoft Corporation that works with mobile computing devices and also with traditional desktop and laptop PCs.

The three major tasks of an operating system are to:

- Manage your computer's hardware—the printers, scanners, disk drives, monitors, and other hardware attached to it.
- Manage the application software installed on your computer—programs like those in Microsoft Office and other programs you might install to edit photos and videos, play games, and so on.
- Manage the *data* generated from your application software. Data refers to the documents, worksheets, pictures, songs, and so on that you create and store during the day-to-day use of your computer.

The Windows 10 operating system continues to perform these three tasks, and additionally is optimized for touchscreens; for example, tablets of all sizes and convertible laptop computers. Windows 10 works equally well with any input device, including a mouse, keyboard, touchscreen, and *pen*—a pen-shaped stylus that you tap on a computer screen.

In most instances, when you purchase a computer, the operating system software is already installed. The operating system consists of many smaller programs, stored as system files, which transfer data to and from the disk and transfer data in and out of your computer's memory. Other functions performed by the operating system include hardware-specific tasks such as checking to see if a key has been pressed on the keyboard and, if it has, displaying the appropriate letter or character on the screen.

Windows 10, in the same manner as other operating systems and earlier versions of the Windows operating system, uses a *graphical user interface*—abbreviated as *GUI* and pronounced *GOO-ee*. A graphical user interface uses graphics such as an image of a file folder or wastebasket that you click to activate the item represented. A GUI commonly incorporates the following:

- A *pointer*—any symbol that displays on your screen in response to moving your mouse and with which you can select objects and commands.

- An *insertion point*—a blinking vertical line that indicates where text will be inserted when you type or where an action will take place.

- A *pointing device*, such as a mouse or touchpad, to control the pointer.

- *Icons*—small images that represent commands, files, applications, or other windows.

- A *desktop*—a simulation of a real desk that represents your work area; here you can arrange icons such as shortcuts to programs, files, folders, and various types of documents in the same manner you would arrange physical objects on top of a desk.

In Windows 10, you also have a Start menu with tiles that display when you click the Start button in the lower left corner of your screen. The array of tiles serves as a connected dashboard to all of your important programs, sites, and services. On the Start menu, your view is tailored to your information and activities.

The physical parts of your computer such as the central processing unit (CPU), memory, and any attached devices such as a printer, are collectively known as *resources*. The operating system keeps track of the status of each resource and decides when a resource needs attention and for how long.

Application programs enable you to do work on, and be entertained by, your computer—programs such as Word and Excel found in the Microsoft Office suite of products, Adobe Photoshop, and computer games. No application program, whether a larger desktop app or smaller *Microsoft Store app*—a smaller app that you download from the Store—can run on its own; it must run under the direction of an operating system.

For the everyday use of your computer, the most important and most often used function of the operating system is managing your files and folders—referred to as *data management*. In the same manner that you strive to keep your paper documents and file folders organized so that you can find information when you need it, your goal when organizing your computer files and folders is to group your files so that you can find information easily. Managing your data files so that you can find your information when you need it is one of the most important computing skills you can learn.

Activity 1.20 | Recognizing User Accounts in Windows 10

On a single computer, Windows 10 can have multiple user accounts. This is useful because you can share a computer with other people in your family or organization and each person can have his or her own information and settings—none of which others can see. Each user on a single computer is referred to as a ***user account***. Figure 1.45 shows the Settings screen where you can add additional users to your computer.

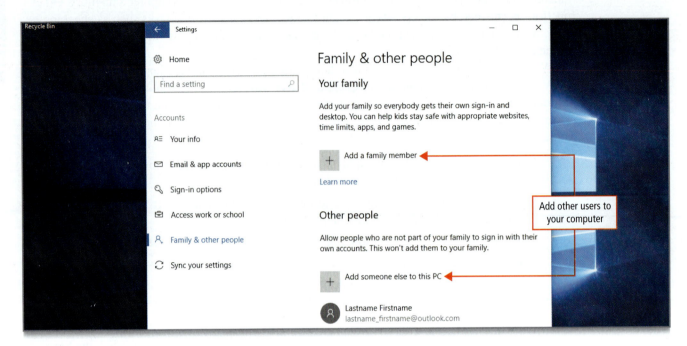

Figure 1.45

With Windows 10, you can create a ***Microsoft account***, and then use that account to sign in to *any* Windows 10 computer on which you have, or create, a user account. By signing in with a Microsoft account you can:

• Download apps from the Microsoft Store
• Get your online content—email, social network updates, updated news—automatically displayed in an app when you sign in

Optionally, you can create a local account for use only on a specific PC. On your own Windows 10 computer, you must establish and then sign in with either a local account or a Microsoft account. Regardless of which one you select, you must provide an email address to associate with the user account name. If you create and then sign in with a local account, you can still connect to the internet, but you will not have the advantage of having your personal arrangement of apps displayed on your Start menu every time you sign in to that PC. You can use any email address to create a local account—similar to other online services where an email address is your user ID. You can also use any email address to create a Microsoft account.

To enjoy and get the full benefit of Windows 10, Microsoft Office, Skype, and free OneDrive cloud storage, if you have not already done so, create a Microsoft account. To do so, in your preferred web search engine, search for *create a Microsoft account.*

You can create an account using any email address. By signing in with a Microsoft account, your computer becomes your connected device where *you*—not your files—are the center of activity. At your college or place of employment, sign-in requirements will vary, because those computers are controlled by the organization's IT (Information Technology) professionals who are responsible for maintaining a secure computing environment for the entire organization.

Activity 1.21 | **Turning On Your Computer, Signing In, and Exploring the Windows 10 Environment**

Before you begin any computer activity, you must, if necessary, turn on your computer. This process is commonly referred to as ***booting the computer***. Because Windows 10 does not require you to completely shut down your computer except to install or repair a hardware device, in most instances moving the mouse or pressing a key will wake your computer in a few seconds. So, most of the time you will skip the lengthier boot process.

In this Activity, you will turn on your computer and sign in to Windows 10. Within an organization, the sign-in process may differ from that of your own computer.

ALERT The look and features of Windows 10 will differ between your own PC and a PC you might use at your college or workplace.

The Activities in this project assume that you are working on your own PC and signed in with a Microsoft account, or that you are working on a PC at your college or workplace where you are permitted to sign into Windows 10 with your own Microsoft account.

If you do not have a Microsoft account, or are working at a computer where you are unable to sign in with your Microsoft account, you can still complete the Activities, but some steps will differ.

On your own computer, you created your user account when you installed Windows 10 or when you set up your new computer that came with Windows 10. In a classroom or lab, check with your instructor to see how you will sign in to Windows 10.

NOTE Create your Microsoft account if you have not already done so.

To benefit from this instruction and understand your own computer, be sure that you know your Microsoft account login and password and use that to set up your user account. If you need to create a Microsoft account, in your preferred web search engine, search for *create a Microsoft account* and click the appropriate link.

1 If necessary, turn on your computer, and then examine Figure 1.46.

The Windows 10 *lock screen* fills your computer screen with a background—this might be a default picture from Microsoft such as one of the ones shown in the Lock screen settings in Figure 1.46 or a picture that you selected if you have personalized your system already. You can also choose to have a slide show of your own photos display on the lock screen.

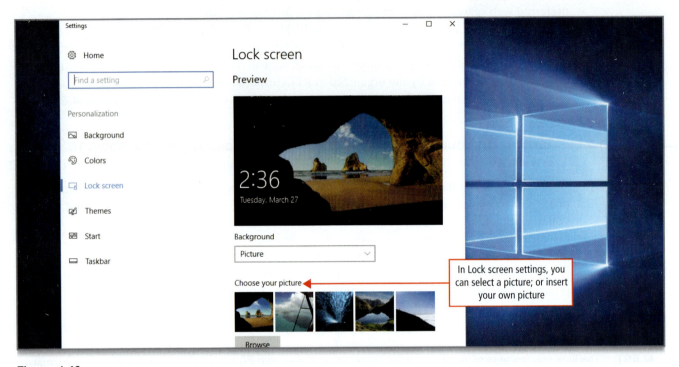

Figure 1.46

2 Determine whether you are working with a mouse and keyboard system or with a touchscreen system. If you are working with a touchscreen, determine whether you will use a stylus pen or the touch of your fingers.

NOTE   This Book Assumes You Are Using a Mouse and Keyboard, but You Can Also Use Touch

This instruction uses terminology that assumes you are using a mouse and keyboard, but you need only touch gestures (described at the beginning of Project 1A in this chapter) to move through the instruction easily using touch. If a touch gesture needs more clarification, a *By Touch* box will assist you in using the correct gesture. Because more precision is needed for desktop operations, touching with a stylus pen may be preferable to touch using your fingers. When working with Microsoft Store apps, finger gestures are usually precise enough.

---

3 Press Enter to display the Windows 10 sign-in screen. If you are already signed in, go to Step 5.

BY TOUCH   On the lock screen, swipe upward to display the sign-in screen. Tap your user image if necessary to display the Password box.

---

4 If you are the displayed user, type your password (if you have established one) and press Enter. If you are not the displayed user, click your user image if it displays or click the Switch user arrow →   and then click your user image. Type your password.

The Windows 10 desktop displays with a default desktop background, a background you have selected, or perhaps a background set by your college or workplace.

BY TOUCH   Tap the Password box to display the onscreen keyboard, type your password using the onscreen keyboard, and then at the right, tap the arrow.

5▸ In the lower left corner of your screen, move the mouse pointer over—*point to*—**Start** ▦ and then *click*—press the left button on your mouse pointing device—to display the **Start menu**. Compare your screen with Figure 1.47, and then take a moment to study the table in Figure 1.48. If your list of programs does not display, in the upper left, click the ≡.

The *mouse pointer* is any symbol that displays on your screen in response to moving your mouse.

The Windows 10 *Start menu* displays a list of installed programs on the left and a customizable group of square and rectangular boxes—referred to as *tiles*—on the right. You can customize the arrangement of tiles from which you can access apps, websites, programs, folders, and tools for using your computer by simply clicking or tapping them.

Think of the right side of the Start menu as your connected *dashboard*—a one-screen view of links to information and programs that matter to *you*—through which you can connect with the people, activities, places, and apps that you care about.

Some tiles are referred to as *live tiles*, because they are constantly updated with fresh information relevant to you—the number of new email messages you have or new sports scores that you are interested in. Live tiles are at the center of your Windows 10 experience.

Figure 1.47

Parts of the Windows 10 Start Menu	
Create	Apps pinned to the Start menu that relate to your own information; for example, your Mail, your Calendar, and apps with which you create things; for example, your Office apps.
Apps list	Displays a list of the apps available on your system (yours will differ).
Play and Explore	Apps pinned to the Start menu that relate to games or news apps that you have installed; you can change this heading or delete it.
Power button	Enables you to set your computer to Sleep, Shut down, or Restart.
Settings	Displays the Settings menu to change any Windows 10 setting.
Signed-in User	Displays the icon for the signed-in user.

Figure 1.48

6 Click **Start** ⊞ again to close the Start menu. Compare your screen with Figure 1.49, and then take a moment to study the parts of the Windows desktop as shown in the table in Figure 1.50.

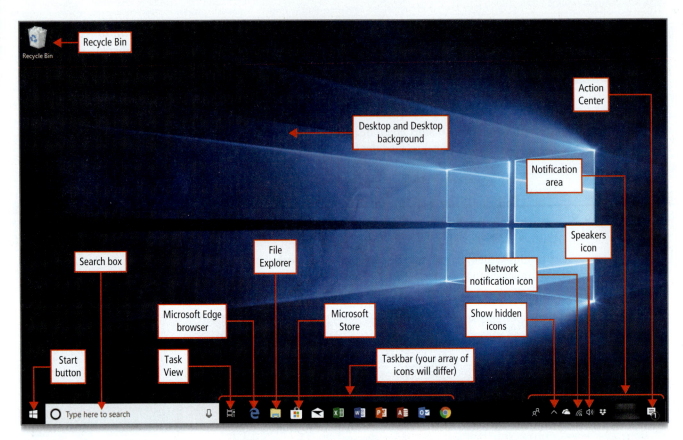

Figure 1.49

Parts of the Windows 10 Desktop	
Action Center	Displays the Action Center in a vertical pane on the right of your screen where you can see notifications—such as new mail or new alerts from social networks—at the top and access commonly used settings at the bottom.
Desktop	Serves as a surface for your work, like the top of an actual desk. Here you can arrange icons— small pictures that represent a file, folder, program, or other object.
Desktop background	Displays the colors and graphics of your desktop; you can change the desktop background to look the way you want it, such as using a picture or a solid color. Also referred to as *wallpaper*.
File Explorer	Launches the File Explorer program, which displays the contents of folders and files on your computer and on connected locations and also enables you to perform tasks related to your files and folders such as copying, moving, and renaming. If your File Explorer icon does not display, search for it, right-click its name in the search results, and then click Pin to taskbar.
Microsoft Edge browser	Launches Microsoft Edge, the web browser program developed by Microsoft that is included with Windows 10.
Microsoft Store	Opens the Microsoft Store where you can select and download Microsoft Store apps.
Network notification icon	Displays the status of your network.
Notification area	Displays notification icons and the system clock and calendar; sometimes referred to as the *system tray*.
Recycle Bin	Contains files and folders that you delete. When you delete a file or folder, it is not actually deleted; it stays in the Recycle Bin if you want it back, until you take an action to empty the Recycle Bin.
Search box	If *Cortana*—Microsoft's intelligent personal assistant—is enabled, a small circle will display on the left edge of the Search box. If Cortana is not enabled, a search icon displays at the left edge.

Parts of the Windows 10 Desktop	
Show hidden icons	Displays additional icons related to your notifications.
Speakers icon	Displays the status of your computer's speakers (if any).
Start button	Displays the Start menu.
Task View	Displays your desktop background with a small image of all open programs and apps. Click once to open, click again to close. May also display the Timeline.
Taskbar	Contains buttons to launch programs and buttons for all open programs; by default, it is located at the bottom of the desktop, but you can move it. You can customize the number and arrangement of buttons.

Figure 1.50

Activity 1.22 | Pinning a Program to the Taskbar

Snipping Tool is a program within Windows 10 that captures an image of all or part of your computer's screen. A *snip*, as the captured image is called, can be annotated, saved, copied, or shared via email. Any capture of your screen is referred to as a *screenshot*, and there are many other ways to capture your screen in addition to the Snipping Tool.

NOTE   Snip & Sketch Offers Improved Snipping Capabilities

Although Snipping Tool will be available for several more years, a newer tool for snipping, called Snip & Sketch, will roll out to Windows 10 users. Find it by typing Snip & Sketch in the search box.

---

1 In the lower left corner of your screen, click in the **Search box**.

Search relies on *Bing*, Microsoft's search engine, which enables you to conduct a search on your PC, your apps, and the web.

2 With your insertion point in the search box, type **snipping** Compare your screen with Figure 1.51.

BY TOUCH   On a touchscreen, tap in the Search box to display the onscreen keyboard, and then begin to type *snipping*.

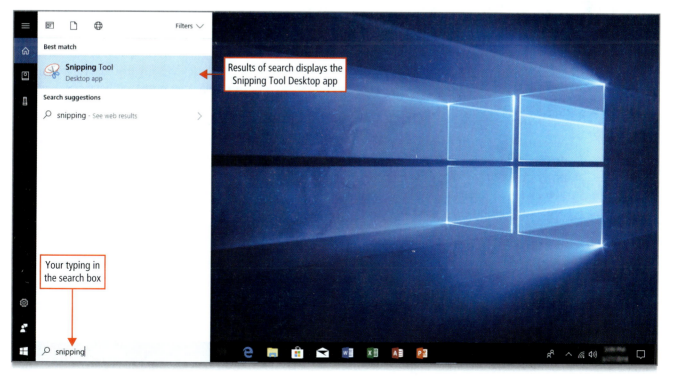

Results of search displays the Snipping Tool Desktop app

Your typing in the search box

Figure 1.51

3 With the **Snipping Tool Desktop app** shaded and displayed at the top of the search results, press Enter one time.

> The Snipping Tool program's *dialog box*—a small window that displays options for completing a task—displays on the desktop, and on the taskbar, the Snipping Tool program button displays underlined and framed in a lighter shade to indicate that the program is open.

BY TOUCH   In the search results, tap the Snipping Tool app.

4 On the taskbar, point to the **Snipping Tool** button and then *right-click*—click the right mouse button one time. On the displayed **Jump List**, click **Pin to taskbar**.

> A *Jump List* displays destinations and tasks from a program's taskbar icon when you right-click the icon.

BY TOUCH   On the taskbar, use the *Swipe to select* technique—swipe upward with a short quick movement—to display the Jump List. On the list, tap *Pin to taskbar*.

5 Point to the upper right corner of the **Snipping Tool** dialog box, and then click **Close** ☒.

> Because Snipping Tool is a useful tool, while completing the Projects in this textbook, it is recommended that you leave Snipping Tool pinned to your taskbar.

Objective 8 | Prepare to Work with Folders and Files

A *file* is a collection of information stored on a computer under a single name. Examples of a file include a Word document, an Excel workbook, a picture, a song, or a program. A *folder* is a container in which you store files. Windows 10 organizes and keeps track of your electronic files by letting you create and label electronic folders into which you can place your files.

Activity 1.23 | Creating a New Folder to Store a File

In this Activity, you will create a new folder and save it in a location of your choice. You might decide to use a *removable storage device*, such as a USB flash drive, which is commonly used to transfer information from one computer to another. Such devices are also useful when you want to work with your files on different computers. For example, you probably have files that you work with at your college, at home, and possibly at your workplace.

A *drive* is an area of storage that is formatted with a file system compatible with your operating system and is identified by a drive letter. For example, your computer's *hard disk drive*—the primary storage device located inside your computer where some of your files and programs are typically stored—is usually designated as drive *C*. Removable storage devices that you insert into your computer will be designated with a drive letter—the letter designation varies depending on how many input ports you have on your computer.

You can also use *cloud storage*—storage space on an internet service that can also display as a drive on your computer. When you create a Microsoft account, free cloud storage called *OneDrive* is provided to you. If you are signed in with your Microsoft account, you can access OneDrive from File Explorer.

Increasingly, the use of removable storage devices for file storage is becoming less common, because having your files stored in the cloud where you can retrieve them from any device is more convenient and efficient.

1 ▶ Be sure your Windows desktop is still displayed. If you want to do so, insert your USB flash drive. If necessary, close any messages.

Plugging in a device results in a chime sound—if sound is enabled. You might see a message in the taskbar or on the screen that the device software is being installed.

2 ▶ On your taskbar, check to see if the **File Explorer** icon ▣ displays. If it does, move to Step 3. If not, in the search box, type **file explorer** under **Best match**, point to **File Explorer Desktop app**, right-click, and then click **Pin to taskbar**.

In an enterprise environment such as a college or business, File Explorer may not be pinned to the taskbar by default, so you might have to pin it there each time you use the computer. Windows 10 Home, the version of Windows that comes on most consumer PCs, typically has File Explorer pinned to the taskbar by default.

3 ▶ On the taskbar, click **File Explorer** ▣. If necessary, in the upper right corner of the **File Explorer** window, click Expand the Ribbon ▢.

File Explorer is the program that displays the contents of locations, folders, and files on your computer and also in your OneDrive and other cloud storage locations.

The *ribbon* is a user interface in Windows 10 that groups commands for performing related tasks on tabs across the upper portion of a window. Commands for common tasks include copying and moving, creating new folders, emailing and zipping items, and changing the view.

Use the *navigation pane*—the area on the left side of File Explorer window—to get to locations—your OneDrive, folders on your PC, devices and drives connected to your PC, and other PCs on your network.

4 On the ribbon at the top of the window, click the **View tab**, and then in the **Layout group**, click **Tiles**. Compare your screen with Figure 1.52, and then take a moment to study the parts of the File Explorer window as shown in the table in Figure 1.53.

The *File Explorer window* displays with the Quick access area selected by default. A File Explorer window displays the contents of the current location and contains helpful parts so you can *navigate*—explore within the file organizing structure of Windows. A *location* is any disk drive, folder, network, or cloud storage area in which you can store files and folders.

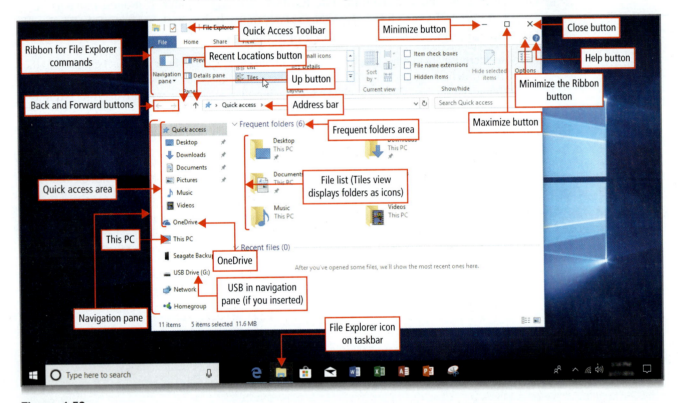

Figure 1.52

Parts of the File Explorer Window

Address bar	Displays your current location in the folder structure as a series of links separated by arrows.
Back and Forward buttons	Provides the ability to navigate to other folders you have already opened without closing the current folder window. These buttons work with the address bar; that is, after you use the address bar to change folders, you can use the Back button to return to the previous folder.
Close button	Closes the window.
File list	Displays the contents of the current folder or location; if you type text into the Search box, only the folders and files that match your search will display here—including files in subfolders.
Frequent folders area	When Quick access is selected in the navigation pane, displays the folders you use frequently.
Help button	Opens a Bing search for Windows 10 help.
Maximize button	Increases the size of a window to fill the entire screen.
Minimize button	Removes the window from the screen without closing it; minimized windows can be reopened by clicking the associated button in the taskbar.

Parts of the File Explorer Window

Minimize the Ribbon button	Collapses the ribbon so that only the tab names display.
Navigation pane	Displays—for the purpose of navigating to locations—the Quick access area, your OneDrive if you have one and are signed in, locations on the PC at which you are working, any connected storage devices, and network locations to which you might be connected.
OneDrive	Provides navigation to your free file storage and file sharing service provided by Microsoft that you get when you sign up for a Microsoft account; this is your personal cloud storage for files.
Quick access area	Displays commonly accessed locations—such as Documents and Desktop—that you want to access quickly.
Quick Access Toolbar	Displays commonly used commands; you can customize this toolbar by adding and deleting commands and by showing it below the ribbon instead of above the ribbon.
Recent Locations button	Displays the path to locations you have visited recently so that you can go back to a previously working directory quickly.
Ribbon for File Explorer commands	Groups common tasks such as copying and moving, creating new folders, emailing and zipping items, and changing views.
Search box	Locates files stored within the current folder when you type a search term.
This PC	Provides navigation to your internal storage and attached storage devices including optical media such as a DVD drive.
Up button	Opens the location where the folder you are viewing is saved—also referred to as the *parent folder*.

Figure 1.53

5 In the **navigation pane**, click **This PC**. On the right, under **Devices and drives**, locate **Windows (C:)**—or **OS (C:)**—point to the device name to display the ⬚ pointer, and then right-click to display a shortcut menu. Compare your screen with Figure 1.54.

A *shortcut menu* is a context-sensitive menu that displays commands and options relevant to the active object. The Windows logo on the C: drive indicates this is where the Windows 10 operating system is stored.

BY TOUCH Press and hold briefly to display a shaded square and then release.

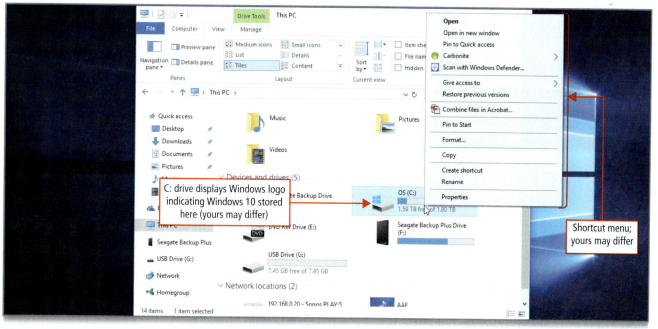

Figure 1.54

6 On the shortcut menu, click **Open** to display the *file list* for this drive.

A file list displays the contents of the current location. This area is also referred to as the *content pane*. If you enter a search term in the search box, your results will also display here. Here, in the C: drive, Windows 10 stores various files related to your operating system.

ANOTHER WAY Point to the device name and double-click to display the file list for the device.

7 On the ribbon, notice that the **Drive Tools** tab displays above the **Manage tab**.

This is a *contextual tab*, which is a tab added to the ribbon automatically when a specific object is selected and that contains commands relevant to the selected object.

8 To the left of the **address bar**, click **Up** ⬆ to move up one level in the drive hierarchy and close the file list.

The *address bar* displays your current location in the folder structure as a series of links separated by arrows. Use the address bar to enter or select a location. You can click a part of the path to go to that level. Or, click at the end of the path to select the path for copying.

9 Under **Devices and drives**, click your **USB flash drive** to select it—or click the folder or location where you want to store your file for this project—and notice that the drive or folder is highlighted in blue, indicating it is selected. At the top of the window, on the ribbon, click the **Computer tab**, and then in the **Location group**, click **Open**. Compare your screen with Figure 1.55.

The file list for the selected location displays. There may be no files or only a few files in the location you have selected. You can open a location by double-clicking its name, using the shortcut menu, or by using this ribbon command.

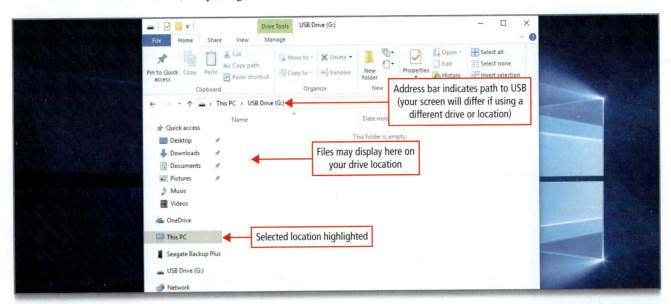

Figure 1.55

10 On the ribbon, on the **Home tab**, in the **New group**, click **New folder**.

11 With the text *New folder* highlighted, type **Windows 10 Chapter 1** and then press Enter to confirm the folder name and select—highlight—the new folder. With the folder selected, press Enter again to open the File Explorer window for your **Windows 10 Chapter 1** folder. Compare your screen with Figure 1.56.

> Windows creates a new folder in the location you selected. The address bar indicates the *path* from This PC to your folder. A path is a sequence of folders that leads to a specific file or folder.
>
> To *select* means to specify, by highlighting, a block of data or text on the screen with the intent of performing some action on the selection.

BY TOUCH You may have to tap the keyboard icon in the lower right corner of the taskbar to display the onscreen keyboard.

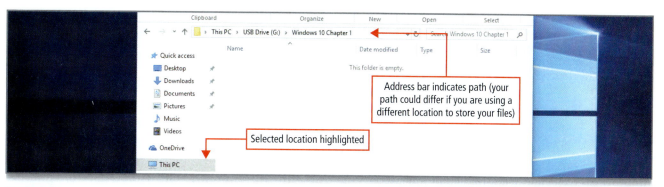

Figure 1.56

MORE KNOWLEDGE **Use OneDrive as Cloud Storage**

OneDrive is Microsoft's *cloud storage* product. Cloud storage means that your data is stored on a remote server that is maintained by a company so that you can access your files from anywhere and from any device. The idea of having all your data on a single device—your desktop or laptop PC—has become old fashioned. Because cloud storage from large companies like Microsoft are secure, many computer users now store their information on cloud services like OneDrive. Anyone with a Microsoft account has a large amount of free storage on OneDrive, and if you have an Office 365 account—free to most college students—you have 1 terabyte or more of OneDrive storage that you can use across all Microsoft products. That amount of storage is probably all you will ever need—even if you store lots of photos on your OneDrive. OneDrive is integrated into the Windows 10 operating system.

Activity 1.24 | Creating and Saving a File

1 In the upper right corner of your **Windows 10 Chapter 1** folder window, click **Close** ⊠.

2 In the lower left corner, click **Start** ⊞.

3 ▶ Point to the right side of the **apps list** to display a **scroll bar**, and then drag the **scroll box** down to view apps listed under **T**. Compare your screen with Figure 1.57.

To *drag* is to move something from one location on the screen to another while holding down the left mouse button; the action of dragging includes releasing the mouse button at the desired time or location.

A vertical *scroll bar* displays on the right side of the menu area. A scroll bar displays when the contents of a window or pane are not completely visible. A scroll bar can be vertical as shown or horizontal and displayed at the bottom of a window.

Within the scroll bar, you can move the *scroll box* to bring the contents of the window into view. The position of the scroll box within the scroll bar indicates your relative position within the window's contents. You can click the *scroll arrow* at either end of the scroll bar to move within the window in small increments.

Figure 1.57

MORE KNOWLEDGE   **Jump to a Lettered Section of the Apps List Quickly**

To move quickly to an alphabetic section of the apps list, click an alphabetic letter on the list to display an onscreen alphabet, and then click the letter of the alphabet to which you want to jump.

---

4 ▶ Click **Tips**. If necessary, in the upper right, click **Maximize** ☐ so that the **Tips** window fills your entire screen. Then, move your mouse pointer to the right edge of the screen to display the **scroll bar**. Compare your screen with Figure 1.58.

In any window, the *Maximize* button will maximize the size of the window to fill the entire screen.

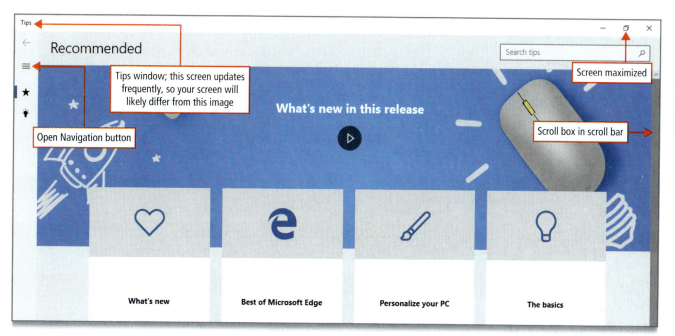

Figure 1.58

> **5** In the upper left corner, click **Open Navigation** ≡.

This icon is commonly referred to as a *menu icon* or a *hamburger menu* or simply a *hamburger*. The name derives from the three lines that bring to mind a hamburger on a bun. This type of button is commonly used in mobile applications because it is compact to use on smaller screens.

When you click the hamburger icon, a menu expands to identify the icons on the left—Recommended and Collections.

> **6** Click **Collections**, and then click **Windows**. Click **Get organized**. Move your mouse within the center right side of the screen to display a slideshow arrow ▷, and then click the arrow until you get to the tip **Snap apps side by side**; if this tip is not available, pause at another interesting tip. Compare your screen with Figure 1.59.

To find interesting new things about Windows, Office, Microsoft Mixed Reality, and other topics, take time to explore the Tips app.

Figure 1.59

7 On the taskbar, click **Snipping Tool** 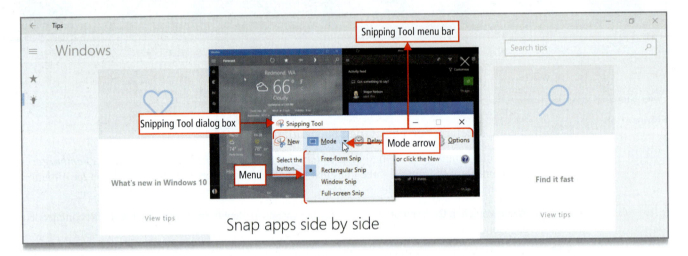 to display the small **Snipping Tool** dialog box over the screen.

8 On the **menu bar** of the **Snipping Tool** dialog box, to the right of *Mode*, click the **arrow**. Compare your screen with Figure 1.60.

> This *menu*—a list of commands within a category—displays four types of snips. A group of menus at the top of a program window is referred to as the *menu bar*.
>
> Use a *free-form snip* to draw an irregular line such as a circle around an area of the screen. Use a *rectangular snip* to draw a precise box by dragging the mouse pointer around an area of the screen to form a rectangle. Use a *window snip* to capture the entire displayed window. Use a *full-screen snip* to capture the entire screen.

Figure 1.60

9 On the menu, click **Rectangular Snip**, and move your mouse slightly. Notice that the screen dims and your pointer takes the shape of a plus sign ⊞.

10 Move the ⊞ pointer to the upper left corner of the slide portion of the screen, hold down the left mouse button, and then drag down and to the right until you have captured the slide portion of the screen, as shown in Figure 1.61 and then release the mouse button. If you are not satisfied with your result, close the Snipping Tool window and begin again.

> The Snipping Tool mark-up window displays the portion of the screen that you snipped. Here you can annotate—mark or make notes on—save, copy, or share the snip.

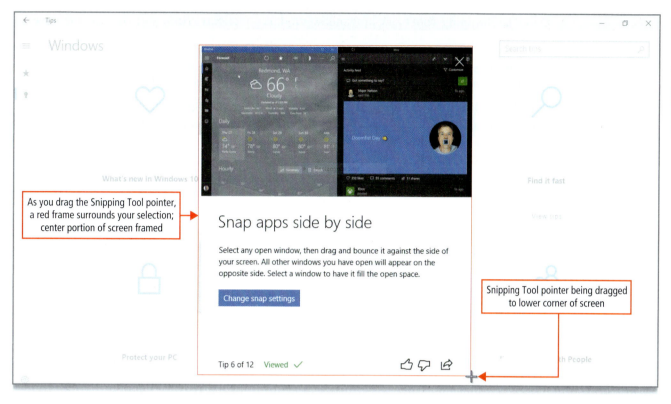

As you drag the Snipping Tool pointer, a red frame surrounds your selection; center portion of screen framed

Snipping Tool pointer being dragged to lower corner of screen

Figure 1.61

11 On the toolbar of the displayed **Snipping Tool** mark-up window, click the **Pen button arrow** , and then click **Red Pen**. Notice that your mouse pointer displays as a red dot.

12 On the snip—remember that you are now looking at a picture of the portion of the screen you captured—use the red mouse pointer to draw a circle around the text *Snap apps side by side*—or whatever the name of the tip you selected is. The circle need not be precise. If you are not satisfied with your circle, on the toolbar, click the Eraser button , point anywhere on the red circle, click to erase, and then begin again. Compare your screen with Figure 1.62.

Snipping Tool markup window

Pen markup tool

Snipping Tool markup menu bar

Snipping Tool toolbar

Your image may differ if you selected a different tip

Snipping Tool creates a picture of the portion of the screen you captured.

Red circle created with Red Pen markup tool

Figure 1.62

13 On the **Snipping Tool** mark-up window's toolbar, click **Save Snip** 🖫 to display the **Save As** dialog box.

14 In the **Save As** dialog box, in the **navigation pane**, drag the scroll box down as necessary to find and then click the location where you created your **Windows 10 Chapter 1** folder.

15 In the **file list**, scroll as necessary, locate and *double-click*—press the left mouse button two times in rapid succession while holding the mouse still—your **Windows 10 Chapter 1** folder. Compare your screen with Figure 1.63.

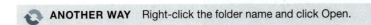

ANOTHER WAY Right-click the folder name and click Open.

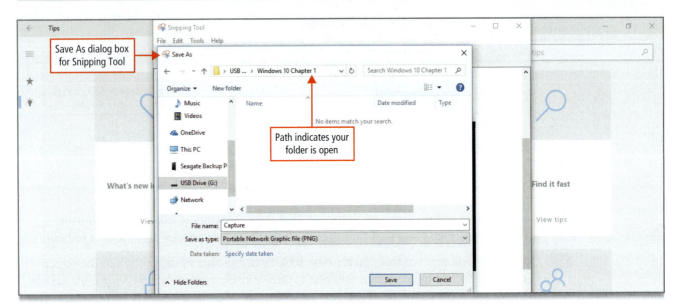

Figure 1.63

NOTE   Successful Double-Clicking Requires a Steady Hand

Double-clicking needs a steady hand. The speed of the two clicks is not as important as holding the mouse still between the two clicks. If you are not satisfied with your result, try again.

---

16 At the bottom of the **Save As** dialog box, locate **Save as type**, click anywhere in the box to display a list, and then on the displayed list click **JPEG file**.

> *JPEG*, which is commonly pronounced *JAY-peg* and stands for Joint Photographic Experts Group, is a common file type used by digital cameras and computers to store digital pictures. JPEG is popular because it can store a high-quality picture in a relatively small file.

17 At the bottom of the **Save As** dialog box, click in the **File name** box to select the text *Capture*, and then using your own name, type **Lastname_Firstname_1B_Tip_Snip**

> Within any Windows-based program, text highlighted in blue—selected—in this manner will be replaced by your typing.

NOTE   File Naming in This Textbook

Windows 10 recognizes file names with spaces. You can use spaces in file names, however, some programs, especially when transferring files over the internet, may insert the extra characters %20 in place of a space. In this instruction you will be instructed to save files using an underscore instead of a space. The underscore key is the shift of the ⌐ key—on most keyboards located two or three keys to the left of ⌫Backspace.

---

18 In the lower right corner of the window, click **Save**.

19 **Close** ☒ the **Snipping Tool** mark-up window, and then **Close** ☒ the **Tips** window.

20 Close any open windows and display your Windows desktop.

You have successfully created a folder and saved a file within that folder.

MORE KNOWLEDGE **The Hamburger** ☰

For a brief history of the hamburger icon, visit http://blog.placeit.net/history-of-the-hamburger-icon

---

For Non-MyLab Submissions

Start PowerPoint and click Blank Presentation. Click the File tab, on the left click Save As, click Browse, and then navigate to your Windows 10 Chapter 1 folder. At the bottom of the Save As dialog box, in the File name box, using your own name, name the file **Lastname_Firstname_Windows_10_1B_Hotel_Files** and then click Save. Move to Activity 1.26.

Activity 1.25 | Downloading and Extracting Zipped Files

1 If the Microsoft PowerPoint application is not pinned to your taskbar, use the same technique you used to search for and pin the Snipping Tool application to search for and pin the PowerPoint application to your taskbar.

2 Sign in to your MyLab IT course. In your course, locate and click **Windows 10 1B Hotel Files**, click Download Materials, and then click Download All Files. Using the Chrome browser (if you are using a different browser see notes below), use the steps below to extract the zipped folder to your **Windows 10 Chapter 1** (or use your favorite method to download and extract files):

- In the lower left, next to the downloaded zipped folder, click the small **arrow**, and then click **Show in folder**. The zipped folder displays in *File Explorer*—the Windows program that displays the contents of locations, folders, and files on your computer—in the Downloads folder. (Unless you have changed default settings, downloaded files go to the Downloads folder on your computer.)
- With the zipped folder selected, on the ribbon, under **Compressed Folder Tools**, click the **Extract tab**, and then at the right end of the ribbon, click **Extract all**.
- In the displayed **Extract Compressed (Zipped) Folders** dialog box, click **Browse**. In the **Select a destination** dialog box, use the navigation pane on the left to navigate to your **Windows 10 Chapter 1 folder**, and double-click its name to open the folder and display its name in the **Address bar**.
- In the lower right, click **Select Folder**, and then in the lower right, click **Extract**; when complete, a new File Explorer window displays showing the extracted files in your chapter folder. For this Project, you will see a PowerPoint file with your name and another zipped folder named **win01_1B_Bell_Orchid**, which you will extract later, a result file to check against, and an Instruction file. Take a moment to open **Windows_10_1B_Hotel_Files_Instructions**; note any recent updates to the book.
- **Close** ☒ both File Explorer windows, close the Grader download screens, and close any open documents For this Project, you should close MyLab and any other open windows in your browser.

3 From the taskbar, click **File Explorer**, navigate to and reopen your **Windows 10 Chapter 1 folder**, and then double-click the PowerPoint file you downloaded from MyLab IT that displays your name—**Student_Windows_10_1B_Hotel_Files**. In your blank PowerPoint presentation, if necessary, at the top click **Enable Editing**.

Activity 1.26 | Locating and Inserting a Saved File Into a PowerPoint Presentation

1 Be sure your PowerPoint presentation with your name is displayed. Then, on the **Home tab**, in the **Slides group**, click **Layout**. In the displayed gallery, click **Title Only**. If necessary, on the right, close the Design Ideas pane. Click anywhere in the text *Click to add title*, and then type **Tip Snip**

2 Click anywhere in the empty space below the title you just typed. Click the **Insert tab**, and then in the **Images group**, click **Pictures**. In the **navigation pane**, click the location of your **Windows 10 Chapter 1** folder, open the folder, and then in the **Insert Picture** dialog box, click one time to select your **Lastname_Firstname_1B_Tip_Snip** file. In the lower right corner of the dialog box, click **Insert**. If necessary, close the Design Ideas pane on the right. If necessary, drag the image to the right so that your slide title *Tip Snip* displays.

3 On the Quick Access Toolbar, click **Save** 🖫, and then in the upper right corner of the PowerPoint window, click **Minimize** ⎯ so that PowerPoint remains open but not displayed on your screen; you will need your PowerPoint presentation as you progress through this project.

4 **Close** ☒ the File Explorer window and close any other open windows.

Activity 1.27 | Using Snap and Task View

Use *Snap* to arrange two or more open windows on your screen so that you can work with multiple screens at the same time.

Snap with the mouse by dragging the *title bar*—the bar across the top of the window that displays the program, file, or app name—of one app to the left until it snaps into place, and then dragging the title bar of another app to the right until it snaps into place.

Snap with the keyboard by selecting the window you want to snap, and then pressing ⊞ + ←. Then select another window and press ⊞ + →. This is an example of a *keyboard shortcut*—a combination of two or more keyboard keys used to perform a task that would otherwise require a mouse.

1 From your desktop, click **Start** ⊞. In the list of apps, click the letter **A** to display the alphabet, and then click **W**. Under **W**, click **Weather**. If necessary, personalize your weather content by typing your zip code into the Search box, selecting your location, and clicking Start.

2 By using the same technique to display the alphabet, click **C**, and then click **Calculator**. On the taskbar, notice that icons display to show that the Weather app and the Calculator app are open. Notice also that on the desktop, the most recently opened app displays on top and is also framed on the taskbar. Compare your screen with Figure 1.64.

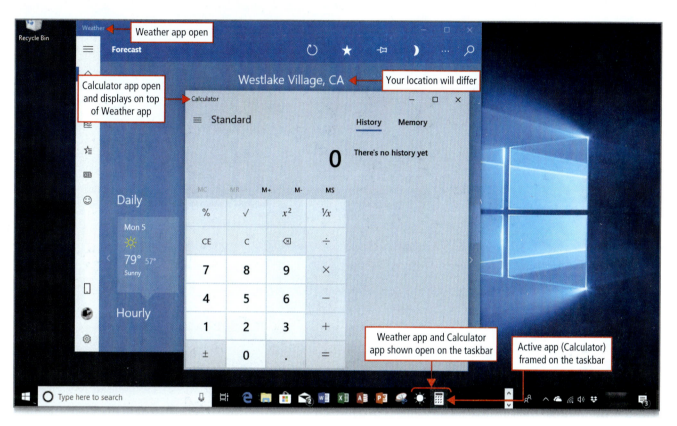

Figure 1.64

3 ▶ Point to the word *Calculator* at the top of this open app, hold down your left mouse button, drag your mouse pointer to the left edge of your screen until an outline displays to show where the window will snap, and then release the mouse button. Compare your screen with Figure 1.65.

On the right, all open windows display—your PowerPoint presentation and the Weather app. This feature is ***Snap Assist***—after you have snapped a window, all other open windows display as ***thumbnails*** in the remaining space. A thumbnail is a reduced image of a graphic.

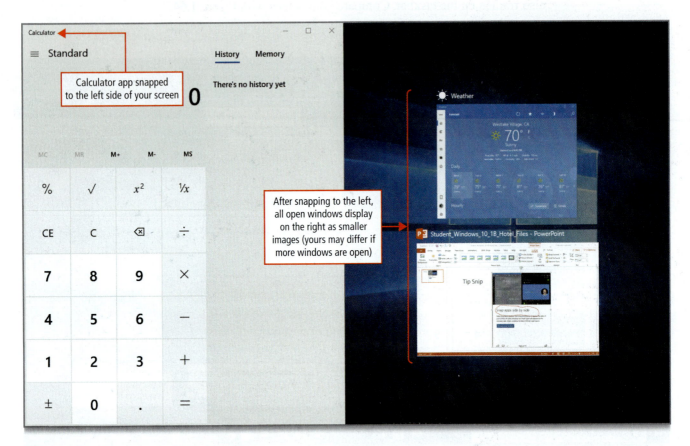

Figure 1.65

4 ▶ Click the **Weather** app to have it fill the right half of your screen.

5 ▶ In the lower left of your keyboard, press and hold down ⊞ and then in upper right of your keyboard, locate and press and release [PrintScrn]. Notice that your screen dims momentarily.

This is another method to create a screenshot. This screenshot file is automatically stored in the Screenshots folder in the Pictures folder of your hard drive; it is also stored on the Clipboard if you want to copy it immediately.

A screenshot captured in this manner is saved as a ***.png*** file, which is commonly pronounced PING, and stands for Portable Network Graphic. This is an image file type that can be transferred over the internet.

6 On the taskbar, click **Task View** 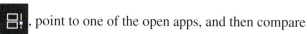, point to one of the open apps, and then compare your screen with Figure 1.66.

Use the *Task View* button on the taskbar to see and switch between open apps—including desktop apps. You may see the Windows 10 feature *Timeline*, with which, when you click the Task View button, you can see your activities and files you have recently worked on across your devices. For example, you can find a document, image, or video you worked on yesterday or a week ago.

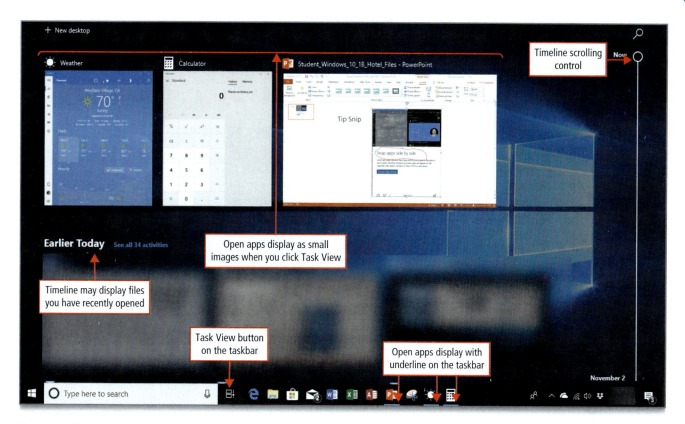

Figure 1.66

7 From **Task View**, click your **PowerPoint** window. On the **Home tab**, in the **Slides group**, click the upper portion of the **New Slide** button to insert a new slide in the same layout as your previous slide.

An arrow attached to a button will display a menu when clicked. Such a button is referred to as a *split button*—clicking the main part of the button performs a command and clicking the arrow opens a menu with choices.

8 As the title type **Side by Side** and then click in the blank space below the title. On the ribbon, on the **Home tab**, in the **Clipboard group**, click the upper portion of the **Paste** button to paste your screenshot into the slide.

Recall that by creating a screenshot using the ⊞ + (PrintScrn) command, a copy was placed on the Clipboard. A permanent copy is also stored in the Screenshots folder of your Pictures folder. This is a convenient way to create a quick screenshot.

9 With the image selected, on the ribbon, under **Picture Tools**, click **Format**. In the **Size group**, click in the **Shape Height** box ▯0.05", type 5 and press Enter. Drag the image down and into the center of the space so that your slide title is visible. Compare your screen with Figure 1.67.

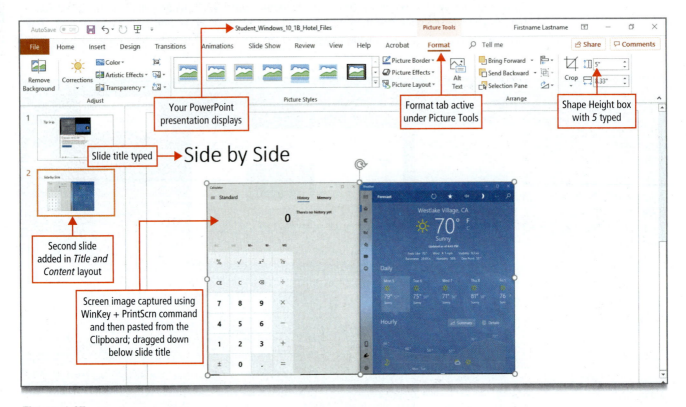

Figure 1.67

10 On the Quick Access Toolbar, click **Save** 🖫, and then in the upper right corner of the PowerPoint window, click **Minimize** ‒ so that PowerPoint remains open but not displayed on your screen.

11 Close ☒ the **Calculator** app and the **Weather** app to display your desktop.

Objective 9 **Use File Explorer to Extract Zipped Files and to Display Locations, Folders, and Files**

A file is the fundamental unit of storage that enables Windows 10 to distinguish one set of information from another. A folder is the basic organizing tool for files. In a folder, you can store files that are related to one another. You can also place a folder inside of another folder, which is then referred to as a *subfolder*.

Windows 10 arranges folders in a structure that resembles a *hierarchy*—an arrangement where items are ranked and where each level is lower in rank than the item above it. The hierarchy of folders is referred to as the *folder structure*. A sequence of folders in the folder structure that leads to a specific file or folder is a *path*.

Activity 1.28 | Navigating with File Explorer

Recall that File Explorer is the program that displays the contents of locations, folders, and files on your computer and also in your OneDrive and other cloud storage locations. File Explorer also enables you to perform tasks related to your files and folders such as copying, moving, and renaming. When you open a folder or location, a window displays to show its contents. The design of the window helps you navigate—explore within the file structure so you can find your files and folders—and so that you can save and find your files and folders efficiently.

In this Activity, you will open a folder and examine the parts of its window.

1 With your desktop displayed, on the taskbar, *point to* but do not click **File Explorer** 📁, and notice the ScreenTip *File Explorer*.

A *ScreenTip* displays useful information when you perform various mouse actions, such as pointing to screen elements.

2 Click **File Explorer** 📁 to display the **File Explorer** window.

File Explorer is at work anytime you are viewing the contents of a location or the contents of a folder stored in a specific location. By default, the File Explorer button on the taskbar opens with the *Quick access* location—a list of files you have been working on and folders you use often—selected in the navigation pane and in the address bar.

The default list will likely display the Desktop, Downloads, Documents, and Pictures folders, and then folders you worked on recently or work on frequently will be added automatically, although you can change this behavior.

The benefit of the Quick access list is that you can customize a list of folders that you go to often. To add a folder to the list quickly, you can right-click a folder in the file list and click Pin to Quick Access.

For example, if you are working on a project, you can pin it—or simply drag it—to the Quick access list. When you are done with the project and not using the folder so often, you can remove it from the list. Removing it from the list does not delete the folder, it simply removes it from the Quick access list.

3 On the left, in the **navigation pane**, scroll down if necessary, and then click **This PC** to display folders, devices, and drives in the **file list** on the right. Compare your screen with Figure 1.68.

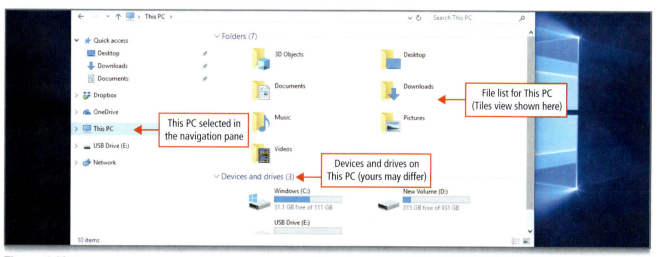

Figure 1.68

4 If necessary, in the upper right corner, click Expand the Ribbon ☑. In the **file list**, under **Folders**—click **Documents** one time to select it, and then on the ribbon, on the **Computer tab**, in the **Location group**, click **Open**.

5 On the ribbon, click the **View tab**. In the **Show/Hide group**, be sure that **Item check boxes** is selected—select it if necessary, and then in the **Layout group**, if necessary, click **Details**.

The window for the Documents folder displays. You may or may not have files and folders already stored here. Because this window typically displays the file list for a folder, it is also referred to as the *folder window*. Item check boxes make it easier to select items in a file list and also to see which items are selected in a file list.

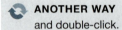 **ANOTHER WAY** Point to Documents, right-click to display a shortcut menu, and then click Open; or, point to Documents and double-click.

6 Compare your screen with Figure 1.69, and then take a moment to study the parts of the window as described in the table in Figure 1.70.

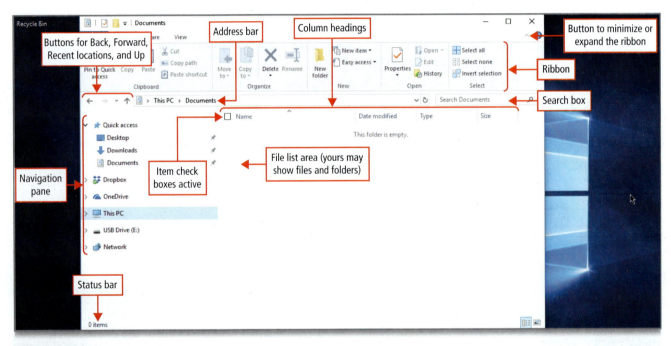

Figure 1.69

Parts of the File Explorer Window	
Window Part	**Function**
Address bar	Displays your current location in the file structure as a series of links separated by arrows. Tap or click a part of the path to go to that level or tap or click at the end to select the path for copying.
Back, Forward, Recent locations, and Up buttons	Enable you to navigate to other folders you have already opened without closing the current window. These buttons work with the address bar; that is, after you use the address bar to change folders, you can use the Back button to return to the previous folder. Use the Up button to open the location where the folder you are viewing is saved—also referred to as the *parent folder*.
Column headings	Identify the columns in Details view. By clicking the column heading name, you can change how the files in the file list are organized; by clicking the arrow on the right, you can select various sort arrangements in the file list. By right-clicking a column heading, you can select other columns to add to the file list.
File list	Displays the contents of the current folder or location. If you type text into the Search box, a search is conducted on the folder or location only, and only the folders and files that match your search will display here—including files in subfolders.
Minimize the Ribbon or Expand the Ribbon button	Changes the display of the ribbon. When minimized, the ribbon shows only the tab names and not the full ribbon.
Navigation pane	Displays locations to which you can navigate; for example, your OneDrive, folders on This PC, devices and drives connected to your PC, folders listed under Quick access, and possibly other PCs on your network. Use Quick access to open your most commonly used folders and searches. If you have a folder that you use frequently, you can drag it to the Quick access area so that it is always available.
Ribbon	Groups common tasks such as copying and moving, creating new folders, emailing and zipping items, and changing views of the items in the file list.
Search box	Enables you to type a word or phrase and then searches for a file or subfolder stored in the current folder that contains matching text. The search begins as soon as you begin typing; for example, if you type *G*, all the file and folder names that start with the letter *G* display in the file list.
Status bar	Displays the total number of items in a location, or the number of selected items and their total size.

Figure 1.70

7 Move your [pointer icon] pointer anywhere into the **navigation pane**, and notice that a downward pointing arrow ˅ displays to the left of *Quick access* to indicate that this item is expanded, and a right-pointing arrow > displays to the left of items that are collapsed.

You can click these arrows to collapse and expand areas in the navigation pane.

Activity 1.29 | Using File Explorer to Extract Zipped Files

For Non-MyLab Users
From your instructor or from www.pearsonhighered.com/go download the zipped folder **win01_1B_Bell_Orchid** to your **Windows 10 Chapter 1** folder.

1 In the **navigation pane**, if necessary expand **This PC**, scroll down if necessary, and then click your **USB flash drive** (or the location where you have stored your chapter folder) one time to display its contents in the **file list**. Double-click to open your **Windows 10 Chapter 1 folder** and locate the zipped folder **win01_1B_Bell_Orchid**.

2 Use the steps below to extract this zipped folder to your **Windows 10 Chapter 1 folder** as follows (or use your favorite method to unzip):

- On the **Home tab**, click **New folder**, and then name the folder **win01_1B_Bell_Orchid**
- Click the zipped folder **win01_1B_Bell_Orchid** one time to select it.

- With the zipped folder selected, on the ribbon, under **Compressed Folder Tools**, click the **Extract tab**, and then at the right end of the ribbon, click **Extract all**.
- In the displayed **Extract Compressed (Zipped) Folders** dialog box, click **Browse**. In the **Select a destination** dialog box, use the navigation pane on the left to navigate to your **Windows 10 Chapter 1 folder**, and then double-click the name of the new folder you just created to open the folder and display its name in the **Address bar**.
- In the lower right, click **Select Folder**, and then in the lower right, click **Extract**. When complete, click the Up button ⬆ one time. You will see the extracted folder and the zipped folder.
- To delete the unneeded zipped version, click it one time to select it, and then on the **Home tab**, in the **Organize group**, click **Delete**. If necessary, click Yes. Now that the files are extracted, you do not need the zipped copy.

3 **Close** ⊠ all File Explorer windows to display your desktop.

Activity 1.30 | Using File Explorer to Display Locations, Folders, and Files

1 From the taskbar, open **File Explorer** 📁. In the **navigation pane**, if necessary expand **This PC**, scroll down if necessary, and then click your **USB flash drive** (or the location where you have stored your chapter folder) one time to display its contents in the **file list**. In the **file list**, double-click your **Windows 10 Chapter 1 folder** to display its contents. Compare your screen with Figure 1.71.

In the navigation pane, *This PC* displays all of the drive letter locations attached to your computer, including the internal hard drives, CD or DVD drives, and any connected devices such as a USB flash drive.

Your PowerPoint file, your *Tip_Snip* file, and your extracted folder *win01_1B_Bell_Orchid* folder display if this is your storage location.

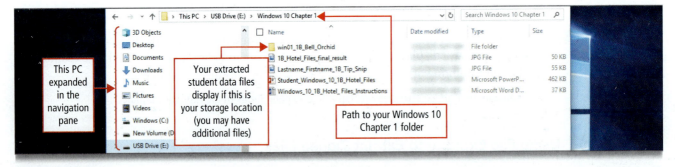

Figure 1.71

> **2** In the **file list**, double-click the **win01_1B_Bell_Orchid** folder to display the subfolders and files.

Recall that the corporate office of the Bell Orchid Hotels is in Boston. The corporate office maintains subfolders labeled for each of its large hotels in Honolulu, Orlando, San Diego, and Santa Barbara.

ANOTHER WAY   Right-click the folder, and then click Open; or, select the folder and then on the ribbon, on the Home tab, in the Open group, click Open.

> **3** In the **file list**, double-click **Orlando** to display the subfolders, and then look at the **address bar** to view the path. Compare your screen with Figure 1.72.

Within each city's subfolder, there is a structure of subfolders for the Accounting, Engineering, Food and Beverage, Human Resources, Operations, and Sales and Marketing departments.

Because folders can be placed inside of other folders, such an arrangement is common when organizing files on a computer.

In the address bar, the path from the flash drive to the win01_1B_Bell_Orchid folder to the Orlando folder displays as a series of links.

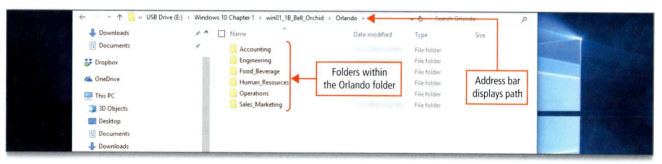

Figure 1.72

> **4** In the **address bar**, to the right of **win01_1B_Bell_Orchid**, click the ⬚ arrow to display a list of the subfolders in the **win01_1B_Bell_Orchid** folder. On the list that displays, notice that **Orlando** displays in bold, indicating it is open in the file list. Then, on the list, click **Honolulu**.

The subfolders within the Honolulu folder display.

> **5** In the **address bar**, to the right of **win01_1B_Bell_Orchid**, click the ⬚ arrow again to display the subfolders in that folder. Then, on the **address bar**—not on the list—point to **Honolulu** and notice that the list of subfolders in the **Honolulu** folder displays.

After you display one set of subfolders in the address bar, all of the links are active and you need only point to them to display the list of subfolders.

Clicking an arrow to the right of a folder name in the address bar displays a list of the subfolders in that folder. You can click a subfolder name to display its contents. In this manner, the address bar is not only a path, but it is also an active control with which you can step from the current folder directly to any other folder above it in the folder structure just by clicking a folder name.

6 On the list of subfolders for **Honolulu**, click **Sales_Marketing** to display its contents in the **file list**. On the **View tab**, in the **Layout group**, if necessary, click **Details**. Compare your screen with Figure 1.73.

🔄 **ANOTHER WAY** In the file list, double-click the Sales_Marketing folder.

The files in the Sales_Marketing folder for Honolulu display in the Details layout. To the left of each file name, an icon indicates the program that created each file. Here, there is one PowerPoint file, one Excel file, one Word file, and four JPEG images.

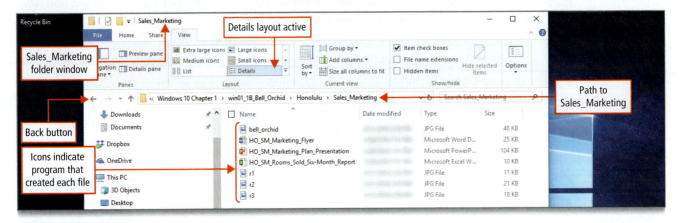

Figure 1.73

7 In the upper left portion of the window, click **Back** [←] one time.

The Back button retraces each of your clicks in the same manner as clicking the Back button when you are browsing the internet.

8 In the **file list**, point to the **Human_Resources** folder, and then double-click to open the folder.

9 In the **file list**, click one time to select the PowerPoint file **HO_HR_New_Employee_Presentation**, and then on the ribbon, click the **View tab**. In the **Panes group**, click **Details pane**, and then compare your screen with Figure 1.74.

The *Details pane* displays the most common *file properties* associated with the selected file. File properties refer to information about a file, such as the author, the date the file was last changed, and any descriptive *tags*—properties that you create to help you find and organize your files.

Additionally, a thumbnail image of the first slide in the presentation displays, and the status bar displays the number of items in the folder.

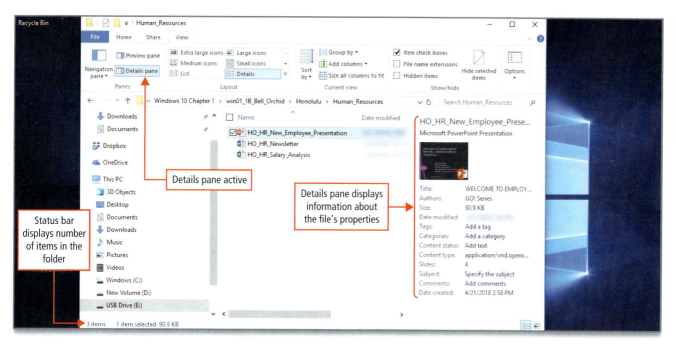

Figure 1.74

10 On the right, in the **Details pane**, click **Add a tag**, type **New Employee meeting** and then at the bottom of the pane click **Save**.

Because you can search for tags, adding tags to files makes them easier to find.

ANOTHER WAY With the file selected, on the Home tab, in the Open group, click Properties to display the Properties dialog box for the file, and then click the Details tab.

11 On the ribbon, on the **View tab**, in the **Panes group**, click **Preview pane** to replace the **Details pane** with the **Preview pane**. Compare your screen with Figure 1.75.

In the Preview pane that displays on the right, you can use the scroll bar to scroll through the slides in the presentation; or, you can click the up or down scroll arrow to view the slides as a miniature presentation.

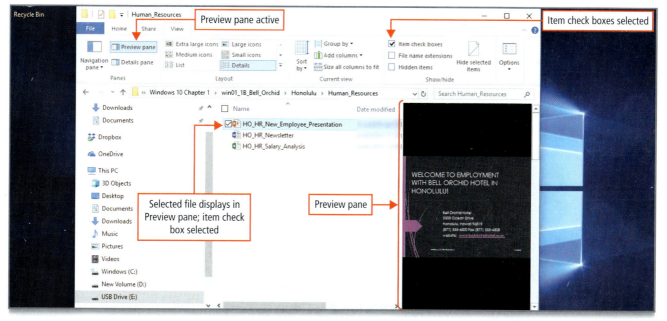

Figure 1.75

12 On the ribbon, click **Preview pane** to close the right pane.

Use the Details pane to see a file's properties and the Preview pane when you want to look at a file quickly without actually opening it.

13 Close ⊠ the **Human_Resources** window.

Objective 10 | Start Programs and Open Data Files

When you are using the software programs installed on your computer, you create and save data files—the documents, workbooks, databases, songs, pictures, and so on that you need for your job or personal use. Therefore, most of your work with Windows 10 desktop applications is concerned with locating and starting your programs and locating and opening your files.

Activity 1.31 | Starting Programs

You can start programs from the Start menu or from the taskbar by pinning a program to the taskbar. You can open your data files from within the program in which they were created, or you can open a data file from a window in File Explorer, which will simultaneously start the program and open your file.

1 Be sure your desktop displays and that your PowerPoint presentation is still open but minimized on the taskbar. You can point to the PowerPoint icon to have a small image of the active slide display. Click **Start** ⊞ to place the insertion point in the search box, type **wordpad** and then click the **WordPad Desktop app**.

2 With the insertion point blinking in the document window, type your first and last name.

3 From the taskbar, open your PowerPoint presentation. On the **Home tab**, click the upper portion of the **New Slide** button to insert a blank slide in the Title Only layout. Click anywhere in the text *Click to add title*, and then type **Wordpad**

4 Click anywhere in the lower portion of the slide. On the **Insert tab**, in the **Images group**, click **Screenshot**, and then under **Available Windows**, click the image of the WordPad program with your name typed to insert the image in the PowerPoint slide. Click in a blank area of the slide to deselect the image; if necessary, close the Design Ideas pane on the right. As necessary, drag the image down so that the title displays, and if necessary, use the Shape Height box to decrease the size of the screenshot slightly. Compare your screen with Figure 1.76.

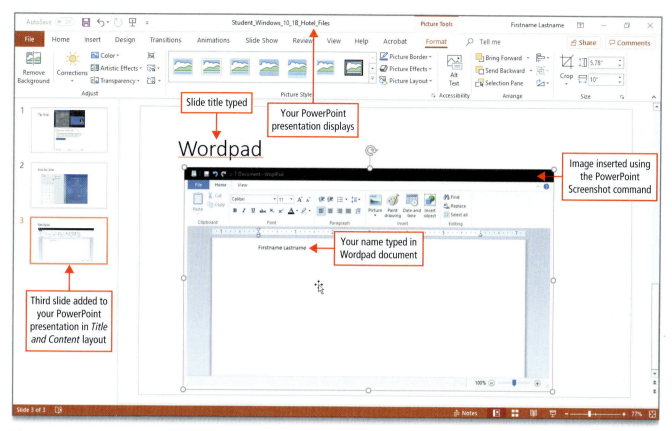

Figure 1.76

> **5** On the Quick Access toolbar, click **Save** 🖫 and then in the upper right corner of the PowerPoint window, click **Minimize** ☐ so that PowerPoint remains open but not displayed on your screen.

> **6** **Close** ☒ **WordPad**, and then click **Don't Save**.

Activity 1.32 | Opening Data Files

1 ▶ Open **Microsoft Word** from your taskbar, or click **Start** ⊞, type **Microsoft word** and then open the **Word** desktop app. Compare your screen with Figure 1.77.

> The Word program window has features that are common to other programs you have opened; for example, commands are arranged on tabs. When you create and save data in Word, you create a Word document file.

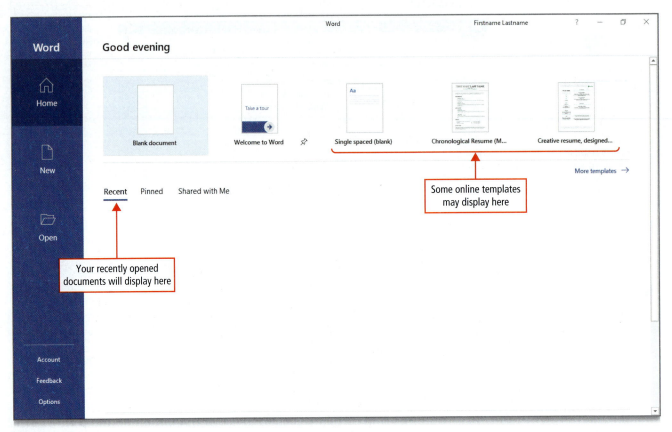

Figure 1.77

2 ▶ On the left, click **Open**. Notice the list of places from which you can open a document, including your OneDrive if you are logged in. Click **Browse** to display the **Open** dialog box. Compare your screen with Figure 1.78, and then take a moment to study the table in Figure 1.79.

> Recall that a dialog box is a window containing options for completing a task; the layout of the Open dialog box is similar to that of a File Explorer window. When you are working in a desktop application, use the Open dialog box to locate and open existing files that were created in the desktop application.

> When you click Browse, typically the Documents folder on This PC displays. You can use the skills you have practiced to navigate to other locations on your computer, such as your removable USB flash drive.

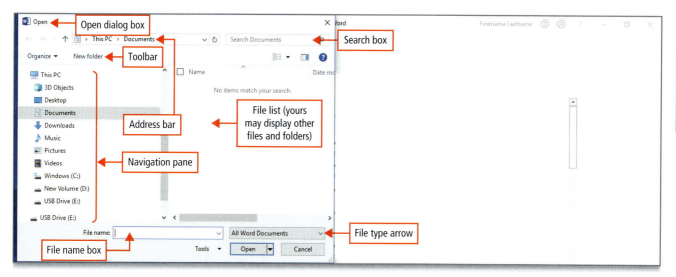

Figure 1.78

Dialog Box Element	Function
Address bar	Displays the path in the folder structure.
File list	Displays the list of files and folders that are available in the folder indicated in the address bar.
File name box	Enables you to type the name of a specific file to locate it—if you know it.
File type arrow	Enables you to restrict the type of files displayed in the file list; for example, the default *All Word Documents* restricts (filters) the type of files displayed to only Word documents. You can click the arrow and adjust the restrictions (filters) to a narrower or wider group of files.
Navigation pane	Navigate to files and folders and get access to Quick access, OneDrive, and This PC.
Search box	Search for files in the current folder. Filters the file list based on text that you type; the search is based on text in the file name (and for files on the hard drive or OneDrive, in the file itself), and on other properties that you can specify. The search takes place in the current folder, as displayed in the address bar, and in any subfolders within that folder.
Toolbar	Displays relevant tasks; for example, creating a new folder.

Figure 1.79

3 In the **navigation pane**, scroll down as necessary, and then under **This PC**, click your **USB flash drive** or whatever location where you have stored your files for this project. In the **file list**, double-click your **win01_1B_Bell_Orchid** folder to open it and display its contents.

4 In the upper right portion of the **Open** dialog box, click the **More options arrow** ▾ , and then set the view to **Large icons**. Compare your screen with Figure 1.80.

The Live Preview feature indicates that each folder contains additional subfolders.

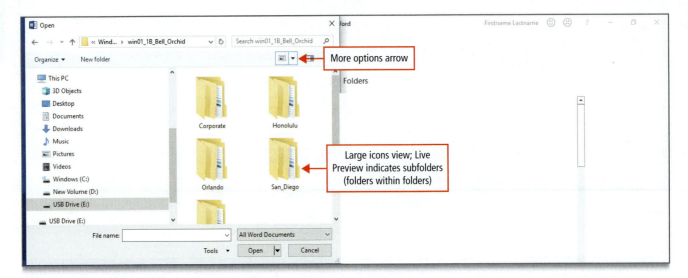

Figure 1.80

5 In the **file list**, double-click the **Corporate** folder, and then double-click the **Accounting** folder.

The view returns to the Details view.

6 In the **file list**, notice that only one document—a Word document—displays. In the lower right corner, locate the **File type** button, and notice that *All Word Documents* displays as the file type. Click the **File type arrow**, and then on the displayed list, click **All Files**. Compare your screen with Figure 1.81.

When you change the file type to *All Files*, you can see that the Word file is not the only file in this folder. By default, the Open dialog box displays only the files created in the active program; however, you can display variations of file types in this manner.

Microsoft Office file types are identified by small icons, which is a convenient way to differentiate one type of file from another. Although you can view all the files in the folder, you can open only the files that were created in the active program, which in this instance is Microsoft Word.

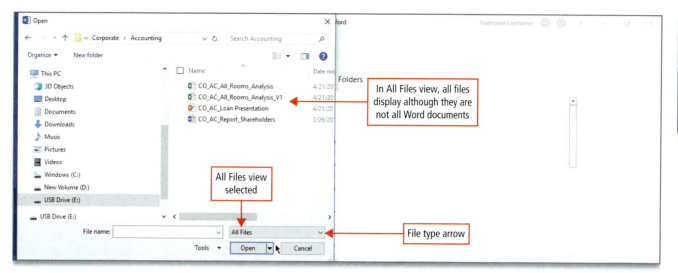

Figure 1.81

7 ▶ Change the file type back to **All Word Documents**. Then, in the **file list**, double-click the **CO_AC_Report_Shareholders** Word file to open the document. Take a moment to scroll through the document. If necessary, Maximize ☐ the window.

8 ▶ **Close** ☒ the Word window.

9 ▶ Click **Start** ▦, and then search for **.txt** At the top, click **Filters**, click **Documents**, and then on the list, click **Structure.txt in Future_Hotels**.

The file opens using the Windows 10 *Notepad* desktop app—a basic text-editing program included with Windows 10 that you can use to create simple documents.

In the search box, you can search for files on your computer, and you can search for a file by its *file name extension*—a set of characters at the end of a file name that helps Windows understand what kind of information is in a file and what program should open it. A *.txt file* is a simple file consisting of lines of text with no formatting that almost any computer can open and display.

10 ▶ **Close** ☒ the Notepad program.

MORE KNOWLEDGE **Do Not Clutter Your Desktop by Creating Desktop Shortcuts or Storing Files**

On your desktop, you can add or remove *desktop shortcuts*, which are desktop icons that can link to items accessible on your computer such as a program, file, folder, disk drive, printer, or another computer. In previous versions of Windows, many computer users commonly did this.

Now the Start menu is your personal dashboard for all your programs and online activities, and increasingly you will access programs and your own files in the cloud. So do not clutter your desktop with shortcuts—doing so is more confusing than useful. Placing desktop shortcuts for frequently used programs or folders directly on your desktop may seem convenient, but as you add more icons, your desktop becomes cluttered and the shortcuts are not easy to find. A better organizing method is to use the taskbar for shortcuts to programs. For folders and files, the best organizing structure is to create a logical structure of folders within your Documents folder or your cloud-based OneDrive.

You can also drag frequently-used folders to the Quick access area in the navigation pane so that they are available any time you open File Explorer. As you progress in your use of Windows 10, you will discover techniques for using the taskbar and the Quick access area of the navigation pane to streamline your work instead of cluttering your desktop.

Activity 1.33 | Searching, Pinning, Sorting, and Filtering in File Explorer

1 From the taskbar, open **File Explorer** 📁. On the right, at the bottom, you may notice that under **Recent files**, you can see files that you have recently opened.

2 In the **navigation pane**, click your **USB flash drive**—or click the location where you have stored your files for this project. Double-click your **Windows 10 Chapter 1 folder** to open it. In the upper right, click in the **Search** box, and then type **pool** Compare your screen with Figure 1.82.

Files that contain the word *pool* in the title display. If you are searching a folder on your hard drive or OneDrive, files that contain the word *pool* within the document will also display. Additionally, Search Tools display on the ribbon.

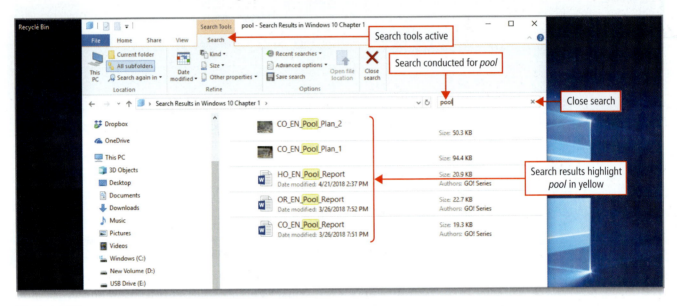

Figure 1.82

3 In the search box, clear the search by clicking ☒, and then in the search box type **Paris.jpg** Notice that you can also search by using a file extension as part of the search term.

4 **Clear** ☒ the search. Double-click your **win01_1B_Bell_Orchid** folder to open it.

5 On the **Home tab**, in the **Clipboard group**, click **Pin to Quick access**. If necessary, scroll up in the navigation pane. Compare your screen with Figure 1.83.

You can pin frequently used folders to the Quick access area, and then unpin them when you no longer need frequent access. Folders that you access frequently will also display in the Quick access area without the pin image. Delete them by right-clicking the name and clicking Unpin from Quick access.

Figure 1.83

 ANOTHER WAY In the file list, right-click a folder name, and then click Pin to Quick access; or, drag the folder to the Quick access area in the navigation pain and release the mouse button when the ScreenTip displays Pin to Quick access.

6 In the **file list**—double-click the **Corporate** folder and then double-click the **Engineering** folder.

7 On the **View tab**, in the **Current view group**, click **Sort by**, and then click **Type**. Compare your screen with Figure 1.84.

> Use this technique to sort files in the file list by type. Here, the JPG files display first, and then the Microsoft Excel files, and so on—in alphabetic order by file type.

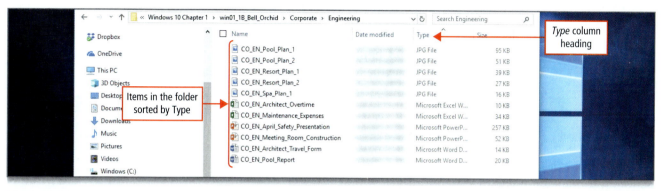

Figure 1.84

8 Point to the column heading **Type**, and then click **^**.

9 Point to the column heading **Type** again, and on the right, click ⌄. On the displayed list, click **Microsoft PowerPoint Presentation**, and notice that the file list is filtered to show only PowerPoint files.

> A *filtered list* is a display of files that is limited based on specified criteria.

10 To the right of the **Type** column heading, click the check mark and then click **Microsoft PowerPoint Presentation** again to clear the Microsoft PowerPoint filter and redisplay all of the files.

11 **Close** ⊠ the File Explorer window.

ALERT   Allow Time to Complete the Remainder of This Project in One Session

If you are working on a computer that is not your own, for example in a college lab, plan your time to complete the remainder of this project in one working session. Allow 45 to 60 minutes.

Because you will need to store and then delete files on the hard disk drive of the computer at which you are working, it is recommended that you complete this project in one working session—*unless you are working on your own computer or you know that the files will be retained*. In your college lab, files you store on the computer's hard drive will not be retained after you sign off.

Objective 11 **Create, Rename, and Copy Files and Folders**

File management includes organizing, copying, renaming, moving, and deleting the files and folders you have stored in various locations—both locally and in the cloud.

Activity 1.34 | **Copying Files from a Removable Storage Device to the Documents Folder on the Hard Disk Drive**

Barbara and Steven have the assignment to transfer and then organize some of the corporation's files to a computer that will be connected to the corporate network. Data on such a computer can be accessed by employees at any of the hotel locations through the use of sharing technologies. For example, *SharePoint* is a Microsoft technology that enables employees in an organization to access information across organizational and geographic boundaries.

1 Close any open windows, but leave your open PowerPoint presentation minimized on the taskbar.

2 From the taskbar, open **File Explorer** 📁. In the **navigation pane**, if necessary expand **This PC**, and then click your USB flash drive or the location where you have stored your chapter folder to display its contents in the file list.

> Recall that in the navigation pane, under This PC, you have access to all the storage areas inside your computer, such as your hard disk drives, and to any devices with removable storage, such as CDs, DVDs, or USB flash drives.

3 Open your **Windows 10 Chapter 1** folder, and then in the **file list**, click **win01_1B_Bell_Orchid** one time to select the folder. Compare your screen with Figure 1.85.

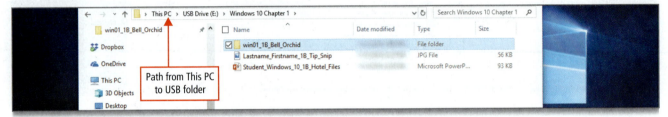

Figure 1.85

4 With the **win01_1B_Bell_Orchid** folder selected, on the ribbon, on the **Home tab**, in the **Clipboard group**, click **Copy**.

> The Copy command places a copy of your selected file or folder on the *Clipboard* where it will be stored until you use the Paste command to place the copy somewhere else. The Clipboard is a temporary storage area for information that you have copied or moved from one place and plan to use somewhere else.

> In Windows 10, the Clipboard can hold only one piece of information at a time. Whenever something is copied to the Clipboard, it replaces whatever was there before. In Windows 10, you cannot view the contents of the Clipboard nor place multiple items there in the manner that you can in Microsoft Word.

🔄 **ANOTHER WAY**   With the item selected in the file list, press Ctrl + C to copy the item to the clipboard.

5 To the left of the address bar, click **Up** ⬆ two times. In the **file list**, double-click your **Documents** folder to open it, and then on the **Home tab**, in the **Clipboard group**, click **Paste**.

> A *progress bar* displays in a dialog box and also displays on the taskbar button with green shading. A progress bar indicates visually the progress of a task such as a copy process, a download, or a file transfer.

> The Documents folder is one of several folders within your *personal folder* stored on the hard disk drive. For each user account—even if there is only one user on the computer—Windows 10 creates a personal folder labeled with the account holder's name.

🔄 **ANOTHER WAY**   With the destination location selected, press Ctrl + V to paste the item from the clipboard to the selected location. Or, on the Home tab, in the Organize group, click Copy to, find and then click the location to which you want to copy. If the desired location is not on the list, use the Choose location command at the bottom.

6 **Close** ☒ the **Documents** window.

Barbara and Steven can see that various managers have been placing files related to new European hotels in the *Future_Hotels* folder. They can also see that the files have not been organized into a logical structure. For example, files that are related to each other are not in separate folders; instead they are mixed in with other files that are not related to the topic.

In this Activity, you will create, name, and rename folders to begin a logical structure of folders in which to organize the files related to the European hotels project.

1 From the taskbar, open **File Explorer** 🔲, and then use any of the techniques you have practiced to display the contents of the **Documents** folder in the **file list**.

NOTE   **Using the Documents Folder and OneDrive Instead of Your USB Drive**

In this modern computing era, you should limit your use of USB drives to those times when you want to quickly take some files to another computer without going online. Instead of using a USB drive, use your computer's hard drive, or better yet, your free OneDrive cloud storage that comes with your Microsoft account.

There are two good reasons to stop using USB flash drives. First, searching is limited on a USB drive—search does not look at the content inside a file. When you search files on your hard drive or OneDrive, the search extends to words and phrases actually *inside* the files. Second, if you delete a file or folder from a USB drive, it is gone and cannot be retrieved. Files you delete from your hard drive or OneDrive go to the Recycle Bin where you can retrieve them later.

---

2 In the **file list**, double-click the **win01_1B_Bell_Orchid** folder, double-click the **Corporate** folder, double-click the **Information_Technology** folder, and then double-click the **Future_Hotels** folder to display its contents in the file list; sometimes this navigation is written as *Documents > win01_1B_Bell_Orchid > Corporate > Information_Technology > Future_Hotels*.

Some computer users prefer to navigate a folder structure by double-clicking in this manner. Others prefer using the address bar as described in the following Another Way box. Use whatever method you prefer—double-clicking in the file list, clicking in the address bar, or expanding files in the Navigation pane.

ANOTHER WAY   In the navigation pane, click Documents, and expand each folder in the navigation pane. Or, In the address bar, to the right of Documents, click >, and then on the list, click win01_1B_Bell_Orchid. To the right of win01_1B_Bell_Orchid, click the > and then click Corporate. To the right of Corporate, click > and then click Information_ Technology. To the right of Information_Technology, click >, and then click Future_Hotels.

3 In the **file list**, be sure the items are in alphabetical order by **Name**. If the items are not in alphabetical order, recall that by clicking the small arrow in the column heading name, you can change how the files in the file list are ordered.

4 On the ribbon, click the **View tab**, and then in the **Layout group**, be sure **Details** is selected.

The *Details view* displays a list of files or folders and their most common properties.

ANOTHER WAY   Right-click in a blank area of the file list, point to View, and then click Details.

5 On the ribbon, click the **Home tab**, and then in the **New group**, click **New folder**. With the text *New folder* selected, type **Paris** and press Enter. Click **New folder** again, type **Venice** and then press Enter. Create a third **New folder** named **London**

In a Windows 10 file list, folders are listed first, in alphabetic order, followed by individual files in alphabetic order.

6 Click the **Venice** folder one time to select it, and then on the ribbon, on the **Home tab**, in the **Organize group**, click **Rename**. Notice that the text *Venice* is selected. Type **Rome** and press Enter.

ANOTHER WAY   Point to a folder or file name, right-click, and then on the shortcut menu, click Rename.

7 In the **file list**, click one time to select the Word file **Architects**. With the file name selected, click the file name again to select all the text. Click the file name again to place the insertion point within the file name, edit the file name to **Architects_Local** and press Enter. Compare your screen with Figure 1.86.

You can use any of the techniques you just practiced to change the name of a file or folder.

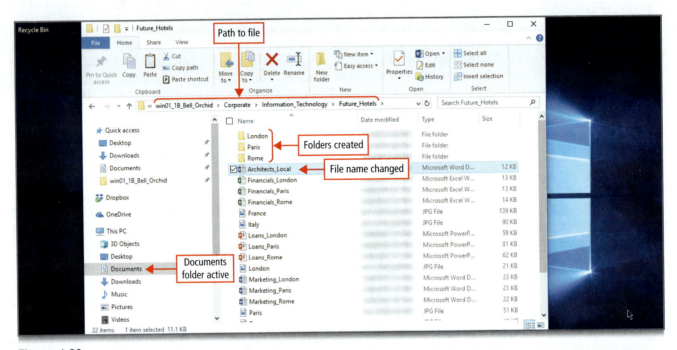

Figure 1.86

8 On the taskbar, click the **PowerPoint** icon to redisplay your **Windows_10_1B_Hotel_Files** presentation, and then on the **Home tab**, click the upper portion of the **New Slide** button to insert a new slide with the Title Only layout.

9 Click anywhere in the text *Click to add title*, type **Europe Folders** and then click anywhere in the empty space below the title.

10 On the **Insert tab**, in the **Images group**, click **Screenshot**, and then under **Available Windows**, click the image of your file list. On the **Picture Tools Format tab**, in the **Size group**, click in the **Shape Height** box, type **5** and then press Enter. As necessary, drag the image down so that the title you typed is visible; your presentation contains four slides.

11 Above the **File tab**, on the Quick Access toolbar, click **Save**, and then in the upper right corner, click **Minimize** so that PowerPoint remains open but not displayed on your screen.

12 Close the **Future_Hotels** window.

Copying, moving, renaming, and deleting files and folders comprise the most heavily used features within File Explorer. Probably half or more of the steps you complete in File Explorer relate to these tasks, so mastering these techniques will increase your efficiency.

When you *copy* a file or a folder, you make a duplicate of the original item and then store the duplicate in another location. In this Activity, you will assist Barbara and Steven in making copies of the Staffing_Plan file, and then placing the copies in each of the three folders you created—London, Paris, and Rome.

1 From the taskbar, open **File Explorer** 🗂, and then by double-clicking in the file list or following the links in the address bar, navigate to **This PC > Documents > win01_1B_Bell_ Orchid > Corporate > Information_Technology > Future_Hotels**.

2 In the upper right corner, **Maximize** ☐ the window. On the **View tab**, if necessary set the **Layout** to **Details**, and then in the **Current view group**, click **Size all columns to fit** ⊞.

3 In the **file list**, click the file **Staffing_Plan** one time to select it, and then on the **Home tab**, in the **Clipboard group**, click **Copy**.

4 At the top of the **file list**, double-click the **London folder** to open it, and then in the **Clipboard group**, click **Paste**. Notice that the copy of the **Staffing_Plan** file displays. Compare your screen with Figure 1.87.

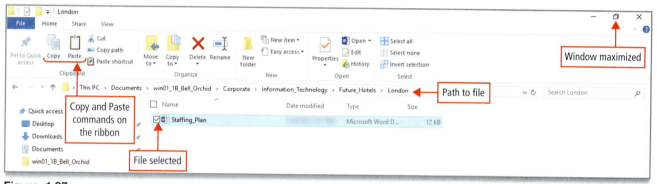

Figure 1.87

🔄 **ANOTHER WAY** Right-click the file you want to copy, and on the menu click Copy. Then right-click the folder into which you want to place the copy, and on the menu click Paste. Or, select the file you want to copy, press [Ctrl] + [C] to activate the Copy command, open the folder into which you want to paste the file, and then press [Ctrl] + [V] to activate the Paste command.

---

5 With the **London** window open, by using any of the techniques you have practiced, rename this copy of the **Staffing_Plan** file to **London_Staffing_Plan**

6 To the left of the **address bar**, click **Up** ⬆ to move up one level in the folder structure and to redisplay the **file list** for the **Future_Hotels** folder.

🔄 **ANOTHER WAY** In the address bar, click Future_Hotels to redisplay this window and move up one level in the folder structure.

---

7 Click the **Staffing_Plan** file one time to select it, hold down Ctrl, and then drag the file upward over the **Paris** folder until the ScreenTip + *Copy to Paris* displays, and then release the mouse button and release Ctrl.

> When dragging a file into a folder, holding down Ctrl engages the Copy command and places a *copy* of the file at the location where you release the mouse button. This is another way to copy a file or copy a folder.

8 Open the **Paris** folder, and then rename the **Staffing_Plan** file **Paris_Staffing_Plan** Then, move up one level in the folder structure to redisplay the **Future_Hotels** window.

9 Double-click the **Rome** folder to open it. With your mouse pointer anywhere in the **file list**, right-click, and then from the shortcut menu click **Paste**.

> A copy of the Staffing_Plan file is copied to the folder. Because a copy of the Staffing_Plan file is still on the Clipboard, you can continue to paste the item until you copy another item on the Clipboard to replace it.

10 Rename the file **Rome_Staffing_Plan**

11 On the **address bar**, click **Future_Hotels** to move up one level and open the **Future_Hotels** window—or click Up ↑ to move up one level. Leave this folder open for the next Activity.

Activity 1.37 | Moving Files

When you *move* a file or folder, you remove it from the original location and store it in a new location. In this Activity, you will move items from the Future_Hotels folder into their appropriate folders.

1 With the **Future_Hotels** folder open, in the **file list**, click the Excel file **Financials_London** one time to select it. On the **Home tab**, in the **Clipboard group**, click **Cut**.

> The file's Excel icon dims. This action places the item on the Clipboard.

> **ANOTHER WAY** Right-click the file or folder, and then on the shortcut menu, click Cut; or, select the file or folder, and then press Ctrl + X.

2 Double-click the **London** folder to open it, and then on the **Home tab**, in the **Clipboard group**, click **Paste**.

> **ANOTHER WAY** Right-click the folder, and then on the shortcut menu, click Paste; or, select the folder, and then press Ctrl + V.

3 Click Up ↑ to move up one level and redisplay the **Future_Hotels** folder window. In the **file list**, point to **Financials_Paris**, hold down the left mouse button, and then drag the file upward over the **Paris** folder until the ScreenTip *Move to Paris* displays, and then release the mouse button.

4 Open the **Paris** folder, and notice that the file was moved to this folder. Click Up ↑—or on the address bar, click Future_Hotels to return to that folder.

5 ▶ In the **file list**, click **Loans_London** one time to select it. hold down Ctrl, and then click the photo image **London** and the Word document **Marketing_London** to select the three files. Release the Ctrl key. Compare your screen with Figure 1.88.

Use this technique to select a group of noncontiguous items in a list.

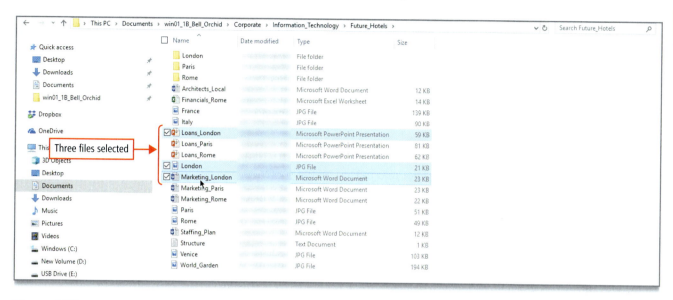

Figure 1.88

6 ▶ Point to any of the selected files, hold down the left mouse button, and then drag upward over the **London** folder until the ScreenTip →*Move to London* displays and *3* displays over the files being moved, and then release the mouse button.

You can see that by keeping related files together—for example, all the files that relate to the London hotel—in folders that have an appropriately descriptive name, it will be easier to locate information later.

7 ▶ By dragging, move the **Architects_Local** file into the **London** folder.

8 ▶ In an empty area of the file list, right-click, and then click **Undo Move**. Leave the **Future_Hotels** window open for the next Activity.

Any action that you make in a file list can be undone in this manner.

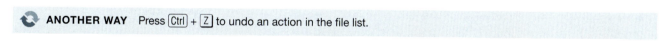

ANOTHER WAY   Press Ctrl + Z to undo an action in the file list.

MORE KNOWLEDGE   **Using Shift + Click to Select Files**

If a group of files to be selected are contiguous (next to each other in the file list), click the first file to be selected, hold down Shift and then click the left mouse button on the last file to select all of the files between the top and bottom file selections.

Activity 1.38 | Copying and Moving Files by Snapping Two Windows

Sometimes you will want to open, in a second window, another instance of a program that you are using; that is, two copies of the program will be running simultaneously. This capability is especially useful in the File Explorer program, because you are frequently moving or copying files from one location to another.

In this Activity, you will open two instances of File Explorer, and then use snap, which you have already practiced in this chapter, to display both instances on your screen.

To copy or move files or folders into a different level of a folder structure, or to a different drive location, the most efficient method is to display two windows side by side and then use drag and drop or copy (or cut) and paste commands.

In this Activity, you will assist Barbara and Steven in making copies of the Staffing_Plan files for the corporate office.

1. In the upper right corner, click **Restore Down** ⬜ to restore the **Future_Hotels** window to its previous size and not maximized on the screen.

    Use the **Restore Down** command ⬜ to resize a window to its previous size.

2. Hold down ⊞ and press ← to snap the window so that it occupies the left half of the screen.

3. On the taskbar, *point* to **File Explorer** 📁 and then right-click. On the jump list, click **File Explorer** to open another instance of the program. With the new window active, hold down ⊞ and press → to snap the window so that it occupies the right half of the screen.

4. In the window on the right, click in a blank area to make the window active. Then navigate to **Documents > win01_1B_Bell_Orchid > Corporate > Human_Resources**. Compare your screen with Figure 1.89.

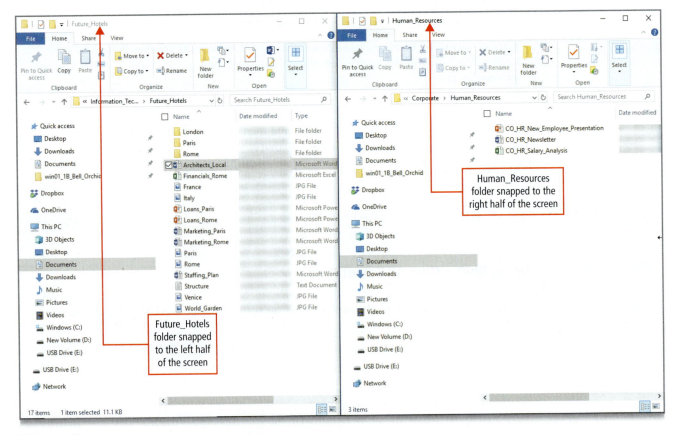

Figure 1.89

5 In the left window, double-click to open the **Rome** folder, and then click one time to select the file **Rome_Staffing_Plan**.

6 Hold down Ctrl, and then drag the file into the right window, into an empty area of the **Human_Resources file list**, until the ScreenTip + *Copy to Human_Resources* displays and then release the mouse button and Ctrl.

7 In the left window, on the **address bar**, click **Future_Hotels** to redisplay that folder. Open the **Paris** folder, point to **Paris_Staffing_Plan** and right-click, and then click **Copy**.

> You can access the Copy command in various ways; for example, from the shortcut menu, on the ribbon, or by using the keyboard shortcut Ctrl + C.

8 In the right window, point anywhere in the **file list**, right-click, and then click **Paste**.

9 On the taskbar, click the PowerPoint icon to redisplay your **Windows_10_1B_Hotel_Files** presentation, and then on the **Home tab**, click the upper portion of the **New Slide** button to insert a new slide with the **Title Only** layout; this will be your fifth slide.

10 Click anywhere in the text *Click to add title*, type **Staffing Plan Files** and then click anywhere in the empty space below the title.

11 On the **Insert tab**, in the **Images group**, click **Screenshot**, and then click **Screen Clipping**. When the dimmed screen displays, move the ⊞ pointer to the upper left corner of the screen, hold down the left mouse button, and drag to the lower right corner but do not include the taskbar. Then release the mouse button.

> Because you have two windows displayed side by side, each window displays under Available Windows. Recall that to capture an entire screen that contains more than one window, use the Screen Clipping tool with which you can capture a snapshot of your screen.

12 If necessary, close the Design Ideas pane on the right. On the **Picture Tools Format tab**, in the **Size group**, click in the **Shape Height** box ⟦‡ 0.05"⟧, type **5** and press Enter. As necessary, drag the image down so that the title you typed is visible.

13 Click outside of the image to deselect it, and then press Ctrl + Home to display the first slide in your presentation; your presentation contains five slides.

14 In the upper right, **Close** ⊠ the **PowerPoint** window, and when prompted, click **Save**.

15 **Close** ⊠ all open windows.

For Non-MyLab Submissions Determine What Your Instructor Requires for Submission
As directed by your instructor, submit your completed PowerPoint file.

---

16 In **MyLab IT**, locate and click the Grader Project **Windows 10 1B Hotel Files**. In **step 3**, under **Upload Completed Assignment**, click **Choose File**. In the **Open** dialog box, navigate to your **Windows 10 Chapter 1 folder**, and then click your **Student_Windows_10_1B_ Hotel_Files** file one time to select it. In the lower right corner of the **Open** dialog box, click **Open**.

> The name of your selected file displays above the Upload button.

17 To submit your file to MyLab IT for grading, click **Upload**, wait a moment for a green **Success!** message, and then in **step 4**, click the blue **Submit for Grading** button. Click **Close Assignment** to return to your list of **Course Materials**.

It is good practice to delete files and folders that you no longer need from your hard disk drive and removable storage devices. Doing so makes it easier to keep your data organized and also frees up storage space.

When you delete a file or folder from any area of your computer's hard disk drive or from OneDrive, the file or folder is not immediately deleted. Instead, the deleted item is stored in the *Recycle Bin* and remains there until the Recycle Bin is emptied. Thus, you can recover an item deleted from your computer's hard disk drive or OneDrive so long as the Recycle Bin has not been emptied. Items deleted from removable storage devices like a USB flash drive and from some network drives are immediately deleted and cannot be recovered from the Recycle Bin.

To permanently delete a file without first moving it to the Recycle Bin, click the item, hold down Shift, and then press Delete. A message will display indicating *Are you sure you want to permanently delete this file?* Use caution when using Shift + Delete to permanently delete a file because this action is not reversible.

You can restore items by dragging them from the file list of the Recycle Bin window to the file list of the folder window in which you want to restore. Or, you can restore them to the location they were deleted from by right-clicking the items in the file list of the Recycle Bin window and selecting Restore.

You have completed Project 1B | END

wavebreakmedia/Shutterstock, Monkey Business Images/Fotolia, Ivanko80/Shutterstock, Monkey Business Images/Shutterstock

Microsoft Office Specialist (MOS) Skills in this Chapter
Project 1A
Microsoft Word
1.1.1 Search for text
1.2.1 Set up document pages
1.2.4 Configure page background elements
1.2.4 Modify basic document properties
1.3.1 Modify basic document properties
1.4.1 Locate and remove hidden properties and personal information
1.4.2 Locate and correct accessibility issues
1.4.3 Locate and correct compatibility issues
2.2.5 Clear formatting
5.2.6 Format 3D models
5.4.3 Add alternative text to objects for accessibility
Microsoft Excel
5.3.3 Add alternative text to charts for accessibility

Build Your E-Portfolio

An E-Portfolio is a collection of evidence, stored electronically, that showcases what you have accomplished while completing your education. Collecting and then sharing your work products with potential employers reflects your academic and career goals. Your completed documents from the following projects are good examples to show what you have learned: 1A and 1B.

GO! for Job Success

Discussion: Managing Your Computer Files

Your instructor may assign this discussion to your class, and then ask you to think about, or discuss with your classmates, these questions:

g-stockstudio/Shutterstock

> Why do you think it is important to follow specific guidelines when naming and organizing your files?

> Why is it impractical to store files and shortcuts to programs on your desktop?

> How are you making the transition from storing all your files on physical media, such as flash drives or the hard drive of your computer, to storing your files in the cloud where you can access them from any computer with an internet connection?

End of Chapter

Summary

Many Office features and commands, such as accessing the Open and Save As dialog boxes, performing commands from the ribbon and from dialog boxes, and using the Clipboard are the same in all Office desktop apps.

A desktop app is installed on your computer and requires a computer operating system such as Microsoft Windows or Apple's macOS to run. The programs in Microsoft Office 365 and Office 2019 are considered to be desktop apps.

The Windows 10 Start menu is your connected dashboard—this is your one-screen view of information that updates continuously with new information and personal communications that are important to you.

File Explorer is at work anytime you are viewing the contents of a location, a folder, or a file. Use File Explorer to navigate your Windows 10 folder structure that stores and organizes the files you create.

GO! Learn It Online

Review the concepts, key terms, and MOS skills in this chapter by completing these online challenges, which you can find at **MyLab IT**.

Chapter Quiz: Answer matching and multiple-choice questions to test what you have learned in this chapter.

Lessons on the GO!: Learn how to use all the new apps and features as they are introduced by Microsoft.

Quiz: Answer questions to review the MOS skills that you practiced in this chapter.

Monkey Business Images/Fotolia

Glossary

Glossary of Chapter Key Terms

.png file An image file type that can be transferred over the internet, an acronym for Portable Network Graphic.

.txt file A simple file consisting of lines of text with no formatting that almost any computer can open and display.

3D models A new kind of shape that you can insert from an online library of ready-to-use three-dimensional graphics.

Address bar In a File Explorer window, the area that displays your current location in the folder structure as a series of links separated by arrows.

Alignment The placement of text or objects relative to the margins.

Alignment guides Green lines that display when you move an object to assist in alignment.

Alt text Text added to a picture or object that helps people using a screen reader understand what the object is; also called *alternative text*.

Alternative text Text added to a picture or object that helps people using a screen reader understand what the object is; also called *alt text*.

Application A computer program that helps you perform a task for a specific purpose.

AutoSave An Office 365 feature that saves your document every few seconds—if saved on OneDrive, OneDrive for Business, or SharePoint Online—and enables you to share the document with others for real-time co-authoring.

Backstage tabs The area along the left side of Backstage view with tabs to display screens with related groups of commands.

Backstage view A centralized space for file management tasks; for example, opening, saving, printing, publishing, or sharing a file.

Bing Microsoft's search engine.

Bookmark A command that marks a word, section, or place in a document so that you can jump to it quickly without scrolling.

Booting the computer The process of turning on the computer.

Center alignment The alignment of text or objects centered horizontally between the left and right margin.

Check Accessibility A command that checks a document for content that people with disabilities might find difficult to read.

Check Compatibility A command that searches your document for features that may not be supported by older versions of Office.

Click The action of pressing the left button of the mouse pointing device.

Clipboard A temporary storage area that holds text or graphics that you select and then cut or copy.

Cloud computing Applications and services that are accessed over the internet.

Cloud storage Online storage of data so that you can access your data from different places and devices.

Commands An instruction to a computer program that causes an action to be carried out.

Compressed Folder Tools A command available in File Explorer with which you can extract compressed files.

Compressed files Files that have been reduced in size, take up less storage space, and can be transferred to other computers faster than uncompressed files.

Content pane In a File Explorer window, another name for the file list.

Context menus Menus that display commands and options relevant to the selected text or object; also called *shortcut menus*.

Context-sensitive commands Commands that display on a shortcut menu that relate to the object or text that is selected.

Contextual tab A tab added to the ribbon automatically when a specific object is selected and that contains commands relevant to the selected object.

Copy A command that duplicates a selection and places it on the Clipboard.

Cortana Microsoft's intelligent personal assistant in Windows 10 and also available on other devices; named for the intelligent female character in the video game Halo.

Cut A command that removes a selection and places it on the Clipboard.

Dashboard The right side of the Start menu that is a one-screen view of links to information and programs that matter to you.

Data The documents, worksheets, pictures, songs, and so on that you create and store during the day-to-day use of your computer.

Data management The process of managing files and folders.

Default The term that refers to the current selection or setting that is automatically used by a computer program unless you specify otherwise.

Deselect The action of canceling the selection of an object or block of text by clicking outside of the selection.

Desktop A simulation of a real desk that represents your work area; here you can arrange icons such as shortcuts to files, folders, and various types of documents in the same manner you would arrange physical objects on top of a desk.

Desktop app A computer program that is installed on your PC and requires a computer operating system such as Microsoft Windows to run; also known as a *desktop application*.

Desktop application A computer program that is installed on your PC and requires a computer operating system such as Microsoft Windows to run; also known as a *desktop app*.

Desktop shortcuts Desktop icons that can link to items accessible on your computer such as a program, file, folder, disk drive, printer, or another computer.

Details pane When activated in a folder window, displays—on the right—the most common file properties associated with the selected file.

Details view A command that displays a list of files or folders and their most common properties.

Dialog box A small window that displays options for completing a task.

Dictate A feature in Word, PowerPoint, Outlook, and OneNote for Windows 10; when you enable Dictate, you start talking and as you talk, text appears in your document or slide.

Dialog Box Launcher A small icon that displays to the right of some group names on the ribbon and that opens a related dialog box or pane providing additional options and commands related to that group.

Document properties Details about a file that describe or identify it, including the title, author name, subject, and keywords that identify the document's topic or contents; also known as *metadata*.

Double-click The action of pressing the left mouse button two times in rapid succession while holding the mouse still.

Glossary

Download The action of transferring or copying a file from another location—such as a cloud storage location, your college's Learning Management System, or from an internet site—to your computer.

Drag The action of holding down the left mouse button while moving your mouse.

Drive An area of storage that is formatted with a file system compatible with your operating system and is identified by a drive letter.

Edit The process of making changes to text or graphics in an Office file.

Editor A digital writing assistant in Word and Outlook that displays misspellings, grammatical mistakes, and writing style issues.

Ellipsis A set of three dots indicating incompleteness; an ellipsis following a command name indicates that a dialog box will display if you click the command.

Enhanced ScreenTip A ScreenTip that displays useful descriptive information about the command.

Extract To decompress, or pull out, files from a compressed form.

File Information stored on a computer under a single name.

File Explorer The Windows program that displays the contents of locations, folders, and files on your computer.

File Explorer window A window that displays the contents of the current location and contains helpful parts so that you can navigate—explore within the file organizing structure of Windows.

File list In a File Explorer window, the area that displays the contents of the current location.

File name extension A set of characters at the end of a file name that helps Windows understand what kind of information is in a file and what program should open it.

File properties Information about a file, such as the author, the date the file was last changed, and any descriptive tags.

Fill The inside color of an object.

Filtered list A display of files that is limited based on specified criteria.

Folder A container in which you can store files.

Folder structure The hierarchy of folders.

Folder window A window that typically displays the File List for a folder.

Font A set of characters with the same design and shape.

Font styles Formatting emphasis such as bold, italic, and underline.

Footer A reserved area for text or graphics that displays at the bottom of each page in a document.

Format Painter The command to copy the formatting of specific text or to copy the formatting of a paragraph and then apply it in other locations in your document; when active, the pointer takes the shape of a paintbrush.

Formatting The process of applying Office commands to make your documents easy to read and to add visual touches and design elements to make your document inviting to the reader; establishes the overall appearance of text, graphics, and pages in an Office file—for example, in a Word document.

Formatting marks Characters that display on the screen, but do not print, indicating where the Enter key, the Spacebar, and the Tab key were pressed; also called *nonprinting characters*.

Free-form snip From the Snipping Tool, a command that draws an irregular line such as a circle around an area of the screen.

Full-screen snip From the Snipping Tool, a command that captures the entire screen.

Gallery An Office feature that displays a list of potential results.

Gradient fill A fill effect in which one color fades into another.

Graphical user interface Graphics such as an image of a file folder or wastebasket that you click to activate the item represented.

Groups On the Office ribbon, the sets of related commands that you might need for a specific type of task.

GUI An abbreviation of the term graphical user interface.

Hamburger Another name for a hamburger menu.

Hamburger menu Another name for a menu icon, deriving from the three lines that bring to mind a hamburger on a bun.

Hard disk drive The primary storage device located inside your computer where some of your files and programs are typically stored, usually designated as drive C.

Hierarchy An arrangement where items are ranked and where each level is lower in rank than the item above it

Icons Small images that represent commands, files, applications, or other windows.

Info tab The tab in Backstage view that displays information about the current file.

Insertion point A blinking vertical line that indicates where text or graphics will be inserted.

Inspect Document A command that searches your document for hidden data of personal information that you might not want to share publicly.

JPEG An acronym that stands for *Joint Photographic Experts Group* and that is a common file type used by digital cameras and computers to store digital pictures.

Jump List A display of destinations and tasks from a program's taskbar icon when you right-click the icon.

Keyboard shortcut A combination of two or more keyboard keys, used to perform a task that would otherwise require a mouse.

KeyTip The letter that displays on a command in the ribbon and that indicates the key you can press to activate the command when keyboard control of the ribbon is activated.

Keywords Custom file properties in the form of words that you associate with a document to give an indication of the document's content.

Landscape orientation A page orientation in which the paper is wider than it is tall.

Layout Options A button that displays when an object is selected and that has commands to choose how the object interacts with surrounding text.

Live Preview A technology that shows the result of applying an editing or formatting change as you point to possible results— *before* you actually apply it.

Live tiles Tiles that are constantly updated with fresh information.

Location Any disk drive, folder, or other place in which you can store files and folders.

Lock screen A background that fills the computer screen when the computer boots up or wakes up from sleep mode.

Maximize A window control button that will enlarge the size of the window to fill the entire screen.

Menu A list of commands within a category.

Menu bar A group of menus at the top of a program window.

Menu icon A button consisting of three lines that, when clicked, expands a menu; often used in mobile applications because it is compact to use on smaller screens— also referred to a *hamburger menu*.

Glossary

Metadata Details about a file that describe or identify it, including the title, author name, subject, and keywords that identify the document's topic or contents; also known as *document properties*.

Microsoft account A user account with which you can sign in to any Windows 10 computer on which you have, or create, an account.

Microsoft Store app A smaller app that you download from the Microsoft Store.

Mini toolbar A small toolbar containing frequently used formatting commands that displays as a result of selecting text or objects.

Minimize A window control button that will keep a program open but will remove it from screen view.

Move In File Explorer, the action of removing a file or folder from its original location and storing it in a new location.

Mouse pointer Any symbol that displays on the screen in response to moving the mouse.

MRU Acronym for *most recently used*, which refers to the state of some commands that retain the characteristic most recently applied; for example, the Font Color button retains the most recently used color until a new color is chosen.

Navigate A process for exploring within the file organizing structure of Windows.

Navigation pane The area on the left side of the File Explorer window to access your OneDrive, folders on your PC, devices and drives connected to your PC, and other PCs on your network.

Nonprinting characters Characters that display on the screen, but do not print, indicating where the Enter key, the Spacebar, and the Tab key were pressed; also called *formatting marks*.

Notepad A basic text-editing program included with Windows 10 that you can use to create simple documents.

Object A text box, picture, table, or shape that you can select and then move and resize.

Office 365 A version of Microsoft Office to which you subscribe for an annual fee.

OneDrive Microsoft's free cloud storage for anyone with a free Microsoft account.

Operating system A specific type of computer program that manages the other programs on a computing device such as a desktop computer, a laptop computer, a smartphone, a tablet computer, or a game console.

Option button In a dialog box, a round button that enables you to make one choice among two or more options.

Page Width A command that zooms the document so that the width of the page matches the width of the window.

Paragraph symbol The symbol ¶ that represents the end of a paragraph.

Parent folder The location in which the folder you are viewing is saved.

Paste The action of placing text or objects that have been copied or cut from one location to another location.

Paste Options gallery A gallery of buttons that provides a Live Preview of all the Paste options available in the current context.

Path A sequence of folders that leads to a specific file or folder.

PDF The acronym for Portable Document Format, which is a file format that creates an image that preserves the look of your file, but that cannot be easily changed; a popular format for sending documents electronically, because the document will display on most computers.

Pen A pen-shaped stylus that you tap on a computer screen.

Personal folder The folder created on the hard drive for each Windows 10 user account on a computer; for each user account—even if there is only one user on the computer—Windows 10 creates a personal folder labeled with the account holder's name.

Point to The action of moving the mouse pointer over a specific area.

Pointer Any symbol that displays on your screen in response to moving your mouse.

Pointing device A mouse or touchpad used to control the pointer.

Points A measurement of the size of a font; there are 72 points in an inch.

Portable Document Format A file format that creates an image that preserves the look of your file, but that cannot be easily changed; a popular format for sending documents electronically, because the document will display on most computers.

Portrait orientation A page orientation in which the paper is taller than it is wide.

Print Preview A view of a document as it will appear when you print it.

Program A set of instructions that a computer uses to accomplish a task.

Progress bar A bar that displays in a dialog box—and also on the taskbar button—that indicates visually the progress of a task such as a copy process, a download, or a file transfer.

pt The abbreviation for *point* when referring to a font size.

Quick access In the navigation pane in a File Explorer window, a list of files you have been working on and folders you use often.

Real-time co-authoring A process where two or more people work on the same file at the same time and see changes made by others in seconds.

Rectangular snip From the Snipping Tool, a command that draws a precise box by dragging the mouse pointer around an area of the screen to form a rectangle.

Recycle Bin The area where deleted items are stored until you empty the bin; enables you to recover deleted items until the bin is emptied.

Removable storage device A device such as a USB flash drive used to transfer information from one computer to another.

Resources The collection of the physical parts of your computer such as the central processing unit (CPU), memory, and any attached devices such as a printer.

Restore Down A command that resizes a window to its previous size.

Ribbon In Office applications, displays a group of task-oriented tabs that contain the commands, styles, and resources you need to work in an Office desktop app. In a File Explorer window, the area at the top that groups common tasks on tabs. such as copying and moving, creating new folders, emailing and zipping items, and changing the view on related tabs.

Right-click The action of clicking the right mouse button one time.

Sans serif font A font design with no lines or extensions on the ends of characters.

Screen reader Software that enables visually impaired users to read text on a computer screen to understand the content of pictures.

Screenshot Any captured image of your screen.

ScreenTip A small box that displays useful information when you perform various mouse actions such as pointing to screen elements or dragging.

Glossary

Scroll arrow An arrow found at either end of a scroll bar that can be clicked to move within the window in small increments.

Scroll bar A vertical bar that displays when the contents of a window or pane are not completely visible; a scroll bar can be vertical, displayed at the side of the window, or horizontal, displayed at the bottom of a window.

Scroll box Within a scroll bar, a box that you can move to bring the contents of the window into view.

Select To specify, by highlighting, a block of data or text on the screen with the intent of performing some action on the selection.

Selecting Highlighting, by dragging with your mouse, areas of text or data or graphics, so that the selection can be edited, formatted, copied, or moved.

Serif font A font design that includes small line extensions on the ends of the letters to guide the eye in reading from left to right.

SharePoint A Microsoft technology that enables employees in an organization to access information across organizational and geographic boundaries.

Shortcut menu A menu that displays commands and options relevant to the selected text or object; also called a *context menu*.

Sizing handles Small circles or squares that indicate a picture or object is selected.

Snap An action to arrange two or more open windows on your screen so that you can work with multiple screens at the same time.

Snap Assist A feature that displays all other open windows after one window is snapped.

Snip An image captured by the Snipping tool that can be annotated, saved, copied, or shared via email.

Snipping tool A Windows 10 program that captures an image of all or part of your computer's screen.

Split button A button divided into two parts and in which clicking the main part of the button performs a command and clicking the arrow opens a menu with choices.

Start menu A Windows 10 menu that displays as a result of clicking the Start button and that displays a list of installed programs on the left and a customizable group of tiles on the right that can act as a user dashboard.

Style A group of formatting commands, such as font, font size, font color, paragraph alignment, and line spacing that can be applied to a paragraph with one command.

Subfolder The term for a folder placed within another folder.

Synchronization The process of updating computer files that are in two or more locations according to specific rules—also called *syncing*.

Syncing The process of updating computer files that are in two or more locations according to specific rules—also called *synchronization*.

System tray Another term for the notification area on the taskbar that displays notification icons and the system clock and calendar.

Tabs (ribbon) On the Office ribbon, the name of each activity area.

Tags Custom file properties in the form of words that you associate with a document to give an indication of the document's content; used to help find and organize files. Also called keywords.

Task View A taskbar button that displays your desktop background with small images of all open programs and apps and from which you can see and switch between open apps, including desktop apps.

Taskbar The bar at the bottom of your Windows screen that contains buttons to launch programs and buttons for all open apps.

Tell Me A search feature for Microsoft Office commands that you activate by typing what you are looking for in the Tell Me box.

Tell me more A prompt within a ScreenTip that opens the Office online Help system with explanations about how to perform the command referenced in the ScreenTip.

Template A preformatted document that you can use as a starting point and then change to suit your needs.

Theme A predesigned combination of colors, fonts, and effects that look good together and that is applied to an entire document by a single selection.

Timeline A Windows 10 feature that when you click the Task view button, you can see activities you have worked on across your devices; for example, you can find a document, image, or video you worked on yesterday or a week ago.

Thumbnail A reduced image of a graphic.

Tiles A group of square and rectangular boxes that display on the start menu.

Title bar The bar across the top of the window that displays the program, file, or app name.

Toggle button A button that can be turned on by clicking it once and then turned off by clicking it again.

Toolbar A row, column, or block of buttons or icons that displays across the top of a window and that contains commands for tasks you perform with a single click.

Triple-click The action of clicking the left mouse button three times in rapid succession.

Undo On the Quick Access Toolbar, the command that reverses your last action.

Unzip The process of extracting files that have been compressed.

User account A user on a single computer.

Wallpaper Another term for the Desktop background.

Window snip From the Snipping Tool, a command that captures the entire displayed window.

Windows 10 An operating system developed by Microsoft Corporation that works with mobile computing devices and also with traditional desktop and laptop PCs.

XML Paper Specification A Microsoft file format that creates an image of your document and that opens in the XPS viewer.

XPS The acronym for *XML Paper Specification*—a Microsoft file format that creates an image of your document and that opens in the XPS viewer.

Zip The process of compressing files.

Zoom The action of increasing or decreasing the size of the viewing area on the screen.

Introducing Microsoft Word 2019

WORD 2019

TippaPatt/Shutterstock

Word 2019: Introduction

Introduction to Word

Content! Defined by Merriam-Webster's online dictionary as "the topic or matter treated in a written work" and also as "the principal substance (as written matter, illustrations, or music) offered by a World Wide Web site," content is what you consume when you read on paper or online, when you watch video, or when you listen to any kind of music—live or recorded.

Content is what you *create* when your own words or performances are recorded in some form. For creating content in the form of words, Microsoft Word is a great choice. Rather than just a tool for word processing, Word is now a tool for you to communicate and collaborate with others. When you want to communicate with pictures or images, Microsoft Word has many features to help you do so. You can use Word to complete complex tasks, such as creating sophisticated tables, embedding graphics, writing blogs, and creating publications. Word is a program that you can learn gradually, and then add more advanced skills one at a time.

Best of all, Microsoft Word is integrated into the cloud. If you save your documents to your cloud-based storage that comes with any free Microsoft account, you can retrieve them from any device and continue to work with and share your documents.

Creating Documents with Microsoft Word

1

WORD 2019

Roman Belogorodov/Shutterstock

In This Chapter

 GO! To Work with Word

In this chapter, you will begin your study of Microsoft Word, one of the most popular computer software applications and one that almost everyone has a reason to use. You can use Microsoft Word to perform basic word processing tasks, such as writing a memo, a report, or a letter. In this chapter, you will insert and format objects such as pictures, text boxes, SmartArt, and shapes, to improve the appearance of your documents and to better communicate your message. You will also practice formatting fonts, paragraphs, and the layout of your pages.

The projects in this chapter relate to **Sturgeon Point Productions**, an independent film company based in Miami with offices in Detroit and Milwaukee. The film professionals produce effective broadcast and branded content for many industries and provide a wide array of film and video production services. Sturgeon Point Productions has won awards for broadcast advertising, business media, music videos, and social media. The mission of the company is to help clients tell their stories— whether the story is about a social issue, a new product, a geographical location, a company, or a person.

PROJECT
1A Flyer

Project Activities

In Activities 1.01 through 1.16, you will create a flyer for Sharon Matsuo, Creative Director for Sturgeon Point Productions, announcing two internships for a short documentary. Your completed document will look similar to Figure 1.1.

 ## Project Files for MyLab IT Grader

1. In your storage location, create a folder named **Word Chapter 1**.
2. In your **MyLab IT** course, locate and click **Word 1A Flyer**, Download Materials, and then Download All Files.
3. Extract the zipped folder to your Word Chapter 1 folder. Close the Grader download screens.
4. Take a moment to open the downloaded **Word_1A_Flyer_Instructions**; note any recent updates to the book.

Project Results

GO Project 1A
Where We're Going

Figure 1.1 Project 1A Internship Flyer

For Non-MyLab Submissions
For Project 1A, you will need:
New blank Word Document
w01A_Bird
w01A_Text

In your storage location, create a folder named **Word Chapter 1**
In your Word Chapter 1 folder, save your document as:
Lastname_Firstname_1A_Flyer

Start a new, blank Word document. After you have named and saved your document, on the next page begin with Step 2.

NOTE   If You Are Using a Touch Screen

Tap an item to click it.

Press and hold for a few seconds to right-click; release when the information or commands display.

Touch the screen with two or more fingers and then pinch together to zoom out or stretch your fingers apart to zoom in.

Slide your finger on the screen to scroll—slide left to scroll right and slide right to scroll left.

Slide to rearrange—similar to dragging with a mouse.

Swipe to select—slide an item a short distance with a quick movement—to select an item and bring up commands, if any.

Objective 1   **Create a New Document and Insert Text**

ALERT   Because Office 365 is a cloud-based subscription service that receives continuous updates, you may encounter some variations in what appears on your screen and what is shown in this instruction. Microsoft Office 365 is fully installed on your PC or Mac; no internet access is necessary to create or edit documents. When you *are* connected to the internet, you will receive monthly upgrades and new features, so you always have the latest versions of Office apps as soon as they are available. Your subscription gives you continuous free access to the latest innovations and refinements.

GO! Learn How
Video W1-1

When you create a new document, you can type all the document text, or you can type some of the text and then insert additional text from another source. Sharon Matsuo, Creative Director for Sturgeon Point Productions, created some of the document text in a Word document that you can insert in the flyer you are creating.

Activity 1.01 │ Creating a New Word Document

MOS
1.1.4

1 Navigate to your **Word Chapter 1 folder**, and then double-click the Word file you downloaded from **MyLab IT** that displays your name—**Student_Word_1A_Flyer**. In your blank document, if necessary, at the top click **Enable Editing**.

MAC TIP   If you are not submitting your file in MyLab IT, from the student data files that accompany this project, open the file Mac_w01A_Flyer. This is a blank document with default settings necessary to complete this project.

2 On the **Home tab**, in the **Paragraph group**, if necessary click Show/Hide ¶ so that it is active and the formatting marks display. If the rulers do not display, click the View tab, and then in the Show group, select the Ruler check box.

MAC TIP   To display group names on the ribbon, display the menu, click Word, click Preferences, click View, select the Show group titles check box.

3 Type **Internships Available** and then press Enter two times. Then, type the following text: **This summer, Sturgeon Point Productions will be filming a short documentary in Costa Rica about its native birds and has positions available for two interns.**

As you type, the insertion point moves to the right, and when it approaches the right margin, Word determines whether the next word in the line will fit within the established right margin. If the word does not fit, Word moves the entire word down to the next line. This is **word wrap** and means that you press Enter *only* when you reach the end of a paragraph—it is not necessary to press Enter at the end of each line of text.

NOTE **Spacing Between Sentences**

Although you might have learned to add two spaces following end-of-sentence punctuation, the common practice now is to space only one time at the end of a sentence. Be sure to press Spacebar only one time following end-of-sentence punctuation.

4 Press Spacebar and then take a moment to study the table in Figure 1.2 to become familiar with the default document settings in Microsoft Word. Compare your screen with Figure 1.3.

When you press Enter, Spacebar, or Tab on your keyboard and Show/Hide is active, characters display in your document to represent these keystrokes. These characters do not print and are referred to as *formatting marks* or *nonprinting characters*. These marks will display throughout this instruction.

Default Document Settings in a New Word Document	
Setting	**Default format**
Font and font size	The default font is Calibri, and the default font size is 11 points.
Margins	The default left, right, top, and bottom page margins are 1 inch.
Line spacing	The default line spacing is 1.08, which provides slightly more space between lines than single spacing does.
Paragraph spacing	The default spacing after a paragraph is 8 points, which is slightly less than the height of one blank line of text.
View	The default view is Print Layout view, which displays the page borders and displays the document as it will appear when printed.

Figure 1.2

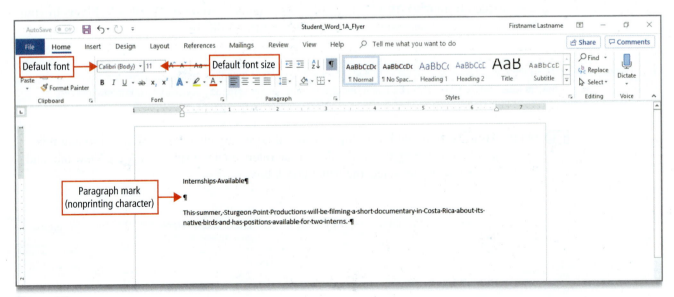

Figure 1.3

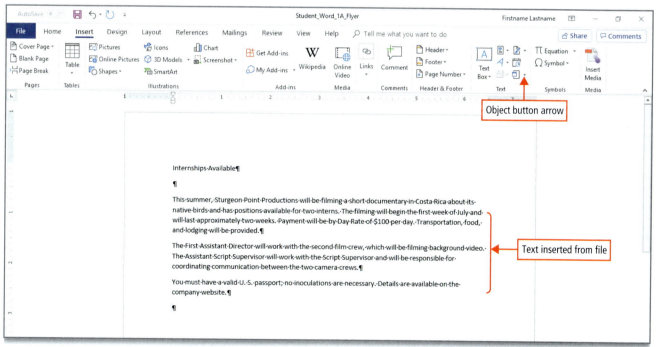

MORE KNOWLEDGE | **Word's Default Settings Are Easier to Read Online**

Until just a few years ago, word processing programs used single spacing, an extra blank paragraph to separate paragraphs, and 12 pt Times New Roman as the default formats. Now, studies show that individuals find the Word default formats described in Figure 1.2 to be easier to read online, where many documents are now viewed and read.

Activity 1.02 | Inserting Text from Another Document

You can create text in one Word document and insert it in another. Sharon Matsuo, Creative Director for Sturgeon Point Productions, created some of the document text for your flyer. You will insert the text from her document into the flyer you are creating.

1 On the ribbon, click the **Insert tab**. In the **Text group**, click the **Object button arrow**, and then click **Text from File**.

ALERT **Does the Object dialog box display?**

If the Object dialog box displays, you probably clicked the Object *button* instead of the Object *button arrow*. Close the Object dialog box, and then in the Text group, click the Object button arrow, as shown in Figure 1.4. Click *Text from File*, and then continue with Step 2.

2 In the **Insert File** dialog box, navigate to the files you downloaded for this project, locate and select **w01A_Text**, and then click **Insert**. Compare your screen with Figure 1.4.

A *copy* of the text from the w01A_Text file displays at the insertion point location; the text is not removed from the original file.

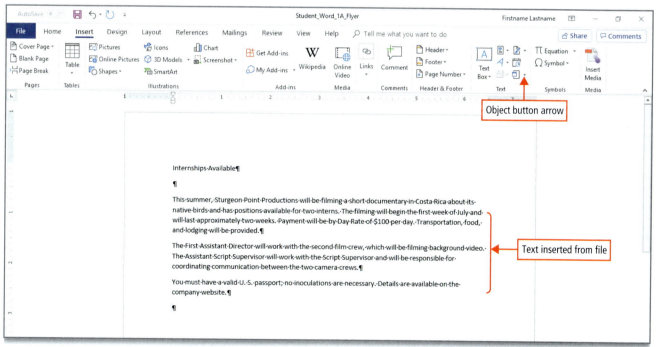

Object button arrow

Text inserted from file

Figure 1.4

ANOTHER WAY Open the file, copy the required text, close the file, and then paste the text into the current document.

3 On the **Quick Access Toolbar**, click **Save**.

GO! Learn How

Video W1-2

To add visual interest to a document, insert *graphics*. Graphics include pictures, online pictures, charts, and *drawing objects*—shapes, diagrams, lines, and so on. For additional visual interest, you can apply an attractive graphic format to text; add, resize, move, and format pictures; and add a page border.

Activity 1.03 │ Formatting Text by Using Text Effects

Text effects are decorative formats, such as shadowed or mirrored text, text glow, 3-D effects, and colors that make text stand out. The flyer you are creating will be printed and posted online, and the use of text effects will draw attention to some of the important information.

1 ▶ Including the paragraph mark, select the first paragraph of text—*Internships Available*. On the **Home tab**, in the **Font group**, click **Text Effects and Typography** [A⁻].

2 ▶ In the **Text Effects and Typography** gallery, in the third row, click the first effect to apply it to the selection.

3 ▶ With the text still selected, in the **Font group**, click in the **Font Size** box [11 ⁻] to select the existing font size. Type **52** and then press [Enter].

When you want to change the font size of selected text to a size that does not display in the Font Size list, type the number in the Font Size box and press [Enter] to confirm the new font size.

4 ▶ With the text still selected, in the **Paragraph group**, click **Center** [≡] to center the text. Compare your screen with Figure 1.5.

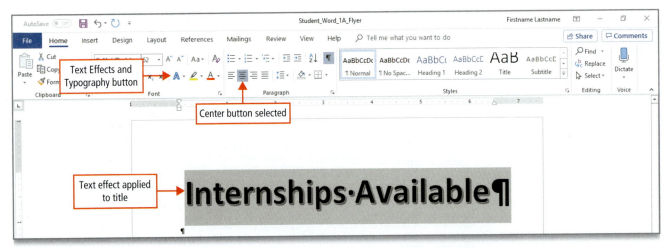

Figure 1.5

5 ▶ With the text still selected, in the **Font group**, click the **Font Color button arrow** [A⁻] to display the Font Color palette. Under **Theme Colors**, in the sixth column, click the first color.

6 ▶ With the text still selected, in the **Font group**, click **Text Effects and Typography** [A⁻]. Point to **Shadow**, and then under **Outer**, in the second row, click the third style.

7 ▶ Click anywhere in the document to deselect the text, click **Save** [💾], and then compare your screen with Figure 1.6.

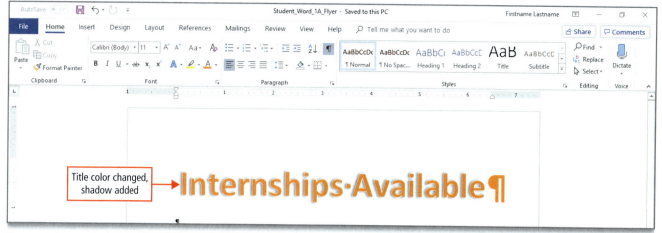

Figure 1.6

MORE KNOWLEDGE   **Clear Existing Formatting**

If you do not like your text effect, you can remove all formatting from any selected text. To do so, on the Home tab, in the Font group, click Clear All Formatting .

Activity 1.04 | Inserting Pictures

MOS
5.1.2

Pictures that reflect document content can focus the reader's attention on the message. Sharon Matsuo asked that you insert a picture in the flyer that depicts the types of images that a photographer might capture during the internship.

1 In the paragraph that begins *This summer*, click to position the insertion point at the beginning of the paragraph.

2 On the **Insert tab**, in the **Illustrations group**, click **Pictures**. In the **Insert Picture** dialog box, navigate to the files you downloaded for this project, locate and click **w01A_Bird**, and then click **Insert**.

Word inserts the picture as an *inline object*; that is, the picture is positioned directly in the text at the insertion point, just like a character in a sentence. The Layout Options button displays to the right of the picture. You can change the *Layout Options* to control the manner in which text wraps around a picture or other object. Sizing handles surround the picture indicating it is selected.

MAC TIP   To insert the picture, on the Insert tab, click Pictures, and then click Picture from File.

3 Notice the sizing handles around the selected picture, as shown in Figure 1.7.

The corner sizing handles resize the graphic proportionally. The center sizing handles resize a graphic vertically or horizontally only; however, sizing with these will distort the graphic. A *rotation handle*, with which you can rotate the graphic to any angle, displays above the top center sizing handle.

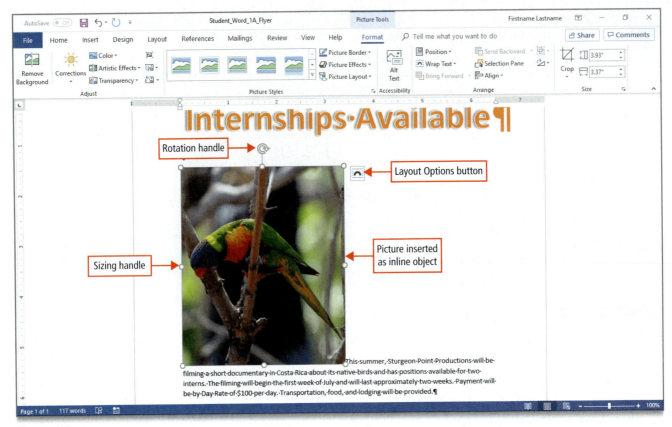

Figure 1.7

Activity 1.05 | Wrapping Text Around a Picture Using Layout Options

MOS
5.4.2

Recall that Layout Options enable you to control ***text wrapping***—the manner in which text displays around an object.

1 Be sure the picture is selected—you know it is selected if the sizing handles display.

2 To the right of the picture, click **Layout Options** 🖾 to display a gallery of text wrapping arrangements. Point to each icon layout option to view its ScreenTip.

Each icon visually depicts how text will wrap around an object.

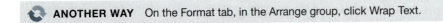

ANOTHER WAY On the Format tab, in the Arrange group, click Wrap Text.

MAC TIP On the Picture Format tab, click Wrap Text, and then choose the layout option that you want to apply.

3 From the gallery, under **With Text Wrapping**, click the first layout—**Square**. Compare your screen with Figure 1.8.

Select Square text wrapping when you want to wrap the text to the left or right of an image. To the left of the picture, an ***object anchor*** displays, indicating that the selected object is anchored to the text at this location in the document.

Figure 1.8

> **4** Close ⊠ the **Layout Options**, and then **Save** 🖫 your document.

Activity 1.06 | Resizing Pictures and Using Live Layout

When you move or size a picture, *Live Layout* reflows text as you move or size an object so that you can view the placement of surrounding text.

> **1** If necessary, scroll your document so the entire picture displays. At the lower right corner of the picture, point to the sizing handle until the ⤡ pointer displays. Drag slightly upward and to the left. As you drag, a green alignment guide may display. Compare your screen with Figure 1.9.

Alignment guides may display when you are moving or sizing a picture to help you with object placement, and Live Layout shows you how the document text will flow and display on the page.

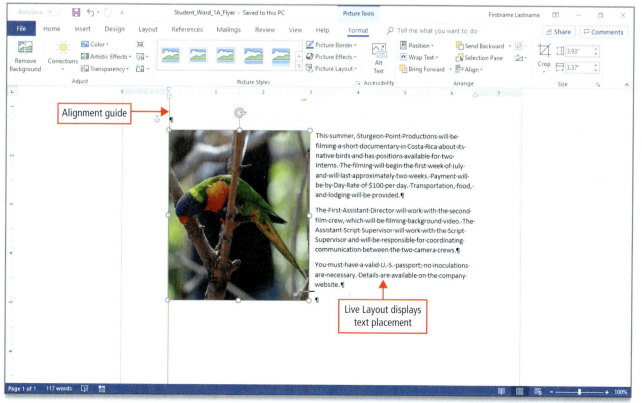

Figure 1.9

2 Continue to drag up and to the left until the bottom of the graphic is aligned at approximately **4 inches on the vertical ruler**. Notice that the graphic is proportionally resized.

3 On the **Quick Access Toolbar**, click **Undo** ↶ to restore the picture to its original size.

ANOTHER WAY On the Format tab, in the Adjust group, click Reset Picture.

4 On the ribbon, under **Picture Tools**, on the **Format tab**, in the **Size group**, click in the **Shape Height box** to select the number. Type **3.8** and then press Enter. If necessary, scroll down to view the entire picture on your screen, and then compare your screen with Figure 1.10.

When you use the Shape Height and Shape Width boxes to change the size of a graphic, the graphic will resize proportionally; that is, the width adjusts as you change the height and vice versa.

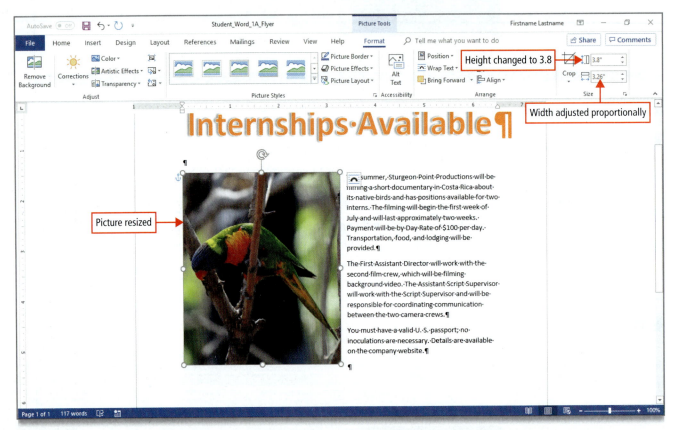

Figure 1.10

ANOTHER WAY A *spin box* is a small box with an upward- and downward-pointing arrow that lets you move rapidly through a set of values by clicking. You can change the height or width of a picture or object by clicking the Shape Height or Shape Width spin box arrows.

5 Save 💾 your document.

Activity 1.07 | Positioning a Picture

5.4.1

There are two ways to move a picture in a document. You can point to the picture and then drag it to a new position. You can also change the picture settings in a dialog box, which gives you more precise control over the picture location.

1 Be sure the picture is selected. On the ribbon, click the **Format tab**. In the **Arrange group**, click **Position**, and then click **More Layout Options**.

2 In the **Layout** dialog box, be sure the **Position tab** is selected. Under **Horizontal**, click the **Alignment** option button. To the right of **Alignment**, click the **arrow**, and then click **Right**. To the right of **relative to**, click the **arrow**, and then click **Margin**.

3 Under **Vertical**, click the **Alignment** option button. Change the **Alignment** options to **Top relative to Line**. Compare your screen with Figure 1.11.

> With these alignment settings, the picture will move to the right margin of the page and the top edge will align with the top of the first line of the paragraph to which it is anchored.

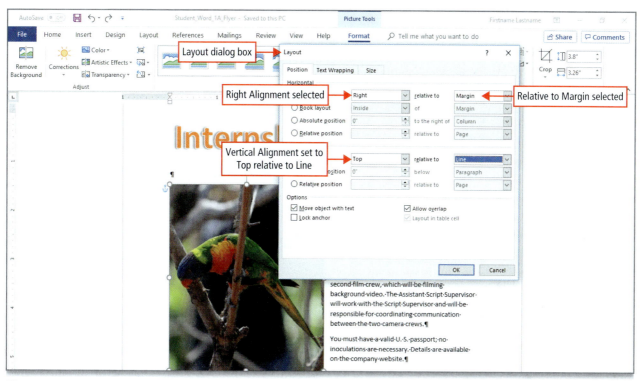

Figure 1.11

4 At the bottom of the **Layout** dialog box, click **OK**, and then on the **Quick Access Toolbar**, click **Save** 🖫. Notice that the picture moves to the right margin, and the text wraps on the left side of the picture. Compare your screen with Figure 1.12.

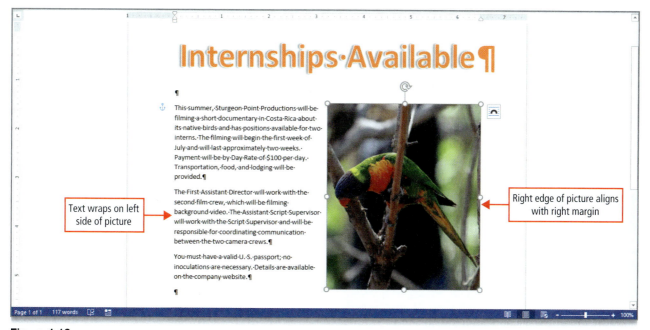

Figure 1.12

Activity 1.08 | Applying Picture Effects

Picture styles include shapes, shadows, frames, borders, and other special effects with which you can stylize an image. *Picture Effects* enhance a picture with effects such as a shadow, glow, reflection, or 3-D rotation.

1 Be sure the picture is selected. On the **Format tab**, in the **Picture Styles group**, click **Picture Effects**.

2 Point to **Soft Edges**. Use the ScreenTips to locate and then click **5 Point**.

The Soft Edges feature fades the edges of the picture. The number of points you choose determines how far the fade goes inward from the edges of the picture.

3 Compare your screen with Figure 1.13, and then **Save** 💾 your document.

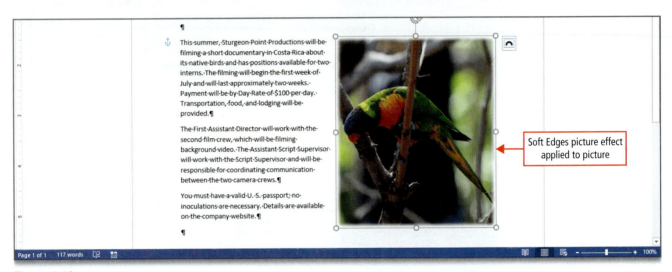

Figure 1.13

MORE KNOWLEDGE | **Applying Picture Styles**

To apply a picture style, select the picture. On the Format tab, in the Picture Styles group, click More, and then click the Picture Style that you want to apply.

Activity 1.09 | Applying Artistic Effects

Artistic effects are formats that make pictures look more like sketches or paintings.

1 Be sure the picture is selected. On the **Format tab**, in the **Adjust group**, click **Artistic Effects**.

2 In the first row of the gallery, point to, but do not click, the third effect.

Live Preview displays the picture with the third effect added.

3 In the second row of the gallery, click the third effect—**Paint Brush**. Paint Brush may be in another location in the gallery. If necessary, use the ScreenTips to locate the Paint Brush effect.

4 **Save** 💾 your document, and then notice that the picture looks more like a painting than a photograph. Compare your screen with Figure 1.14.

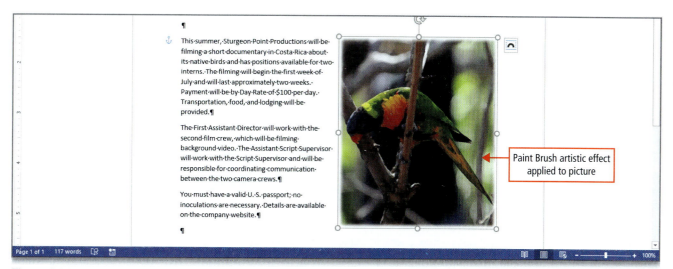

Figure 1.14

Activity 1.10 | Adding a Page Border

Page borders frame a page and help to focus the information on the page.

1 Click anywhere outside the picture to deselect it. On the **Design tab**, in the **Page Background group**, click **Page Borders**.

2 In the **Borders and Shading** dialog box, on the **Page Border tab**, under **Setting**, click **Box**. Under **Style**, scroll the list and click the seventh style—double lines.

3 Click the **Color arrow**, and then in the sixth column, click the first color.

4 Under **Apply to**, be sure *Whole document* is selected, and then compare your screen with Figure 1.15.

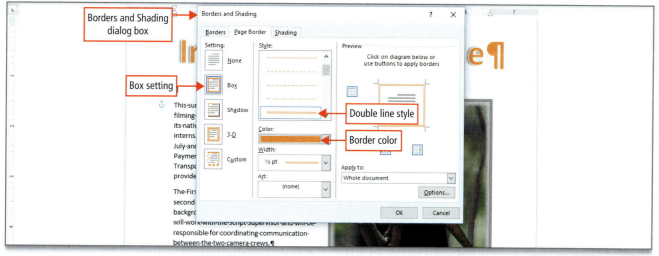

Figure 1.15

5 At the bottom of the **Borders and Shading** dialog box, click **OK**. Press Ctrl + Home to move to the top of the document.

MAC TIP To move to the top of a document, press command ⌘ + fn + ←.

6 **Save** 💾 your document, and then compare your screen with Figure 1.16.

Page border applied to document

Internships·Available¶

¶

This·summer,·Sturgeon·Point·Productions·will·be·
filming·a·short·documentary·in·Costa·Rica·about·
its·native·birds·and·has·positions·available·for·two·
interns.·The·filming·will·begin·the·first·week·of·

Figure 1.16

> **MAC TIP**   If your document page border does not display as shown in Figure 1.16, you may need to adjust the border margins. On the Design tab, click Page Borders. In the lower right corner of the Borders and Shading dialog box, click Options, and then change all the margins to 24 pt measured from Edge of page.

Objective 3 | Insert and Modify Text Boxes and Shapes

GO! Learn How
Video W1-3

Word has predefined *shapes* and *text boxes* that you can add to your documents. A shape is an object such as a line, arrow, box, callout, or banner. A text box is a movable, resizable container for text or graphics. Use these objects to add visual interest to your document.

Activity 1.11 | Inserting, Sizing, and Positioning a Shape

MOS
5.1.1

Important information in a document needs to be easily recognized and noticed. Ms. Matsuo asked that you insert a shape with text in it to draw attention to the important information in the flyer.

1 Click in the blank paragraph below the title. Press Enter four times to create additional space for a text box, and then notice that the picture anchored to the paragraph moves with the text.

2 Press Ctrl + End to move to the bottom of the document, and then notice that your insertion point is positioned in the empty paragraph at the end of the document. Press Delete to remove the blank paragraph.

> **MAC TIP**   To move to the bottom of a document, press command ⌘ + fn + →.

3 Click the **Insert tab**, and then in the **Illustrations group**, click **Shapes** to display the Shapes gallery. Compare your screen with Figure 1.17.

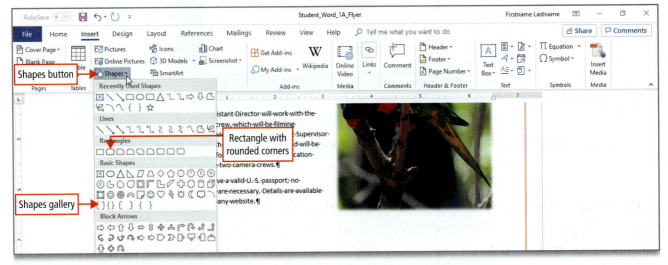

Figure 1.17

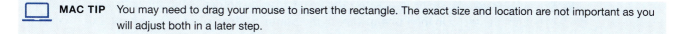

4 Under **Rectangles**, click the second shape—the rectangle that includes rounded corners, and then move your pointer. Notice that the ⊞ pointer displays.

5 Position the ⊞ pointer near the left margin at approximately **8 inches** on the vertical ruler. Click one time to insert a 1-inch by 1-inch rounded rectangle. The exact location is not important.

A blue rectangle with rounded edges displays.

> 💻 **MAC TIP** You may need to drag your mouse to insert the rectangle. The exact size and location are not important as you will adjust both in a later step.

6 To the right of the rectangle object, click **Layout Options** 🔲, and then at the bottom of the gallery, click **See more** to display the Layout dialog box.

> 💻 **MAC TIP** On the Shape Format tab, click Arrange, click Position, and then click More Layout Options.

7 In the **Layout** dialog box, under **Horizontal**, click **Alignment**. To the right of **Alignment**, click the **arrow**, and then click **Centered**. To the right of **relative to**, click the **arrow**, and then click **Page**. Under **Vertical**, select the existing number in the **Absolute position** box. Type **1** and then to the right of **below**, be sure that **Paragraph** displays. Click **OK**.

This action centers the rectangle on the page and positions the rectangle one inch below the last paragraph.

8 On the **Format tab**, in the **Shape Height box** ↕ 0.29" ⇅ select the existing number. Type **1.5** and then click in the **Shape Width box** ↔ 1.07" ⇅. Select the existing number, type **4.5** and then press Enter.

9 Compare your screen with Figure 1.18, and then **Save** 🖫 your document.

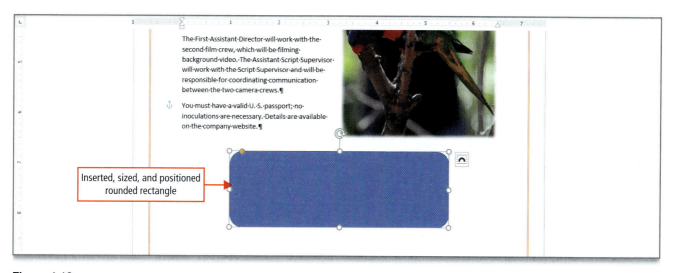

Figure 1.18

Activity 1.12 | Typing Text in a Shape and Formatting a Shape

MOS
5.2.4 and 5.3.2

1 If necessary, select the rectangle shape. Type **To set up an interview, apply online at:** and then press Enter. Type **www.SturgeonPointProductions.com**

2 Press Ctrl + A to select all of the text in the shape. Right-click over the selected text to display the mini toolbar, and then click **Bold** B. With the text still selected, click **Increase Font Size** A˄ three times to increase the font size to **16 pt**.

Use the keyboard shortcut Ctrl + A to select all of the text in a text box.

3 With the text still selected, on the **Home tab**, click the **Font Color button arrow**. Under **Theme Colors**, in the second column, click the first color.

4 Click outside the shape to deselect the text. Click the border of the shape to select the shape but not the text. On the **Format tab**, in the **Shape Styles group**, click **Shape Fill**. In the sixth column, click the fourth color.

5 With the shape still selected, in the **Shape Styles group**, click **Shape Outline**. In the sixth column, click the first color. Compare your screen with Figure 1.19, and then **Save** 🖫 your document.

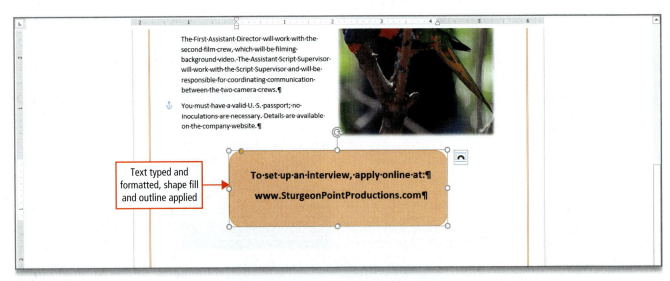

Figure 1.19

Activity 1.13 | Inserting a Text Box

MOS
5.1.6

A text box is useful to differentiate portions of text from other text on the page. Because it is a *floating object*—a graphic that can be moved independently of the surrounding text characters—you can place a text box anywhere on the page.

1 Press `Ctrl` + `Home` to move to the top of the document.

2 On the **Insert tab**, in the **Text group**, click **Text Box**. At the bottom of the gallery, click **Draw Text Box**.

3 Position the ⊞ pointer over the first blank paragraph—aligned with the left margin and at approximately 1 inch on the vertical ruler. Drag down and to the right to create a text box approximately **1.5 inches** high and **4 inches** wide—the exact size and location need not be precise.

4 With the insertion point blinking in the text box, type the following, pressing [Enter] after each of the first *two* lines to create a new paragraph:

> **Interviews will be held:**
> **Friday and Saturday, January 14 and 15**
> **In the Career Services Conference Room**

5 Compare your screen with Figure 1.20, and then **Save** 💾 your document

Figure 1.20

Activity 1.14 | Sizing and Positioning a Text Box and Formatting a Text Box Using Shape Styles

5.2.4

1 Point to the text box border to display the ⟨🔳⟩ pointer. In the space below the *Internships Available* title, by dragging, move the text box until a horizontal green alignment guide displays above the first blank paragraph mark and a vertical green alignment guide displays in the center of the page, as shown in Figure 1.21. If the alignment guides do not display, drag the text box to position it approximately as shown in the figure.

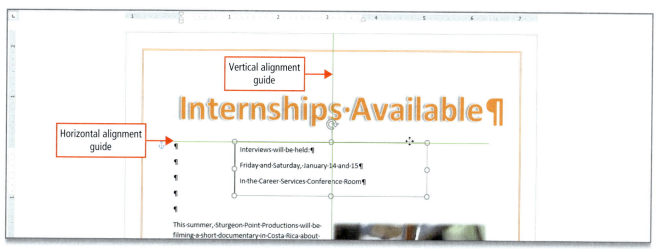

Figure 1.21

2 To place the text box precisely, on the **Format tab**, in the **Arrange group**, click **Position**, and then click **More Layout Options**.

3 In the **Layout** dialog box, under **Horizontal**, click **Alignment**. To the right of **Alignment**, click the **arrow**, and then click **Centered**. To the right of **relative to**, click the **arrow**, and then click **Page**.

4 Under **Vertical**, click in the **Absolute position** box, select the existing number, and then type **1.25** To the right of **below**, click the **arrow**, and then click **Margin**.

5 In the **Layout** dialog box, click the **Size tab**. Under **Height**, select the number in the **Absolute** box. Type **1.25** and then under **Width**, select the number in the **Absolute** box. Type **4** and then click **OK**.

The text box is sized correctly, centered horizontally, and the top edge is positioned 1.25 inches below the top margin of the document.

6 On the **Format tab**, in the **Shape Styles group**, click **More** ⊡, and then in the first row, click the third style.

💻 **MAC TIP**   The More button is located below the Shape Styles.

---

7 On the **Format tab**, in the **Shape Styles group**, click **Shape Effects**. Point to **Shadow**, and then under **Outer**, in the first row, click the first effect.

8 Click in the text box, and then select all the text in the text box. On the **Home tab**, change the **Font Size** to **16** and apply **Bold** B . In the **Paragraph group**, click **Center** ☰.

🔄 **ANOTHER WAY**   The keyboard shortcut to center text in a document is Ctrl + E .

---

9 Click anywhere in the document to deselect the text box. Compare your screen with Figure 1.22, and then **Save** 💾 your document.

Text formatted and centered, text box sized and positioned, shape style and Shadow effect applied

Internships·Available¶

Interviews·will·be·held:¶

Friday·and·Saturday,·January·14·and·15¶

In·the·Career·Services·Conference·Room¶

Figure 1.22

| Objective 4 | **Preview and Print a Document** |

GO! Learn How
Video W1-4

While you are creating your document, it is useful to preview your document periodically to be sure that you are getting the result you want. Then, before printing or distributing electronically, make a final preview to be sure the document layout is what you intended.

Activity 1.15 | Adding a File Name to the Footer by Inserting a Field

MOS

1.3.4

Information in headers and footers helps to identify a document when it is printed or displayed electronically. Recall that a header is information that prints at the top of every page and a footer is information that prints at the bottom of every page. In this text book, you will insert the file name in the footer of every Word document.

1 ▶ Click the **Insert tab**, and then in the **Header & Footer group**, click **Footer**.

2 ▶ At the bottom of the gallery, click **Edit Footer**.

The footer area displays with the insertion point blinking at the left edge, and on the ribbon, the Header & Footer Tools display.

ANOTHER WAY At the bottom edge of the page, right-click; from the shortcut menu, click Edit Footer.

3 ▶ On the ribbon, under the **Header & Footer Tools**, on the **Design tab**, in the **Insert group**, click **Document Info**, and then click **File Name**. Compare your screen with Figure 1.23.

MAC TIP To insert the filename in the footer, on the Insert tab, click Footer, and then click Edit Footer. On the Header & Footer tab, click Field, and then under Categories, click Document Information. Under Field Names, click FileName, and then click OK.

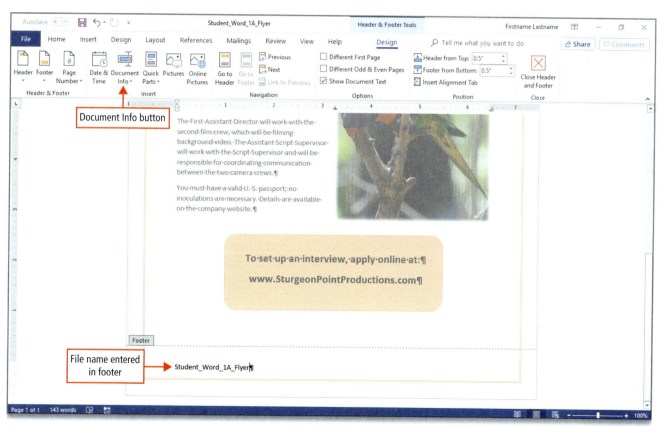

Figure 1.23

4 ▶ On the **Design tab**, click **Close Header and Footer**, and then **Save** 🖫 your document.

When the body of the document is active, the footer text is dimmed—it displays in gray. Conversely, when the footer area is active, the footer text is not dimmed; instead, the document text is dimmed.

ANOTHER WAY Double-click in the document outside of the footer area to close the footer and return to the document.

Activity 1.16 | Adding Document Properties and Previewing and Printing a Document

1.3.2 and 1.3.3

1 Press `Ctrl` + `Home` to move the insertion point to the top of the document. In the upper left corner of your screen, click the **File tab** to display **Backstage** view. Click **Info**, and then at the bottom of the **Properties** list, click **Show All Properties**.

2 As the **Tags** type **internship, documentary** In the **Subject** box, type your course name and section number. Be sure that your name displays in the **Author** box and edit if necessary.

MAC TIP To enter document properties, click File. At the bottom of the menu, click Properties, and then click the Summary tab. Click in the Keywords box to type the tags internship, documentary. Click in the Subject box, type your course name and section number, edit the Author if necessary, and then click OK. To print, click File, and then click Print.

---

3 On the left, click **Print** to display the **Print Preview**. Compare your screen with Figure 1.24.

Here you can select any printer connected to your system and adjust the settings related to how you want to print. On the right, Print Preview displays your document exactly as it will print; the formatting marks do not display. At the bottom of the Print Preview area, the number of pages and arrows with which you can move among the pages in Print Preview display. On the right, Zoom settings enable you to shrink or enlarge the Print Preview.

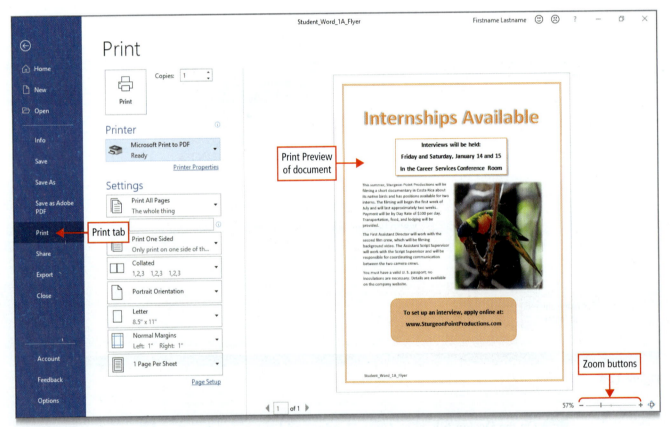

Figure 1.24

4 In the lower right corner of the window, click **Zoom In** ➕ several times to view the document at a larger size, and notice that a larger preview is easier to read. Click **Zoom to Page** 🔲 to view the entire page.

5 If you want to print your document on paper using the default printer on your system, in the upper left portion of the screen, click **Print**. If you do not print, click Save.

> The document will print on your default printer; if you do not have a color printer, colors will print in shades of gray. Backstage view closes and your file redisplays in the Word window.

6 Save 🖫 your document. In the upper right corner of the Word window, click **Close** ⊠.

For Non-MyLab Submissions Determine What Your Instructor Requires
As directed by your instructor, submit your completed Word file.

7 In **MyLab IT**, locate and click the Grader Project **Word 1A Flyer**. In **step 3**, under **Upload Completed Assignment**, click **Choose File**. In the **Open** dialog box, navigate to your **Word Chapter 1 folder**, and then click your **Student_Word_1A_Flyer** file one time to select it. In the lower right corner of the **Open** dialog box, click **Open**.

> The name of your selected file displays above the Upload button.

8 To submit your file to **MyLab IT** for grading, click **Upload**, wait a moment for a green **Success!** message, and then in **step 4**, click the blue **Submit for Grading** button. Click **Close Assignment** to return to your list of **Course Materials**.

You have completed Project 1A **END**

»» GO! With Google Docs

Objective	Create a Flyer Using Google Docs

ALERT   **Working with Web-Based Applications and Services**

Computer programs and services on the web receive continuous updates and improvements, so the steps to complete this web-based Activity may differ from the ones shown. You can often look at the screens and the information presented to determine how to complete the Activity.

If you do not already have a Google account, you will need to create one before you begin this Activity. Go to **http://google.com** and in the upper right corner, click Sign In. On the Sign In screen, click Create Account. On the Create your Google Account page, complete the form, read and agree to the Terms of Service and Privacy Policy, and then click Next step. On the Welcome screen, click Get Started.

Activity | Creating a Flyer

In this Activity, you will use Google Docs to create a flyer.

1 From the desktop, open your browser, navigate to http://google.com, and then sign in to your Google account. In the upper right corner of your screen, click **Google apps**, and then click **Drive**.

2 To create a folder in which to store your web projects, click **New**, and then click **Folder**. In the **New folder** box, type **GO! Web Projects** and then click **Create** to create a folder on your Google drive. Double-click your **GO! Web Projects** folder to open it.

3 In the left pane, click **New**, and then click **Google Docs** to open a new tab in your browser and to start an Untitled document. At the top of the window, click **Untitled document** and then, using your own name as the file name, type **Lastname_Firstname WD_1A_Web** and then press Enter to change the file name.

4 To the right of the file name, point to the small file folder to display the ScreenTip **Move to**. Click the file folder and notice that your file is saved in the GO! Web Projects folder. Compare your screen with Figure A.

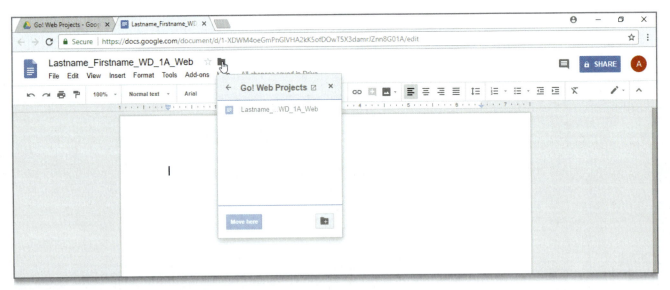

Figure A

5 Click in your document to close the Move to folder dialog box and to position the insertion point at the top of the document. Type **Internships Available** and then press Enter two times. Type **Interviews will be held Friday and Saturday, January 14 and 15 in the Career Services Conference Room.**

6 Press Ctrl + A to select all of the text. Click the **Font size arrow** 10 , and then click **24**. With the text still selected, click **Center** .

7 Press Ctrl + End to move to the end of the document, and then press Enter. Click **Insert**, and then click **Image**. Click **Upload from computer**, and then navigate to your student data files. Click **w01A_Bird**, and then click **Open** to insert the picture.

8 Click the picture to select it, and then point to the square sizing handle at the upper left corner of the picture. Drag down and to the right until the sizing handle aligns with approximately **3 inches on the ruler**.

9 If necessary scroll up to view the image and the text above it. Click to the right of the picture and then press Enter twice. Type **Join our production crew in Costa Rica as we film a short documentary about its native birds. We are hiring two interns!**

10 Select the title *Internships Available* and then click **Text color** . In the first column, click the last color, and then apply **Bold** . Your document will look similar to Figure B.

11 Your document will be saved automatically. Sign out of your Google account. Submit as instructed by your instructor.

Internships Available

Interviews will be held Friday and Saturday, January 14 and 15 in the Career Services Conference Room.

Join our production crew in Costa Rica as we film a short documentary about its native birds. We are hiring two interns!

Figure B

PROJECT 1B Information Handout

Project Activities

In Activities 1.17 through 1.29, you will format an information handout from Sturgeon Point Productions that describes internships available to students. Your completed document will look similar to Figure 1.25.

Project Files for MyLab IT Grader

1. In your **MyLab IT** course, locate and click **Word 1B Programs**, Download Materials, and then Download All Files.
2. Extract the zipped folder to your Word Chapter 1 folder. Close the Grader download screens.
3. Take a moment to open the downloaded **Word_1B_Programs_Instructions**; note any recent updates to the book.

Project Results

GO! Project 1B
Where We're Going

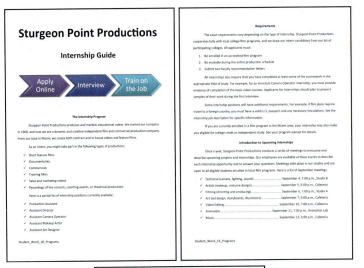

Figure 1.25 Project 1B Information Handout

For Non-MyLab Submissions

For Project 1B, you will need:

w01B_Programs

In your Word Chapter 1 folder, save your document as:

Lastname_Firstname_1B_Programs

After you have named and saved your document, on the next page continue with Step 2.

GO! Learn How

Video W1-5

Document layout includes *margins*—the space between the text and the top, bottom, left, and right edges of the paper. Paragraph layout includes line spacing, indents, and tabs. In Word, the information about paragraph formats is stored in the paragraph mark at the end of a paragraph. When you press [Enter], the new paragraph mark contains the formatting of the previous paragraph, unless you take steps to change it.

Activity 1.17 | Setting Margins

1.2.1

1 ▶ Navigate to your **Word Chapter 1 folder**, and then double-click the Word file you downloaded from **MyLab IT** that displays your name —**Student_Word_1B_Programs**. If necessary, at the top click **Enable Editing**. On the **Home tab**, in the **Paragraph group**, be sure **Show/Hide** ¶ is active so that you can view the formatting marks.

2 ▶ Click the **Layout tab**. In the **Page Setup group**, click **Margins**, and then take a moment to study the settings in the Margins gallery.

> If you have recently used custom margins settings, they will display at the top of this gallery. Other commonly used settings also display.

3 ▶ At the bottom of the **Margins** gallery, click the command followed by an ellipsis—**Custom Margins . . .** —to display the **Page Setup** dialog box.

4 ▶ In the **Page Setup** dialog box, under **Margins**, press [Tab] as necessary to select the value in the **Left** box, and then, with *1.25"* selected, type **1**

> This action will change the left margin to 1 inch on all pages of the document. You do not need to type the inch (") mark.

5 ▶ Press [Tab] to select the margin in the **Right** box, and then type **1** At the bottom of the dialog box, notice that the new margins will apply to the **Whole document**. Compare your screen with Figure 1.26.

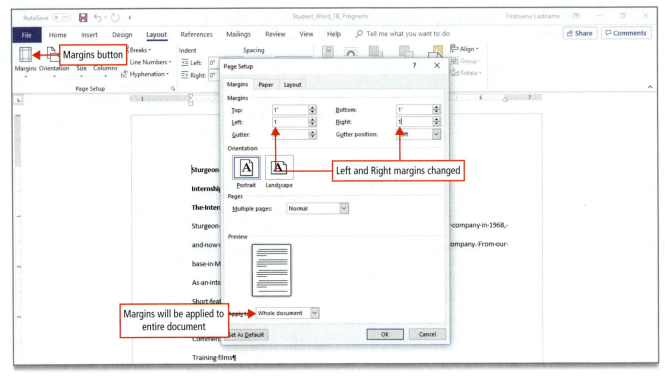

Figure 1.26

6 ▸ Click **OK** to apply the new margins and close the dialog box. If the ruler below the ribbon is not displayed, on the View tab, in the Show group, select the Ruler check box.

7 ▸ Scroll to position the bottom of **Page 1** and the top of **Page 2** on your screen. Notice that the page edges display, and the page number and total number of pages display on the left side of the status bar.

8 ▸ Near the bottom edge of **Page 1**, point anywhere in the bottom margin area, right-click, and then click **Edit Footer** to display the footer area. On the ribbon, under the **Header & Footer Tools**, on the **Design tab**, in the **Insert group**, click **Document Info**, and then click **File Name**.

> **MAC TIP** In the bottom margin area, hold down [control] and then click to display the shortcut menu. Click Edit Footer. On the Header & Footer tab, click Field, and then under Categories, click Document Information. Under Field Names, click FileName, and then click OK.

9 ▸ Double-click anywhere in the document to close the footer area, and then **Save** 🖫 your document.

Activity 1.18 | Aligning Paragraphs

Alignment refers to the placement of paragraph text relative to the left and right margins. Most paragraph text uses *left alignment*—aligned at the left margin, leaving the right margin uneven. Three other types of paragraph alignment are: *center alignment*—centered between the left and right margins; *right alignment*—aligned at the right margin with an uneven left margin; and *justified alignment*—text aligned evenly at both the left and right margins. The table in Figure 1.27 shows examples of these alignment types.

Types of Paragraph Alignment		
Alignment	**Button**	**Description and Example**
Align Left	☰	Align Left is the default paragraph alignment in Word. Text in the paragraph aligns at the left margin, and the right margin is uneven.
Center	☰	Center alignment aligns text in the paragraph so that it is centered between the left and right margins.
Align Right	☰	Align Right aligns text at the right margin. Using Align Right, the left margin, which is normally even, is uneven.
Justify	☰	The Justify alignment option adds additional space between words so that both the left and right margins are even. Justify is often used when formatting newspaper-style columns.

Figure 1.27

1 Scroll to position the middle of **Page 2** on your screen, look at the left and right margins, and notice that the text is justified—both the right and left margins of multiple-line paragraphs are aligned evenly at the margins. On the **Home tab**, in the **Paragraph group**, notice that **Justify** ☰ is active.

> To achieve a justified right margin, Word adjusts the size of spaces between words, which can result in unattractive spacing in a document that spans the width of a page. Many individuals find such spacing difficult to read.

2 Press Ctrl + A to select all the text in the document, and then on the **Home tab**, in the **Paragraph group**, click **Align Left** ☰.

ANOTHER WAY   On the Home tab, in the Editing group, click Select, and then click Select All.

MAC TIP   Use command ⌘ + A to select all the text in a document.

3 Press Ctrl + Home to move to the beginning of the document. In the left margin area, point to the left of the first paragraph—*Sturgeon Point Productions*—until the ⇗ pointer displays, and then click one time to select the paragraph.

> Use this technique to select entire lines of text.

4 On the mini toolbar, in the **Font Size** box, select the existing number, type **40** and then press Enter.

> Use this technique to change the font size to a size that is not available on the Font Size list.

MAC TIP   On the Home tab, in the Font Size, select the existing number and type 40.

5 Select the second paragraph—*Internship Guide*—and then using the mini toolbar or the ribbon, change the **Font Size** to **26 pt**. Point to the left of the first paragraph—*Sturgeon Point Productions*—to display the ⇗ pointer again, and then drag down to select the first two paragraphs, which form the title and subtitle of the document.

6 On the **Home tab**, in the **Paragraph group**, click **Center** ☰ to center the title and subtitle between the left and right margins, and then compare your screen with Figure 1.28.

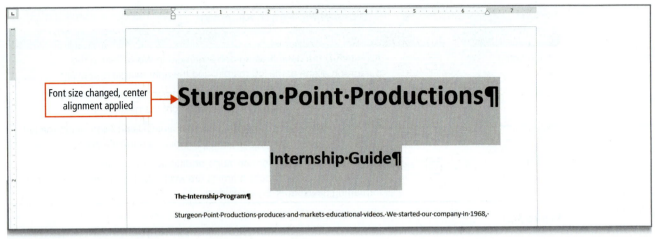

Figure 1.28

 7 Near the top of **Page 1**, locate the first bold subheading—*The Internship Program*. Point to the left of the paragraph to display the ⟨🔺⟩ pointer, and then click one time to select the text.

8 With *The Internship Program* selected, use your mouse wheel or the vertical scroll bar to bring the bottom portion of **Page 1** into view. Locate the subheading *Requirements*. Move the pointer to the left of the paragraph to display the ⟨🔺⟩ pointer, hold down Ctrl, and then click one time. Release Ctrl, and then scroll to the middle of **Page 2**. Use the same technique to select the third subheading—*Introduction to Upcoming Internships*.

Three subheadings are selected; in Windows-based programs, you can hold down Ctrl to select multiple items.

⌨️ **MAC TIP**   Hold down command ⌘ when selecting multiple items.

---

9 Click **Center** ☰ to center all three subheadings, and then click **Save** 💾.

Activity 1.19 | Setting Line Spacing

MOS
2.2.3

Line spacing is the distance between lines of text in a paragraph. Three of the most commonly used line spacing options are shown in the table in Figure 1.29.

Line Spacing Options	
Spacing	**Description, Example, and Information**
Single spacing	**This text in this example uses single spacing.** Single spacing was once the most commonly used spacing in business documents. Now, because so many documents are read on a computer screen rather than on paper, single spacing is becoming less popular.
Multiple 1.08 spacing	**This text in this example uses multiple 1.08 spacing.** The default line spacing in Microsoft Word is 1.08, which is slightly more than single spacing to make the text easier to read on a computer screen. Many individuals now prefer this spacing, even on paper, because the lines of text appear less crowded.
Double spacing	**This text in this example uses double spacing.** College research papers and draft documents that need space for notes are commonly double-spaced; there is space for a full line of text between each document line.

Figure 1.29

1 ▶ Move to the beginning of the document, and then press `Ctrl` + `A` to select all of the text in the document.

2 ▶ With all of the text in the document selected, on the **Home tab**, in the **Paragraph group**, click **Line and Paragraph Spacing** ![icon], and notice that the text in the document is double spaced—**2.0** is checked. Compare your screen with Figure 1.30.

👉 **BY TOUCH** Tap the ribbon commands.

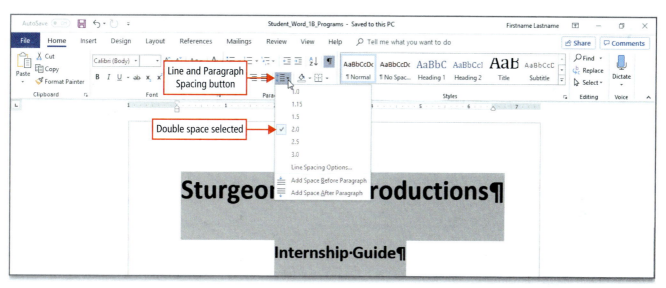

Figure 1.30

3 ▶ On the **Line Spacing** menu, click **1.5**, and then click anywhere in the document to deselect the text. Compare your screen with Figure 1.31, and then **Save** ![icon] your document.

Figure 1.31

Activity 1.20 | Indenting Text

MOS
2.2.3

Indenting the first line of each paragraph is a common technique to distinguish paragraphs.

1 ▶ Below the title and subtitle of the document, click anywhere in the paragraph that begins *Sturgeon Point Productions produces*.

2 ▶ On the **Home tab**, in the **Paragraph group**, click the **Dialog Box Launcher** ![icon].

💻 **MAC TIP** Click the Line and Paragraph Spacing button, and then click Line Spacing Options.

3 In the **Paragraph** dialog box, on the **Indents and Spacing tab**, under **Indentation**, click the **Special arrow**, and then click **First line** to indent the first line by 0.5", which is the default indent setting. Compare your screen with Figure 1.32.

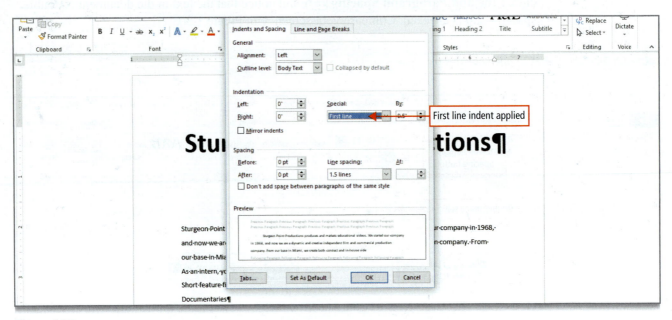

Figure 1.32

4 Click **OK**, and then click anywhere in the next paragraph, which begins *As an intern*. On the ruler under the ribbon, drag the **First Line Indent** marker ▽ to **0.5 inches on the horizontal ruler**, and then compare your screen with Figure 1.33.

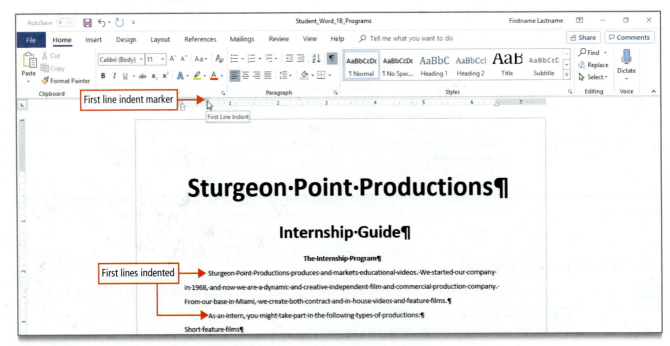

Figure 1.33

5 By using either of the techniques you just practiced, apply a first line indent of **0.5"** to the paragraph that begins *Here is a partial*.

6 **Save** 🖫 your document.

Activity 1.21 | Setting Space Before and After Paragraphs

2.2.3

Adding space after each paragraph is another technique to differentiate paragraphs.

1 Press ⌃Ctrl + Ⓐ to select all the text in the document. Click the **Layout tab**, and then in the **Paragraph group**, under **Spacing**, click the **After spin box up arrow** one time to change the value to **6 pt**.

To change the value in the box, you can also select the existing number, type a new number, and then press ⏎Enter. This document will use 6 pt spacing after paragraphs to add space.

🔄 **ANOTHER WAY** On either the Home tab or the Layout tab, display the Paragraph dialog box from the Paragraph group, and then under Spacing, click the spin box arrows as necessary.

2 Press ⌃Ctrl + Ⓗome, and then compare your screen with Figure 1.34.

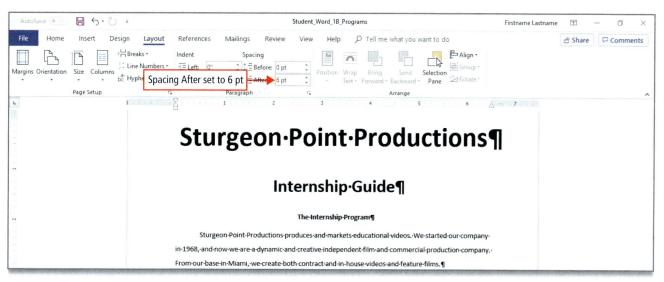

Figure 1.34

3 Near the top of **Page 1**, select the subheading *The Internship Program*, including the paragraph mark following it. Scroll down using the vertical scroll bar, hold down ⌃Ctrl, and then select the *Requirements* and *Introduction to Upcoming Internships* subheadings.

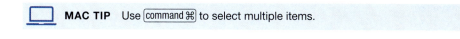
💻 **MAC TIP** Use ⌘command ⌘ to select multiple items.

ALERT **Did your screen zoom when you were selecting?**

Holding down ⌃Ctrl and using the mouse wheel at the same time will zoom your screen.

4 With all three subheadings selected, in the **Paragraph group**, under **Spacing**, click the **Before up spin box arrow** two times to set the **Spacing Before** to **12 pt**. Compare your screen with Figure 1.35, and then **Save** 🖫 your document.

This action increases the amount of space above each of the subheadings, which will make them easy to distinguish in the document. The formatting is applied only to the selected paragraphs.

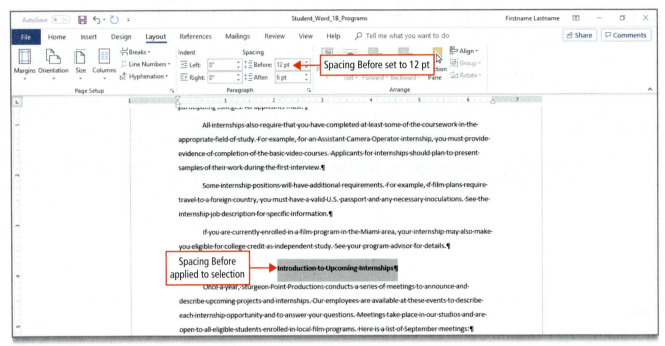

Figure 1.35

Objective 6   Create and Modify Lists

GO! Learn How
Video W1-6

To display a list of information, you can choose a ***bulleted list***, which uses ***bullets***—text symbols such as small circles or check marks—to introduce each item in a list. You can also choose a ***numbered list***, which uses consecutive numbers or letters to introduce each item in a list.

Use a bulleted list if the items in the list can be introduced in any order; use a numbered list for items that have definite steps, a sequence of actions, or are in chronological order.

Activity 1.22 │ Creating a Bulleted List

MOS
3.3.1

1 In the upper portion of **Page 1**, locate the paragraph *Short feature films*, and then point to this paragraph from the left margin area to display the 𝄃 pointer. Drag down to select this paragraph and the next five paragraphs—ending with the paragraph *Recordings of live concerts*.

2 On the **Home tab**, in the **Paragraph group**, click **Bullets** ☰⁝ to change the selected text to a bulleted list.

The spacing between each of the bulleted points is removed and each bulleted item is automatically indented.

3 On the ruler, point to **First Line Indent** ▽ and read the ScreenTip, and then point to **Hanging Indent** △. Compare your screen with Figure 1.36.

By default, Word formats bulleted items with a first line indent of 0.25" and adds a Hanging Indent at 0.5". The hanging indent maintains the alignment of text when a bulleted item is more than one line.

You can modify the list indentation by using Decrease Indent ◀≣ or Increase Indent ▶≣. Decrease Indent moves your paragraph closer to the margin. Increase Indent moves your paragraph farther away from the margin.

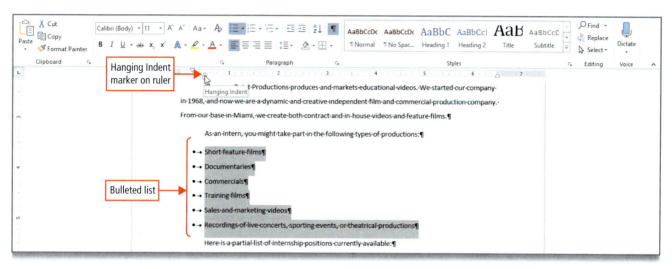

Figure 1.36

4 Scroll down slightly, and then by using the ⌐▞ pointer from the left margin area, select the five internship positions, beginning with *Production Assistant* and ending with *Assistant Set Designer*. In the **Paragraph group**, click **Bullets** ▤ ▾.

5 Scroll down to view **Page 2**. Apply bullets to all of the paragraphs that indicate the September meetings and meeting dates, beginning with *Technical* and ending with *Music*.

6 **Save** 🖫 your document.

Activity 1.23 | Creating a Numbered List

3.3.1

1 Under the subheading *Requirements*, in the paragraph that begins *The exact requirements*, click to position the insertion point at the *end* of the paragraph, following the colon. Press Enter to create a blank paragraph. Notice that the paragraph is indented because the First Line Indent from the previous paragraph carried over to the new paragraph.

2 To change the indent formatting for this paragraph, on the ruler, drag the **First Line Indent** marker ▽ to the left so that it is positioned directly above the lower button.

3 Being sure to include the period, type **1.** and press Spacebar. Compare your screen with Figure 1.37.

Word determines that this paragraph is the first item in a numbered list and formats the new paragraph accordingly, indenting the list in the same manner as the bulleted list. The space after the number changes to a tab, and the AutoCorrect Options button displays to the left of the list item. The tab is indicated by a right arrow formatting mark.

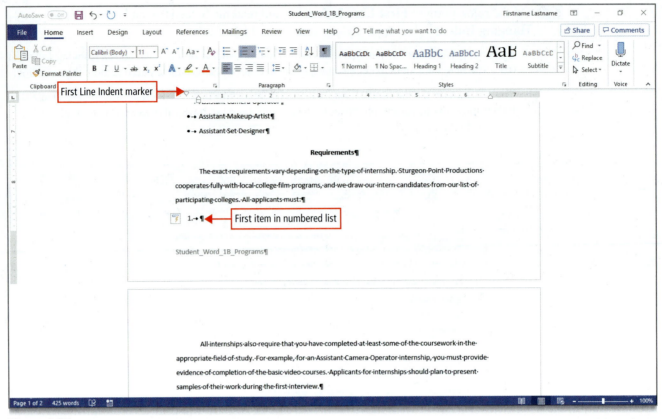

Figure 1.37

4 ▶ Click **AutoCorrect Options** ⚡, and then compare your screen with Figure 1.38.

From the displayed list, you can remove the automatic formatting here, or stop using the automatic numbered lists option in this document. You also have the option to open the AutoCorrect dialog box to *Control AutoFormat Options*.

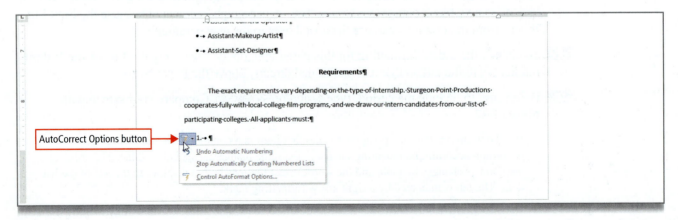

Figure 1.38

5 Click **AutoCorrect Options** ⚡ again to close the menu without selecting any of the commands. Type **Be enrolled in an accredited film program** and press Enter. Notice that the second number and a tab are added to the next line.

6 Type **Be available during the entire production schedule** and press Enter. Type **Submit two faculty recommendation letters** and then compare your screen with Figure 1.39. **Save** 💾 your document.

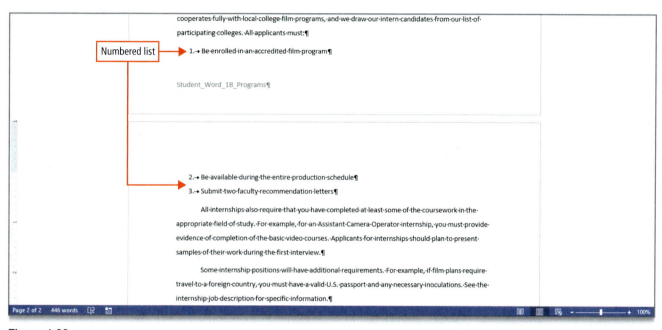

cooperates·fully·with·local·college·film·programs,·and·we·draw·our·intern·candidates·from·our·list·of·
participating·colleges.·All·applicants·must:¶

Numbered list → 1.→ Be·enrolled·in·an·accredited·film·program¶

Student_Word_1B_Programs¶

2.→ Be·available·during·the·entire·production·schedule¶
3.→ Submit·two·faculty·recommendation·letters¶

All·internships·also·require·that·you·have·completed·at·least·some·of·the·coursework·in·the·
appropriate·field·of·study.·For·example,·for·an·Assistant·Camera·Operator·internship,·you·must·provide·
evidence·of·completion·of·the·basic·video·courses.·Applicants·for·internships·should·plan·to·present·
samples·of·their·work·during·the·first·interview.¶

Some·internship·positions·will·have·additional·requirements.·For·example,·if·film·plans·require·
travel·to·a·foreign·country,·you·must·have·a·valid·U.S.·passport·and·any·necessary·inoculations.·See·the·
internship·job·description·for·specific·information.¶

Page 2 of 2   446 words

Figure 1.39

MORE KNOWLEDGE | **To End a List**

To turn a list off, you can press Backspace, click the Numbering or Bullets button, or press Enter two times. Both list buttons— Numbering and Bullets—act as *toggle buttons*; that is, clicking the button one time turns the feature on, and clicking the button again turns the feature off.

Activity 1.24 | Customizing Bullets

MOS

3.3.2

You can use any symbol from any font for your bullet characters.

1 Press Ctrl + End to move to the end of the document, and then scroll up as necessary to display the bulleted list containing the list of meetings.

2 Point to the left of the first list item to display the 🖋 pointer, and then drag down to select all six meetings in the list—the bullet symbols are not selected.

3 On the mini toolbar, click the **Bullets button arrow** to display the Bullet Library, and then compare your screen with Figure 1.40.

💻 **MAC TIP** On the Home tab, click the Bullets button arrow.

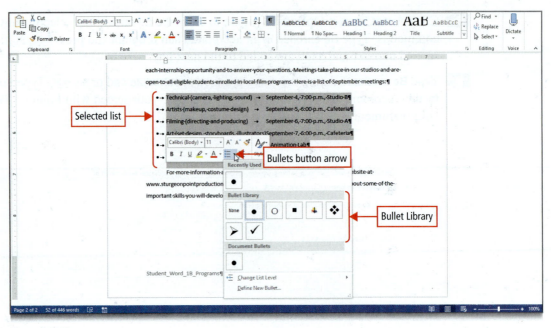

Figure 1.40

4 ▶ Under **Bullet Library**, click the **check mark** symbol.

MAC TIP   If the check mark bullet is not available, click Define New Bullet. Click Bullet, click the Font arrow, click Wingdings, and then locate and click the check mark symbol. Click OK two times.

5 ▶ With the bulleted list still selected, on the **Home tab**, in the **Clipboard group**, double-click **Format Painter** 🖌 to activate it for multiple use.

6 ▶ Use the vertical scroll bar or your mouse wheel to scroll to view **Page 1**. Move the pointer to the left of the first item in the first bulleted list to display the 🔏 pointer, and then drag down to select all six items in the list and to apply the format of the third bulleted list—the check mark bullets—to this list. Repeat this procedure to change the bullets in the second list to check marks. Press Esc to turn off **Format Painter**, and then **Save** 🖫 your document. Compare your screen with Figure 1.41.

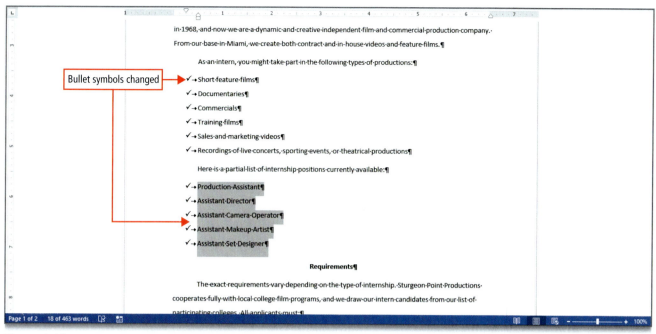

Figure 1.41

Objective 7 | Set and Modify Tab Stops

GO! Learn How
Video W1-7

Tab stops mark specific locations on a line of text. Use tab stops to indent and align text and use the ⟨Tab⟩ key to move to tab stops.

Activity 1.25 | Setting Tab Stops

1 ▶ Scroll to view **Page 2**, and then by using the pointer at the left of the first item, select all the items in the bulleted list. Notice that there is a tab mark between the name of the meeting and the date.

The arrow that indicates a tab is a nonprinting formatting mark.

2 ▶ To the left of the horizontal ruler, point to **Tab Alignment** ⌊ to display the *Left Tab* ScreenTip, and then compare your screen with Figure 1.42.

Project 1B: Information Handout | **Word** 139

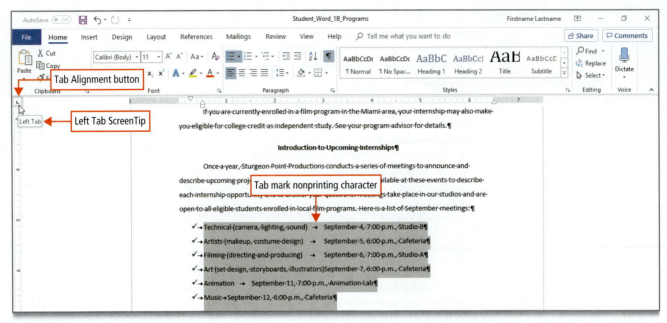

Figure 1.42

> **3** ▸ Click **Tab Alignment** ⌐ several times to view the tab alignment options shown in the table in Figure 1.43.

Tab Alignment Options		
Type	**Tab Alignment Button Displays This Marker**	**Description**
Left	⌐	Text is left aligned at the tab stop and extends to the right.
Center	⊥	Text is centered around the tab stop.
Right	⌐	Text is right aligned at the tab stop and extends to the left.
Decimal	⊥	The decimal point aligns at the tab stop.
Bar	I	A vertical bar displays at the tab stop.
First Line Indent	▽	Text in the first line of a paragraph indents.
Hanging Indent	△	Text in all lines indents except for the first line in the paragraph.

Figure 1.43

> **4** ▸ Display **Left Tab** ⌐. Along the lower edge of the horizontal ruler, point to and then click at **3.5 inches on the horizontal ruler**. Notice that all of the dates left align at the new tab stop location, and the right edge of the column is uneven.

> **5** ▸ Compare your screen with Figure 1.44, and then **Save** 🖫 your document.

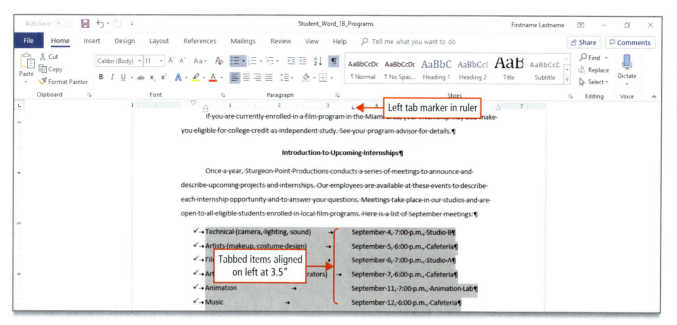

Figure 1.44

Activity 1.26 | Modifying Tab Stops

Tab stops are a form of paragraph formatting. Therefore, the information about tab stops is stored in the paragraph mark in the paragraphs to which they were applied.

1 With the bulleted list still selected, on the ruler, point to the new tab marker at *3.5 inches on the horizontal ruler*, and then when the *Left Tab* ScreenTip displays, drag the tab marker to **4 inches on the horizontal ruler**.

In all of the selected lines, the text at the tab stop left aligns at 4 inches.

2 On the ruler, point to the tab marker that you moved to display the *Left Tab* ScreenTip, and then double-click to display the **Tabs** dialog box.

ANOTHER WAY On the Home tab, in the Paragraph group, click the Dialog Box Launcher. At the bottom of the Paragraph dialog box, click the Tabs button.

3 In the **Tabs** dialog box, under **Tab stop position**, if necessary select *4"*, and then type **6**

MAC TIP At the bottom of the Tabs dialog box, click Clear All. In the Tab stops box type 6. Under Alignment, click Right. Under Leader, click the option that is a series of dots, and then skip to step 6.

4 Under **Alignment**, click the **Right** option button. Under **Leader**, click the **2** option button. Near the bottom of the **Tabs** dialog box, click **Set**.

Because the Right tab will be used to align the items in the list, the tab stop at 4" is no longer necessary.

5 In the **Tabs** dialog box, in the **Tab stop position** box, click **4"** to select this tab stop, and then in the lower portion of the **Tabs** dialog box, click the **Clear** button to delete this tab stop, which is no longer necessary. Compare your screen with Figure 1.45.

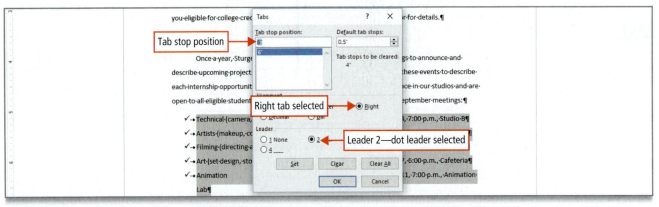

Figure 1.45

6 Click **OK**. On the ruler, notice that the left tab marker at *4″* no longer displays, a right tab marker displays at *6″*, and a series of dots—a **dot leader**—displays between the columns of the list. Notice also that the right edge of the column is even. Compare your screen with Figure 1.46.

A **leader character** creates a solid, dotted, or dashed line that fills the space to the left of a tab character and draws the reader's eyes across the page from one item to the next. When the character used for the leader is a dot, it is commonly referred to as a dot leader.

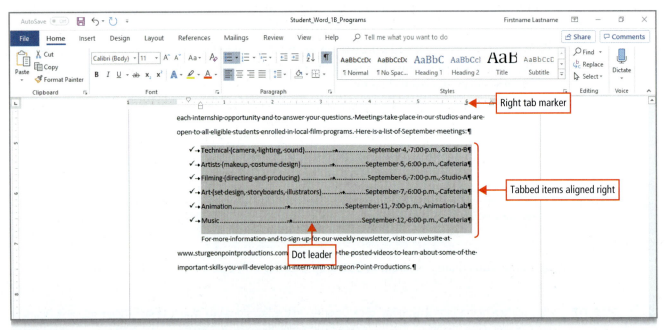

Figure 1.46

7 In the bulleted list that uses dot leaders, locate the *Art* meeting, and then click to position the insertion point at the end of that line, after the word *Cafeteria*. Press Enter to create a new blank bullet item.

8 Type **Video Editing** and press Tab. Notice that a dot leader fills the space to the tab marker location.

9 Type **September 10, 7:00 p.m., Cafeteria** and notice that the text moves to the left to maintain the right alignment of the tab stop.

10 **Save** 🖫 your document.

Objective 8   Insert and Format a SmartArt Graphic and an Icon

GO! Learn How
Video W1-8

SmartArt graphics are designer-quality visual representations of information, and Word provides many different layouts from which you can choose. *Icons* are pictures composed of straight and curved lines. SmartArt graphics and icons can communicate your messages or ideas more effectively than plain text, and these objects add visual interest to a document or web page.

Activity 1.27 | Inserting a SmartArt Graphic

5.1.4 and 5.3.3

1 ▶ Press [Ctrl] + [Home] to move to the top of the document, and then click to the right of the subtitle *Internship Guide*.

2 ▶ Click the **Insert tab**, and then in the **Illustrations group**, point to **SmartArt** to display its ScreenTip. Read the ScreenTip, and then click **SmartArt**.

3 ▶ In the center portion of the **Choose a SmartArt Graphic** dialog box, examine the numerous types of SmartArt graphics available.

4 ▶ On the left, click **Process**, and then by using the ScreenTips, locate and click **Basic Chevron Process**. Compare your screen with Figure 1.47.

At the right of the dialog box, a preview and description of the SmartArt displays.

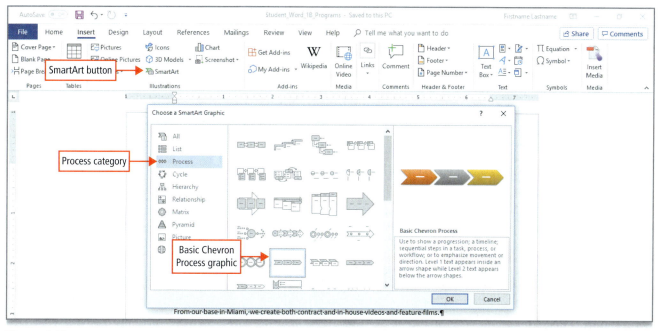

Figure 1.47

5 ▶ Click **OK** to insert the SmartArt graphic.

To the left of the inserted SmartArt graphic, the text pane may display. The ***text pane*** is used to type text and edit text in your SmartArt graphic. If you choose not to use the text pane to enter text, you can close it.

6 ▶ On the ribbon, under **SmartArt Tools**, on the **Design tab**, in the **Create Graphic group**, notice the Text Pane button. If the text pane button is selected, click **Text Pane** to close the pane.

7 ▶ In the SmartArt graphic, in the first blue arrow, click **[Text]**, and notice that *[Text]* is replaced by a blinking insertion point.

The word *[Text]* is called ***placeholder text***, which is nonprinting text that indicates where you can type.

8 ▸ Type **Apply Online**

9 ▸ Click the placeholder text in the middle arrow. Type **Interview** and then click the placeholder text in the third arrow. Type **Train on the Job** and then compare your screen with Figure 1.48.

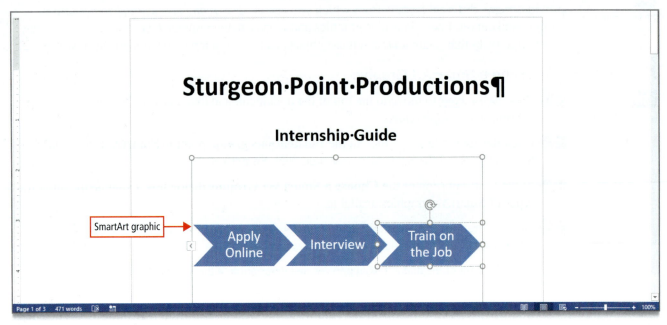

Figure 1.48

10 ▸ Save 🖫 your document.

Activity 1.28 | **Sizing and Formatting a SmartArt Graphic**

5.2.5

1 ▸ Click the **SmartArt solid border** to select it. Be sure that none of the arrows have sizing handles around their border, which would indicate the arrow was selected, not the entire graphic.

2 ▸ Click the **SmartArt Tools Format tab**, and then in the **Size group**, if necessary, click Size to display the Shape Height and Shape Width boxes.

3 ▸ Set the **Height** to **1.75"** and the **Width** to **6.5"**, and then compare your screen with Figure 1.49.

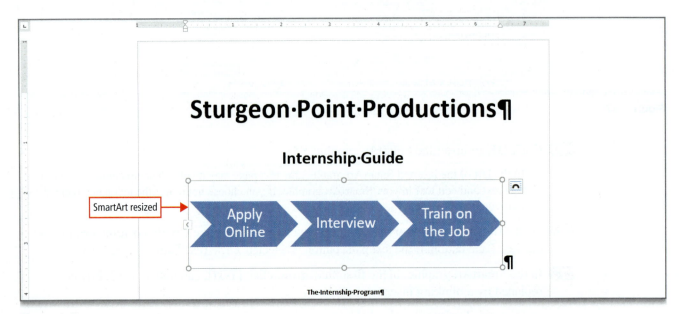

Figure 1.49

4 With the SmartArt graphic still selected, click the **SmartArt Tools Design tab**, and then in the **SmartArt Styles group**, click **Change Colors**. Under **Colorful**, click the fourth style—**Colorful Range - Accent Colors 4 to 5**.

5 On the **SmartArt Tools Design tab**, in the **SmartArt Styles group**, click **More** [⋮]. Under **3-D**, click the second style—**Inset**. Compare your screen with Figure 1.50.

Figure 1.50

6 **Save** 🖫 your document.

Activity 1.29 | Inserting an Icon

Many of the marketing materials at Sturgeon Point Productions use a clapperboard icon to represent the filmmaking and video production aspect of the business. In this Activity, you will insert a clapperboard icon at the end of the document.

1 Press [Ctrl] + [End] to move to the end of the document. Press [Enter] to insert a blank line and notice that a first line indent is applied. On the ruler, drag the **First Line Indent** marker back to the left margin.

2 On the **Insert tab**, in the **Illustrations group**, click **Icons**. On the left side of the **Insert Icons** dialog box, click **Arts**. Under **Arts**, click the **clapperboard icon** as shown in Figure 1.51 so that a check mark displays.

💻 **MAC TIP** In the Icons pane, click the Jump to arrow, and then click Arts. Click the Clapperboard icon.

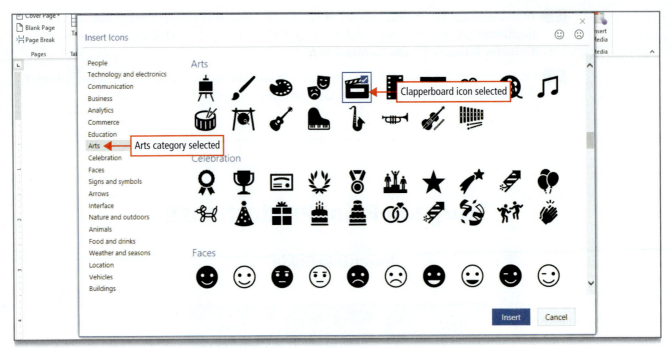

Figure 1.51

> **3** ▶ Click **Insert** to insert the icon. On the **Home tab**, in the **Paragraph group**, click **Center**.

> **4** ▶ **Save** 🖫 your document. In the upper right corner of the Word window, click **Close** ☒.

For Non-MyLab Submissions Determine What Your Instructor Requires
As directed by your instructor, submit your completed Word file.

> **5** ▶ In **MyLab IT**, locate and click the Grader Project **Word 1B Programs**. In step 3, under **Upload Completed Assignment**, click **Choose File**. In the **Open** dialog box, navigate to your **Word Chapter 1 folder**, and then click your **Student_Word_1B_Programs** file one time to select it. In the lower right corner of the **Open** dialog box, click **Open**.

> The name of your selected file displays above the Upload button.

> **6** ▶ To submit your file to **MyLab IT** for grading, click **Upload**, wait a moment for a green **Success!** message, and then in **step 4**, click the blue **Submit for Grading** button. Click **Close Assignment** to return to your list of **Course Materials**.

You have completed Project 1B   **END**

Objective	Create an Information Handout

ALERT   **Working with Web-Based Applications and Services**

Computer programs and services on the web receive continuous updates and improvements, so the steps to complete this web-based Activity may differ from the ones shown. You can often look at the screens and the information presented to determine how to complete the Activity.

If you do not already have a Google account, you will need to create one before you begin this Activity. Go to http://google .com and in the upper right corner, click **Sign In**. On the Sign In screen, click **Create Account**. On the Create your Google Account page, complete the form, read and agree to the Terms of Service and Privacy Policy, and then click **Next step**. On the Welcome screen, click **Get Started**.

Activity | Creating a Handout with Bulleted and Numbered Lists

In this Activity, you will use Google Docs to create an information handout.

1 From the desktop, open your browser, navigate to http://google.com. In the upper right corner of your screen, click **Google apps** ⊞, and then click **Drive** ▲. Sign in to your Google account, and then double-click your **GO! Web Projects** folder to open it. If you have not created this folder, refer to the instructions in the first Google Docs project in this chapter.

2 Click **New**, and then click **Google Docs**. Click **File**, and then click **Open**. Click **Upload**, and then click **Select a file from your computer**. From your student data files, click **w01_1B_Web** and then click **Open**.

3 In the upper left corner of the Google Docs window, select **w01_1B_Web**. Type **Lastname_Firstname_WD_1B_Web** and then press Enter to rename the file.

4 Press Ctrl + A to select all of the text. Click **Line spacing** ⥮, and then click **1.5**. Click **Left align** ☰.

5 Select the six lines of text beginning with *Short feature films* and ending with *Recording of live concerts*, and then click **Bulleted list** ⬛ to apply bullets to the selected text. Select the list of internship positions beginning with *Production Assistant* and ending with *Assistant Set Designer*, and then click **Bulleted list**. Compare your screen with Figure A.

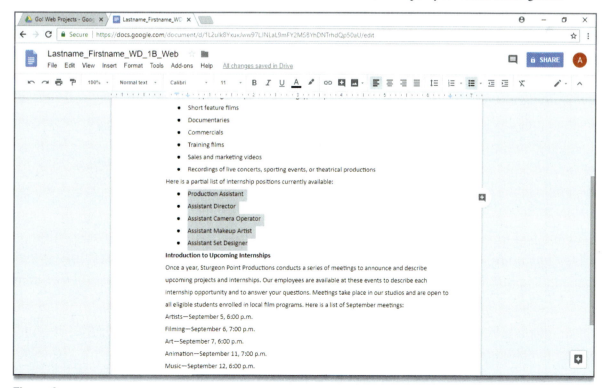

Figure A

»» **GO!** With Google continues on next page

6 Select the last five lines of the document beginning with *Artists* and ending with *Music*. To create a numbered list from the selection, click **Numbered list** 📋.

7 Select the first three lines of text in the document, and then click **Center** 🖹. Click in the *Introduction to Upcoming Internships* heading, and then click **Center**.

8 Click at the beginning of the paragraph that begins *Sturgeon Point Production produces and markets*, and then press ⎵Tab. Look at the ruler and notice that the first line indent is applied.

9 With the insertion point in the same paragraph, double-click **Paint format** 🖌. Then, click in the paragraphs that begin *As an intern*, *Here is a partial list*, and *Once a year* to apply the first line indent to each of the paragraphs. Click **Paint format** 🖌 to turn it off. Compare your document with Figure B.

10 Your document will be saved automatically. Sign out of your Google account, and then submit as instructed by your instructor.

Sturgeon Point Productions

Internship Guide

The Internship Program

Sturgeon Point Productions produces and markets educational videos. We started our company in 1968, and now we are a dynamic and creative independent film and commercial production company. From our base in Miami, we create both contract and in-house videos and feature films.

As an intern, you might take part in the following types of productions:

- Short feature films
- Documentaries
- Commercials
- Training films
- Sales and marketing videos
- Recordings of live concerts, sporting events, or theatrical productions

Here is a partial list of internship positions currently available:

- Production Assistant
- Assistant Director
- Assistant Camera Operator
- Assistant Makeup Artist
- Assistant Set Designer

Introduction to Upcoming Internships

Once a year, Sturgeon Point Productions conducts a series of meetings to announce and describe upcoming projects and internships. Our employees are available at these events to describe each internship opportunity and to answer your questions. Meetings take place in our studios and are open to all eligible students enrolled in local film programs. Here is a list of September meetings:

1. Artists—September 5, 6:00 p.m.
2. Filming—September 6, 7:00 p.m.
3. Art—September 7, 6:00 p.m.
4. Animation—September 11, 7:00 p.m.
5. Music—September 12, 6:00 p.m.

Figure B

wavebreakmedia/Shutterstock, Monkey Business Images/Fotolia, Ivanko80/Shutterstock, Monkey Business Images/Shutterstock

1
WORD

Microsoft Office Specialist (MOS) Skills in this Chapter

Project A	Project B
1.1.4 Show or hide formatting symbols and hidden text	**1.2.1** Set up document pages
1.2.3 Insert and modify headers and footers	**2.2.3** Set line and paragraph spacing and indentation
1.3.2 Modify basic document properties	**3.3.1** Format paragraphs as numbered and bulleted lists
1.3.3 Modify print settings	**3.3.2** Change bullet characters and number formats
5.1.1 Insert shapes	**5.1.4** Insert SmartArt graphics
5.1.2 Insert pictures	**5.2.5** Format SmartArt graphics
5.1.6 Insert text boxes	**5.3.3** Add and modify SmartArt graphic content
5.2.1 Apply artistic effects	
5.2.2 Apply picture effects and picture styles	
5.2.4 Format graphic elements	
5.3.2 Add and modify text in shapes	
5.4.1 Position objects	
5.4.2 Wrap text around objects	

Build Your E-Portfolio

An E-Portfolio is a collection of evidence, stored electronically, that showcases what you have accomplished while completing your education. Collecting and then sharing your work products with potential employers reflects your academic and career goals. Your completed documents from the following projects are good examples to show what you have learned: 1G, 1K, and 1L

 ## Go! For Job Success

Video: How to Succeed in an Interview

Your instructor may assign this video to your class, and then ask you to think about, or discuss with your classmates, these questions:

g-stockstudio/Shutterstock

Can you think of two or three behaviors that Lee might want to change before he interviews with another company?

If you were going on an interview, which of Connie's behaviors would you imitate?

If you were the interviewer, Maria, would you have handled anything differently with either candidate?

End of Chapter

Summary

In this chapter, you started Word and practiced navigating the Word window, and you entered, edited, and formatted text. You also inserted text from another Word file.

Graphics include pictures, shapes, and text boxes. In this chapter, you formatted objects by applying styles, effects, and text-wrapping options, and you sized and positioned objects on the page.

SmartArt graphics visually represent your ideas, and there are many SmartArt graphics from which to choose. You added an icon to your document to provide visual interest.

Word documents can be formatted to display your information attractively. You can add a page border, add bulleted and numbered lists, change margins and tabs, and modify paragraph and line spacing.

GO! Learn It Online

Review the concepts, key terms, and MOS skills in this chapter by completing these online challenges, which you can find at **MyLab IT**.

Chapter Quiz: Answer matching and multiple-choice questions to test what you learned in this chapter.

Lessons on the GO!: Learn how to use all the new apps and features as they are introduced by Microsoft.

MOS Prep Quiz: Answer questions to review the MOS skills that you practiced in this chapter.

GO! Collaborative Team Project (Available in Instructor Resource Center)

If your instructor assigns this project to your class, you can expect to work with one or more of your classmates—either in person or by using Internet tools—to create work products similar to those that you created in this chapter. A *team* is a group of workers who work together to solve a problem, make a decision, or create a work product. *Collaboration* is when you work together with others as a team in an intellectual endeavor to complete a shared task or achieve a shared goal.

Monkey Business Images/Fotolia

Project Guide for Word Chapter 1

Your instructor will assign Projects from this list to ensure your learning and assess your knowledge.

	Project Guide for Word Chapter 1		
Project	**Apply Skills from These Chapter Objectives**	**Project Type**	**Project Location**
1A MyLab IT	Objectives 1–4 from Project 1A	**1A Instructional Project (Grader Project)** Instruction Guided instruction to learn the skills in Project A.	In **MyLab IT** and in text
1B MyLab IT	Objectives 5–8 from Project 1B	**1B Instructional Project (Grader Project)** Instruction Guided instruction to learn the skills in Project B.	In **MyLab IT** and in text
1C	Objectives 1–4 from Project 1A	**1C Skills Review (Scorecard Grading)** Review A guided review of the skills from Project 1A.	In text
1D	Objectives 5–8 from Project 1B	**1D Skills Review (Scorecard Grading)** Review A guided review of the skills from Project 1B.	In text
1E MyLab IT	Objectives 1–4 from Project 1A	**1E Mastery (Grader Project)** Mastery and Transfer of Learning A demonstration of your mastery of the skills in Project 2A with extensive decision-making.	In **MyLab IT** and in text
1F MyLab IT	Objectives 5–8 from Project 1B	**1F Mastery (Grader Project)** Mastery and Transfer of Learning A demonstration of your mastery of the skills in Project 1B with extensive decision-making.	In **MyLab IT** and in text
1G MyLab IT	Objectives 1–8 from Projects 1A and 1B	**1G Mastery (Grader Project)** Mastery and Transfer of Learning A demonstration of your mastery of the skills in Projects 1A and 1B with extensive decision-making.	In **MyLab IT** and in text
1H	Combination of Objectives from Projects 1A and 1B	**1H GO! Fix It (Scorecard Grading)** Critical Thinking A demonstration of your mastery of the skills in Projects 1A and 1B by creating a correct result from a document that contains errors you must find.	IRC
1I	Combination of Objectives from Projects 1A and 1B	**1I GO! Make It (Scorecard Grading)** Critical Thinking A demonstration of your mastery of the skills in Projects 1A and 1B by creating a result from a supplied picture.	IRC
1J	Combination of Objectives from Projects 1A and 1B	**1J GO! Solve It (Rubric Grading)** Critical Thinking A demonstration of your mastery of the skills in Projects 1A and 1B, your decision-making skills, and your critical thinking skills. A task-specific rubric helps you self-assess your result.	IRC
1K	Combination of Objectives from Projects 1A and 1B	**1K GO! Solve It (Rubric Grading)** Critical Thinking A demonstration of your mastery of the skills in Projects 1A and 1B, your decision-making skills, and your critical thinking skills. A task-specific rubric helps you self-assess your result.	In text
1L	Combination of Objectives from Projects 1A and 1B	**1L GO! Think (Rubric Grading)** Critical Thinking A demonstration of your understanding of the chapter concepts applied in a manner that you would outside of college. An analytic rubric helps you and your instructor grade the quality of your work by comparing it to the work an expert in the discipline would create.	In text
1M	Combination of Objectives from Projects 1A and 1B	**1M GO! Think (Rubric Grading)** Critical Thinking A demonstration of your understanding of the chapter concepts applied in a manner that you would outside of college. An analytic rubric helps you and your instructor grade the quality of your work by comparing it to the work an expert in the discipline would create.	IRC
1N	Combination of Objectives from Projects 1A and 1B	**1N You and GO! (Rubric Grading)** Critical Thinking A demonstration of your understanding of the chapter concepts applied in a manner that you would in a personal situation. An analytic rubric helps you and your instructor grade the quality of your work.	IRC
1O	Combination of Objectives from Projects 1A and 1B	**1O Cumulative Group Project for Word Chapter 1** A demonstration of your understanding of concepts and your ability to work collaboratively in a group role-playing assessment, requiring both collaboration and self-management.	IRC

Glossary

Glossary of Chapter Key Terms

Alignment The placement of paragraph text relative to the left and right margins.

Alignment guide A green vertical or horizontal line that displays when you are moving or sizing an object to assist you with object placement.

Artistic effects Formats applied to images that make pictures resemble sketches or paintings.

Bulleted list A list of items with each item introduced by a symbol such as a small circle or check mark, and which is useful when the items in the list can be displayed in any order.

Bullets Text symbols such as small circles or check marks that precede each item in a bulleted list.

Center alignment The alignment of text or objects that is centered horizontally between the left and right margin.

Collaboration The action of working together with others as a team in an intellectual endeavor to complete a shared task or achieve a shared goal.

Dot leader A series of dots preceding a tab that guides the eye across the line.

Drawing objects Graphic objects, such as shapes, diagrams, lines, or circles.

Floating object A graphic that can be moved independently of the surrounding text characters.

Formatting marks Characters that display on the screen, but do not print, indicating where the Enter key, the Spacebar, and the Tab key were pressed; also called nonprinting characters.

Graphics Pictures, charts, or drawing objects.

Icons Pictures composed of straight and curved lines.

Inline object An object or graphic inserted in a document that acts like a character in a sentence.

Justified alignment An arrangement of text in which the text aligns evenly on both the left and right margins.

Layout Options Picture formatting options that control the manner in which text wraps around a picture or other object.

Leader character Characters that form a solid, dotted, or dashed line that fills the space preceding a tab stop.

Left alignment An arrangement of text in which the text aligns at the left margin, leaving the right margin uneven.

Line spacing The distance between lines of text in a paragraph.

Live Layout A feature that reflows text as you move or size an object so that you can view the placement of surrounding text.

Margins The space between the text and the top, bottom, left, and right edges of the paper.

Nonprinting characters Characters that display on the screen, but do not print; also called formatting marks.

Numbered list A list that uses consecutive numbers or letters to introduce each item in a list.

Object anchor The symbol that indicates to which paragraph an object is attached.

Picture effects Effects that enhance a picture, such as a shadow, glow, reflection, or 3-D rotation.

Picture styles Frames, shapes, shadows, borders, and other special effects that can be added to an image to create an overall visual style for the image.

Placeholder text Nonprinting text that holds a place in a document where you can type.

Right alignment An arrangement of text in which the text aligns at the right margin, leaving the left margin uneven.

Rotation handle A symbol with which you can rotate a graphic to any angle; displays above the top center sizing handle.

Shapes Lines, arrows, stars, banners, ovals, rectangles, and other basic shapes with which you can illustrate an idea, a process, or a workflow.

SmartArt A designer-quality visual representation of your information that you can create by choosing from among many different layouts to effectively communicate your message or ideas.

Spin box A small box with an upward- and downward-pointing arrow that lets you move rapidly through a set of values by clicking.

Tab stop A specific location on a line of text, marked on the Word ruler, to which you can move the insertion point by pressing the Tab key, and which is used to align and indent text.

Team A group of workers tasked with working together to solve a problem, make a decision, or create a work product.

Text box A movable resizable container for text or graphics.

Text effects Decorative formats, such as shadowed or mirrored text, text glow, 3-D effects, and colors that make text stand out.

Text pane A pane that displays to the left of a SmartArt graphic and is used to type text and edit text in a SmartArt graphic.

Text wrapping The manner in which text displays around an object.

Toggle button A button that can be turned on by clicking it once, and then turned off by clicking it again.

Word wrap The feature that moves text from the right edge of a paragraph to the beginning of the next line as necessary to fit within the margins.

Chapter Review

Skills Review | Project 1C Photography

Apply 1A skills from these Objectives:

1. Create a New Document and Insert Text
2. Insert and Format Graphics
3. Insert and Modify Text Boxes and Shapes
4. Preview and Print a Document

In the following Skills Review, you will create a flyer advertising a photography internship with Sturgeon Point Productions. Your completed document will look similar to Figure 1.52.

Project Files

For Project 1C, you will need the following files:

New blank Word document

w01C_Building

w01C_Job_Description

You will save your document as:

Lastname_Firstname_1C_Photography

Project Results

Internship Available for

Still Photographer

This position requires skill in the use of:

Professional full-frame DSLR cameras

Tilt-shift lenses for tall buildings

This fall, Sturgeon Point Productions will film a documentary on the historic architecture in and around Milwaukee, Wisconsin.

The filming will take place during the last two weeks of September. If the weather is not conducive to outdoor shooting, it is possible that filming will continue into the first week of October.

The still photographer will accompany the director during the first two weeks of September to scout locations and take photographs for the purpose of planning the filming schedule. The photographer will also accompany the film crew throughout filming.

Photographs taken during pre-production and filming will be used for advertising and marketing and published in an upcoming book on the history of the city of Milwaukee.

Submit Your Application by June 30!

Student_Word_1C_Photography

Figure 1.52

Chapter Review

1 Start Word and then click **Blank document**. On the **Home tab**, in the **Paragraph group**, if necessary, click Show/Hide to display the formatting marks. If the rulers do not display, click the View tab, and then in the Show group, select the Ruler check box. (Mac users, from your student data files, open Mac_w01C_Photography and use this file instead of a new blank document.) **Save** the file in your **Word Chapter 1** folder as **Lastname_Firstname_1C_Photography**

   a. Type **Internship Available for Still Photographer** and then press Enter two times. Type the following text: **This fall, Sturgeon Point Productions will film a documentary on the historic architecture in and around Milwaukee, Wisconsin.** Press Enter.

   b. On the ribbon, click the **Insert tab**. In the **Text group**, click the **Object button arrow**, and then click **Text from File**. In the **Insert File** dialog box, from your student data files, locate and select **w01C_Job_Description**, and then click **Insert**. Delete the blank paragraph at the end of the document.

   c. Including the paragraph mark, select the first paragraph of text—*Internship Available for Still Photographer*. On the **Home tab**, in the **Font group**, click **Text Effects and Typography**. In the **Text Effects and Typography** gallery, in the first row, click the fourth effect.

   d. With the text still selected, in the **Font group**, click in the **Font Size** box to select the existing font size. Type **44** and then press Enter. In the **Font group**, click the **Font Color button arrow**. Under **Theme Colors**, in the fourth column, click the first color.

   e. With the text still selected, in the **Font group**, click **Text Effects and Typography**. Point to **Shadow**, and then under **Outer**, in the second row, click the third style. In the **Paragraph group**, click **Center**.

2 In the paragraph that begins *The filming*, click to position the insertion point at the beginning of the paragraph. On the **Insert tab**, in the **Illustrations group**, click **Pictures**. (Mac users, after clicking Pictures, click Picture form File.) In the **Insert Picture** dialog box, navigate to your student data files, locate and click **w01C_Building**, and then click **Insert**.

   a. To the right of the selected picture, click the **Layout Options** button, and then under **With Text Wrapping**, click the first option—**Square**. **Close** the Layout Options. (Mac users, on the Picture Format tab, click Wrap Text.)

   b. On the **Format tab**, in the **Size group**, click in the **Shape Height** box to select the value, type **2.7** and then press Enter.

   c. With the picture selected, on the **Format tab**, in the **Arrange group**, click **Position**, and then click **More Layout Options**. In the **Layout** dialog box, on the **Position tab**, in the middle of the dialog box under **Vertical**, click the **Alignment** option button. To the right of **Alignment**, click the arrow, and then click **Top**. To the right of **relative to**, click the arrow, and then click **Line**. Click **OK**.

   d. On the **Format tab**, in the **Picture Styles group**, click **Picture Effects**. Point to **Soft Edges**, and then click **5 Point**. On the **Format tab**, in the **Adjust group**, click **Artistic Effects**. Use the ScreenTips to locate and click **Crisscross Etching**.

   e. Click anywhere outside the picture to deselect it. On the **Design tab**, in the **Page Background group**, click **Page Borders**. In the **Borders and Shading** dialog box, on the **Page Border tab**, under **Setting**, click **Box**. Under **Style**, scroll the list and then click the third style from the bottom—a black line that fades to gray.

   f. Click the **Color arrow**, and then in the next to last column, click the first color. Under **Apply to**, be sure **Whole document** is selected, and then click **OK**. Click **Save**.

3 Click the **Insert tab**, and then in the **Illustrations group**, click **Shapes** to display the gallery. Under **Basic Shapes**, use the ScreenTips to locate and then click **Frame**.

   a. Position the ⊞ pointer anywhere in the blank area at the bottom of the document. Click one time to insert a 1" by 1" frame. The exact location need not be precise. To the right of the shape, click the **Layout Options** button, and at the bottom, click **See more**. (Mac users, drag a 1 × 1 shape, click to insert the shape. To display the Layout dialog box, on the Shape Format tab, click Arrange, click Position, click More Layout Options.)

   b. In the **Layout** dialog box, under **Horizontal**, click the **Alignment** option button. To the right of **Alignment**, click the arrow, and then click **Centered**. To the right of **relative to**, click the arrow, and then click **Page**. Under **Vertical**, click the **Absolute position** option button. In the **Absolute position** box, select the existing number, and then type **1** To the right of **below**, click the arrow, and then click **Paragraph**. Click **OK**.

(continues on next page)

Chapter Review

c. On the **Format tab**, click in the **Shape Height** box. Type **1.5** and then select the number in the **Shape Width** box. Type **5.5** and then press [Enter].

d. If necessary, select the frame shape. On the **Format tab**, in the **Shape Styles group**, click **More**. In the **Shape Styles** gallery, in the first row, click the sixth style. With the shape selected, type **Submit Your Application by June 30!** Select the text you just typed, and then change the **Font Size** to **22**.

4 Click outside of the frame to deselect it, and then to move to the top of the document. Click in the blank paragraph below the title. Press [Enter] four times to make space for a text box.

a. On the **Insert tab**, in the **Text group**, click **Text Box**. At the bottom of the gallery, click **Draw Text Box**. Position the ⊞ pointer over the first blank paragraph at the left margin. Drag down and to the right to create a text box approximately 1.5 inches high and 4 inches wide—the exact size and location need not be precise.

b. With the insertion point blinking in the text box, type the following, pressing [Enter] after the first two lines to create a new paragraph:

This position requires skill in the use of:
Professional full-frame DSLR cameras
Tilt-shift lenses for tall buildings

c. To precisely place the text box, on the **Format tab**, in the **Arrange group**, click **Position**, and then click **More Layout Options**. In the **Layout** dialog box, under **Horizontal**, click the **Alignment** button. To the right of **Alignment**, click the arrow, and then click **Centered**. To the right of **relative to**, click the arrow, and then click **Page**.

d. Under **Vertical**, click the **Absolute position** button. In the **Absolute position** box, select the existing number. Type **2** To the right of **below**, click the arrow, and then click **Margin**.

e. In the **Layout** dialog box, click the **Size tab**. Under **Height**, select the number in the **Absolute** box. Type **1** and then under **Width**, select the number in the **Absolute** box. Type **3.75** and then click **OK**.

f. In the text box, select all of the text. On the **Home tab**, change the **Font Size** to **12**, apply **Bold**, and then **Center** the text.

g. On the **Format tab**, in the **Shape Styles group**, click **Shape Effects**. Point to **Shadow**, and then under **Outer**, in the first row, click the first style.

h. In the **Shape Styles group**, click **Shape Outline**. In the fifth column, click the first color to change the color of the text box border. Click **Shape Fill**, and then in the fifth column, click the second color. Click **Save**.

5 Click the **Insert tab**, and then in the **Header & Footer group**, click **Footer**. At the bottom of the menu, click **Edit Footer**. On the **Header & Footer Tools Design tab**, in the **Insert group**, click **Document Info**, and then click **File Name**. Double-click in the document outside of the footer area to close the footer and return to the document. (Mac users, on the Header & Footer tab, click Field, click Document Information, click FileName.)

a. In the upper left corner of your screen, click the **File tab** to display **Backstage** view. Click **Info**, and then at the bottom of the **Properties list**, click **Show All Properties**. On the list of Properties, click to the right of **Tags**, and then type **internship, documentary** Click to the right of **Subject**, and then type your course name and section #. Under **Related People**, be sure that your name displays as the author. If necessary, right-click the author name, click Edit Property, type your name, and click OK. ((Mac users, click File, click Properties, click Summary. In the Keywords box type the tags. Type the Subject and Author. Click OK.)

b. **Save** and **Close** your document. Print or submit your workbook electronically as directed by your instructor.

You have completed Project 1C **END**

Chapter Review

Apply 1B skills from these Objectives:

5. Change Document and Paragraph Layout
6. Create and Modify Lists
7. Set and Modify Tab Stops
8. Insert and Format a SmartArt Graphic and an Icon

Skills Review | Project 1D Internship

In the following Skills Review, you will edit an information handout regarding production and development internships with Sturgeon Point Productions. Your completed document will look similar to Figure 1.53.

Project Files

For Project 1D, you will need the following file:

w01D_Internship

You will save your document as:

Lastname_Firstname_1D_Internship

Project Results

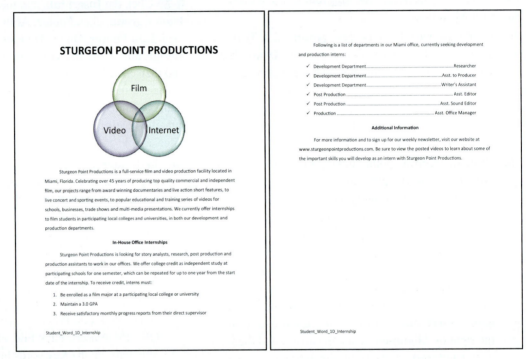

Figure 1.53

(continues on next page)

Chapter Review

Skills Review: Project 1D Internship (continued)

1 From your student data files, open **w01D_Internship**. On the **Home tab**, in the **Paragraph group**, be sure **Show/Hide** is active. **Save** the document to your **Word Chapter 1** folder, as **Lastname_Firstname_1D_Internship**

a. Click the **Layout tab**. In the **Page Setup group**, click **Margins**, and then click **Custom Margins**. In the **Page Setup** dialog box, press Tab as necessary to select the value in the **Left** box. Type **1** and then press Tab to select the value in the **Right** box. Type **1** and then click **OK**.

b. Scroll down to view the bottom of **Page 1**, point anywhere in the bottom margin area, right-click, and then click **Edit Footer** to display the footer area. On the **Header & Footer Tools Design tab**, in the **Insert group**, click **Document Info**, and then click **File Name**. Double-click anywhere in the document to close the footer area. (Mac users, double-click in the footer area. On the Header & Footer tab, click Field.)

c. Press Ctrl + A to select all the text in the document. (Mac users, press command ⌘ + A.) On the **Home tab**, in the **Paragraph group**, click **Align Left**.

d. Press Ctrl + Home. (Mac users, press command ⌘ + fn + ←.) Select the document title, and then on the **Home tab**, in the **Paragraph group**, click **Center**.

e. Locate the first bold subheading—*In-House Office Internships*. Point to the left of the paragraph to display the ⟰ pointer, and then click one time to select the text. With *In-House Office Internships* selected, locate the subheading *Additional Information*. Move the pointer to the left of the paragraph to display the ⟰ pointer, hold down Ctrl, and then click one time to select both paragraphs. (Mac users, press command ⌘.) In the **Paragraph group**, click **Center**.

f. Select all of the text in the document. On the **Home tab**, in the **Paragraph group**, click **Line and Paragraph Spacing**, and then click **1.5**.

2 Below the title of the document, click anywhere in the paragraph that begins *Sturgeon Point Productions is a full-service*. On the **Home tab**, in the **Paragraph group**, click the **Dialog Box Launcher**. (Mac users, on the Home tab, click Line and Paragraph Spacing, click Line Spacing Options.)

a. In the **Paragraph** dialog box, on the **Indents and Spacing tab**, under **Indentation**, click the **Special arrow**, and then click **First line** to indent the first line by 0.5". Click **OK**, and then click anywhere in the paragraph that begins *Sturgeon Point Productions is looking for*. On the ruler under the ribbon, drag the **First Line Indent** marker to **0.5 inches on the horizontal ruler**.

b. Select all the text in the document. Click the **Layout tab**, and then in the **Paragraph group**, under **Spacing**, click the **After spin box up arrow** one time to change the value to **6 pt**.

c. Select the subheading *In-House Office Internships*, including the paragraph mark following it. Scroll down, hold down Ctrl, and then select the subheading *Additional Information*. With both subheadings selected, in the **Paragraph group**, under **Spacing**, click the **Before up spin box arrow** two times to set the **Spacing Before** to **12 pt**. **Save** your document.

3 Locate the first paragraph that begins *Development Department*, and then point to this paragraph from the left margin area to display the ⟰ pointer. Drag down to select this paragraph and the next five paragraphs so that six paragraphs are selected. On the **Home tab**, in the **Paragraph group**, click **Bullets** to change the selected text to a bulleted list.

a. Under the subheading *In-House Office Internships*, in the paragraph that begins *Sturgeon Point Productions is looking*, click to position the insertion point at the *end* of the paragraph, following the colon. Press Enter to create a blank paragraph. On the ruler, drag the **First Line Indent** marker to the left so that it is positioned directly above the lower button. Being sure to include the period, type **1.** and then press Spacebar to create the first item in a numbered list.

b. Type **Be enrolled as a film major at a participating local college or university** and then press Enter. Type **Maintain a 3.0 GPA** and then press Enter. Type **Receive satisfactory monthly progress reports from their direct supervisor**

c. Scroll down to view the bulleted list of departments, and then select all six bulleted items in the list. On the mini toolbar, click the **Bullets button arrow**, and then under **Bullet Library**, click the **check mark** symbol. If the check mark is not available, choose another bullet symbol.

4 With the list selected, move the pointer to the horizontal ruler, and then point to and click at **3.5 inches on the horizontal ruler** to align the job titles at the tab mark.

a. With the bulleted list still selected, on the ruler, point to the new tab marker at **3.5 inches on the horizontal ruler**, and then when the *Left Tab* ScreenTip displays, drag the tab marker to **4 inches on the horizontal ruler**.

(continues on next page)

Chapter Review

b. With the list still selected, on the ruler, point to the tab marker that you moved to display the *Left Tab* ScreenTip, and then double-click to display the **Tabs** dialog box.

c. In the **Tabs** dialog box, under **Tab stop position**, if necessary select *4"*, and then type **6** Under **Alignment**, click the **Right** option button. Under **Leader**, click the **2** option button. Near the bottom of the **Tabs** dialog box, click **Set**. Under **Tab stop position**, select *4"*, and then click **Clear** to delete the tab stop. (Mac users, click Clear All. In the Tab stops box, type 6, click Right, and then Under Leader, click the dot leader style.) Click **OK**. **Save** your document.

5 Press Ctrl + Home to move to the top of the document, and then in the title, click to the right of the *S* in *PRODUCTIONS*.

a. Click the **Insert tab**, and then in the **Illustrations group**, click **SmartArt**. On the left, click **Relationship**, and then scroll the list to the bottom. Locate and then click **Basic Venn**. Click **OK** to insert the SmartArt graphic. If necessary, close the Text Pane.

b. In the SmartArt graphic, click on *[Text]* in the top circle shape. Type **Film** and then in the lower left shape, click on the placeholder *[Text]*. Type **Video** and then in the third circle, type **Internet**

c. Click the SmartArt graphic border to select it. Click the **Format tab**, and then in the **Size group**, if necessary click **Size** to display the **Shape Height** and **Shape Width** boxes. Set the **Height** to **3"**.

d. With the SmartArt graphic still selected, on the ribbon, under **SmartArt Tools**, click the **Design tab**, and then in the **SmartArt Styles group**, click **Change Colors**. (Mac users, use the SmartArt Design tab.) Under **Colorful**, click the third style—**Colorful Range - Accent Colors 3 to 4**. On the **Design tab**, in the **SmartArt Styles group**, click **More**. Under **3-D**, click **Cartoon**.

e. Click the **File tab**, click **Info**, and then, click **Show All Properties**. In the **Tags** box, type **internship** and in the **Subject** box type your course name and section number. If necessary, in the **Author** box, replace the existing text with your first and last name. Click **Save**.

f. Click the **File tab** to display **Backstage** view, and then click **Print** to display **Print Preview**. At the bottom of the preview, click the **Next Page** and **Previous Page** buttons to move between pages. If necessary, return to the document and make any necessary changes.

g. **Save** and **Close** your document. Print or submit your workbook electronically as directed by your instructor.

You have completed Project 1D **END**

MyLab IT Grader | **Mastering Word** **Project 1E Documentary**

In the following Mastery project, you will create a flyer announcing a special event being hosted by Sturgeon Point Productions. Your printed results will look similar to those in Figure 1.54.

Project Files for MyLab IT Grader

1. In your **MyLab IT** course, locate and click **Word 1E Documentary**, Download Materials, and then Download All Files.
2. Extract the zipped folder to your Word Chapter 1 folder. Close the Grader download screens.
3. Take a moment to open the downloaded **Word_1E_Documentary_Instructions**; note any recent updates to the book.

Project Results

Sturgeon Point Productions

Presents Aria Pacheco

Sturgeon Point Productions will be hosting its *5th Annual Script to Screen* series, every Friday night this April in our Studio G screening room. All employees, interns, and film students with current school ID are welcome to share in this totally free, exciting evening, where our award-winning filmmakers from our Documentary and Short Feature Film Departments give a first-hand account of the filmmaking process and the challenges that went into their particular projects, from the script phase through production and finally, in distribution and marketing.

This year, we are proud to kick off the series with Aria Pacheco, who will discuss her multi-award winning documentary, **"Through the Cold."** This film documents the perils and triumphs of a team of scientists living in Antarctica. This compelling story, rich in visual complexity, follows the team as they prepare for the six months of darkness in the winter season. Celebrated film critic, Georges Harold, will be conducting an interview with Ms. Pacheco and select members of her crew following a screening of the film, which will take place on Friday, April 5th at 8 p.m. This event is guaranteed to fill up fast, so we suggest you get in line at least one hour prior to the screening.

"Through the Cold" has been heralded by critics across the country. Don't miss this chance to meet one of our greatest documentary filmmakers.

Date: April 5

Time 8 p.m.

Place: Studio G Screening Room

Student_Word_1E_Documentary

Figure 1.54 (Volodymyr Goinyk/Shutterstock)

For Non-MyLab Submissions

For Project 1E, you will need:
New blank Word Document
w01E_Antarctica
w01E_Filmmaker

In your Word Chapter 1 folder, save your document as:
Lastname_Firstname_1E_Documentary

Start with a new blank document. After you have named and saved your document, on the next page, begin with Step 2.
After Step 16, save and submit your file as directed by your instructor.

Mastering Word: Project 1E Documentary (continued)

1 Navigate to your **Word Chapter 1 folder**, and then double-click the Word file you downloaded from **MyLab IT** that displays your name—**Student_Word_1E_Documentary**. In your document, if necessary, at the top click **Enable Editing**. Display the rulers and verify that **Show/Hide** is active. (Mac users, If you are not submitting your file in **MyLab IT**, from the student data files that accompany this project, open the file **Mac_w01E_Documentary**.)

2 Type **Sturgeon Point Productions Presents Aria Pacheco** and then press [Enter]. From your downloaded files, insert the text file **w01E_Filmmaker**.

3 Select the title and then from the **Text Effects and Typography** gallery, in the first row apply the second effect. Change the **Font Size** to **36**.

4 With the title still selected, display the **Font Color** palette, and then in the fourth column apply the first color. Then, from the **Shadow** gallery, under **Outer**, apply the first **Shadow** style. **Center** the title.

5 Position the insertion point at the beginning of the paragraph that begins with *This year*, and then from your downloaded files, insert the picture **w01E_Antarctica**.

6 Change the **Layout Options** to **Square** and then change the **Height** of the picture to **2.25**

7 Using the **Position** command, display the **Layout** dialog box, and then change the **Horizontal Alignment** to **Right relative to** the **Margin**.

8 Apply a **10 Point Soft Edges** picture effect to the image, and then display the **Artistic Effects** gallery. Apply the **Paint Brush** effect.

9 Deselect the picture. Apply a **Page Border** to the document using the **Shadow** setting, and then select the double lines style.

10 Below the last paragraph, draw a **Text Box** and then change the **Height** to **1.5** and the **Width** to **4.5**

11 To precisely place the text box, display the **Layout** dialog box. Change the **Horizontal Alignment** to **Centered, relative to** the **Page**, and then change the **Vertical Absolute position** to **0.5** below the **Paragraph**.

12 In the text box, type the following text:

Date: April 5

Time: 8 p.m.

Place: Studio G Screening Room

13 In the text box, change the font size of all the text to **18**. Apply **Bold** and **Center**.

14 Apply a **Shape Style** to the text box—under **Theme Styles**, in the last row, select the second style.

15 Insert the **File Name** in the footer, and then display the document properties. As the **Tags**, type **documentary, interview** and as the **Subject**, type your course and section number. Be sure your name is indicated as the **Author**. **Save** your file.

16 Display the **Print Preview** and, if necessary, return to the document and make any necessary changes. **Save** your document and **Close** Word.

17 In **MyLab IT**, locate and click the Grader Project **Word 1E Documentary**. In **step 3**, under **Upload Completed Assignment**, click **Choose File**. In the **Open** dialog box, navigate to your **Word Chapter 1 folder**, and then click your **Student_Word_1E_Documentary** file one time to select it. In the lower right corner of the **Open** dialog box, click **Open**.

The name of your selected file displays above the Upload button.

18 To submit your file to **MyLab IT** for grading, click **Upload**, wait a moment for a green **Success!** message, and then in step 4, click the blue **Submit for Grading** button. Click **Close Assignment** to return to your list of **Course Materials**.

You have completed Project 1E | **END**

Content-Based Assessments (Mastery and Transfer of Learning)

MyLab IT Grader

Mastering Word   **Project 1F Pitch Festival**

Apply 1B skills from these Objectives:

5. Change Document and Paragraph Layout
6. Create and Modify Lists
7. Set and Modify Tab Stops
8. Insert and Format a SmartArt Graphic and an Icon

In the following Mastery project, you will edit a document with information regarding an event that Sturgeon Point Productions is holding for college students. Your printed results will look similar to those in Figure 1.55.

Project Files for MyLab IT Grader

1. In your **MyLab IT** course, locate and click **Word 1F Pitch Festival**, Download Materials, and then Download All Files. Close the Grader download screens.
2. Extract the zipped folder to your Word Chapter 1 folder. Close the Grader download screens.
3. Take a moment to open the downloaded **Word_1F_Pitch_Festival_Instructions**; note any recent updates to the book.

Project Results

Pitch Festival!

Do you have a story that must be told? Pitch us your project during the Sturgeon Point Productions annual Pitch Festival! We're setting up several days of conference video calls for college students that are currently enrolled in an accredited film production program anywhere in the United States. If your idea is selected, you will be flown to our studios in Miami, Florida to pitch your idea to our staff of producers and development executives.

Do You Have an Idea to Pitch?
We are looking for fresh and interesting film documentary subjects and creative ways to implement them!

Sturgeon Point Productions is one of the leading independent film and video companies in the Miami area. We are currently looking for new, fresh, exciting ideas for short and full-length feature films and documentaries. We like character driven stories that can be shot on an independent budget within one or two locations, preferably either in our studios or in the Miami area. We are currently looking for scripts, ideas, and concepts that are in one of the following categories:

1. Human interest or educational
2. Political or journalistic
3. Biographical or documentary

The Pitch Festival will take place at our secure website on the following dates and times. There are no entry fees to pitch; this unique opportunity to pitch to our staff of professional filmmakers is absolutely free for college film students. Sign up now at www.sturgeonpointproductions.com/pitchfest for one of the following pitch sessions:

- September 12, 11 a.m...Short and Feature Film Pitches
- September 13, 8 p.m....................................Biographical and Documentary Film Pitches
- September 14, 7 p.m...Educational Series Pitches

Your Ideas + Our Experts = Pitch Festival!

Student_Word_1F_Pitch_Festival

Figure 1.55

For Non-MyLab Submissions

For Project 1F, you will need:
w01F_Pitch_Festival

In your Word Chapter 1 folder, save your document as:
Lastname_Firstname_1F_Pitch_Festival

After you have named and saved your document, on the next page, begin with Step 2.
After Step 13, save and submit your file as directed by your instructor.

Mastering Word: Project 1F Pitch Festival (continued)

1 Navigate to your **Word Chapter 1 folder**, and then double-click the Word file you downloaded from **MyLab IT** that displays your name—**Student_Word_1F_Pitch_Festival**. In your document, if necessary, at the top, click **Enable Editing**. Display the rulers and verify that **Show/Hide** is active.

2 Insert the **File Name** in the footer, and then change the **Line Spacing** for the entire document to **1.5. Center** the document title, and then change the title font size to **24**. Change the **Top** and **Bottom** margins to **0.5**

3 Select the paragraph below the title, and then apply a **First line** indent of **0.5"**. Then, apply the same indent to the paragraphs below the picture that begin *Sturgeon Point Productions* and *The Pitch Festival*.

4 Select the entire document, and then change the **Spacing Before** to **6 pt** and the **Spacing After** to **6 pt**.

5 Select the last three paragraphs containing the dates, and then apply the filled square bullets. With the bulleted list selected, set a **Right** tab with **dot leaders** at **6"**.

6 Locate the paragraph that begins *Sturgeon Point Productions*, and then click at the end of the paragraph, after the colon. Press Enter and remove the first line indent from the new paragraph.

7 In the blank line you inserted, create a numbered list with the following three numbered items:

Human interest or educational
Political or journalistic
Biographical or documentary

8 Position the insertion point at the end of the document after the word *Pitches*. Do *not* insert a blank line. Display the **SmartArt** gallery and the **Process** category. Select and insert the **Equation** SmartArt. Select the outside border of the SmartArt, and then change the **Height** of the SmartArt to **1** and the **Width** to **6.5**

9 With the SmartArt selected, change the layout to **Square**, and change the **Horizontal Alignment** to **Centered relative to** the **Page**. Change the **Vertical Alignment** to **Bottom relative to** the **Margin**.

10 In the first circle, type **Your Ideas** and in the second circle, type **Our Experts** In the third circle, type **Pitch Festival!**

11 Change the SmartArt color to **Colorful Range – Accent Colors 4 to 5**. Apply the **3-D Polished** style.

12 Display the document properties. As the **Tags**, type **pitch festival** and in the **Subject** box, type your course name and section number. In the **Author** box, replace the existing text with your first and last name. **Save** the file.

13 Display the **Print Preview** and if necessary, return to the document and make any necessary changes. **Save** your document and **Close** Word.

14 In **MyLab IT**, locate and click the Grader Project **Word 1F Pitch Festival**. In **step 3**, under **Upload Completed Assignment**, click **Choose File**. In the **Open** dialog box, navigate to your **Word Chapter 1 folder**, and then click your **Student_Word_1F_Pitch_Festival** file one time to select it. In the lower right corner of the **Open** dialog box, click **Open**.

The name of your selected file displays above the Upload button.

15 To submit your file to **MyLab IT** for grading, click **Upload**, wait a moment for a green **Success!** message, and then in step 4, click the blue **Submit for Grading** button. Click **Close Assignment** to return to your list of **Course Materials**.

You have completed Project 1F **END**

| MyLab IT Grader | **Mastering Word** | **Project 1G Educational Website** |

In the following Mastery project, you will create a flyer that details a new educational website that Sturgeon Point Productions has developed for instructors. Your printed results will look similar to those in Figure 1.56.

Apply 1A and 1B skills from these Objectives:

1. Create a New Document and Insert Text
2. Insert and Format Graphics
3. Insert and Modify Text Boxes and Shapes
4. Preview and Print a Document
5. Change Document and Paragraph Layout
6. Create and Modify Lists
7. Set and Modify Tab Stops
8. Insert and Format a SmartArt Graphic and an Icon

Project Files for MyLab IT Grader

1. In your **MyLab IT** course, locate and click **Word 1G Educational Website**, Download Materials, and then Download All Files. Close the Grader download screens.
2. Extract the zipped folder to your Word Chapter 1 folder. Close the Grader download screens.
3. Take a moment to open the downloaded **Word_1G_Educational_Website_Instructions**; note any recent updates to the book.

Project Results

Figure 1.56

For Non-MyLab Submissions

For Project 1G, you will need:

New blank document
w01G_Education
w01G_Media

In your Word Chapter 1 folder, save your document as:

Lastname_Firstname_1G_Educational_Website

After you have named and saved your document, on the next page, begin with Step 2.
After Step 19, save and submit your file as directed by your instructor.

(continues on next page)

Mastering Word: Project 1G Educational Website (continued)

1 Navigate to your **Word Chapter 1 folder**, and then double-click the Word file you downloaded from **MyLab IT** that displays your name—**Student_Word_1G_Educational_Website**. In your document, if necessary, at the top click **Enable Editing**. Display the rulers and verify that **Show/Hide** is active. (Mac users, If you are not submitting your file in MyLab IT, from the student data files that accompany this project, open the file **Mac_w01G_Educational_Website**.)

2 Type **Educational Websites** and then press Enter. Type **Sturgeon Point Productions is offering website tie-ins with every educational video in our catalog, at no additional cost.** Press Spacebar, and then with the insertion point positioned at the end of the sentence that you typed, insert the text from your downloaded file **w01G_Education**.

3 Change the **Line Spacing** for the entire document to **1.5** and the spacing **After** to **6 pt**. To each of the four paragraphs that begin *Sturgeon Point Productions*, *As educators*, *When submitting*, and *Additional information*, apply a **First Line** indent of **0.5"**.

4 Change the **font size** of the title to **50** and the **Line Spacing** to **1.0. Center** the title. With the title selected, display the **Text Effects and Typography** gallery. In the first row, apply the second effect.

5 Click at the beginning of the paragraph below the title, and then from your downloaded files, insert the picture **w01G_Media**. Change the picture **Height** to **2** and the **Layout Options** to **Square**. Format the picture with **Soft Edges** in **10 Point**.

6 Use the **Position** command to display the **Layout** dialog box. Change the picture position so that the **Horizontal Alignment** is **Right relative to** the **Margin**. Change the **Vertical Alignment** to **Top relative to** the **Line**.

7 Select the five paragraphs beginning with *Historic interactive timelines* and ending with *Quizzes and essay exams*, and then apply checkmark bullets. (Mac users, if the check mark bullet style does not display, click Define New Bullet, click Bullet, change the font to Wingdings, click the check mark symbol, and then click OK.)

8 In the paragraph below the bulleted list, click after the colon. Press Enter and remove the first line indent. Type a numbered list with the following three numbered items:

> **The title in which you are interested**
> **The name of the class and subject**
> **Online tools you would like to see created**

9 With the insertion point located at the end of the numbered list, insert a **SmartArt** graphic. In the **Process** category, locate and select the **Basic Chevron Process**. In the first shape, type **View** In the second shape, type **Interact** and in the third shape, type **Assess**

10 Change the SmartArt color to **Colorful Range – Accent Colors 4 to 5**, and then apply the **3-D Flat Scene** style. Change the **Height** of the SmartArt to **1** and the **Width** to **6.5** Change the **Layout Options** to **Square**, the **Horizontal Alignment** to **Centered relative to** the **Page**, and the **Vertical Alignment** to **Bottom relative to** the **Margin**.

11 Select the days and times at the end of the document, and then set a **Right** tab with **dot leaders** at **6"**.

12 In the middle of **Page 2**, insert a **Shape**—the rectangle with rounded corners. The exact location need not be precise. Change the **Shape Height** to **1.5** and the **Shape Width** to **6.5** and then display the **Shape Styles** gallery. In the first row, apply the second style.

13 Use the **Position** command to display the **Layout** dialog box, and then change the position so that both the **Horizontal** and **Vertical Alignment** are **Centered relative to** the **Margin**. In the rectangle, type **Sturgeon Point Productions** and then press Enter. Type **Partnering with Educators to Produce Rich Media Content** and then change the font size to **16**.

14 Move to the top of the document and insert a **Text Box** above the title. The exact location need not be precise. Change the **Height** of the text box to the **0.5** and the **Width** to **3.7** Type **Sturgeon Point Productions** and then change the font size of all the text in the text box to **22. Center** the text.

15 Use the **Position** command to display the **Layout** dialog box, and then position the text box so that the **Horizontal Alignment** is **Centered relative to** the **Page** and the **Vertical Absolute position** is **0.5 below** the **Page**.

16 With the text box selected, display the **Shape Fill** gallery, and then in the next to last column, select the second color. Change the **Shape Outline** to the same color.

17 Deselect the text box. Apply a **Page Border** to the document. Use the **Box** setting, and then choose the first style. Display the **Color** palette, and then in the second to last column, apply the first color.

18 Change the **Top** margin to **1.25** and insert the **File Name** in the footer.

(continues on next page)

19 Display the document properties. As the **Tags**, type **website** and as the **Subject**, type your course and section number. Be sure your name displays in the **Author** box. **Save** your document and **Close** Word.

20 In **MyLab IT**, locate and click the Grader Project **Word 1G Educational Website**. In **step 3**, under **Upload Completed Assignment**, click **Choose File**. In the **Open** dialog box, navigate to your **Word Chapter 1 folder**, and then click your **Student_Word_1G_Educational_ Website** file one time to select it. In the lower right corner of the **Open** dialog box, click **Open**.

The name of your selected file displays above the Upload button.

21 To submit your file to **MyLab IT** for grading, click **Upload**, wait a moment for a green **Success!** message, and then in step 4, click the blue **Submit for Grading** button. Click **Close Assignment** to return to your list of **Course Materials**.

You have completed Project 1G   **END**

Content-Based Assessments (Critical Thinking)

Apply a combination of the **1A** and **1B** skills	GO! Fix It	**Project 1H Casting Call**	IRC
	GO! Make It	**Project 1I Development Team**	IRC
	GO! Solve It	**Project 1J Softball**	IRC
	GO! Solve It	**Project 1K Production**	

Project Files

For Project 1K, you will need the following files:

w01K_Production

w01K_Studio

You will save your document as:

Lastname_Firstname_1K_Production

The Marketing Director for Sturgeon Point Productions is developing marketing materials aimed at filmmakers. From the student files that accompany this textbook, locate and open the file w01K_Production. Format the document using techniques you learned in this chapter to create an appropriate flyer aimed at filmmakers. From your student data files, insert the picture w01K_Studio, and then format the picture with an artistic effect. Insert a SmartArt graphic that illustrates two or three important points about the company. Use text effects so that the flyer is easy to read and understand and has an attractive design. Save the file in your Word Chapter 1 folder as **Lastname_Firstname_1K_Production** and submit it as directed.

		Performance Level		
		Exemplary: You consistently applied the relevant skills	**Proficient: You sometimes, but not always, applied the relevant skills.**	**Developing: You rarely or never applied the relevant skills.**
Performance Criteria	**Use text effects**	Text effects applied to text in an attractive and appropriate manner.	Text effects are applied but do not appropriately display text.	Text effects not used.
	Insert and format a picture	The picture is inserted; text wrapping and an artistic effect are applied.	The picture is inserted but not formatted properly.	No picture is inserted in the document.
	Insert and format SmartArt	The SmartArt is inserted and appropriately formatted.	The SmartArt is inserted but no formatting is applied.	A SmartArt is not inserted in the document.

You have completed Project 1K | **END**

Outcomes-Based Assessments (Critical Thinking)

Rubric

The following outcomes-based assessments are *open-ended assessments*. That is, there is no specific correct result; your result will depend on your approach to the information provided. Make *Professional Quality* your goal. Use the following scoring rubric to guide you in *how* to approach the problem and then to evaluate *how well* your approach solves the problem.

The *criteria*—Software Mastery, Content, Format and Layout, and Process—represent the knowledge and skills you have gained that you can apply to solving the problem. The *levels of performance*—Professional Quality, Approaching Professional Quality, or Needs Quality Improvements—help you and your instructor evaluate your result.

	Your completed project is of Professional Quality if you:	Your completed project is Approaching Professional Quality if you:	Your completed project Needs Quality Improvements if you:
1-Software Mastery	Choose and apply the most appropriate skills, tools, and features and identify efficient methods to solve the problem.	Choose and apply some appropriate skills, tools, and features, but not in the most efficient manner.	Choose inappropriate skills, tools, or features, or are inefficient in solving the problem.
2-Content	Construct a solution that is clear and well organized, contains content that is accurate, appropriate to the audience and purpose, and is complete. Provide a solution that contains no errors of spelling, grammar, or style.	Construct a solution in which some components are unclear, poorly organized, inconsistent, or incomplete. Misjudge the needs of the audience. Have some errors in spelling, grammar, or style, but the errors do not detract from comprehension.	Construct a solution that is unclear, incomplete, or poorly organized, contains some inaccurate or inappropriate content, and contains many errors of spelling, grammar, or style. Do not solve the problem.
3-Format and Layout	Format and arrange all elements to communicate information and ideas, clarify function, illustrate relationships, and indicate relative importance.	Apply appropriate format and layout features to some elements, but not others. Overuse features, causing minor distraction.	Apply format and layout that does not communicate information or ideas clearly. Do not use format and layout features to clarify function, illustrate relationships, or indicate relative importance. Use available features excessively, causing distraction.
4-Process	Use an organized approach that integrates planning, development, self-assessment, revision, and reflection.	Demonstrate an organized approach in some areas, but not others; or, use an insufficient process of organization throughout.	Do not use an organized approach to solve the problem.

Outcomes-Based Assessments (Critical Thinking)

Apply a combination of the 1A and 1B skills.

GO! Think	Project 1L Classes

Project Files

For Project 1L, you will need the following file:

New blank Word document

You will save your document as:

Lastname_Firstname_1L_Classes

The Human Resources director at Sturgeon Point Productions needs to create a flyer to inform full-time employees of educational opportunities beginning in September. The courses are taught each year by industry professionals and are designed to improve skills in motion picture and television development and production. Employees who have been with Sturgeon Point Productions for at least two years are eligible to take the courses free of cost. The classes provide employees with opportunities to advance their careers, gain valuable skills, and achieve technical certification. All courses take place in Studio G. Interested employees should contact Elana Springs in Human Resources to sign up. Information meetings are being held at 5:30 according to the following schedule: television development on June 15; motion picture production on June 17; and recording services on June 21.

Create a flyer with basic information about the courses and information meetings. Be sure the flyer is easy to read and understand and has an attractive design. Save the document as **Lastname_Firstname_1L_Classes** and submit it as directed.

You have completed Project 1L	END

GO! Think	Project 1M Store	IRC

You and GO!	Project 1N Family Flyer	IRC

GO! Cumulative Team Project	Project 1O Bell Orchid Hotels	IRC

Introducing Microsoft Excel 2019

Excel 2019: Introduction

 Introduction to Excel

Quantitative information! Defined as a type of information that can be counted or that communicates the quantity of something, quantitative information can be either easy or hard to understand—depending on how it is presented. According to Stephen Few, in his book *Show Me the Numbers:* "Quantitative information forms the core of what businesses must know to operate effectively."

Excel 2019 is a tool to communicate quantitative business information effectively. Sometimes you need to communicate quantitative relationships. For example, the number of units sold per geographic region shows a relationship of sales to geography. Sometimes you need to summarize numbers. A list of every student enrolled at your college along with his or her major is not as informative as a summary of the total number of students in each major. In business, the most common quantitative information is some measure of money—costs, sales, payroll, expenses and so on.

Rather than just a tool for making calculations, Excel is also a tool for you to communicate and collaborate with others. When you want to communicate visually with tables and graphs, Excel 2019 has many features to help you do so. If you engage in Business Intelligence activities, you will find rich tools for forecasting and for delivering insights about your organization's data.

Creating a Worksheet and Charting Data

1

EXCEL 2019

Wavebreakmedia/Shutterstock

In This Chapter

GO! To Work with Excel

In this chapter, you will use Microsoft Excel to create and analyze data organized into columns and rows. After entering data in a worksheet, you can perform complex calculations, analyze the data to make logical decisions, and create attractive charts that help readers visualize your data in a way they can understand and that is meaningful. In this chapter, you will create and modify Excel workbooks. You will practice the basics of worksheet design, create a footer, enter and edit data in a worksheet, and chart data. You will save, preview, and print workbooks, and you will construct formulas for mathematical operations.

The projects in this chapter relate to **Pro Fit Marietta**, a distributor of fitness equipment and apparel to private gyms, personal trainers, health clubs, corporate wellness centers, hotels, college athletic facilities, physical therapy practices, and multi-unit residential properties. The company's mission is to find, test, and distribute the highest quality fitness products in the world to its customers for the benefit of consumers. The company's blog provides useful tips on how to use the latest workout and fitness equipment. The company is in Marietta, Georgia, which is metropolitan Atlanta's largest suburb.

Sales Report with Embedded Column Chart and Sparklines

MyLab IT

Project 1A Grader for Instruction

Project 1A Simulation for Training and Review

Project Activities

In Activities 1.01 through 1.17, you will create an Excel worksheet for Michelle Barry, the President of Pro Fit Marietta. The worksheet displays the second quarter sales of cardio equipment for the current year and includes a chart to visually represent the data. Your completed worksheet will look similar to Figure 1.1.

Project Files for MyLab IT Grader

1. In your storage location, create a folder named **Excel Chapter 1**.
2. In your MyLab IT course, locate and click **Excel 1A Quarterly Sales**, Download Materials, and then Download All Files.
3. Extract the zipped folder to your Excel Chapter 1 folder. Close the Grader download screens.
4. Take a moment to open the downloaded **Excel_1A_Quarterly_Sales_Instructions**; note any recent updates to the book.

Project Results

GO! Project 1A

Where We're Going

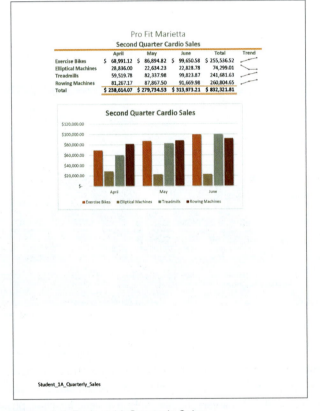

Figure 1.1 Project 1A Quarterly Sales

For Non-MyLab Submissions

For Project 1A, you will need:

New blank Excel workbook

In your storage location, create a folder named **Excel Chapter 1**

In your Excel Chapter 1 folder, save your workbook as:

Lastname_Firstname_1A_Quarterly_Sales

If your instructor requires a workbook with formulas, save as:

Lastname_Firstname_1A_Quarterly_Sales_formulas

After you have named and saved your workbook, on the next page begin with Step 2.

Objective 1   Create, Save, and Navigate an Excel Workbook

ALERT   Because Office 365 is a cloud-based subscription service that receives continuous updates, you may encounter some variations in what appears on your screen and what is shown in this instruction. Microsoft Office 365 is fully installed on your PC or Mac; no internet access is necessary to create or edit documents. When you *are* connected to the internet, you will receive monthly upgrades and new features, so you always have the latest versions of Office apps as soon as they are available. Your subscription gives you continuous free access to the latest innovations and refinements.

GO Learn How
Video E1-1

On startup, Excel displays a new blank **workbook**—the Excel document that stores your data—which contains one or more pages called a **worksheet**. A worksheet—or **spreadsheet**—is stored in a workbook and is formatted as a pattern of uniformly spaced horizontal rows and vertical columns. The intersection of a column and a row forms a box referred to as a **cell**.

Activity 1.01 | Starting Excel, Navigating Excel, and Naming and Saving a Workbook

1 ▶ Navigate to your **Excel Chapter 1 folder**, and then double-click the Excel file you downloaded from **MyLab IT** that displays your name—**Student_Excel_1A_Quarterly_Sales**. In your blank workbook, if necessary, at the top click **Enable Editing**.

2 ▶ In the lower right corner of the window, on the status bar, if necessary, click the **Normal** button ⊞, and then to the right, locate the zoom—magnification—level.

Your zoom level should be 100%, although some figures in this textbook may be shown at a higher zoom level. The **Normal view** maximizes the number of cells visible on your screen and keeps the column letters and row numbers closer.

3 Compare your screen with Figure 1.2, and then take a moment to study the Excel window parts in the table in Figure 1.3.

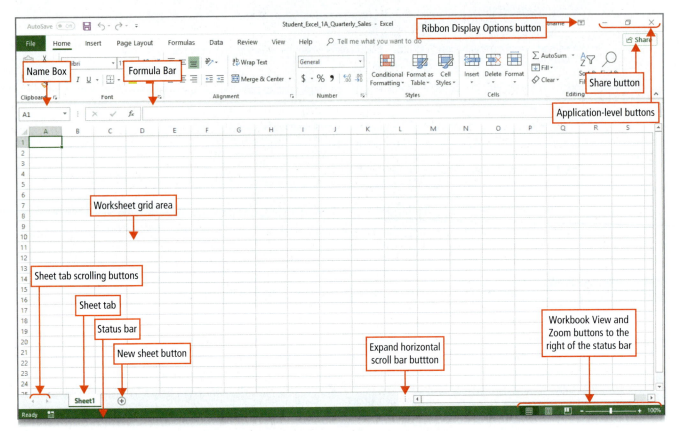

Figure 1.2

Parts of the Excel Window	
Screen Part	**Description**
Application-level buttons	Minimize, close, or restore the previous size of the displayed workbook window.
Expand horizontal scroll bar button	Increases or decreases the width of the horizontal scroll bar by sliding left or right.
Formula Bar	Displays the value or formula contained in the active cell; also permits entry or editing.
Name Box	Displays the name of the selected cell, table, chart, or object.
New sheet button	Inserts an additional worksheet.
Ribbon Display Options button	Displays various ways you can display the ribbon—Show Tabs and Commands is shown here.
Share button	Opens the Share dialog box or the Share pane from which you can save your file to the cloud—for example, your OneDrive—and then share it with others so you can collaborate.
Sheet tab	Identifies the worksheet in the workbook.
Sheet tab scrolling buttons	Display sheet tabs that are not in view when there are numerous sheet tabs.
Status bar	Displays the current cell mode (here in Ready mode) and possibly Macro information as shown here. To the right of the status bar, Workbook View buttons and Zoom buttons display. Here, numerical data and common calculations such as Sum and Average may display.
Worksheet grid area	Displays the columns and rows that intersect to form the worksheet's cells.

Figure 1.3

4 Take a moment to study Figure 1.4 and the table in Figure 1.5 to become familiar with the Excel workbook window.

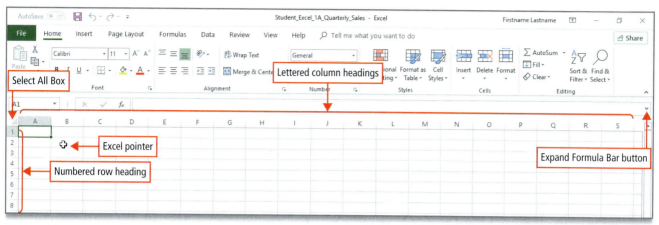

Figure 1.4

Excel Workbook Window Elements	
Workbook Window Element	**Description**
Excel pointer	Displays the location of the pointer.
Expand Formula Bar button	Increases the height of the Formula Bar to display lengthy cell content.
Lettered column headings	Indicate the column letter.
Numbered row headings	Indicate the row number.
Select All box	Selects all the cells in a worksheet.

Figure 1.5

5 In the lower right corner of the screen, in the horizontal scroll bar, click the **right scroll arrow** one time to shift **column A** out of view.

A *column* is a vertical group of cells in a worksheet. Beginning with the first letter of the alphabet, *A*, a unique letter identifies each column—this is called the *column heading*. Clicking one of the horizontal scroll bar arrows shifts the window either left or right one column at a time.

6 Point to the **right scroll arrow**, and then hold down the left mouse button until the columns begin to scroll rapidly to the right; release the mouse button when you begin to see pairs of letters as the column headings.

MAC TIP For rapid scrolling, swipe your finger to the left or right on the mouse or track pad.

BY TOUCH Anywhere on the worksheet, slide your finger to the left to scroll to the right.

7 Slowly drag the horizontal scroll box to the left, and notice that just above the scroll box, ScreenTips with the column letters display as you drag. Drag the horizontal scroll box left or right—or click the left or right scroll arrow—as necessary to position **column Z** near the center of your screen.

Column headings after column Z use two letters starting with AA, AB, and so on through ZZ. After that, columns begin with three letters beginning with AAA. This pattern provides 16,384 columns. The last column is XFD.

MAC TIP Drag the scroll box, there are no ScreenTips.

8 In the vertical scroll bar, click the **down scroll arrow** one time to move **row 1** out of view.

A *row* is a horizontal group of cells. Beginning with number 1, a unique number identifies each row—this is the *row heading*, located at the left side of the worksheet. A single worksheet can have 1,048,576 rows of data.

9 Use the skills you just practiced to scroll horizontally to display **column A**, and if necessary, **row 1**.

10 Point to and then click the cell at the intersection of **column A** and **row 1** to make it the *active cell*—the cell is outlined and ready to accept data.

The intersecting column letter and row number form the *cell reference*—also called the *cell address*. When a cell is active, its column letter and row number are highlighted. The cell reference of the selected cell, *A1*, displays in the Name Box.

11 With cell **A1** as the active cell, type the worksheet title **Pro Fit Marietta** and then press ⏎. Compare your screen with Figure 1.6. Click **Save** 💾.

Text or numbers in a cell are referred to as *data*. You must confirm the data you type in a cell by pressing ⏎ or by some other keyboard movement, such as pressing ⏭ or an arrow key. Pressing ⏎ moves the active cell to the cell below.

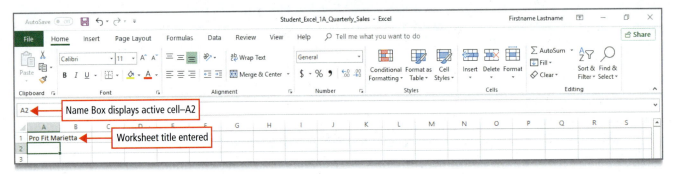

Figure 1.6

| Objective 2 | Enter Data in a Worksheet |

GO! Learn How
Video E1-2

Cell content, which is anything you type in a cell, can be one of two things: either a *constant value*—referred to simply as a *value*—or a *formula*. A formula is an equation that performs mathematical calculations on values in your worksheet. The most commonly used values are *text values* and *number values*, but a value can also include a date or a time of day. A text value is also referred to as a *label*.

Activity 1.02 | **Entering Text, Using AutoComplete, and Using the Name Box to Select a Cell**

MOS
1.2.2

A text value usually provides information about number values in other worksheet cells. In this worksheet for Pro Fit Marietta, the title *Second Quarter Cardio Sales* gives the reader an indication that data in the worksheet relates to information about sales of cardio equipment during the three-month period April through June.

1 In cell **A1**, notice that the text does not fit; the text extends into cell **B1** to the right.

If text is too long for a cell and cells to the right are empty, the text will display. If the cells to the right contain other data, only the text that will fit in the cell displays.

2 In cell **A2**, type the worksheet subtitle **Second Quarter Cardio Sales** and then press ⏎. Compare your screen with Figure 1.7.

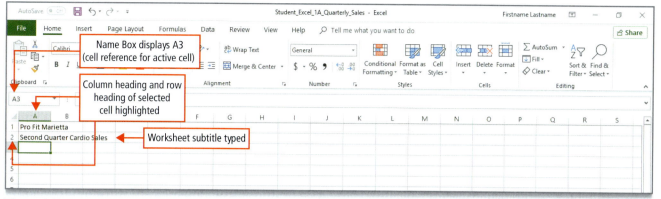

Figure 1.7

The text characters that you typed align at the left edge of the cell—referred to as *left alignment*—and cell A5 becomes the active cell. Left alignment is the default for text values. You can type a cell address in the Name Box and press [Enter] to move to a specific cell quickly.

4 In cell **A5**, type **E** and notice the text from the previous cell displays.

If the first characters you type in a cell match an existing entry in the column, Excel fills in the remaining characters for you. This feature, called *AutoComplete*, assists only with alphabetic values.

5 Continue typing the remainder of the row title **lliptical Machines** and press [Enter].

The AutoComplete suggestion is removed when the entry you are typing differs from the previous value.

6 In cell **A6**, type **Treadmills** and press [Enter]. In cell **A7**, type **Rowing Machines** and press [Enter]. In cell **A8**, type **Total** and press [Enter]. On the Quick Access Toolbar, click **Save** 🖫.

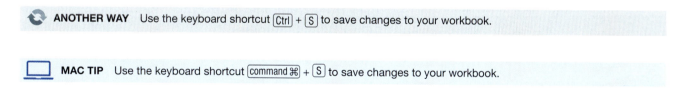

ANOTHER WAY   Use the keyboard shortcut [Ctrl] + [S] to save changes to your workbook.

MAC TIP   Use the keyboard shortcut [command ⌘] + [S] to save changes to your workbook.

Activity 1.03 | Using Auto Fill and Keyboard Shortcuts

2.1.2

1 Click cell **B3**. Type **A** and notice that when you begin to type in a cell, on the **Formula Bar**, the **Cancel** and **Enter** buttons become active, as shown in Figure 1.8.

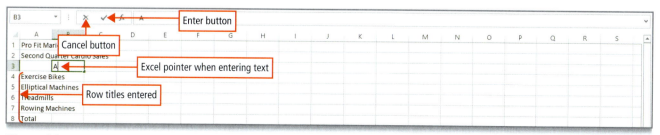

Figure 1.8

2 Continue to type **pril** On the **Formula Bar**, notice that values you type in a cell also display there, and then on the **Formula Bar**, click **Enter** ☑ to confirm the entry and keep cell **B3** active.

3 With cell **B3** active, locate the small square in the lower right corner of the selected cell.

You can drag this *fill handle*—the small square in the lower right corner of a selected cell—to adjacent cells to fill the cells with values based on the first cell.

4 Point to the **fill handle** until the ➕ pointer displays, hold down the left mouse button, drag to the right to cell **D3**, and as you drag, notice the ScreenTips *May* and *June*. Release the mouse button.

5 Under the text that you just filled, click the **Auto Fill Options** button ⊞ that displays, and then compare your screen with Figure 1.9.

Auto Fill generates and extends a *series* of values into adjacent cells based on the value of other cells. A series is a group of things that come one after another in succession; for example, *April, May, June*.

The Auto Fill Options button displays options to fill the data; options vary depending on the content and program from which you are filling, and the format of the data you are filling.

Fill Series is selected, indicating the action that was taken. Because the options are related to the current task, the button is referred to as being *context sensitive*.

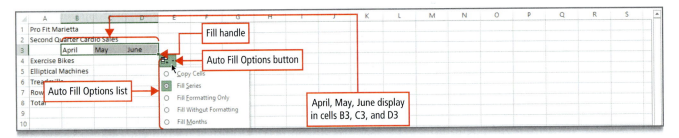

Figure 1.9

6 Click in any cell to cancel the display of the list.

The list no longer displays; the button will display until you perform some other screen action.

7 Press Ctrl + Home, which is the keyboard shortcut to make cell **A1** active.

MAC TIP Press control + fn + ← to make cell A1 active.

8 On the Quick Access Toolbar, click **Save** 🖫 to save the changes you have made to your workbook.

9 Take a moment to study the table in Figure 1.10 to become familiar with keyboard shortcuts with which you can navigate the Excel worksheet.

Keyboard Shortcuts to Navigate the Excel Window		
To Move the Location of the Active Cell:	**On a Windows PC Press:**	**On a Mac Press:**
Up, down, right, or left one cell	↑, ↓, →, ←	↑, ↓, →, ←
Down one cell	Enter	enter
Up one cell	Shift + Enter	shift + enter
Up one full screen	PgUp	fn + ↑
Down one full screen	PgDn	fn + ↓
To column A of the current row	Home	fn + ←
To the last cell on a worksheet, to the lowest used row of the rightmost used column	Ctrl + End	control + fn + →
To cell A1	Ctrl + Home	control + fn + ←
Right one cell	Tab	tab
Left one cell	Shift + Tab	shift + tab
To one screen to the right in a worksheet	Alt + PgDn	fn + option + ↓
To one screen to the left in a worksheet	Alt + PgUp	fn + option + ↑

Figure 1.10

Activity 1.04 | Aligning Text and Adjusting the Size of Columns

MOS
1.3.2

1 ▶ In the **column heading area**, point to the vertical line between **column A** and **column B** to display the ⊞ pointer, press and hold down the left mouse button, and then compare your screen with Figure 1.11.

A ScreenTip displays information about the width of the column. The default width of a column is 64 *pixels*. A pixel, short for *picture element*, is a point of light measured in dots per square inch. Sixty-four pixels equal 8.43 characters, which is the average number of characters that will fit in a cell using the default font. The default font in Excel is Calibri and the default font size is 11.

🖥 **MAC TIP** The default font size on a Mac is 12.

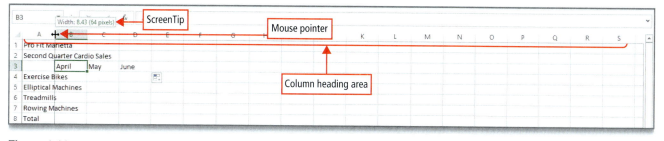

Figure 1.11

2 Drag to the right, and when the number of pixels indicated in the ScreenTip reaches **120 pixels**, release the mouse button. If you are not satisfied with your result, click Undo 🔄 on the Quick Access Toolbar and begin again.

> This width accommodates the longest row title in cells A4 through A8—*Elliptical Machines*. The worksheet subtitle in cell A2 spans more than one column and still does not fit in column A.

💻 **MAC TIP** Change the width to 16.50 (104 pixels).

---

3 Point to cell **B3** and then drag across to select cells **B3**, **C3**, and **D3**. Compare your screen with Figure 1.12; if you are not satisfied with your result, click anywhere and begin again.

> The three cells, B3 through D3, are selected and form a *range*—two or more cells on a worksheet that are adjacent (next to each other) or nonadjacent (not next to each other). This range of cells is referred to as *B3:D3*. When you see a colon (:) between two cell references, the range includes all the cells between the two cell references.
>
> A range of cells you select this way is indicated by a dark border, and Excel treats the range as a single unit so you can make the same changes to more than one cell at a time. The selected cells in the range are highlighted except for the first cell in the range, which displays in the Name Box.
>
> When you select a range of data, the *Quick Analysis tool* displays in the lower right corner of the selected range, with which you can analyze your data by using Excel tools such as charts, color-coding, and formulas.

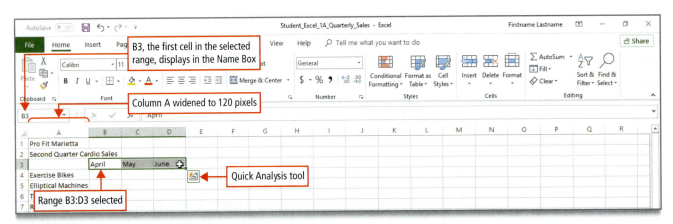

Figure 1.12

👉 **BY TOUCH** To select a range, tap and hold the first cell, and then when the circular gripper displays, drag it to the right, or to the right and down, to define the beginning and end of a range.

---

4 With the range **B3:D3** selected, point anywhere over the selected range, right-click, and then on the mini toolbar, click **Center** 🔲. On the Quick Access Toolbar, click **Save** 💾.

> The column titles *April*, *May*, *June* align in the center of each cell.

💻 **MAC TIP** Press ⌘ command ⌘ + E to center align.

Activity 1.05 | Entering Numbers

MOS
2.2.5

To type number values, use either the number keys across the top of your keyboard or the numeric keypad if you have one—laptop computers may not have a numeric keypad.

In this Activity, you will enter the data that Michelle has given you that represents the sales of cardio equipment in the second quarter of the year.

1 ▶ Under *April*, click cell **B4**, type **68991.12** and then on the **Formula Bar**, click **Enter** ☑ to maintain cell **B4** as the active cell. Compare your screen with Figure 1.13.

By default, *number* values align at the right edge of the cell. The default ***number format***—a specific way in which Excel displays numbers—is the ***general format***. In the default general format, whatever you type in the cell will display, with the exception of trailing zeros to the right of a decimal point. For example, in the number 237.50 the *0* following the *5* is a trailing zero and would not display.

Data that displays in a cell is the ***displayed value***. Data that displays in the Formula Bar is the ***underlying value***. The number of digits or characters that display in a cell—the displayed value—depends on the width of the column. Calculations on numbers will always be based on the underlying value, not the displayed value.

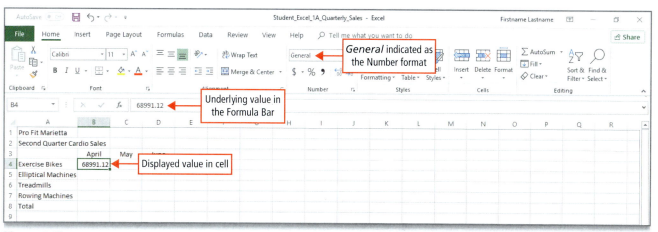

Figure 1.13

2 ▶ Press ⎋Tab to make cell **C4** active. Type **86894.82** and then press ⎋Tab to move to cell **D4**. Type **99650.58** and then press ⎋Enter to move to cell **B5** in the next row. Then, by using the same technique, enter the remaining sales numbers as shown:

	April	May	June
Elliptical Machines	28836	22634.23	22828.78
Treadmills	59519.78	82337.98	99823.87
Rowing Machines	81267.17	87867.50	91669.98

3 ▶ Compare the numbers you entered with Figure 1.14, and then **Save** 🖫 your workbook.

In the default General format, trailing zeros to the right of a decimal point will not display. For example, when you type *87867.50*, the cell displays 87867.5 instead.

Figure 1.14

Objective 3   Construct and Copy Formulas and Use the SUM Function

GO! Learn How
Video E1-3

A cell contains either a constant value (text or numbers) or a formula. A formula is an equation that performs mathematical calculations on values in other cells, and then places the result in the cell containing the formula. You can create formulas or use a *function*—a prewritten formula that looks at one or more values, performs an operation, and then returns a value.

Activity 1.06 │ Constructing a Formula and Using the SUM Function

4.2.1

In this Activity, you will practice three different ways to sum a group of numbers in Excel so that Michelle can see totals for each month and for each category of equipment sold.

1 ▶ Click cell **B8** to make it the active cell and type **=**

The equal sign (=) displays in the cell with the insertion point blinking, ready to accept more data.

All formulas begin with the = sign, which signals Excel to begin a calculation. The Formula Bar displays the = sign, and the Formula Bar Cancel and Enter buttons display.

2 ▶ At the insertion point, type **b4** and then compare your screen with Figure 1.15.

A list of Excel functions that begin with the letter *B* may briefly display—as you progress in your study of Excel, you will use functions of this type. A blue border with small corner boxes surrounds cell B4, which indicates that the cell is part of an active formula. The color used in the box matches the color of the cell reference in the formula.

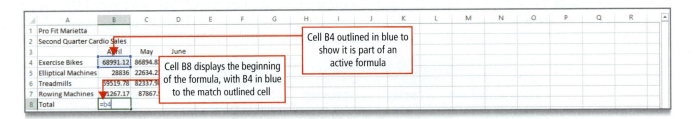

Figure 1.15

3 ▶ At the insertion point, type **+** and then type **b5**

A border of another color surrounds cell B5, and the color matches the color of the cell reference in the active formula. When typing cell references, it is not necessary to use uppercase letters.

4 ▶ At the insertion point, type **+b6+b7** and then press Enter.

The result of the formula calculation—*238614.1*—displays in the cell. Recall that in the default General format, trailing zeros do not display. (Mac users: yours may display *238614.07*)

5 Click cell **B8** again, look at the **Formula Bar**, and then compare your screen with Figure 1.16.

> The formula adds the values in cells B4 through B7, and the result displays in cell B8. In this manner, you can construct a formula by typing. Although cell B8 displays the *result* of the formula, the formula itself displays in the Formula Bar. This is referred to as the ***underlying formula***.

> Always view the Formula Bar to be sure of the exact content of a cell—*a displayed number may actually be a formula.*

Figure 1.16

6 Click cell **C8** and type **=** to signal the beginning of a formula. Then, point to cell **C4** and click one time.

> The reference to the cell C4 is added to the active formula. A moving border surrounds the referenced cell, and the border color and the color of the cell reference in the formula are color coded to match.

7 At the insertion point, type **+** and then click cell **C5**. Repeat this process to complete the formula to add cells **C6** and **C7**, and then press Enter.

> The result of the formula calculation—*279734.5*—displays in the cell. This method of constructing a formula is the ***point and click method*** (Mac users: yours may display *279734.53*).

8 Click cell **D8**. On the **Home tab**, in the **Editing group**, click **AutoSum**, and then compare your screen with Figure 1.17.

> SUM is an Excel function—a prewritten formula. A moving border surrounds the range D4:D7 and *=SUM(D4:D7)* displays in cell D8.

> The = sign signals the beginning of a formula, *SUM* indicates the type of calculation that will take place (addition), and *(D4:D7)* indicates the range of cells on which the sum calculation will be performed. A ScreenTip provides additional information about the action.

MAC TIP To display group names on the ribbon, display the menu, click Excel, click Preferences, click View, under In Ribbon, select the Group Titles check box.

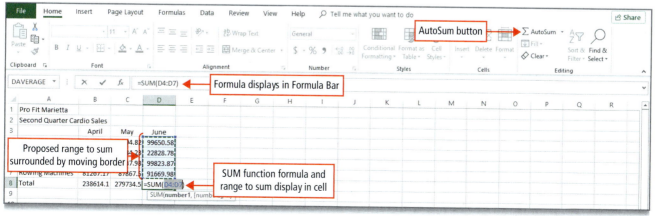

Figure 1.17

> **9** Look at the **Formula Bar** and notice that the formula also displays there. Then, look again at the cells surrounded by the moving border.

When you activate the *Sum function*, Excel first looks *above* the active cell for a range of cells to sum. If no range is above the active cell, Excel will look to the *left* for a range of cells to sum. If the proposed range is not what you want to calculate, you can select a different group of cells.

> **10** Press [Enter] to construct a formula by using the prewritten SUM function.

Your total is *313973.2*. (Mac users: yours may display *313973.21*) Because the Sum function is frequently used, it has its own button in the Editing group on the Home tab of the ribbon. A larger version of the button also displays on the Formulas tab in the Function Library group. This button is also referred to as *AutoSum*.

> **11** Notice that the totals in the range **B8:D8** display only one decimal place. Click **Save** 🖫.

Number values that are too long to fit in the cell do *not* spill over into the unoccupied cell to the right in the same manner as text values. Rather, Excel rounds the number to fit the space.

Rounding is a procedure that determines which digit at the right of the number will be the last digit displayed and then increases it by one if the next digit to its right is 5, 6, 7, 8, or 9.

💻 **MAC TIP**   The total may display 2 decimal places.

Activity 1.07 | Copying a Formula by Using the Fill Handle

4.1.1

You have practiced three ways to create a formula—by typing, by using the point and click technique, and by using a Function button from the ribbon. You can also copy formulas. When you copy a formula from one cell to another, Excel adjusts the cell references to fit the new location of the formula.

> **1** Click cell **E3**, type **Total** and then press [Enter].

The text in cell E3 is centered because the centered format continues from the adjacent cell.

> **2** With cell **E4** as the active cell, hold down [Alt], and then press [=]. Compare your screen with Figure 1.18.

[Alt] + [=] is the keyboard shortcut for the Sum function. Recall that Excel first looks above the selected cell for a proposed range of cells to sum, and if no data is detected, Excel looks to the left and proposes a range of cells to sum.

💻 **MAC TIP**   Press [command ⌘] + [shift] + [T] as the keyboard shortcut to total.

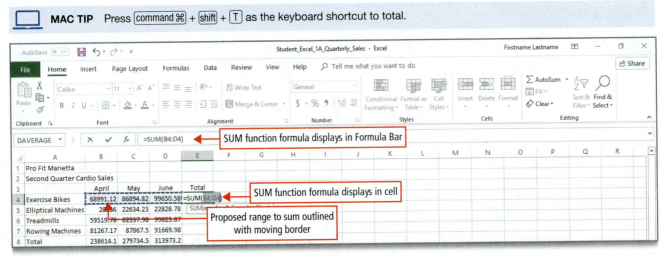

Figure 1.18

3 ▶ On the **Formula Bar**, click **Enter** ☑ to display the result and keep cell **E4** active.

The total dollar amount of *Exercise Bikes* sold in the quarter is *255536.5*. In cells E5:E8, you can see that you need a formula similar to the one in E4, but formulas that refer to the cells in row 5, row 6, and so on.

4 ▶ With cell **E4** active, point to the fill handle in the lower right corner of the cell until the ⊞ pointer displays. Then, drag down through cell **E8**; if you are not satisfied with your result, on the Quick Access Toolbar, click Undo ↶ and begin again. Compare your screen with Figure 1.19.

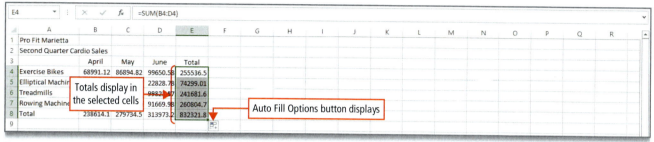

Figure 1.19

5 ▶ Click cell **E5**, look at the **Formula Bar**, and notice the formula =*SUM(B5:D5)*. Click cell **E6**, look at the **Formula Bar**, and then notice the formula =*SUM(B6:D6)*.

In each row, Excel copied the formula but adjusted the cell references *relative to* the row number. This is called a *relative cell reference*—a cell reference based on the relative position of the cell that contains the formula and the cells referred to in the formula.

The calculation is the same, but it is performed on the cells in that particular row. Use this method to insert numerous formulas into spreadsheets quickly.

6 ▶ Click cell **F3**, type **Trend** and then press [Enter]. **Save** 🖫 your workbook.

Objective 4 Format Cells with Merge & Center, Cell Styles, and Themes

GO! Learn How
Video E1-4

Format—change the appearance of—cells to make your worksheet attractive and easy to read.

Activity 1.08 Using Merge & Center and Applying Cell Styles

2.2.1

In this Activity, you will apply formatting to the worksheet so that Michelle and her staff can present a visually attractive worksheet to the company.

1 ▶ Select the range **A1:F1**, and then in the **Alignment group**, click **Merge & Center**. Then, select the range **A2:F2** and click **Merge & Center**.

The *Merge & Center* command joins selected cells into one larger cell and centers the contents in the merged cell; individual cells in the range B1:F1 and B2:F2 can no longer be selected—they are merged into cells A1 and A2, respectively.

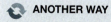 **ANOTHER WAY**   Select the range, right-click over the selection, and then on the mini toolbar, click the Merge & Center button.

2 Click cell **A1**. In the **Styles group**, click **Cell Styles**, and then compare your screen with Figure 1.20.

A *cell style* is a defined set of formatting characteristics, such as font, font size, font color, cell borders, and cell shading.

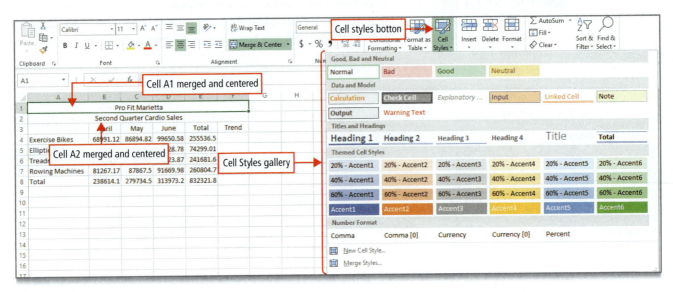

Figure 1.20

3 In the displayed gallery, under **Titles and Headings**, click **Title** and notice that the row height adjusts to accommodate the larger font size.

4 Click cell **A2**, display the **Cell Styles** gallery, and then under **Titles and Headings**, click **Heading 1**.

Use cell styles to maintain a consistent look in a worksheet and across worksheets in a workbook.

5 Select the horizontal range **B3:F3**, hold down Ctrl, and then select the vertical range **A4:A8** to select the column titles and the row titles.

Use this technique to select two or more ranges that are nonadjacent—not next to each other.

MAC TIP Hold down command ⌘ and then select the vertical range.

6 Display the **Cell Styles** gallery, click **Heading 4** to apply this cell style to the column titles and row titles, and then **Save** 🖫 your workbook.

Activity 1.09 | Formatting Financial Numbers

2.2.5, 2.2.7

To present a clear and accurate worksheet, Michelle likes to apply appropriate formatting when reporting financial information such as sales.

In this Activity, you will apply formatting to financial numbers.

1 Select the range **B4:E4**, hold down Ctrl, and then select the range **B8:E8**.

This range is referred to as *b4:e4,b8:e8* with a comma separating the references to the two nonadjacent ranges.

ANOTHER WAY   In the Name Box type b4:e4,b8:e8 and then press Enter.

2 On the **Home tab**, in the **Number group**, click **Accounting Number Format** $ ▾. Compare your screen with Figure 1.21.

The *Accounting Number Format* applies a thousand comma separator where appropriate, inserts a fixed U.S. dollar sign aligned at the left edge of the cell, applies two decimal places, and leaves a small amount of space at the right edge of the cell to accommodate parentheses when negative numbers are present. Excel widens the columns to accommodate the formatted numbers.

At the bottom of your screen, in the status bar, Excel displays the results for some common calculations that might be made on the range; for example, the Average of the numbers selected and the Count—the number of items selected.

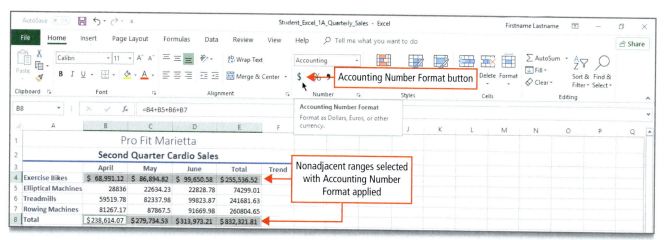

Figure 1.21

ANOTHER WAY   Display the Cell Styles gallery, and under Number Format, click Currency.

3 Select the range **B5:E7**, and then in the **Number group**, click **Comma Style** ▾.

The *Comma Style* inserts a thousand comma separator where appropriate and applies two decimal places. Comma Style also leaves space at the right to accommodate a parenthesis when negative numbers are present.

When preparing worksheets with financial information, the first row of dollar amounts and the total row of dollar amounts are formatted in the Accounting Number Format; that is, with thousand comma separators, dollar signs, two decimal places, and space at the right to accommodate a parenthesis for negative numbers, if any. Rows that are *not* the first row or the total row should be formatted with the Comma Style.

4 Select the range **B8:E8**. In the **Styles group**, display the **Cell Styles** gallery, and then under **Titles and Headings**, click **Total**. Click any blank cell to cancel the selection, and then compare your screen with Figure 1.22.

This is a common way to apply borders to financial information. The single border indicates that calculations were performed on the numbers above, and the double border indicates that the information is complete. Sometimes financial documents do not display values with cents; rather, the values are rounded up. You can do this by selecting the cells, and then clicking the Decrease Decimal button two times.

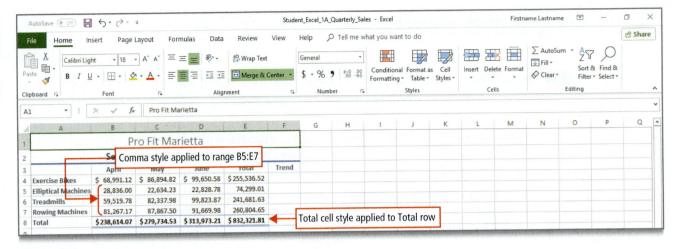

Figure 1.22

Activity 1.10 | Changing the Workbook Theme

A *theme* is a predefined set of colors, fonts, lines, and fill effects that coordinate for an attractive look.

1 ▶ Click the **Page Layout tab**, and then in the **Themes group**, click **Themes**.

2 ▶ Click the **Retrospect** theme, and notice that the cell styles change to match the new theme. Click **Save** 🔲.

MORE KNOWLEDGE **Formatting a Cell's Font, Style, Size, or Color with Individual Commands**

Instead of using Cell Styles, you could use a combination of individual commands to format a cell. For example, on the Home tab, in the Font group, you can change a cell's font by clicking the Font arrow and selecting a different font. You can change the font size by clicking the Font Size arrow and selecting a size. From the same group, you can apply various styles to the cell—such as Bold, Italic, or Underline. To change a cell's font color, in the Font group, click the Font Color arrow and select a different color.

Objective 5 **Chart Data to Create a Column Chart and Insert Sparklines**

GO! Learn How
Video E1-5

A *chart* is a graphic representation of data in a worksheet. Data in a chart is easier to understand than a table of numbers. *Sparklines* are tiny charts embedded in a cell that give a visual trend summary alongside your data. A sparkline makes a pattern more obvious to the eye.

Activity 1.11 | Charting Data and Using Recommended Charts to Select and Insert a Column Chart

MOS

5.1.1, 5.2.2

Recommended Charts is an Excel feature that displays a customized set of charts that, according to Excel's calculations, will best fit your data based on the range of data that you select.

In this Activity, you will create a *column chart* showing the monthly sales of cardio equipment by category during the second quarter. A column chart is useful for illustrating comparisons among related numbers. The chart will enable the company president, Michelle Barry, to see a pattern of overall monthly sales.

1 Select the range **A3:D7**.

When charting data, typically you should *not* include totals—include only the data you want to compare.

2 With the data that you want to compare selected, click the **Insert tab**, and then in the **Charts group**, click **Recommended Charts**. Compare your screen with Figure 1.23.

The Insert Chart dialog box displays a list of recommended charts on the left and a preview of the first chart, which is selected, on the right. The second tab of the Insert Chart dialog box includes all chart types—even those that are not recommended by Excel for this type of data.

By using different *chart types*, you can display data in a way that is meaningful to the reader—common examples are column charts, pie charts, and line charts.

MAC TIP Instead of an Insert Chart dialog box, you may see a drop-down menu of recommended charts; click the second Clustered Column chart.

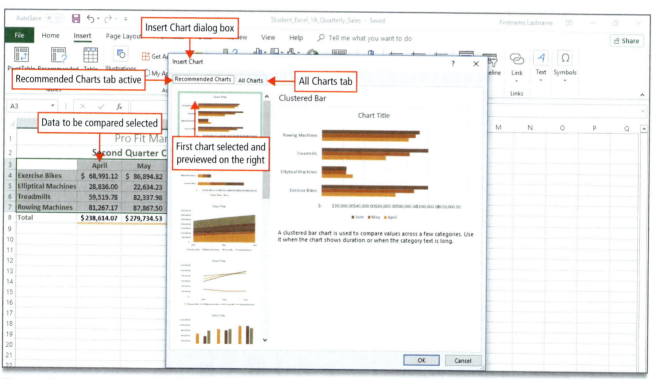

Figure 1.23

3 In the **Insert Chart** dialog box, use the scroll bar to scroll down about one-third of the way, and then click the second Clustered Column chart to view it in the preview area of the **Insert Chart** dialog box. Compare your screen with Figure 1.24.

Here, *each type of cardio equipment* displays its *sales for each month*. A clustered column chart is useful to compare values across a few categories, especially if the order of categories is not important.

MAC TIP Because there is no preview, do not click the chart; if you clicked it and it embedded in your worksheet, on the Quick Access toolbar, click Undo.

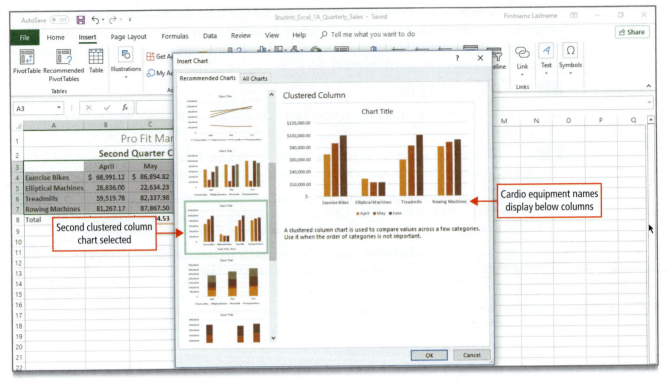

Figure 1.24

> 4 ▸ In the **Insert Chart** dialog box, click the chart directly above the selected chart—the first clustered column chart that shows the month names below the columns. Compare your screen with Figure 1.25.

In this clustered column chart, *each month* displays its *sales for each type of cardio equipment*. When constructing a chart, you can switch the row and column data in this manner to display the data in a way that is most useful to the reader. Here, the president of Pro Fit Marietta wants to compare sales of each type of equipment by month to detect patterns.

The comparison of data—either by month or by type of equipment—depends on the type of analysis you want to perform. You can select either chart, or, after your chart is complete, you can use the *Switch/Row Column* command on the ribbon to swap the data over the axis; that is, data being charted on the vertical axis will move to the horizontal axis and vice versa.

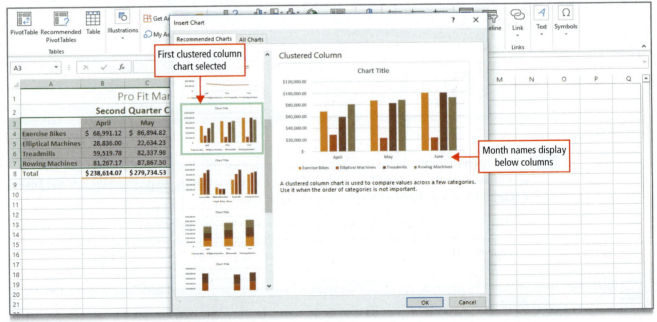

Figure 1.25

5 In the lower right corner of the **Insert Chart** dialog box, click **OK** to insert the selected chart into the worksheet. Compare your screen with Figure 1.26.

Your selected column chart displays in the worksheet, and the charted data is bordered by colored lines. Because the chart object is selected—surrounded by a border and displaying sizing handles—contextual tools named *Chart Tools* display and add contextual tabs next to the standard tabs on the ribbon.

MAC TIP   Click the chart to insert it.

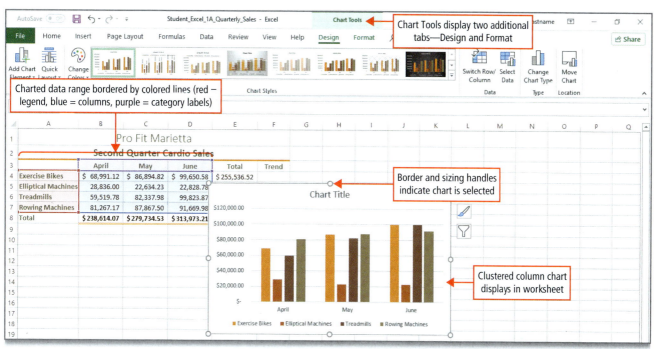

Figure 1.26

Activity 1.12 │ Using the Chart Tools to Apply Chart Styles

5.2.3, 5.3.1

1 On the ribbon, locate the contextual tabs under **Chart Tools—Design** and **Format**.

When a chart is selected, Chart Tools become available and these two tabs provide commands for enhancing the design and format of the chart.

Based on the data you selected in your worksheet and the chart you selected in the Insert Chart dialog box, Excel constructs a column chart and adds *category labels*—the labels that display along the bottom of the chart to identify the category of data. This area is referred to as the *category axis* or the *x-axis*.

Depending on which arrangement of row and column data you select in the Insert Chart dialog box, Excel arranges either the row titles or the column titles as the category names. Here, based on your selection, the column titles that form the category labels are bordered in purple, indicating the cells that contain the category names.

On the left side of the chart, Excel includes a numerical scale on which the charted data is based; this is the *value axis* or the *y-axis*. Along the lower edge of the chart, a *legend*, which is a chart element that identifies the patterns or colors that are assigned to the categories in the chart, displays. Here, the row titles are bordered in red, indicating the cells containing the legend text.

2 To the right of the chart, notice the three buttons, and then point to each button to display its ScreenTip, as shown in Figure 1.27.

The *Chart Elements button* enables you to add, remove, or change chart elements such as the title, legend, gridlines, and data labels.

The *Chart Styles button* enables you to set a style and color scheme for your chart.

The *Chart Filters button* enables you to change which data displays in the chart—for example, to see only the data for *May* and *June* or only the data for *Treadmills* and *Rowing Machines*.

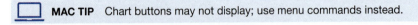
MAC TIP   Chart buttons may not display; use menu commands instead.

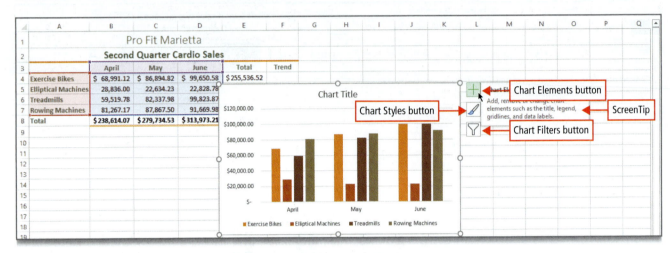

Figure 1.27

3 In the worksheet data, locate the group of cells bordered in blue.

Each of the twelve cells bordered in blue is referred to as a *data point*—a value that originates in a worksheet cell. Each data point is represented in the chart by a *data marker*—a column, bar, area, dot, pie slice, or other symbol in a chart that represents a single data point.

Related data points form a *data series*; for example, there is a data series for *April*, for *May*, and for *June*. Each data series has a unique color or pattern represented in the chart legend.

4 On the **Design tab**, in the **Chart Layouts group**, click **Quick Layout**, and then compare your screen with Figure 1.28.

In the Quick Layout gallery, you can change the overall layout of the chart by selecting a predesigned *chart layout*—a combination of chart elements, which can include a title, legend, labels for the columns, and the table of charted cells.

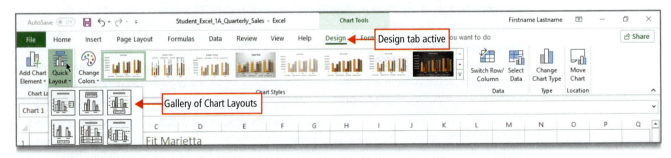

Figure 1.28

5 *Point* to several different layouts to see how Live Preview displays the effect on your chart, and then click the **Quick Layout** button again without changing the layout.

MAC TIP Live Preview may not display.

6 In the chart, click anywhere in the text *Chart Title* to select the title box, watch the **Formula Bar** as you begin to type **Second** and notice that AutoComplete fills in the subtitle for you. Press [Enter] at any point to insert the worksheet subtitle as the chart title.

MAC TIP If necessary, select *Chart Title* and type **Second Quarter Cardio Sales**

7 Click in a white area just slightly *inside* the chart border to deselect the chart title but keep the chart selected. To the right of the chart, click **Chart Styles** 🖊, and then at the top of the **Chart Styles** gallery, be sure that **Style** is selected. Compare your screen with Figure 1.29.

> The **Chart Styles gallery** displays an array of pre-defined *chart styles*—the overall visual look of the chart in terms of its colors, backgrounds, and graphic effects such as flat or shaded columns. You can also select Chart Styles from the Chart Styles group on the ribbon, but having the gallery closer to the chart makes it easier to use a touch gesture on a touch device to format a chart.

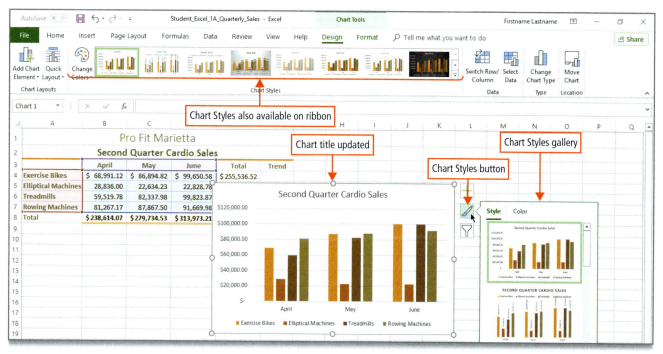

Figure 1.29

8 On the right side of the **Style** gallery, scroll down about halfway, and then by using the ScreenTips as your guide, locate and click **Style 6**.

> This style uses a white background, formats the columns with theme colors, and applies a slight shadowed effect to the columns. With this clear visual representation of the data, the president can see the sales of all product categories in each month, and can see that sales of exercise bikes and treadmills have risen markedly during the quarter.

9 At the top of the gallery, click **Color**. Under **Colorful**, point to the third row of colors to display the ScreenTip, and then click to apply this variation of the theme colors.

MAC TIP Click Change Colors

10 ▶ Point to the top border of the chart to display the pointer, and then drag the upper left corner of the chart just inside the upper left corner of cell **A10**, approximately as shown in Figure 1.30.

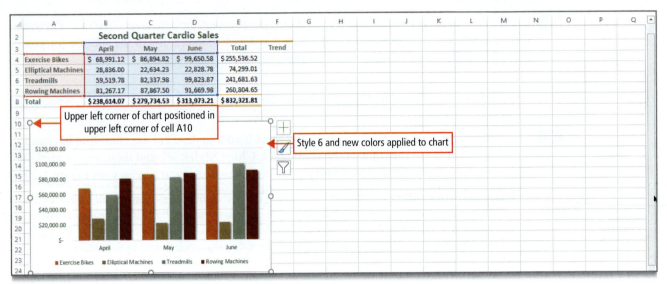

Figure 1.30

11 ▶ Click any cell to deselect the chart, and notice that the chart buttons no longer display to the right of the chart and the Chart Tools no longer display on the ribbon. Click **Save** 🖫.

Contextual tabs display on the ribbon when an object is selected and then are removed from view when the object is deselected.

Activity 1.13 | Creating and Formatting Sparklines

MOS
2.4.1

By creating sparklines, you provide a context for your numbers. Michelle and her colleagues at Pro Fit Marietta will be able to see the relationship between a sparkline and its underlying data quickly.

1 ▶ Select the range **B4:D7**, which represents the monthly sales figures for each product and for each month. Click the **Insert tab**, and then in the **Sparklines group**, click **Line**. In the displayed **Create Sparklines** dialog box, notice that the selected range *B4:D7* displays. Compare your screen with Figure 1.31.

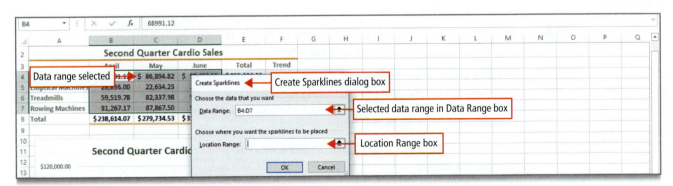

Figure 1.31

2 With the insertion point in the **Location Range** box, type **f4:f7** which is the range of cells where you want the sparklines to display.

ANOTHER WAY In the worksheet, select the range F4:F7 to insert it into the Location Range box.

3 Click **OK** to insert the sparklines in the range **F4:F7**, and then on the **Design tab**, in the **Show group**, click the **Markers** check box to select it.

Alongside each row of data, the sparkline provides a quick visual trend summary for sales of each cardio item over the three-month period. For example, you can see instantly that of the four items, only Elliptical Machines had declining sales for the period.

4 On the **Design tab**, in the **Style group**, click **More** ⬇. In the first row, click the third style. Press Ctrl + Home to deselect the range and make cell **A1** the active range. Click **Save** 🖫, and then compare your screen with Figure 1.32.

Use markers, colors, and styles in this manner to further enhance your sparklines.

MAC TIP Select the third style in the first row of the drop-down gallery, not from the row of styles that remain on the toolbar.

	A	B	C	D	E	F
A1				*fx* Pro Fit Marietta		
1		Pro Fit Marietta				
2		Second Quarter Cardio Sales				
3		April	May	June	Total	Trend
4	Exercise Bikes	$ 68,991.12	$ 86,894.82	$ 99,650.58	$ 255,536.52	
5	Elliptical Machines	28,836.00	22,634.23	22,828.78	74,299.01	
6	Treadmills	59,519.78	82,337.98	99,823.87	241,681.63	
7	Rowing Machines	81,267.17	87,867.50	91,669.98	260,804.65	
8	Total	$ 238,614.07	$ 279,734.53	$ 313,973.21	$ 832,321.81	

Sparklines inserted and formatted

Figure 1.32

Objective 6	**Print a Worksheet, Display Formulas, and Close Excel**

GO! Learn How
Video E1-6

Use the Show Formulas command to display the formula in each cell instead of the resulting value. Use the commands on the Page Layout tab to prepare for printing.

Activity 1.14 | Creating a Footer and Centering a Worksheet

1.3.1

For each Excel project in this textbook, you will create a footer containing the file name, which includes your name and the project name. You will also center the data horizontally on the page to create an attractive result if your worksheet is shared with others electronically or printed.

1 If necessary, click cell **A1** to deselect the chart. Click the **Page Layout tab**, and then in the **Page Setup group**, click **Margins**. At the bottom of the **Margins** gallery, click **Custom Margins** to display the **Page Setup** dialog box. Compare your screen with Figure 1.33.

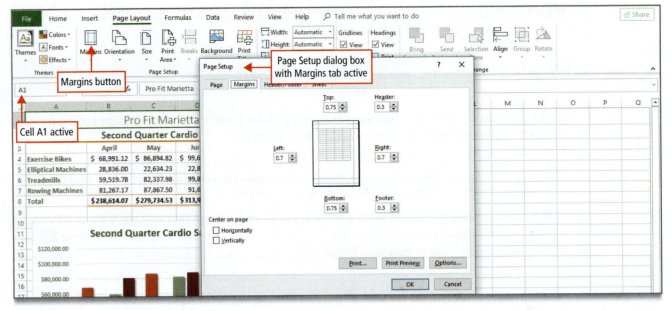

Figure 1.33

2 On the **Margins tab**, under **Center on page**, select the **Horizontally** check box.

This action will center the data and chart horizontally on the page, as shown in the Preview area.

3 Click the **Header/Footer tab**, and then in the center of the dialog box, click **Custom Footer**. In the **Footer** dialog box, with your insertion point blinking in the **Left section**, on the row of buttons, click **Insert File Name**. Compare your screen with Figure 1.34.

&[File] displays in the Left section. Here you can type or insert information from the row of buttons into the left, middle, or right section of the footer. The Custom Header button displays a similar screen to enter information in the header of the worksheet.

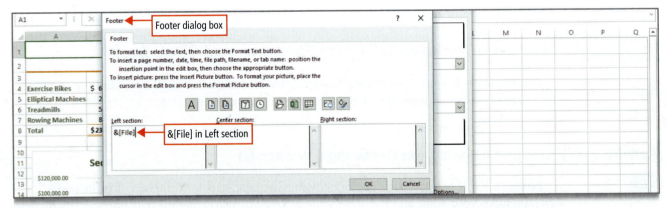

Figure 1.34

4 Click **OK** two times.

The vertical dotted line between columns indicates that as currently arranged, only the columns to the left of the dotted line will print on the first page. The exact position of the vertical line may depend on your default printer setting.

ANOTHER WAY Deselect the chart. On the Insert tab, in the Text group, click Header & Footer to display Page Layout view. Click in the left section of the displayed footer, and then in the Header & Footer Elements group, click File Name. Click any cell in the workbook to deselect the footer area, and then on the status bar, click the Normal button to return to Normal view.

Activity 1.15 | Adding Document Properties and Printing a Workbook

1.4.5

Michelle likes to add tags and other identifying properties to all company documents so they are easily searchable. In this Activity, you will add searchable document properties to the workbook.

1 In the upper left corner of your screen, click the **File tab** to display **Backstage** view. If necessary, on the left, click the **Info tab**. In the lower right corner, click **Show All Properties**.

> **MAC TIP** Click File, at the bottom of the menu, click Properties, click the Summary tab; for Tags use Keywords.

2 As the **Tags**, type **cardio sales** In the **Subject** box, type your course name and section number. Be sure your name displays in the **Author** box and edit if necessary.

3 On the left, click **Print** to view the **Print Preview**. Compare your screen with Figure 1.35.

> **MAC TIP** Click OK to close Properties dialog box first. Click File, then click Print.

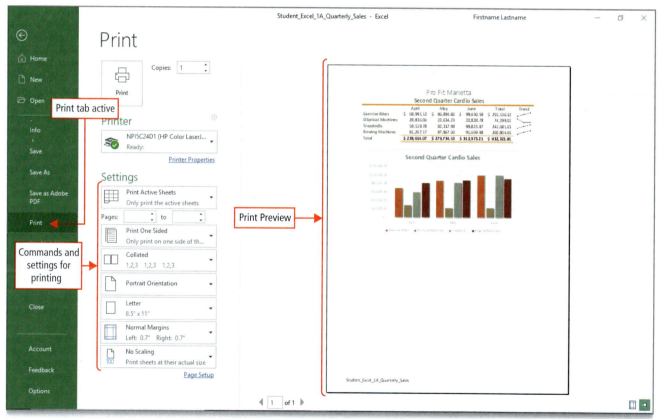

Figure 1.35

4 Note any adjustments that need to be made, and then on the left, click **Save** to save and return to the workbook.

> **MAC TIP** Click Close to close the Print dialog box, then Save your workbook.

Activity 1.16 | Printing a Section of the Worksheet

1.5.1, 1.5.3

From Backstage view, you can print only the portion of the worksheet that you select, and there are times you might want to do this. For example, sometimes Michelle wants to see data for only one or two types of equipment when she is evaluating various brands of equipment.

1 Select the range **A2:F5** to select only the subtitle and the data for *Exercise Bikes* and *Elliptical Machines* and the column titles.

2 Click the **File tab**, on the left, click **Print** to display **Print Preview**, and then under **Settings**, click the first arrow, which currently displays *Print Active Sheets*. On the list that displays, click **Print Selection**, and then compare your screen with Figure 1.36.

 MAC TIP On the File menu, point to Print Area, and then click Set Print Area. When finished, go back to Print Area and click Clear Print Area.

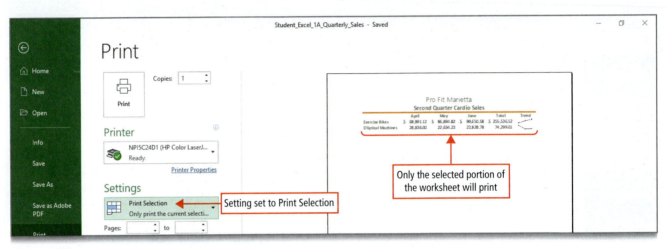

Figure 1.36

 For Non-MyLab Submissions: Determine if Your Instructor Requires a Submission for Printing a Section of a Worksheet
If directed by your instructor, print the selection on paper or create an electronic image. Then press Ctrl + Home and click Save.

3 Click the **Print Selection arrow** again, and then click **Print Active Sheets** to return this setting to the default. In the upper left, click **Back** to return to your document. Press Ctrl + Home to make cell **A1** the active cell, and then click **Save**.

Activity 1.17 | Changing Page Orientation and Displaying, Printing, and Hiding Formulas

1.3.1, 1.3.2,
1.4.6, 1.5.3

When you type a formula in a cell, the cell displays the *results* of the formula calculation. Recall that this value is called the displayed value. You can view and print the underlying formulas in the cells. When you do so, a formula often takes more horizontal space to display than the result of the calculation.

1 If necessary, redisplay your worksheet. Because you will make some temporary changes to your workbook, on the Quick Access Toolbar, click **Save** to be sure your work is saved up to this point.

2 On the **Formulas tab**, in the **Formula Auditing group**, click **Show Formulas**.

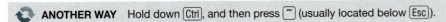 **ANOTHER WAY** Hold down Ctrl, and then press ~ (usually located below Esc).

3 In the **column heading area**, point to the **column A** heading to display the ⬇ pointer, hold down the left mouse button, and then drag to the right to select columns **A:F**. Compare your screen with Figure 1.37.

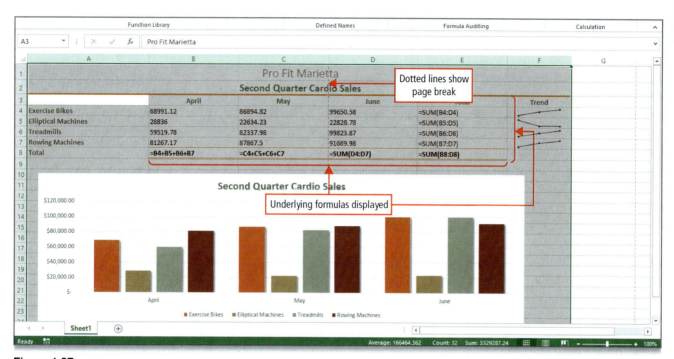

Figure 1.37

NOTE   Turning the Display of Formulas On and Off

The Show Formulas button is a toggle button. Clicking it once turns the display of formulas on—the button will be shaded. Clicking the button again turns the display of formulas off.

---

4 Point to the column heading boundary between any two of the selected columns to display the ➕ pointer, and then double-click to AutoFit the selected columns.

AutoFit adjusts the width of a column to fit the cell content of the *widest* cell in the column.

ANOTHER WAY   With the columns selected, on the Home tab, in the Cells group, click Format, and then click AutoFit Column Width.

---

5 On the **Page Layout tab**, in the **Page Setup group**, click **Orientation**, and then click **Landscape**. In the **Scale to Fit** group, click the **Width arrow**, and then click **1 page** to scale the data to fit onto one page.

Scaling shrinks the width or height of the printed worksheet to fit a maximum number of pages and is convenient for printing formulas. Although it is not always the case, formulas frequently take up more space than the actual data.

ANOTHER WAY   In the Scale to Fit group, click the Dialog Box Launcher button to display the Page tab of the Page Setup dialog box. Then, under Scaling, click the Fit to option button.

---

6 In the **Page Setup group**, click **Margins**, click **Custom Margins**, and then on the **Margins tab**, under **Center on page**, be sure the **Horizontally** check box is selected—select it if necessary.

7 Click **OK** to close the dialog box. Click cell **A1**. Check to be sure your chart is centered below the data and the left and right edges are slightly inside column A and column F—use the ⟦pointer⟧ pointer to drag a chart edge and then deselect the chart if necessary.

8 Click the **File tab**, and then on the left click **Print** to display the **Print Preview**. Under **Settings**, if necessary, switch back to the option to **Print Active Sheets**.

9 On the left, click **Close**, and when prompted, click **Don't Save** so that you do *not* save the changes you made—displaying formulas, changing column widths and orientation, and scaling—to print your formulas.

10 In the upper right corner of your screen, click **Close** ⊠ to close Excel.

For Non-MyLab Submissions: Determine What Your Instructor Requires for Submission
As directed by your instructor, submit your completed Excel workbook.

11 In **MyLab IT**, locate and click the Grader Project **Excel 1A Quarterly Sales**. In **step 3**, under **Upload Completed Assignment**, click **Choose File**. In the **Open** dialog box, navigate to your **Excel Chapter 1 folder**, and then click your **Student_Excel_1A_Quarterly_Sales** file one time to select it. In the lower right corner of the **Open** dialog box, click **Open**.

The name of your selected file displays above the Upload button.

12 To submit your file to **MyLab IT** for grading, click **Upload**, wait a moment for a green **Success!** message, and then in **step 4**, click the blue **Submit for Grading** button. Click **Close Assignment** to return to your list of **Course Materials**.

You have completed Project 1A **END**

Objective	Create a Sales Report with an Embedded Column Chart Using Google Sheets

ALERT **Working with Web-Based Applications and Service**

Computer programs and services on the web receive continuous updates and improvements, so the steps to complete this web-based Activity may differ from the ones shown. You can often look at the screens and the information presented to determine how to complete the Activity.

If you do not already have a Google account, you will need to create one before you begin this Activity. Go to **http://google.com** and in the upper right corner, click Sign In. On the Sign In screen, click Create Account. On the Create your Google Account page, complete the form, read and agree to the Terms of Service and Privacy Policy, and then click Next step. On the Welcome screen, click Get Started.

Activity | Creating a Sales Report with an Embedded Column Chart Using Google Sheets

In this Activity, you will use Google Sheets to create a sales report and chart similar to the one you created in Project 1A.

1 From the desktop, open your browser (use a browser other than Edge), navigate to **https://www.google.com**, and then click the **Google apps** menu. Click **Drive**, and then if necessary, sign in to your Google account.

2 Open your **GO! Web Projects** folder—or click New to create and then open this folder if necessary.

3 In the upper left corner, click **New**, and then click **Google Sheets**. From your Windows taskbar, open **File Explorer**, navigate to the files you downloaded for this chapter, and then in the **File List**, double-click to open **e01A_Web**.

4 In the displayed Excel worksheet, select the range **A1:E8**, right-click over the selection, click **Copy**, and then **Close** Excel. **Close** the **File Explorer** window.

5 In your blank Google Sheet, with cell **A1** active, point to cell **A1**, right-click, and then click **Paste**; by copying and pasting the data, you can create this Project faster without having to do extra typing. In the column heading area, point to the border between **column A** and **column B** to display the ↔ pointer, and then widen **column A** slightly so that all of the data displays.

6 Select the range **A1:E1**. On the toolbar, click **Merge cells**. On the toolbar, click the **Horizontal Align button arrow** and then click **Center**. Repeat for the range **A2:E2**, and then apply **Bold** to cells **A1** and **A2**.

7 Select the range with the month names, center them, and apply **Bold**. Apply **Bold** to the totals in the range **B8:E8**.

8 Select the range **A3:D7**—the data without the totals and without the titles. On the menu bar, click **Insert**, and then click **Chart**. On the right, in the **Chart editor** pane, be sure the **DATA tab** is active.

9 In the Chart editor pane, scroll down as necessary, and then select the **Switch rows/columns** check box.

10 At the top of the **Chart editor** pane, click the **CUSTOMIZE tab**. Click the **Chart & axis titles arrow**, and then click in the **Chart title** box. Type **Second Quarter Cardio Sales**

11 Click the **Legend arrow**, click the **Position arrow**, and then click **None**. Click the **Chart style arrow**, click the **Background color arrow**, and then in the fourth column, click the third color—**light yellow 3**.

12 Point anywhere inside the selected chart, hold down the left mouse button and begin to drag to display the ✋ pointer, and then drag the chart slightly below the data. Then using the corner sizing handles, resize and reposition the chart so that it is the width of columns **A:E** and displays below the data.

13 At the top of the worksheet window, click the text *Untitled spreadsheet*, and then using your own name, type **Lastname_Firstname_EX_1A_Web** and press Enter.

»»» **GO!** With Google continues on next page

»»» GO! With Google Sheets

14 If you are instructed to submit your file to your instructor, you can either share the file through Google Drive, or create a PDF or Excel file. Ask your instructor in what format he or she would like to receive your file.

15 Close ☒ the browser tab—a new Google Sheet always opens in a new window in your browser; your work is automatically saved. Notice that your new Google Sheet displays in the file list on your Google Drive. Sign out of your Google account.

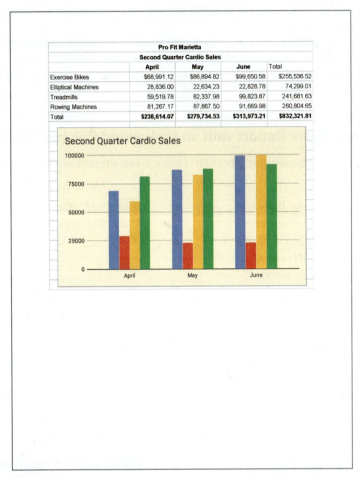

Figure A

PROJECT 1B Inventory Valuation

MyLab IT
Project 1B Grader for Instruction
Project 1B Simulation for Training and Review

Project Activities

In Activities 1.18 through 1.27 you will create a workbook for Josh Feingold, Operations Manager, which calculates the retail value of an inventory of plyometric training products. Your completed worksheet will look similar to Figure 1.38.

Project Files for **MyLab IT Grader**

1. In your MyLab IT course, locate and click **Excel 1B Plyo Products**, Download Materials, and then Download All Files.
2. Extract the zipped folder to your Excel Chapter 1 folder. Close the Grader download screens.
3. Take a moment to open the downloaded **Excel_1B_Plyo_Products_Instructions**; note any recent updates to the book.

Project Results

GO! Project 1B
Where We're Going

Pro Fit Marietta					
Plyometric Products Inventory Valuation					
As of September 30					
	Warehouse Location	Quantity in Stock	Retail Price	Total Retail Value	Percent of Total Retail Value
Power Hurdle	Atlanta	125	$ 32.95	$ 4,118.75	1.41%
Speed Hurdle	Atlanta	995	59.95	59,650.25	20.37%
Stackable Steps	Marietta	450	251.59	113,215.50	38.65%
Pro Jump Rope	Marietta	1,105	49.95	55,194.75	18.84%
Plyometric Box Set	Marietta	255	158.05	40,302.75	13.76%
Plyometric Mat	Atlanta	215	94.99	20,422.85	6.97%
Total Retail Value for All Products				$ 292,904.85	

Student_Excel_1B_Plyo_Products

Figure 1.38 Project 1B Plyo Products

For Non-MyLab Submissions

For Project 1B, you will need:
New blank Excel workbook

In your **Excel Chapter 1** folder, save your workbook as:
Lastname_Firstname_1B_Plyo_Products

If your instructor requires a workbook with formulas, save as:
Lastname_Firstname_1B_Plyo_Products_formulas

After you have named and saved your workbook, on the next page begins with step 2.

Objective 7 | Check Spelling in a Worksheet

ALERT Because Office 365 is a cloud-based subscription service that receives continuous updates, you may encounter some variations in what appears on your screen and what is shown in this instruction. Microsoft Office 365 is fully installed on your PC or Mac; no internet access is necessary to create or edit documents. When you *are* connected to the internet, you will receive monthly upgrades and new features, so you always have the latest versions of Office apps as soon as they are available. Your subscription gives you continuous free access to the latest innovations and refinements.

GO! Learn How
Video E1-7

In Excel, the spelling checker performs similarly to the way it behaves in other Microsoft Office programs.

Activity 1.18 | Checking Spelling in a Worksheet

MOS
2.2.7

1 Navigate to your **Excel Chapter 1 folder**, and then double-click the Excel file you downloaded from **MyLab IT** that displays your name—**Student_Excel_1B_Plyo_ Products**. In your blank workbook, if necessary, at the top click **Enable Editing**.

2 In cell **A1**, type **Pro Fit Marietta** and press Enter. In cell **A2**, type **Plyometric Products Inventory** and press Enter.

MAC TIP To display group names on the ribbon, display the menu, click Excel, click Preferences, click View, under In Ribbon, select the Group Titles check box.

3 Press Tab to move to cell **B3**, type **Quantity** and press Tab. In cell **C3**, type **Average Cost** and press Tab. In cell **D3**, type **Retail Price** and press Tab.

4 Click cell **C3**, and then look at the **Formula Bar**. Notice that in the cell, the displayed value is cut off; however, in the **Formula Bar**, the entire text value—the underlying value—displays. Compare your screen with Figure 1.39.

Text that is too long to fit in a cell extends into cells on the right only if they are empty. If the cell to the right contains data, the text in the cell to the left is truncated—cut off. The entire value continues to exist, but it is not completely visible.

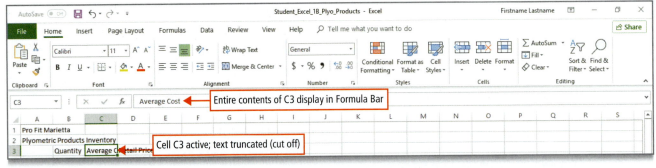

Figure 1.39

5 Click cell **E3**, type **Total Retail Value** and press Tab. In cell **F3**, type **Percent of Total Retail Value** and press Enter.

6 ▸ Click cell **A4**. *Without* correcting the spelling error, type **Powr Hurdle** Press Enter. In the range **A5:A10**, type the remaining row titles shown below. Then compare your screen with Figure 1.40.

Speed Hurdle

Stackable Steps

Pro Jump Rope

Plyometric Box Set

Plyometric Mat

Total Retail Value for All Products

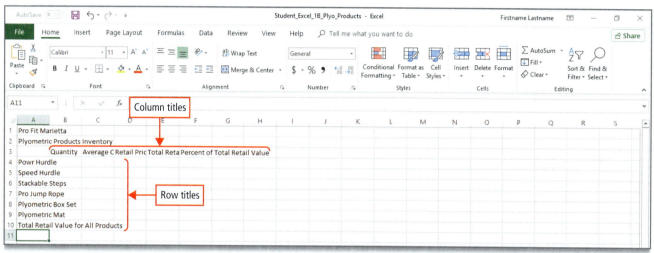

Figure 1.40

7 ▸ In the **column heading area**, point to the right boundary of **column A** to display the ⊞ pointer, and then drag to the right to widen **column A** to **215** pixels.

🖥 **MAC TIP**   Change the width to 30 (185 pixels).

8 ▸ Select the range **A1:F1**, **Merge & Center** the text, and then from the **Cell Styles** gallery, apply the **Title** style.

9 ▸ Select the range **A2:F2**, **Merge & Center** the text, and then from the **Cell Styles** gallery, apply the **Heading 1** style. Press Ctrl + Home to move to cell **A1** at the top of your worksheet.

🖥 **MAC TIP**   Press control + E + ← to move to cell A1.

10 With cell **A1** as the active cell, click the **Review tab**, and then in the **Proofing group**, click **Spelling**. Compare your screen with Figure 1.41.

Figure 1.41

  ANOTHER WAY   Press ⌨F7⌨, which is the keyboard shortcut for the Spelling command.

11 In the **Spelling** dialog box, under **Not in Dictionary**, notice the word *Powr*.

The spelling tool does not have this word in its dictionary. Under *Suggestions*, Excel provides a list of suggested spellings.

12 Under **Suggestions**, if necessary click **Power**, and then click **Change**.

Powr, a typing error, is changed to *Power*. A message box displays *Spell check complete. You're good to go!*—unless you have additional unrecognized words. Because the spelling check begins its checking process starting with the currently selected cell, it is good practice to return to cell A1 before starting the Spelling command.

13 Correct any other errors you may have made. When the message displays, *Spell check complete. You're good to go!*, click **OK. Save** 🖬 your workbook.

Objective 8 Enter Data by Range

GO! Learn How
Video E1-8

You can enter data by first selecting a range of cells. This is a time-saving technique, especially if you use a numeric keypad to enter the numbers.

Activity 1.19 │ Entering Data by Range

1 Select the range **B4:D9**, type **125** and then press ⌨Enter⌨.

The value displays in cell B4, and cell B5 becomes the active cell.

2 With cell **B5** active in the range, and pressing ⌨Enter⌨ after each entry, type the following, and then compare your screen with Figure 1.42:

1125

450

1105

255

215

After you enter the last value and press ⌨Enter⌨, the active cell moves to the top of the next column within the selected range. Although it is not required to enter data in this manner, you can see that selecting the range before you enter data saves time because it confines the movement of the active cell to the selected range. When you select a range of data, the Quick Analysis button displays. (Mac users: you may not see the Quick Analysis button.)

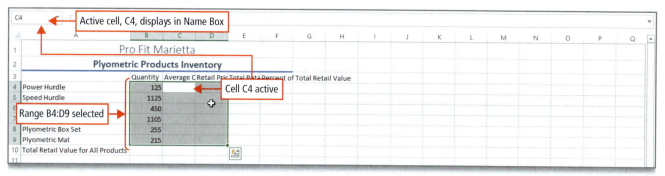

Figure 1.42

3 With the selected range still active, from the following table, beginning in cell **C4** and pressing Enter after each entry, enter the data for the **Average Cost** column and then the **Retail Price** column. If you prefer, deselect the range to enter the values—typing in a selected range is optional.

Average Cost	Retail Price
15.50	32.95
29.55	59.95
125.95	251.59
18.75	49.95
85.25	159.05
49.95	94.99

Recall that the default number format for cells is the *General* number format, in which numbers display exactly as you type them and trailing zeros do not display, even if you type them.

4 Click any blank cell, and then compare your screen with Figure 1.43. Correct any errors you may have made while entering data, and then click **Save** 💾.

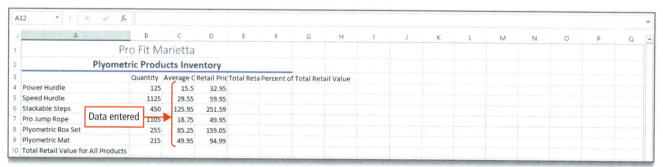

Figure 1.43

Objective 9   Construct Formulas for Mathematical Operations

GO! Learn How
Video E1-9

Operators are symbols with which you can specify the type of calculation you want to perform in a formula.

Activity 1.20 | Using Arithmetic Operators

1 Click cell **E4**, type **=b4*d4** and notice that the two cells are outlined as part of an active formula. Then, press Enter.

The *Total Retail Value* of all *Power Hurdle* items in inventory—*4118.75*—equals the *Quantity* (125) times the *Retail Price* (selling price) of 32.95. In Excel, the asterisk (*) indicates multiplication.

2 Take a moment to study the symbols you will use to perform basic mathematical operations in Excel as shown in the table in Figure 1.44, which are referred to as *arithmetic operators*.

Symbols Used in Excel for Arithmetic Operators	
Operator Symbol	**Operation**
+	Addition
-	Subtraction (also negation)
*	Multiplication
/	Division
%	Percent
^	Exponentiation

Figure 1.44

3 Click cell **E4**.

You can see that in cells E5:E9 you need a formula similar to the one in E4, but one that refers to the cells in row 5, row 6, and so on. Recall that you can copy formulas and the cell references will change *relative to* the row number.

4 With cell **E4** selected, position your pointer over the fill handle in the lower right corner of the cell until the ⊞ pointer displays. Then, drag down through cell **E9** to copy the formula.

5 Select the range **B4:B9**, and then on the **Home tab**, in the **Number group**, click **Comma Style** . In the **Number group**, click **Decrease Decimal** ⌗ two times to remove the decimal places from these values.

Comma Style formats a number with two decimal places; because these are whole numbers referring to quantities, no decimal places are necessary.

↻ **ANOTHER WAY** Select the range, display the Cell Styles gallery, and then under Number Format, click Comma [0].

6 Select the range **E4:E9**, and then at the bottom of your screen, in the status bar, notice the displayed values for **Average**, **Count**, and **Sum**—*50158.89167, 6,* and *300953.35*.

When you select a range of numerical data, Excel's *AutoCalculate* feature displays three calculations in the status bar by default—Average, Count, and Sum. Here, Excel indicates that if you averaged the selected values, the result would be *50158.89167*, there are *6* cells in the selection that contain values, and that if you added the values the result would be *300953.35*.

You can display three additional calculations to this area by right-clicking the status bar and selecting them—Numerical Count, Minimum, and Maximum.

Activity 1.21 | Using the Quick Analysis Tool

2.2.5, 2.2.7

Recall that the Quick Analysis button displays when you select a range of data. Quick Analysis is convenient because it keeps common commands close to your mouse pointer and also displays commands in a format that is easy to touch with your finger if you are using a touchscreen device.

1 With the range **E4:E9** selected, in the lower right corner of the selected range, click **Quick Analysis** ⊞. In the displayed gallery, click **Totals**. *Point to*, but do not click, the first **Sum** button, which shows blue cells at the bottom. Compare your screen with Figure 1.45.

Here, the shaded cells on the button indicate what will be summed and where the result will display, and a preview of the result displays in the cell bordered with a gray shadow.

▭ **MAC TIP** Quick Analysis is not available, use AutoSum.

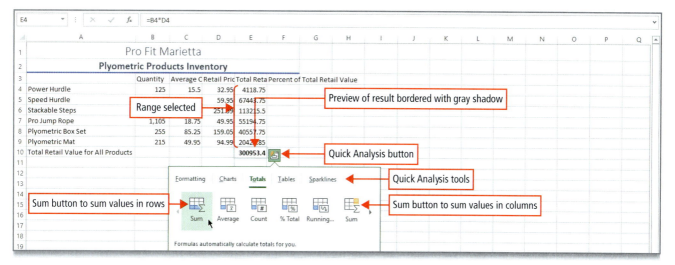

Figure 1.45

2 ▶ Click the first **Sum** button to display the column total *300953.4* formatted in Bold.

Sums calculated using the Quick Analysis tool are formatted in Bold.

💻 **MAC TIP** Select the range E4:E9, and then on the Home tab, click AutoSum. In the Font group, click Bold.

3 ▶ Select the range **C5:E9** and apply the **Comma Style** 🔲 ; notice that Excel widens the columns to accommodate the data.

4 ▶ Select the range **C4:E4**, hold down Ctrl, and then click cell **E10**. Release Ctrl, and then apply the **Accounting Number Format** 🔲 . Notice that Excel widens the columns as necessary.

5 ▶ Click cell **E10**, and then from the **Cell Styles** gallery, apply the **Total** style. Click any blank cell, **Save** 🔲 your workbook, and then compare your screen with Figure 1.46.

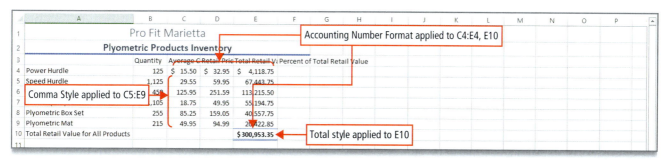

Figure 1.46

Activity 1.22 │ Copying Formulas Containing Absolute Cell References

4.1.1

In a formula, a relative cell reference refers to a cell by its position *relative to* the cell that contains the formula. An **absolute cell reference**, on the other hand, refers to a cell by its *fixed* position in the worksheet, for example, the total in cell E10.

A relative cell reference automatically adjusts when a formula is copied. In some calculations, you do *not* want the cell reference to adjust; rather, you want the cell reference to remain the same when the formula is copied.

1 ▶ Click cell **F4**, type **=** and then click cell **E4**. Type **/** and then click cell **E10**.

The formula *=E4/E10* indicates that the value in cell E4 will be *divided* by the value in cell E10 because Mr. Feingold wants to know the percentage by which each product's Total Retail Value makes up the Total Retail Value for All Products.

Arithmetically, the percentage is computed by dividing the *Total Retail Value* for each product by the *Total Retail Value for All Products*. The result will be a percentage expressed as a decimal.

2 ▶ Press Enter. Click cell **F4** and notice that the formula displays in the **Formula Bar**. Then, point to cell **F4** and double-click.

The formula, with the two referenced cells displayed in color and bordered with the same color, displays in the cell. This feature, called the **range finder**, is useful for verifying formulas because it visually indicates which workbook cells are included in a formula calculation.

3 ▶ Press Enter to redisplay the result of the calculation in the cell, and notice that .013686, which is approximately 1% of the total retail value of the inventory, is made up of Power Hurdles.

4 ▶ Click cell **F4** again, and then drag the fill handle down through cell **F9**. Compare your screen with Figure 1.47.

Each cell displays an error message—*#DIV/0!* and a green triangle in the upper left corner of each cell indicates that Excel detects an error.

Like a grammar checker, Excel uses rules to check for formula errors and flags errors in this manner. Additionally, the Auto Fill Options button displays, from which you can select formatting options for the copied cells.

F4	▼	:	×	✓	fx	=E4/E10										
◢	A		B	C	D	E	F	G	H	I	J	K	L	M	N	O	P
1					Pro Fit Marietta											
2			**Plyometric Products Inventory**													
3			Quantity	Average C	Retail Pric	Total Retail V	Percent of Total Retail Value									
4	Power Hurdle		125	$ 15.50	$ 32.95	$ 4,118.75	0.013686									
5	Speed Hurdle		1,125	29.55	59.95	67,443.75	#DIV/0!									
6	Stackable Steps					13,215.50	#DIV/0!									
7	Pro Jump Rope					55,194.	#DIV/0!									
8	Plyometric Box Set					40,557.75	#DIV/0!									
9	Plyometric Mat		215	49.95	94.99	20,422.85	#DIV/0!									
10	Total Retail Value for All Products					$ 300,953.35										

Cells F5:F9 display error message and green triangles

Auto Fill Options button

Figure 1.47

5 ▶ Click cell **F5**, and then to the left of the cell, point to the **Error Checking** button 🔹 to display its ScreenTip—*The formula or function used is dividing by zero or empty cells.*

In this manner, Excel suggests the cause of an error.

💻 **MAC TIP**   On the Formulas tab, click Error Checking.

6 Look at the **Formula Bar** and examine the formula.

The formula is =E5/E11. The cell reference to E5 is correct, but the cell reference following the division operator (/) is *E11*, and E11 is an *empty* cell.

7 Click cell **F6**, point to the **Error Checking** button 🔷, and in the **Formula Bar**, examine the formula.

Because the cell references are relative, Excel builds the formulas by increasing the row number for each equation. But in this calculation, the divisor must always be the value in cell E10—the *Total Retail Value for All Products*.

8 Point to cell **F4**, and then double-click to place the insertion point within the cell.

9 Within the cell, use the arrow keys as necessary to position the insertion point to the left of *E10*, and then press F4. Compare your screen with Figure 1.48.

Dollar signs ($) display, which changes the reference to cell E10 to an absolute cell reference. The use of the dollar sign to denote an absolute reference is not related in any way to whether or not the values you are working with are currency values. It is simply the symbol that Excel uses to denote an absolute cell reference.

MAC TIP Press command ⌘ + T to make a cell reference in a formula absolute.

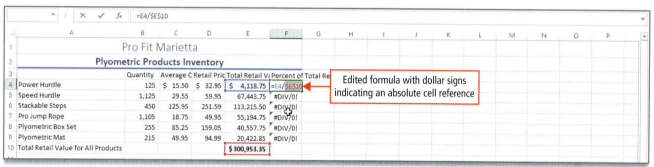

Figure 1.48

ANOTHER WAY Edit the formula so that it indicates =E4/E10.

10 On the **Formula Bar**, click **Enter** ✔ so that **F4** remains the active cell. Then, drag the fill handle to copy the new formula down through cell **F9**. Compare your screen with Figure 1.49.

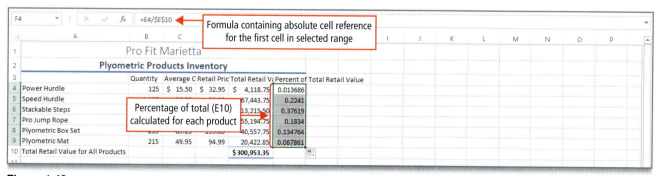

Figure 1.49

11 Click cell **F5**, examine the formula in the **Formula Bar**, and then examine the formulas for cells **F6**, **F7**, **F8**, and **F9**.

For each formula, the cell reference for the *Total Retail Value* of each product changed relative to its row; however, the value used as the divisor—*Total Retail Value for All Products* in cell E10—remained absolute. You can see that by using either relative or absolute cell references, it is easy to duplicate formulas without typing them.

12 Save 🖫 your workbook.

<table>
<tr><td>**MORE KNOWLEDGE**</td><td>**Calculate a Percentage if You Know the Total and the Amount**</td></tr>
</table>

Using the equation *amount/total = percentage*, you can calculate the percentage by which a part makes up a total—with the percentage formatted as a decimal. For example, if on a test you score 42 points correctly out of 50, your percentage of correct answers is 42/50 = 0.84 or 84%.

Objective 10   Edit Values in a Worksheet

GO! Learn How
Video E1-10

Excel performs calculations on numbers; that is why you use Excel. If you make changes to the numbers, Excel automatically *re*-calculates the results. This is one of the most powerful and valuable features of Excel.

Activity 1.23 | Editing Values in a Worksheet

You can edit text and number values directly within a cell or in the Formula Bar.

Josh needs to edit some of the worksheet's information, so in this Activity, you will correct the quantity of Speed Hurdles from 1,125 to 995, change the Retail Price of Plyometric Box Sets from $159.05 to $158.05, edit the subtitle to include the word *Valuation*, and edit the column title in cell B3.

1 In cell **E10**, notice the column total *$300,953.35*. Click cell **B5**, and then change its value by typing **995** Watch cell **E5** and press Enter.

Excel formulas *re-calculate* if you change the value in a cell that is referenced in a formula. It is not necessary to delete the old value in a cell; selecting the cell and typing a new value replaces the old value with your new typing.

The *Total Retail Value* of all *Speed Hurdle* items recalculates to *59,650.25* and the total in cell E10 recalculates to *$293,159.85*. Additionally, all of the percentages in column F recalculate.

2 Point to cell **D8**, and then double-click to place the insertion point within the cell. Use the arrow keys to move the insertion point to the left or right of *9*, and use either Del or Backspace to delete *9* and then type **8** so that the new Retail Price is *158.05*.

3 Watch cell **E8** and **E10** as you press Enter, and then notice the recalculation of the formulas in those two cells.

Excel recalculates the value in cell E8 to *40,302.75* and the value in cell E10 to *$292,904.85*. Additionally, all of the percentages in column F recalculate because the *Total Retail Value for All Products* recalculated.

4 Point to cell **A2** so that the ⊕ pointer is positioned slightly to the right of the word *Inventory*, and then double-click to place the insertion point in the cell. Edit the text to add the word **Valuation** pressing Spacebar as necessary, and then press Enter.

5 ▶ Click cell **B3**, and then in the **Formula Bar**, click to place the insertion point after the letter *y*. Press [Spacebar] one time, type **in Stock** and then on the **Formula Bar**, click **Enter** ✓. Click **Save** 🖫, and then compare your screen with Figure 1.50.

> Recall that if text is too long to fit in the cell and the cell to the right contains data, the text is truncated—cut off—but the entire value still exists as the underlying value.

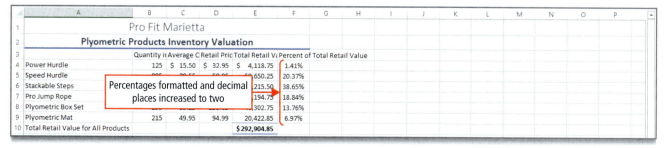

Figure 1.50

Activity 1.24 | Formatting Cells with the Percent Style

MOS

2.2.2

A percentage is part of a whole expressed in hundredths. For example, 75 cents is the same as 75 percent of one dollar. The Percent Style button formats the selected cell as a percentage rounded to the nearest hundredth. In this Activity, you will format the percentage values in column F with the Percent Style.

1 ▶ Click cell **F4**, and then in the **Number group**, click **Percent Style** %.

> Your result is 1%, which is *0.014062* rounded to the nearest hundredth and expressed as a percentage. Percent Style displays the value of a cell as a percentage.

2 ▶ Select the range **F4:F9**. On the **Home tab**, in the **Number group**, click **Percent Style** %, and then click **Increase Decimal** two times. Then in the **Alignment group**, click **Center**.

💻 **MAC TIP** Use commands on the Home tab.

> Percent Style may not offer a percentage precise enough to analyze important financial information—adding additional decimal places to a percentage makes data more precise.

🔄 **ANOTHER WAY** Right-click over the selected range, and then click the commands on the mini toolbar.

3 ▶ Click any cell to cancel the selection, **Save** 🖫 your workbook, and then compare your screen with Figure 1.51.

Figure 1.51

GO! Learn How
Video E1-11

Formatting refers to the process of specifying the appearance of cells and the overall layout of your worksheet. Formatting is accomplished through various commands on the ribbon, for example, applying Cell Styles, and also from commands on shortcut menus, using keyboard shortcuts, and in the Format Cells dialog box.

Activity 1.25 | Inserting and Deleting Rows and Columns

MOS
2.1.3

In the next Activities, you will format the worksheet attractively so that Josh and his staff can view the information easily.

1 In the **row heading area** on the left side of your screen, point to the row heading for **row 3** to display the ➡ pointer, and then right-click to simultaneously select the row and display a shortcut menu.

2 On the shortcut menu, click **Insert** to insert a new **row 3** above the selected row.

The rows below the new row 3 move down one row, and the Insert Options button displays. By default, the new row uses the formatting of the row *above*.

ANOTHER WAY Select the row, on the Home tab, in the Cells group, click the Insert button arrow, and then click Insert Sheet Rows. Or, select the row and click the Insert button—the default setting of the button inserts a new sheet row above the selected row.

3 Click cell **E11**. On the **Formula Bar**, notice that the range changed to sum the new range **E5:E10**. Compare your screen with Figure 1.52.

If you move formulas by inserting additional rows or columns in your worksheet, Excel automatically adjusts the formulas. Here, Excel adjusted all of the formulas in the worksheet that were affected by inserting this new row.

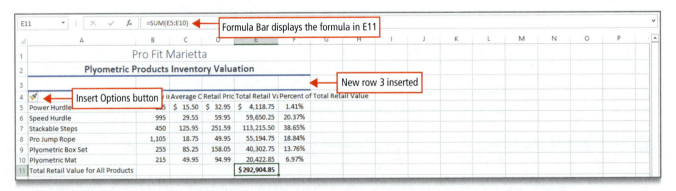

Figure 1.52

4 Click cell **A3**, type **As of September 30** and then on the **Formula Bar**, click **Enter** ✓ to maintain **A3** as the active cell. **Merge & Center** the text across the range **A3:F3**, and then apply the **Heading 2** cell style.

5 In the **column heading area**, point to **column B** to display the ⬇ pointer, right-click, and then click **Insert**.

> A column is inserted to the left of column B. By default, the new column uses the formatting of the column to the *left*.

🔄 **ANOTHER WAY** Select the column, on the Home tab, in the Cells group, click the Insert button arrow, and then click Insert Sheet Columns. Or, select the column and click the Insert button—the default setting of the button inserts a new sheet column to the right of the selected column.

6 Click cell **B4**, type **Warehouse Location** and then press Enter.

7 In cell **B5**, type **Atlanta** and then type **Atlanta** again in cells **B6** and **B10**. Use AutoComplete to speed your typing by pressing Enter as soon as the AutoComplete suggestion displays. In cells **B7**, **B8**, and **B9**, type **Marietta**

8 In the **column heading area**, point to **column D**, right-click, and then click **Delete**.

> The remaining columns shift to the left, and Excel adjusts all the formulas in the worksheet accordingly. You can use a similar technique to delete a row in a worksheet.

9 Compare your screen with Figure 1.53, and then **Save** 💾 your workbook.

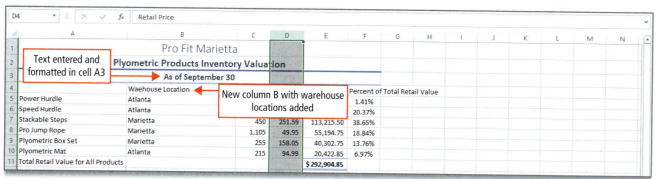

Figure 1.53

Activity 1.26 | Adjusting Column Widths and Wrapping Text

MOS

1.3.2, 2.2.4

Use the Wrap Text command to display the contents of a cell on multiple lines.

1 In the **column heading area**, point to the **column B** heading to display the ⬇ pointer, and then drag to the right to select **columns B:F**.

2 With the columns selected, in the **column heading area**, point to the right boundary of any of the selected columns to display the ➕ pointer, and then drag to set the width to **95 pixels**.

> Use this technique to format multiple columns or rows simultaneously.

💻 **MAC TIP** Set the width of columns B:F to 12.83. (82 pixels)

3 Select the range **B4:F4** that comprises the column headings, and then on the **Home tab**, in the **Alignment group**, click **Wrap Text** 📑. Notice that the row height adjusts to display the column titles on multiple lines.

4 With the range **B4:F4** still selected, in the **Alignment group**, click **Center** ▤ and **Middle Align** ▤. With the range **B4:F4** still selected, apply the **Heading 4** cell style.

> The *Middle Align* command aligns text so that it is centered between the top and bottom of the cell.

5 Select the range **B5:B10**, and then in the **Alignment group**, click **Center** ▤. Click cell **A11**, and then from the **Cell Styles** gallery, under **Themed Cell Styles**, click **40% - Accent1**. Save 🖫 your workbook.

Activity 1.27 | Changing Theme Colors

You can change only the theme *colors* of a workbook—without changing the theme fonts or effects.

1 On the **Page Layout tab**, in the **Themes group**, click **Colors**, and then click **Green** to change the Theme Color. Click any blank cell, and then compare your screen with Figure 1.54.

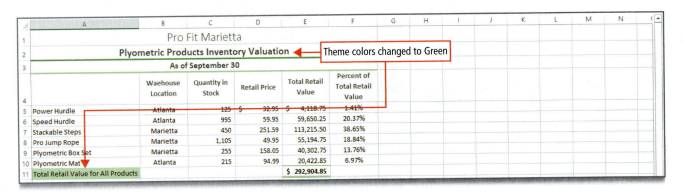

Figure 1.54

2 On the **Page Layout tab**, in the **Page Setup group**, click **Margins**, and then click **Custom Margins**.

3 In the **Page Setup** dialog box, on the **Margins tab**, under **Center on page**, select the **Horizontally** check box.

> This action will center the data and chart horizontally on the page, as shown in the Preview area.

4 Click the **Header/Footer tab**, and then in the center of the dialog box, click **Custom Footer**. In the **Footer** dialog box, with your insertion point blinking in the **Left section**, on the row of buttons, click **Insert File Name** 📄.

> &[File] displays in the Left section. Here you can type or insert information from the row of buttons into the left, middle, or right section of the footer. The Custom Header button displays a similar screen to enter information in the header of the worksheet.

5 Click **OK** two times.

6 Click the **File tab** to display Backstage view, on the left click the **Info tab**, and then in the lower right corner, click **Show All Properties**.

7 ▶ As the **Tags**, type **plyo products, inventory** and as the **Subject**, type your course name and section number. Be sure your name displays in the **Author** box, or edit it if necessary.

8 ▶ On the left, click **Print** to view the **Print Preview**. At the bottom of the **Print Preview**, click **Next Page** ▶, and notice that as currently formatted, the worksheet occupies two pages.

9 ▶ Under **Settings**, click **Portrait Orientation**, and then click **Landscape Orientation**. Compare your screen with Figure 1.55.

You can change the orientation on the Page Layout tab, or here, in Print Preview. Because it is in the Print Preview that you will often see adjustments that need to be made, commonly used settings display on the Print tab in Backstage view.

🖥️ **MAC TIP** At the bottom of the Print dialog box, click Show Details. Select and click the Landscape Orientation button.

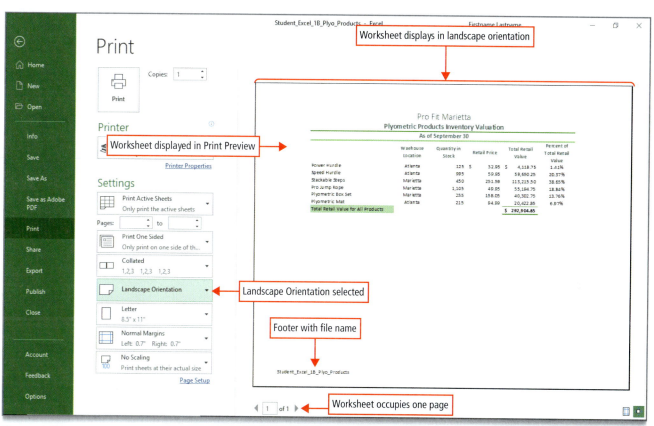

Figure 1.55

10 ▶ On the left, click **Save**.

11 ▶ In the upper right corner of your screen, click **Close** ⊠ to close Excel.

For Non-MyLab Submissions: Determine What Your Instructor Requires for Submission

As directed by your instructor, submit your completed Excel workbook.

12 In **MyLab IT**, locate and click the Grader Project **Excel 1B Plyo Products**. In **step 3**, under **Upload Completed Assignment**, click **Choose File**. In the **Open** dialog box, navigate to your **Excel Chapter 1 folder**, and then click your **Student_Excel_1B_Plyo_Products** file one time to select it. In the lower right corner of the **Open** dialog box, click **Open**.

The name of your selected file displays above the Upload button.

13 To submit your file to **MyLab IT** for grading, click **Upload**, wait a moment for a green **Success!** message, and then in **step 4**, click the blue **Submit for Grading** button. Click **Close Assignment** to return to your list of **Course Materials**.

You have completed Project 1B **END**

Objective | Creating an Inventory Valuation Report

> **ALERT** **Working with Web-Based Applications and Service**
>
> Computer programs and services on the web receive continuous updates and improvements, so the steps to complete this web-based Activity may differ from the ones shown. You can often look at the screens and the information presented to determine how to complete the Activity.
>
> If you do not already have a Google account, you will need to create one before you being this Activity. Go to **http://google.com** and in the upper right corner, click Sign In. On the Sign In screen, click Create Account. On the Create your Google Account page, complete the form, read and agree to the Terms of Service and Privacy Policy, and then click Next step. On the Welcome screen, click Get Started.

Activity | Creating an Inventory Valuation Report Using Google Sheets

In this Activity, you will use Google Sheets to create an inventory valuation report similar to the one you created in Project 1B.

1 From the desktop, open your browser (a browser other than Edge), navigate to **https://www.google.com** and then click the **Google Apps** menu ⊞. Click **Drive**, and then if necessary, sign in to your Google account.

2 Open your **GO! Web Projects** folder—or click New to create and then open this folder if necessary.

3 In the upper left, click **New**, and then click **Google Sheets**. From your Windows taskbar, open **File Explorer**, navigate to the files you downloaded for this chapter, and then in the **File List**, double-click the Word document **e01B_Web**. To complete this project quickly and eliminate extra typing, you will copy the data from a Word document.

4 In the displayed Word document, click anywhere in the text, and then in the upper left corner, click to select the **Table Select** icon ⊞ to select the entire Word table. Right-click anywhere over the selection, and then click **Copy**. **Close** Word. **Close** the **File Explorer** window.

5 In your blank Google Sheet, with cell **A1** active, point to cell **A1**, right-click, and then click **Paste**. In the column heading area, point to the border between **column A** and **column B** to display the ⟷ pointer, and then widen **column A** slightly so that all of the data displays.

6 Select the range **A1:E1** and on the toolbar, click **Merge cells**. On the toolbar, click the **Horizontal Align button arrow** ▤ and then click **Center** ▤. Repeat for the range **A2:E2**, and then apply **Bold** B to cells **A1** and **A2**.

7 Select the range **B3:E3**, on the menu bar click **Format**, point to **Text wrapping**, and then click **Wrap**. **Center** these column titles and apply **Bold** B.

8 Select the range **C4:C9**, on the menu bar click **Format**, point to **Number**, click **Number**, and then on the toolbar, click **Decrease decimal places** .0. two times.

9 Click cell **E4**, type = and then click cell **C4**. Type * and then click cell **D4**. Press Enter. Click cell **E4**, point to the fill handle in the lower right corner of the cell, and then drag down to cell **C9**.

10 Select the range **E4:E9**. On the toolbar, click **Functions** Σ ▾, click **SUM**, and then press Enter to total the column and place the result in cell **E10**.

11 Select the range **D4:E4**, hold down Ctrl, and then select cell **D10**. On the menu bar, click **Format**, point to **Number**, and then click **Currency**.

12 Select cell **A10**, hold down Ctrl, and then select cell **E10**. Apply **Bold** B.

13 Click cell **A1**, hold down Ctrl, and then click cell **A2**, cell **A10**, and cell **E10**. With the four cells selected, on the toolbar, click **Fill color** ◆ ▾, and then in the fourth column, click the third color—**light yellow 3**.

14 At the top of the worksheet, click the text *Untitled spreadsheet*, and then using your own name, type **Lastname_Firstname_Ex_1B_Web** and press Enter.

»»» **GO!** With Google continues on next page

»» GO! With Google Sheets

15 If you are instructed to submit your file to your instructor, you can either share the file through Google Drive, or create a PDF or Excel file. Ask your instructor in what format he or she would like to receive your file.

16 **Close** ▦ the browser tab—a new Google Sheet always opens in a new window in your browser; your work is automatically saved. Notice that your new Google Sheet displays in the file list on your Google Drive. Sign out of your Google account.

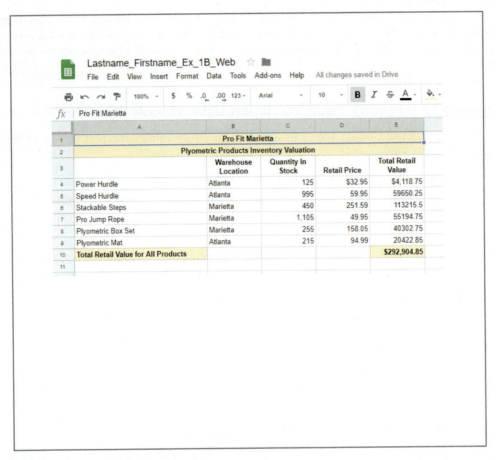

Figure 1A

wavebreakmedia/Shutterstock, Monkey Business Images/Fotolia, Ivanko80/Shutterstock, Monkey Business Images/Shutterstock

Microsoft Office Specialist (MOS) Skills in This Chapter

Project 1A	Project 1B
1.2.2 Navigate to named cells, ranges, or workbook elements	**2.2.2** Modify cell alignment, orientation, and indentation
1.3.1 Modify page setup	**2.2.4** Wrap text within cells
1.3.2 Adjust row height and column width	**2.2.5** Apply number format
1.3.3 Customize headers and footers	**2.2.7** Apply cell styles
1.4.5 Modify basic workbook properties	**4.1.1** Insert relative, absolute, and mixed references
1.4.6 Display formulas	
1.5.1 Set a print area	
1.5.3 Configure print settings	
2.1.2 Fill cells by using Auto Fill	
2.2.1 Merge and unmerge cells	
2.2.5 Apply number format	
2.2.7 Apply cell styles	
2.4.1 Insert Sparklines	
4.1.1 Insert relative, absolute, and mixed references	
4.2.1 Perform calculations by using the SUM function	
5.1.1 Create charts	
5.2.2 Switch between rows and columns in source data	
5.2.3 Add and modify chart elements	
5.3.1 Apply chart layouts	

Build Your E-Portfolio

An E-Portfolio is a collection of evidence, stored electronically, that showcases what you have accomplished while completing your education. Collecting and then sharing your work products with potential employers reflects your academic and career goals. Your completed documents from the following projects are good examples to show what you have learned: 1G, 1K, and 1L.

GO! for Job Success

Video: How to Succeed in an Interview

Your instructor may assign this video to your class, and then ask you to think about, or discuss with your classmates, these questions:

g-stockstudio/ Shutterstock

Can you think of two or three behaviors that Lee might want to change before he interviews with another company?

If you were going on an interview, which of Connie's behaviors would you imitate?

If you were the interviewer, Maria, would you have handled anything differently with either candidate?

End of Chapter

Summary

In Excel, you work with worksheets that are contained in a workbook. A worksheet is formatted as a pattern of uniformly spaced horizontal rows and vertical columns, the intersection of which forms a cell.

A cell can contain a constant value—referred to as a value—or a formula, which is an equation that performs mathematical calculations on the values in your worksheet. Common values are text and numbers.

Charts provide a graphic representation of data in a worksheet. Use the Recommended Charts feature to display customized charts that, according to Excel's calculations, will best represent your data.

You can insert sparklines in an Excel worksheet, which are tiny charts embedded in a cell that give a visual trend summary alongside your data. A sparkline makes a pattern more obvious to the eye.

GO! Learn It Online

Review the concepts, key terms, and MOS skills in this chapter by completing these online challenges, which you can find at **MyLab IT**.

Chapter Quiz: Answer matching and multiple choice questions to test what you learned in this chapter.

Lessons on the GO!: Learn how to use all the new apps and features as they are introduced by Microsoft.

MOS Prep Quiz: Answer questions to review the MOS skills that you practiced in this chapter.

GO! Collaborative Team Project (Available in Instructor Resource Center)

If your instructor assigns this project to your class, you can expect to work with one or more of your classmates—either in person or by using internet tools—to create work products similar to those that you created in this chapter. A team is a group of workers who work together to solve a problem, make a decision, or create a work product. Collaboration is when you work together with others as a team in an intellectual endeavor to complete a shared task or achieve a shared goal.

Monkey Business Images/ Fotolia

Project Guide for Excel Chapter 1

Your instructor will assign Projects from this list to ensure your learning and assess your knowledge.

Project	Apply Skills from These Chapter Objectives	Project Type		Project Location
1A **MyLab IT**	Objectives 1-6 from Project 1A	**1A Instructional Project (Grader Project)** Guided instruction to learn the skills in Project 1A.	**Instruction**	In **MyLab IT** and in text
1B **MyLab IT**	Objectives 7–11 from Project 1B	**1B Instructional Project (Grader Project)** Guided instruction to learn the skills in Project 1B.	**Instruction**	In **MyLab IT** and in text
1C	Objectives 1–6 from Project 1A	**1C Skills Review (Scorecard Grading)** A guided review of the skills from Project 1A.	**Review**	In text
1D	Objectives 7–11 from Project 1B	**1D Skills Review (Scorecard Grading)** A guided review of the skills from Project 1B.	**Review**	In text
1E **MyLab IT**	Objectives 1–6 from Project 1A	**1E Mastery (Grader Project)** A demonstration of your mastery of the skills in Project 1A with extensive decision-making.	**Mastery and Transfer of Learning**	In **MyLab IT** and in text
1F **MyLab IT**	Objectives 7–11 from Project 1B	**1F Mastery (Grader Project)** A demonstration of your mastery of the skills in Project 1B with extensive decision-making.	**Mastery and Transfer of Learning**	In **MyLab IT** and in text
1G **MyLab IT**	Objectives 1–11 from Projects 1A and 1B	**1G Mastery (Grader Project)** A demonstration of your mastery of the skills in Projects 1A and 1B with extensive decision-making.	**Mastery and Transfer of Learning**	In **MyLab IT** and in text
1H	Combination of Objectives from Projects 1A and 1B	**1H GO! Fix It (Scorecard Grading)** A demonstration of your mastery of the skills in Projects 1A and 1B by creating a correct result from a document that contains errors you must find.	**Critical Thinking**	IRC
1I	Combination of Objectives from Projects 1A and 1B	**1I GO! Make It (Scorecard Grading)** A demonstration of your mastery of the skills in Projects 1A and 1B by creating a result from a supplied picture.	**Critical Thinking**	IRC
1J	Combination of Objectives from Projects 1A and 1B	**1J GO! Solve It (Rubric Grading)** A demonstration of your mastery of the skills in Projects 1A and 1B, your decision-making skills, and your critical thinking skills. A task-specific rubric helps you self-assess your result.	**Critical Thinking**	IRC
1K	Combination of Objectives from Projects 1A and 1B	**1K GO! Solve It (Rubric Grading)** A demonstration of your mastery of the skills in Projects 1A and 1B, your decision-making skills, and your critical thinking skills. A task-specific rubric helps you self-assess your result.	**Critical Thinking**	In text
1L	Combination of Objectives from Projects 1A and 1B	**1L GO! Think (Rubric Grading)** A demonstration of your understanding of the Chapter concepts applied in a manner that you would outside of college. An analytic rubric helps you and your instructor grade the quality of your work by comparing it to the work an expert in the discipline would create.	**Critical Thinking**	In text
1M	Combination of Objectives from Projects 1A and 1B	**1M GO! Think (Rubric Grading)** A demonstration of your understanding of the Chapter concepts applied in a manner that you would outside of college. An analytic rubric helps you and your instructor grade the quality of your work by comparing it to the work an expert in the discipline would create.	**Critical Thinking**	IRC
1N	Combination of Objectives from Projects 1A and 1B	**1N You and GO! (Rubric Grading)** A demonstration of your understanding of the Chapter concepts applied in a manner that you would in a personal situation. An analytic rubric helps you and your instructor grade the quality of your work.	**Critical Thinking**	IRC
1O	Combination of Objectives from Projects 1A and 1B	**1O Cumulative Group Project for Excel Chapter 1** A demonstration of your understanding of concepts and your ability to work collaboratively in a group role-playing assessment, requiring both collaboration and self-management.		IRC

Glossary

Glossary of Chapter Key Terms

Absolute cell reference A cell reference that refers to cells by their fixed position in a worksheet; an absolute cell reference remains the same when the formula is copied.

Accounting Number Format The Excel number format that applies a thousand comma separator where appropriate, inserts a fixed U.S. dollar sign aligned at the left edge of the cell, applies two decimal places, and leaves a small amount of space at the right edge of the cell to accommodate a parenthesis for negative numbers.

Active cell The cell, surrounded by a black border, ready to receive data or be affected by the next Excel command.

Arithmetic operators The symbols +, -, *, /, %, and ^ used to denote addition, subtraction (or negation), multiplication, division, percentage, and exponentiation in an Excel formula.

Auto Fill An Excel feature that generates and extends values into adjacent cells based on the values of selected cells.

AutoCalculate A feature that displays three calculations in the status bar by default—Average, Count, and Sum—when you select a range of numerical data.

AutoComplete A feature that speeds your typing and lessens the likelihood of errors; if the first few characters you type in a cell match an existing entry in the column, Excel fills in the remaining characters for you.

AutoFit An Excel feature that adjusts the width of a column to fit the cell content of the widest cell in the column.

AutoSum A button that provides quick access to the SUM function.

Category axis The area along the bottom of a chart that identifies the categories of data; also referred to as the x-axis.

Category labels The labels that display along the bottom of a chart to identify the categories of data; Excel uses the row titles as the category names.

Cell The intersection of a column and a row.

Cell address Another name for a cell reference.

Cell content Anything typed into a cell.

Cell reference The identification of a specific cell by its intersecting column letter and row number.

Cell style A defined set of formatting characteristics, such as font, font size, font color, cell borders, and cell shading.

Chart The graphic representation of data in a worksheet; data presented as a chart is usually easier to understand than a table of numbers.

Chart Elements button A button that enables you to add, remove, or change chart elements such as the title, legend, gridlines, and data labels.

Chart Filters button A button that enables you to change which data displays in the chart.

Chart layout The combination of chart elements that can be displayed in a chart such as a title, legend, labels for the columns, and the table of charted cells.

Chart style The overall visual look of a chart in terms of its graphic effects, colors, and backgrounds; for example, you can have flat or beveled columns, colors that are solid or transparent, and backgrounds that are dark or light.

Chart Styles button A button that enables you to set a style and color scheme for your chart.

Chart Styles gallery A group of predesigned chart styles that you can apply to an Excel chart.

Chart types Various chart formats used in a way that is meaningful to the reader; common examples are column charts, pie charts, and line charts.

Column A vertical group of cells in a worksheet.

Column chart A chart in which the data is arranged in columns and that is useful for showing data changes over a period of time or for illustrating comparisons among items.

Column heading The letter that displays at the top of a vertical group of cells in a worksheet; beginning with the first letter of the alphabet, a unique letter or combination of letters identifies each column.

Comma Style The Excel number format that inserts thousand comma separators where appropriate and applies two decimal places; Comma Style also leaves space at the right to accommodate a parenthesis when negative numbers are present.

Constant value Numbers, text, dates, or times of day that you type into a cell.

Context sensitive A command associated with the currently selected or active object; often activated by right-clicking a screen item.

Data Text or numbers in a cell.

Data marker A column, bar, area, dot, pie slice, or other symbol in a chart that represents a single data point; related data points form a data series.

Data point A value that originates in a worksheet cell and that is represented in a chart by a data marker.

Data series Related data points represented by data markers; each data series has a unique color or pattern represented in the chart legend.

Displayed value The data that displays in a cell.

Excel pointer An Excel window element with which you can display the location of the pointer.

Expand Formula Bar button An Excel window element with which you can increase the height of the Formula Bar to display lengthy cell content.

Expand horizontal scroll bar button An Excel window element with which you can increase the width of the horizontal scroll bar.

Fill handle The small square in the lower right corner of a selected cell.

Format Changing the appearance of cells and worksheet elements to make a worksheet attractive and easy to read.

Formula An equation that performs mathematical calculations on values in a worksheet.

Formula Bar An element in the Excel window that displays the value or formula contained in the active cell; here you can also enter or edit values or formulas.

Function A predefined formula—a formula that Excel has already built for you—that performs calculations by using specific values in a particular order.

General format The default format that Excel applies to numbers; this format has no specific characteristics—whatever you type in the cell will display, with the exception that trailing zeros to the right of a decimal point will not display.

Label Another name for a text value, and which usually provides information about number values.

Glossary

Left alignment The cell format in which characters align at the left edge of the cell; this is the default for text entries and is an example of formatting information stored in a cell.

Legend A chart element that identifies the patterns or colors that are assigned to the categories in the chart.

Lettered column headings The area along the top edge of a worksheet that identifies each column with a unique letter or combination of letters.

Merge & Center A command that joins selected cells in an Excel worksheet into one larger cell and centers the contents in the merged cell.

Middle Align An alignment command that centers text between the top and bottom of a cell.

Name Box An element of the Excel window that displays the name of the selected cell, table, chart, or object.

Normal view A screen view that maximizes the number of cells visible on your screen and keeps the column letters and row numbers close to the columns and rows.

Number format A specific way in which Excel displays numbers in a cell.

Number values Constant values consisting of only numbers.

Numbered row headings The area along the left edge of a worksheet that identifies each row with a unique number.

Operators The symbols with which you can specify the type of calculation you want to perform in an Excel formula.

Picture element A point of light measured in dots per square inch on a screen; 64 pixels equals 8.43 characters, which is the average number of characters that will fit in a cell in an Excel worksheet using the default font.

Pixel The abbreviated name for a picture element.

Point and click method The technique of constructing a formula by pointing to and then clicking cells; this method is convenient when the referenced cells are not adjacent to one another.

Quick Analysis Tool A tool that displays in the lower right corner of a selected range, with which you can analyze your data by using Excel tools such as charts, color-coding, and formulas.

Range Two or more selected cells on a worksheet that are adjacent or nonadjacent; because the range is treated as a single unit, you can make the same changes or combination of changes to more than one cell at a time.

Range finder An Excel feature that outlines cells in color to indicate which cells are used in a formula; useful for verifying which cells are referenced in a formula.

Recommended Charts An Excel feature that displays a customized set of charts that, according to Excel's calculations, will best fit your data based on the range of data that you select.

Relative cell reference In a formula, the address of a cell based on the relative positions of the cell that contains the formula and the cell referred to in the formula.

Rounding A procedure in which you determine which digit at the right of the number will be the last digit displayed and then increase it by one if the next digit to its right is 5, 6, 7, 8, or 9.

Row A horizontal group of cells in a worksheet.

Row heading The numbers along the left side of an Excel worksheet that designate the row numbers.

Scaling The process of shrinking the width and/or height of printed output to fit a maximum number of pages.

Select All box A box in the upper left corner of the worksheet grid that, when clicked, selects all the cells in a worksheet.

Series A group of things that come one after another in succession; for example, January, February, March, and so on.

Sheet tab scrolling buttons Buttons to the left of the sheet tabs used to display Excel sheet tabs that are not in view; used when there are more sheet tabs than will display in the space provided.

Sheet tabs The labels along the lower border of the Excel window that identify each worksheet.

Show Formulas A command that displays the formula in each cell instead of the resulting value.

Sparkline A tiny chart in the background of a cell that gives a visual trend summary alongside your data; makes a pattern more obvious.

Spreadsheet Another name for a worksheet.

Status bar The area along the lower edge of the Excel window that displays, on the left side, the current cell mode, page number, and worksheet information; on the right side, when numerical data is selected, common calculations such as Sum and Average display.

SUM function A predefined formula that adds all the numbers in a selected range of cells.

Switch Row/Column A charting command to swap the data over the axis—data being charted on the vertical axis will move to the horizontal axis and vice versa.

Text values Constant values consisting of only text, and which usually provide information about number values; also referred to as labels.

Theme A predefined set of colors, fonts, lines, and fill effects that coordinate with each other.

Underlying formula The formula entered in a cell and visible only on the Formula Bar.

Underlying value The data that displays in the Formula Bar.

Value Another name for a constant value.

Value axis A numerical scale on the left side of a chart that shows the range of numbers for the data points; also referred to as the y-axis.

Workbook An Excel file that contains one or more worksheets.

Worksheet The primary document that you use in Excel to work with and store data, and which is formatted as a pattern of uniformly spaced horizontal and vertical lines.

Worksheet grid area A part of the Excel window that displays the columns and rows that intersect to form the worksheet's cells.

X-axis Another name for the horizontal (category) axis.

Y-axis Another name for the vertical (value) axis.

Chapter Review

Project 1C Step Sales

Apply 1A skills from these Objectives:

1. Create, Save, and Navigate an Excel Workbook
2. Enter Data in a Worksheet
3. Construct and Copy Formulas and Use the SUM Function
4. Format Cells with Merge & Center, Cell Styles, and Themes
5. Chart Data to Create a Column Chart and Insert Sparklines
6. Print a Worksheet, Display Formulas, and Close Excel

In the following Skills Review, you will create a new Excel worksheet with a chart that summarizes the first quarter sales of fitness equipment for step training. Your completed worksheet will look similar to Figure 1.56.

Project Files

For Project 1C, you will need the following file:

New blank Excel workbook

You will save your workbook as:

Lastname_Firstname_1C_Step_Sales

Project Results

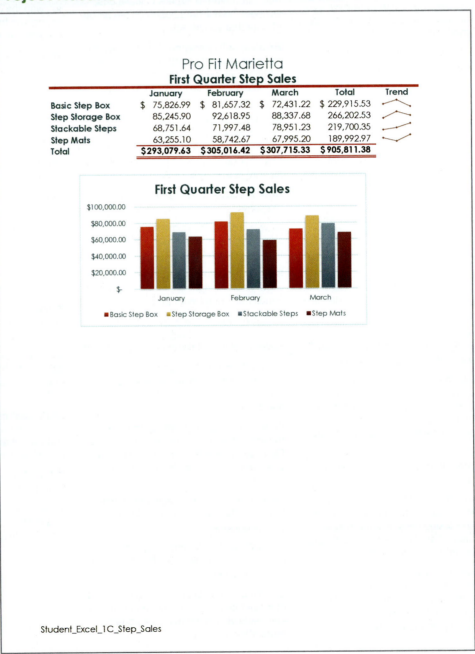

Student_Excel_1C_Step_Sales

Figure 1.56

Chapter Review

1 ▶ Start Excel and open a new blank workbook. Click the **File tab** to display **Backstage** view, click **Save As**, and then navigate to your **Excel Chapter 1** folder. In the **File name** box, using your own name, type **Lastname_Firstname_1C_Step_Sales** and press ⏎.

   a. With cell **A1** as the active cell, type the worksheet title **Pro Fit Marietta** and then press ⏎. In cell **A2**, type the worksheet subtitle **First Quarter Step Sales** and then press ⏎.

   b. Click in cell **A4**, type **Basic Step Box** and then press ⏎. In cell **A5**, type **Step Storage Box** and then press ⏎. In cell **A6**, type **Stackable Steps** and then press ⏎. In cell **A7**, type **Step Mats** and then press ⏎. In cell **A8**, type **Total** and then press ⏎.

   c. Click cell **B3**. Type **January** and then in the **Formula Bar**, click **Enter** to keep cell **B3** the active cell. With **B3** as the active cell, point to the fill handle in the lower right corner of the selected cell, drag to the right to cell **D3**, and then release the mouse button to enter the text *February* and *March*.

   d. Press Ctrl + Home to make cell **A1** the active cell. In the **column heading area**, point to the vertical line between **column A** and **column B** to display the ╬ pointer, hold down the left mouse button, and drag to the right to increase the width of **column A** to **130 pixels**.

   e. Point to cell **B3**, and then drag across to select cells **B3** and **C3** and **D3**. With the range **B3:D3** selected, on the **Home tab**, in the **Alignment group**, click **Center**.

   f. Click cell **B4**, type **75826.99** and press Tab to make cell **C4** active. Enter the remaining values, as shown in **Table 1** below, pressing Tab to move across the rows and pressing ⏎ to move down the columns.

2 ▶ Click cell **B8** to make it the active cell and type **=**

   a. At the insertion point, type **b4** and then type **+** Type **b5** and then type **+b6+b7** Press ⏎. Your result is *293079.6*.

   b. Click in cell **C8**. Type **=** and then click cell **C4**. Type **+** and then click cell **C5**. Repeat this process to complete the formula to add cells **C6** and **C7** to the formula, and then press ⏎. Your result is *305016.4*.

   c. Click cell **D8**. On the **Home tab**, in the **Editing group**, click **AutoSum**, and then press ⏎ to construct a formula by using the SUM function. Your result is *307715.3*.

   d. In cell **E3** type **Total** and press ⏎. With cell **E4** as the active cell, on the **Home tab**, in the **Editing group**, click **AutoSum**. On the **Formula Bar**, click **Enter** to display the result and keep cell **E4** active.

   e. With cell **E4** active, point to the fill handle in the lower right corner of the cell. Drag down through cell **E8**, and then release the mouse button to copy the formula with relative cell references down to sum each row.

3 ▶ Click cell **F3**. Type **Trend** and then press ⏎.

   a. Select the range **A1:F1**, and then on the **Home tab**, in the **Alignment group**, click **Merge & Center**. Select the range **A2:F2** and **Merge & Center** the selection.

   b. Click cell **A1**. In the **Styles group**, click **Cell Styles**. Under **Titles and Headings**, click **Title**. Click cell **A2**, display the **Cell Styles** gallery, and then click **Heading 1**.

   c. Select the range **B3:F3**, hold down Ctrl, and then select the range **A4:A8**. From the **Cell Styles** gallery, click **Heading 4** to apply this cell style to the column and row titles.

   d. Select the range **B4:E4**, hold down Ctrl, and then select the range **B8:E8**. On the **Home tab**, in the **Number group**, click **Accounting Number Format**. Select the range **B5:E7**, and then in the **Number group**, click **Comma Style**. Select the range **B8:E8**. From the **Styles group**, display the **Cell Styles** gallery, and then under **Titles and Headings**, click **Total**.

Table 1			
	January	February	March
Basic Step Box	75826.99	81657.32	72431.22
Step Storage Box	85245.90	92618.95	88337.68
Stackable Steps	68751.64	71997.48	78951.23
Step Mats	63255.10	58742.67	67995.20

Chapter Review

e. On the ribbon, click the **Page Layout tab**, and then in the **Themes group**, click **Themes** to display the **Themes** gallery. Click the **Ion** theme. (This theme widens the columns slightly.) On the Quick Access Toolbar, click **Save**.

4 ▶ Select the range **A3:D7**, which includes the row titles, the column titles and the data without the totals. Click the **Insert tab**, and then in the **Charts group**, click **Recommended Charts**. In the **Insert Chart** dialog box, scroll down and click the **Clustered Column** chart in which *each month* displays its *sales for each type of step training equipment*. Click **OK**.

a. In the chart, click anywhere in the text *Chart Title* to select the text box. Watch the **Formula Bar** as you type **First** and then let AutoComplete complete the title by pressing Enter.

b. Click in a white area just slightly *inside* the chart border to deselect the chart title but keep the chart selected. To the right of the chart, click the second button—the **Chart Styles** button.

Be sure the **Style tab** is active. Use the scroll bar to scroll down, and then by using the ScreenTips, locate and click **Style 6**.

c. At the top of the gallery, click **Color**. Under **Colorful**, click the second row of colors to apply this variation of the theme colors.

d. Point to the top border of the chart to display the pointer, and then drag the upper left corner of the chart just to the center of cell **A10** to visually center it below the data.

5 ▶ Click an empty cell to deselect the chart, and then select the range **B4:D7**. Click the **Insert tab**, and then in the **Sparklines group**, click **Line**. In the **Create Sparklines** dialog box, in the **Location Range** box, type **f4:f7** and then click **OK** to insert the sparklines.

a. On the **Design tab**, in the **Show group**, select the **Markers** check box to display markers in the sparklines.

b. On the **Design tab**, in the **Style group**, click **More** and then in the first row, click the second style.

6 ▶ Click cell **A1** to deselect the chart. Click the **Page Layout tab**, and then in the **Page Setup group**, click **Margins**. Click **Custom Margins**. In the **Page Setup** dialog box, on the **Margins tab**, under **Center on page**, select the **Horizontally** check box.

a. Click the **Header/Footer tab**, and then click **Custom Footer**. With your insertion point in the **Left section**, click **Insert File Name**. Click **OK** two times.

b. Click the **File tab** to display **Backstage** view; if necessary, on the left, click the **Info tab**. In the lower right corner, click **Show All Properties**. As the **Tags**, type **step sales, 1st quarter** In the **Subject** box, type your course name and section number. Be sure your name displays as the author—edit if necessary.

c. On the left, click **Save**.

d. Print or submit your workbook electronically as directed by your instructor. If required by your instructor, print or create an electronic version of your worksheet with formulas displayed by using the instructions at the end of Project 1A. **Close** Excel without saving so that you do not save the changes you made to print formulas. (Mac users: if necessary to fit on one page, on the Page Layout tab, in the Scale to Fit group, set the Width and Height to 1 page.)

You have completed Project 1C **END**

Chapter Review

Skills Review | **Project 1D Band and Tubing Inventory**

Apply **1B** skills from these Objectives:

7. Check Spelling in a Worksheet
8. Enter Data by Range
9. Construct Formulas for Mathematical Operations
10. Edit Values in a Worksheet
11. Format a Worksheet

In the following Skills Review, you will create a worksheet that summarizes the inventory of band and tubing exercise equipment. Your completed worksheet will look similar to Figure 1.57.

Project Files

For Project 1D, you will need the following file:

New blank Excel workbook

You will save your workbook as:

Lastname_Firstname_1D_Band_Inventory

Project Results

Pro Fit Marietta
Band and Tubing Inventory
As of June 30

	Material	Quantity in Stock	Retail Price	Total Retail Value	Percent of Total Retail Value
Super Strength Bands	Latex	225	$ 48.98	$ 11,020.50	25.16%
Medium Tubing	Rubber	198	27.95	5,534.10	12.64%
Resistance Band, Average	Latex	165	42.95	7,086.75	16.18%
Mini Bands, Medium	Latex	245	25.95	6,357.75	14.52%
Mini Bands, Heavy	Rubber	175	32.95	5,766.25	13.17%
Heavy Tubing	Latex	187	42.95	8,031.65	18.34%
Total Retail Value for All Products				$ 43,797.00	

Student_Excel_1D_Band_Inventory

Figure 1.57

Chapter Review

1 Start Excel and display a new blank workbook. **Save** the workbook in your **Excel Chapter 1** folder as **Lastname_Firstname_1D_Band_Inventory** In cell **A1**, type **Pro Fit Marietta** and in cell **A2**, type **Band and Tubing Inventory**

a. Click cell **B3**, type **Quantity in Stock** and press Tab. In cell **C3**, type **Average Cost** and press Tab. In cell **D3**, type **Retail Price** and press Tab. In cell **E3**, type **Total Retail Value** and press Tab. In cell **F3**, type **Percent of Total Retail Value** and press Enter.

b. Click cell **A4**, type **Super Strength Bands** and press Enter. In the range **A5:A10**, type the remaining row titles as shown below, including any misspelled words.

   Medium Tubing
   Resistnce Band, Average
   Mini Bands, Medium
   Mini Bands, Heavy
   Heavy Tubing
   Total Retail Value for All Products

c. Press Ctrl + Home to move to the top of your worksheet. On the **Review tab**, in the **Proofing group**, click **Spelling**. Correct *Resistnce* to **Resistance** and any other spelling errors you may have made, and then when the message displays, *Spell check complete. You're good to go!* click **OK**.

d. In the **column heading area**, point to the right boundary of **column A** to display the ✛ pointer, and then drag to the right to widen **column A** to **225** pixels.

e. In the **column heading area**, point to the **column B** heading to display the ⬇ pointer, and then drag to the right to select **columns B:F**. With the columns selected, in the **column heading area**, point to the right boundary of any of the selected columns, and then drag to the right to set the width to **100 pixels**.

f. Select the range **A1:F1**. On the **Home tab**, in the **Alignment group**, click **Merge & Center**, and then from the **Cell Styles** gallery, apply the **Title** style. Select the range **A2:F2**. **Merge & Center** the text across the selection, and then from the **Cell Styles** gallery, apply the **Heading 1** style.

2 On the **Page Layout tab**, in the **Themes group**, change the **Colors** to **Blue Green**. Select the empty range **B4:D9**. With cell **B4** active in the range, type **225** and then press Enter.

a. With cell **B5** active in the range, and pressing Enter after each entry, type the following data in the *Quantity in Stock* column:

   198
   265
   245
   175
   187

b. With the selected range still active, from the following table, beginning in cell **C4** and pressing Enter after each entry, enter the following data for the **Average Cost** column and then the **Retail Price** column. If you prefer, type without selecting the range first; recall that this is optional.

Average Cost	Retail Price
22.75	48.98
15.95	27.95
26.90	42.95
12.95	25.95
18.75	32.95
26.90	42.95

3 In cell **E4**, type **=b4*d4** and then press Enter to construct a formula that calculates the *Total Retail Value* of the *Super Strength Bands* (Quantity in Stock X Retail Price).

a. Click cell **E4**, position your pointer over the fill handle, and then drag down through cell **E9** to copy the formula with relative cell references.

b. Select the range **B4:B9**, and then on the **Home tab**, in the **Number group**, click **Comma Style**. Then, in the **Number group**, click **Decrease Decimal** two times to remove the decimal places from these non-currency values.

Chapter Review

c. To calculate the *Total Retail Value for All Products*, select the range **E4:E9**, and then in the lower right corner of the selected range, click the **Quick Analysis** button.

d. In the gallery, click **Totals**, and then click the *first* **Sum** button, which visually indicates that the column will be summed with a result at the bottom of the column.

e. Select the range **C5:E9** and apply the **Comma Style**. Select the range **C4:E4**, hold down Ctrl, and then click cell **E10**. With the nonadjacent cells selected, apply the **Accounting Number Format**. Click cell **E10**, and then from the **Cell Styles** gallery, apply the **Total** style.

f. Click cell **F4**, type **=** and then click cell **E4**. Type **/** and then click cell **E10**. Press F4 to make the reference to cell *E10* absolute, and then on the **Formula Bar**, click **Enter** so that cell **F4** remains the active cell. (Mac users: press command ⌘ + T.)

g. Drag the fill handle to copy the formula down through cell **F9**. Point to cell **B6**, and then double-click to place the insertion point within the cell. Use the arrow keys to move the insertion point to the left or right of *2*, and use either Del or Backspace to delete *2*, and then type **1** and press Enter so that the new *Quantity in Stock* is *165*. Notice the recalculations in the worksheet.

4 Select the range **F4:F9**, and then in the **Number group**, click **Percent Style**. Click **Increase Decimal** two times, and then **Center** the selection.

a. In the **row heading area** on the left side of your screen, point to **row 3** to display the ➡ pointer, and then right-click to simultaneously select the row and display a shortcut menu. On the shortcut menu, click **Insert** to insert a new **row 3**.

b. Click cell **A3**, type **As of June 30** and then on the **Formula Bar**, click **Enter** to keep cell **A3** as the active cell. **Merge & Center** the text across the range **A3:F3**, and then apply the **Heading 2** cell style.

5 In the **column heading area**, point to **column B**. When the ⬇ pointer displays, right-click, and then click **Insert** to insert a new column.

a. Click cell **B4**, type **Material** and then press Enter. In cell **B5**, type **Latex** and then press Enter. In cell **B6**, type **Rubber** and then press Enter.

b. Using AutoComplete to speed your typing by pressing Enter as soon as the AutoComplete suggestion displays, in cells **B7**, **B8**, and **B10**, type **Latex** and in cell **B9**, type **Rubber**

c. In the **column heading area**, point to the right boundary of **column B**, and then drag to the left and set the width to **90 pixels**. In the **column heading area**, point to **column D**, right-click, and then click **Delete**.

d. Select the column titles in the range **B4:F4**, and then on the **Home tab**, in the **Alignment group**, click **Wrap Text**, **Center**, and **Middle Align**. With the range still selected, apply the **Heading 4** cell style.

e. Click cell **A11**, and then from the **Cell Styles** gallery, under **Themed Cell Styles**, click **40% - Accent1**.

6 Click the **Page Layout tab**, and then in the **Page Setup group**, click **Margins**. Click **Custom Margins**. In the **Page Setup** dialog box, on the **Margins tab**, under **Center on page**, select the **Horizontally** check box.

a. Click the **Header/Footer tab**, and then click **Custom Footer**. With your insertion point in the **Left section**, click **Insert File Name**. Click **OK** two times.

b. In the **Page Setup group**, click **Orientation**, and then click **Landscape**.

c. Click the **File tab** to display **Backstage** view; if necessary, on the left click the **Info tab**. In the lower right corner, click **Show All Properties**. As the **Tags**, type **bands, tubing, inventory** In the **Subject** box, type your course name and section number. Be sure your name displays as the author—edit if necessary.

d. On the left, click **Save** to be sure that you have saved your work up to this point.

e. Print or submit your workbook electronically as directed by your instructor. (Mac users: if necessary to fit on one page, on the Page Layout tab, in the Scale to Fit group, set the Width and Height to 1 page.)

f. If required by your instructor, print or create an electronic version of your worksheet with formulas displayed by using the instructions at the end of Project 1A. **Close** Excel without saving so that you do not save the changes you made to print formulas.

You have completed Project 1D | **END**

Content-Based Assessments (Mastery and Transfer of Learning)

Apply 1A skills from these Objectives:

1. Create, Save, and Navigate an Excel Workbook
2. Enter Data in a Worksheet
3. Construct and Copy Formulas and Use the SUM Function
4. Format Cells with Merge & Center, Cell Styles, and Themes
5. Chart Data to Create a Column Chart and Insert Sparklines
6. Print a Worksheet, Display Formulas, and Close Excel

In the following Mastering Excel project, you will create a worksheet comparing the sales of different types of home gym equipment sold in the second quarter. Your completed worksheet will look similar to Figure 1.58.

Project Files for MyLab IT Grader

1. In your **MyLab IT** course, locate and click **Excel 1E Gym Sales**, Download Materials, and then Download All Files.
2. Extract the zipped folder to your Excel Chapter 1 folder. Close the Grader download screens.
3. Take a moment to open the downloaded **Excel_1E_Gym_Sales_Instructions**; note any recent updates to the book.

Project Results

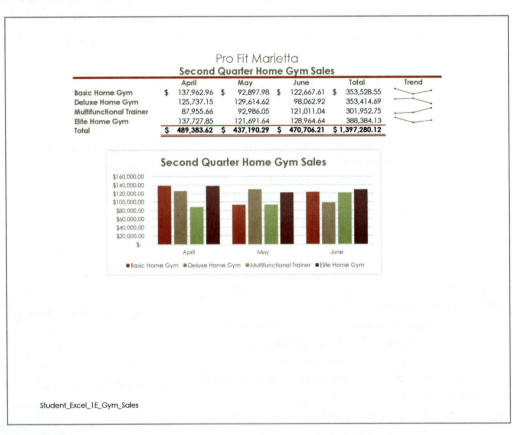

Figure 1.58

For Non-MyLab Submissions

For Project 1E, you will need: In your Excel Chapter 1 folder, save your workbook as:
e01E_Gym_Sales   **Lastname_Firstname_1E_Gym_Sales**

If your instructor requires a workbook with formulas, save as:
Lastname_Firstname_1E_Gym_Sales_formulas

After you have named and saved your workbook, on the next page, begin with Step 2.
After Step 16, submit your file as directed by your instructor.

Mastering Excel: Project 1E Gym Sales (continued)

1 Navigate to your **Excel Chapter 1 folder**, and then double-click the Excel file you downloaded from **MyLab IT** that displays your name—**Student_1E_Gym_Sales**. If necessary, at the top, click **Enable Editing**.

2 Change the workbook theme to **Wisp**. If the Wisp theme is not available on your computer, in the Themes gallery, click Browse for Themes, and then select the theme from your downloaded student files.

3 In cell **B3**, use the fill handle to fill the months *May* and *June* in the range **C3:D3**.

4 **Merge & Center** the title across the range **A1:F1**, and then apply the **Title** cell style. **Merge & Center** the subtitle across the range **A2:F2**, and then apply the **Heading 1** cell style. **Center** the column titles in the range **B3:F3**.

5 Widen **column A** to **180 pixels**, and then widen columns **B:F** to **115 pixels**. (Mac users: set column A to a width of 21.83 or 136 pixels and columns B:F to a width of 13.83 or 88 pixels.) In the range **B7:D7**, enter the monthly sales figures for the Elite Home Gym for April, May, and June as shown in the table below:

	April	May	June
Elite Home Gym	137727.85	121691.64	128964.64

6 In cell **B8**, on the **Home tab**, use the **AutoSum** button to sum the April sales. Copy the resulting formula across to cells **C8:D8** to sum the May monthly sales and the June monthly sales. In cell **E4**, use the **AutoSum** button to sum the *Basic Home Gym* sales. Copy the formula down to cells **E5:E8**.

7 Apply the **Heading 4** cell style to the row titles and the column titles. Apply the **Total** cell style to the totals in the range **B8:E8**.

8 Apply the **Accounting Number Format** to the first row of sales figures and to the total row. Apply the **Comma Style** to the remaining sales figures.

9 To compare the monthly sales of each product visually, select the range that represents the sales figures for the three months, including the month names and the product names—do not include any totals in the range. With this data selected, use the **Recommended Charts** command to insert a **Clustered Column** chart with the month names displayed on the category axis and the product names displayed in the legend.

10 Move the chart so that its upper left corner is positioned in the center of cell **A10**. Then drag the center right sizing handle to the right until the right edge of the chart aligns with the right edge of **column E**; this will display the legend on one row and, after you add the sparklines, center the chart below the data.

11 Apply **Chart Style 6** and change the colors by applying the second row of colors under **Colorful**. Change the **Chart Title** to **Second Quarter Home Gym Sales**

12 In the range **F4:F7**, insert **Line** sparklines that compare the monthly data. Do not include the totals. Show the sparkline **Markers**. Display the sparkline **Style** gallery, and then in the first row, apply the second style.

13 Center the worksheet **Horizontally** on the page, and then insert a **Footer** with the **File Name** in the **left section**.

14 Change the **Orientation** to **Landscape**. Display the document properties, and then as the **Tags** type **home gym, sales** As the **Subject**, type your course name and section number. Be sure your name displays as the **Author**. Check your worksheet by previewing it in **Print Preview**, and then make any necessary corrections.

15 On the left, click **Save**.

16 In the upper right corner of your screen, click **Close** ☒ to close Excel.

17 In **MyLab IT**, locate and click the Grader Project **Excel 1E Gym Sales**. In **step 3**, under **Upload Completed Assignment**, click **Choose File**. In the **Open** dialog box, navigate to your **Excel Chapter 1 folder**, and then click your **Student_Excel_1E_Gym_Sales** file one time to select it. In the lower right corner of the **Open** dialog box, click **Open**.

The name of your selected file displays above the Upload button.

18 To submit your file to **MyLab IT** for grading, click **Upload**, wait a moment for a green **Success!** message, and then in **step 4**, click the blue **Submit for Grading** button. Click **Close Assignment** to return to your list of **Course Materials**.

You have completed Project 1E | **END**

Content-Based Assessments (Mastery and Transfer of Learning)

Mastering Excel   Project 1F Balance Sales

Apply **1B** skills from these Objectives:

7. Check Spelling in a Worksheet
8. Enter Data by Range
9. Construct Formulas for Mathematical Operations
10. Edit Values in a Worksheet
11. Format a Worksheet

In the following Mastering Excel project, you will create a worksheet that summarizes the sales of balance and stabilization equipment that Pro Fit Marietta is marketing. Your completed worksheet will look similar to Figure 1.59.

Project Files for MyLab IT Grader

1. In your **MyLab IT** course, locate and click **Excel 1F Balance Sales**, Download Materials, and then Download All Files.
2. Extract the zipped folder to your Excel Chapter 1 folder. Close the Grader download screens.
3. Take a moment to open the downloaded **Excel_1F_Balance_Sales_Instructions**; note any recent updates to the book.

Project Results

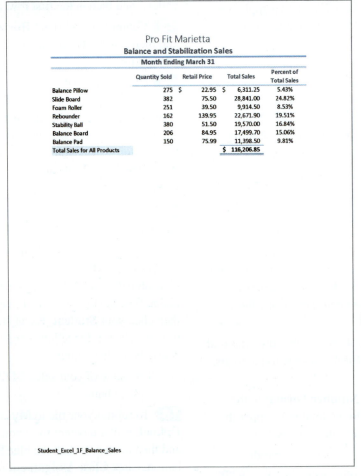

Figure 1.59

For Non-MyLab Submissions

For Project 1F, you will need:
e01F_Gym_Sales

In your Excel Chapter 1 folder, save your workbook as:
Lastname_Firstname_1F_Balance_Sales

If your instructor requires a workbook with formulas, save as:
Lastname_Firstname_1F_Balance_Sales_formulas

After you have named and saved your workbook, on the next page, begin with Step 2.

After Step 18, submit your file as directed by your instructor.

Content-Based Assessments (Mastery and Transfer of Learning)

Mastering Excel: Project 1F Balance Sales (continued)

1 Navigate to your **Excel Chapter 1 folder**, and then double-click the Excel file you downloaded from **MyLab IT** that displays your name—**Student_Excel_1F_Balance_Sales**. If necessary, at the top, click **Enable Editing**.

2 Merge & Center the title and then the subtitle across **columns A:F** and apply the **Title** and **Heading 1** cell styles respectively.

3 Make cell **A1** the active cell, and then check spelling in your worksheet. Correct *Silde* to **Slide**. Widen **column A to 180 pixels** and widen **columns B:F to 95 pixels**. (Mac users: set column A to 141 pixels and widen columns B:F to75 pixels.)

4 In cell **E4**, construct a formula to calculate the *Total Sales* of the *Balance Pillow* by multiplying the *Quantity Sold* times the *Retail Price*. Copy the formula down for the remaining products.

5 Select the range **E4:E10**, and then use the **Quick Analysis** tool to **Sum** the *Total Sales for All Products*, which will be formatted in bold. To the total in cell **E11**, apply the **Total** cell style. (Mac users: instead of the Quick Analysis tool, use the Sum button. Complete the step as specified.)

6 Using absolute cell references as necessary so that you can copy the formula, in cell **F4**, construct a formula to calculate the *Percent of Total Sales* for the first product. Copy the formula down for the remaining products.

7 To the computed percentages, apply **Percent Style** with two decimal places, and then **Center** the percentages.

8 Apply the **Comma Style** with no decimal places to the *Quantity Sold* figures. To cells **D4, E4,** and **E11** apply the **Accounting Number Format**.

9 To the range **D5:E10**, apply the **Comma Style**.

10 Change the *Retail Price* of the *Slide Board* to **75.50** and the *Quantity Sold* of the *Balance Pad* to **150**.

11 Delete **column B**.

12 Insert a new **row 3**. In cell **A3**, type **Month Ending March 31** and then **Merge & Center** the text across the range **A3:E3**. Apply the **Heading 2** cell style.

13 To cell **A12**, apply the **20%-Accent1** cell style.

14 Select the four column titles. Apply **Wrap Text, Middle Align,** and **Center** formatting, and then apply the **Heading 3** cell style.

15 Center the worksheet **Horizontally** on the page, and then insert a **Footer** with the **File Name** in the **left section**.

16 Display the document properties, and then as the **Tags**, type **balance, stability, sales** In the **Subject** box, add your course name and section number. Be sure your name displays as the Author.

17 On the left, click **Save**.

18 In the upper right corner of your screen, click **Close** ☒ to close Excel.

19 In **MyLab IT**, locate and click the Grader Project **Excel 1F Balance Sales**. In **step 3**, under **Upload Completed Assignment**, click **Choose File**. In the **Open** dialog box, navigate to your **Excel Chapter 1 folder**, and then click your **Student_Excel_1F_Balance_Sales** file one time to select it. In the lower right corner of the **Open** dialog box, click **Open**.

The name of your selected file displays above the Upload button.

20 To submit your file to **MyLab IT** for grading, click **Upload**, wait a moment for a green **Success!** message, and then in **step 4**, click the blue **Submit for Grading** button. Click **Close Assignment** to return to your list of **Course Materials**.

You have completed Project 1F | **END**

Content-Based Assessments (Mastery and Transfer of Learning)

MyLab IT Grader	Mastering Excel	Project 1G Regional Sales

Apply a combination of 1A and 1B skills:

1. Create, Save, and Navigate an Excel Workbook
2. Enter Data in a Worksheet
3. Construct and Copy Formulas and Use the SUM Function
4. Format Cells with Merge & Center, Cell Styles, and Themes
5. Chart Data to Create a Column Chart and Insert Sparklines
6. Print a Worksheet, Display Formulas, and Close Excel
7. Check Spelling in a Worksheet
8. Enter Data by Range
9. Construct Formulas for Mathematical Operations
10. Edit Values in a Worksheet
11. Format a Worksheet

In the following Mastering Excel project, you will create a new worksheet that compares annual sales by region. Your completed worksheet will look similar to Figure 1.60.

Project Files for MyLab IT Grader

1. In your **MyLab IT** course, locate and click **Excel 1G Regional Sales**, Download Materials, and then Download All Files.
2. Extract the zipped folder to your Excel Chapter 1 folder. Close the Grader download screens.
3. Take a moment to open the downloaded **Excel_1G_Regional_Sales_Instructions**; note any recent updates to the book.

Project Results

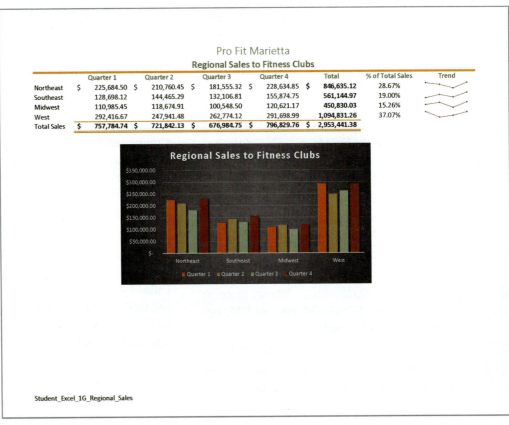

Figure 1.60

For Non-MyLab Submissions

For Project 1G, you will need:
e01G_Regional_Sales

In your Excel Chapter 1 folder, save your workbook as:
Lastname_Firstname_1G_Regional_Sales

If your instructor requires a workbook with formulas, save as:
Lastname_Firstname_1G_Regional_Sales_formulas

After you have named and saved your workbook, on the next page, begin with Step 2.
After Step 18, submit your file as directed by your instructor. (Mac users: if necessary to fit on one page, on the Page Layout tab, in the Scale to Fit group, set the width to 1 page.)

Mastering Excel: Project 1G Regional Sales (continued)

1 Navigate to your **Excel Chapter 1 folder**, and then double-click the Excel file you downloaded from **MyLab IT** that displays your name—**Student_1G_Regional_Sales**. If necessary, at the top, click **Enable Editing**.

2 Change the **Theme** to **Retrospect**. Set the width of **column A** to **80 pixels** and the width of columns **B:H** to **110 pixels**. (Mac users: Set Column A to 68 pixels and columns B:H to 95 pixels.)

3 **Merge & Center** the title across the range **A1:H1**, and then apply the **Title** cell style. **Merge & Center** the subtitle across the range **A2:H2**, and then apply the **Heading 1** cell style.

4 Select the seven column titles, apply **Center** formatting, and then apply the **Heading 4** cell style.

5 By using the **Quick Analysis** tool, **Sum** the *Quarter 1* sales, and then copy the formula across for the remaining Quarters; the Quick Analysis tool formats totals in bold. (Mac users: use AutoSum and apply bold.)

6 Select the *Northeast* sales for the four quarters, and then display the **Quick Analysis** gallery for **Totals**. Click the second **Sum** option—the sixth item in the gallery—which displays the column selection in yellow. Copy the formula down through cell **F7**; recall that the Quick Analysis tool applies bold formatting to sums. (Mac users: use AutoSum and apply bold.)

7 Apply the **Accounting Number Format** to the first row of sales figures and to the total row, and the **Comma Style** to the remaining sales figures. Format the totals in **row 7** with the **Total** cell style.

8 **Insert** a new **row 6** with the row title **Midwest** and the following sales figures for each quarter: **110985.45** and **118674.91** and **100548.50** and **120621.17** Copy the formula in cell **F5** down to cell **F6** to sum the new row.

9 Using absolute cell references as necessary so that you can copy the formula, in cell **G4** construct a formula to calculate the *Percent of Total Sales* for the first region. Copy the formula down for the remaining regions.

10 To the computed percentages, apply **Percent Style** with two decimal places, and then **Center** the percentages.

11 Insert **Line** sparklines in the range **H4:H7** that compare the quarterly data. Do not include the totals. Show the sparkline **Markers** and apply a style to the sparklines using the second style in the second row. (Mac users: Select the first color in the second row.)

12 **Save** your workbook. To compare the quarterly sales of each region visually, select the range that represents the sales figures for the four quarters, including the quarter names and each region—do not include any totals in the range. With this data selected, by using the **Recommended Charts** command, insert a **Clustered Column** with the regions as the category axis and the Quarters as the legend.

13 Apply **Chart Style 8**. Change the colors by applying the third row of colors under Colorful. Position the upper middle sizing handle of the chart on the line between **column D** and **column E** and just below **row 9**.

14 Change the **Chart Title** to **Regional Sales to Fitness Clubs**

15 Deselect the chart. Change the page **Orientation** to **Landscape**, center the worksheet **Horizontally** on the page, and then insert a footer with the file name in the left section.

16 Show the document properties. As the **Tags**, type **fitness clubs, regional sales** In the **Subject** box, type your course name and section number. Be sure your name displays as the Author.

17 On the left, click **Save**.

18 In the upper right corner of your screen, click **Close** ⊗ to close Excel.

19 In **MyLab IT**, locate and click the Grader Project **Excel 1G Regional Sales**. In **step 3**, under **Upload Completed Assignment**, click **Choose File**. In the **Open** dialog box, navigate to your **Excel Chapter 1 folder**, and then click your **Student_Excel_1G_Regional_Sales** file one time to select it. In the lower right corner of the **Open** dialog box, click **Open**.

The name of your selected file displays above the Upload button.

20 To submit your file to **MyLab IT** for grading, click **Upload**, wait a moment for a green **Success!** message, and then in **step 4**, click the blue **Submit for Grading** button. Click **Close Assignment** to return to your list of **Course Materials**.

You have completed Project 1G **END**

Apply a combination of the 1A and 1B skills.

GO! Fix It	**Project 1H Team Sales**	IRC
GO! Make It	**Project 1I Agility Sales**	IRC
GO! Solve It	**Project 1J Kettlebell Sales**	IRC
GO! Solve It	**Project 1K Commission**	

Project Files

For Project 1K, you will need the following file:

e01K_Commission

You will save your workbook as:

Lastname_Firstname_1K_Commission

Open the file e01K_Commission and save it as **Lastname_Firstname_1K_Commission** Complete the worksheet by using Auto Fill to complete the month headings, and then calculating the Total Commission for each month and for each region. Insert and format appropriate sparklines in the Trend column. Format the worksheet attractively with a title and subtitle, check spelling, adjust column width, and apply appropriate financial formatting. Insert a chart that compares the total sales commission for each region with the months displaying as the categories, and format the chart attractively. Include the file name in the footer, add appropriate properties, and submit as directed.

		Performance Level		
		Exemplary: You consistently applied the relevant skills	**Proficient: You sometimes, but not always, applied the relevant skills**	**Developing: You rarely or never applied the relevant skills**
Performance Criteria	**Create formulas**	All formulas are correct and are efficiently constructed.	Formulas are correct but not always constructed in the most efficient manner.	One or more formulas are missing or incorrect; or only numbers were entered.
	Create a chart	Chart created properly.	Chart was created but incorrect data was selected.	No chart was created.
	Insert and format sparklines	Sparklines inserted and formatted properly.	Sparklines were inserted but incorrect data was selected or sparklines were not formatted.	No sparklines were inserted.
	Format attractively and appropriately	Formatting is attractive and appropriate.	Adequately formatted but difficult to read or unattractive.	Inadequate or no formatting.

You have completed Project 1K | END

Outcomes-Based Assessments (Critical Thinking)

Rubric

The following outcomes-based assessments are *open-ended assessments*. That is, there is no specific correct result; your result will depend on your approach to the information provided. Make *Professional Quality* your goal. Use the following scoring rubric to guide you in *how* to approach the problem and then to evaluate *how well* your approach solves the problem.

The *criteria*—Software Mastery, Content, Format and Layout, and Process—represent the knowledge and skills you have gained that you can apply to solving the problem. The *levels of performance*—Professional Quality, Approaching Professional Quality, or Needs Quality Improvements—help you and your instructor evaluate your result.

	Your completed project is of Professional Quality if you:	Your completed project is Approaching Professional Quality if you:	Your completed project Needs Quality Improvements if you:
1-Software Mastery	Choose and apply the most appropriate skills, tools, and features and identify efficient methods to solve the problem.	Choose and apply some appropriate skills, tools, and features, but not in the most efficient manner.	Choose inappropriate skills, tools, or features, or are inefficient in solving the problem.
2-Content	Construct a solution that is clear and well organized, contains content that is accurate, appropriate to the audience and purpose, and is complete. Provide a solution that contains no errors of spelling, grammar, or style.	Construct a solution in which some components are unclear, poorly organized, inconsistent, or incomplete. Misjudge the needs of the audience. Have some errors in spelling, grammar, or style, but the errors do not detract from comprehension.	Construct a solution that is unclear, incomplete, or poorly organized, contains some inaccurate or inappropriate content, and contains many errors of spelling, grammar, or style. Do not solve the problem.
3-Format and Layout	Format and arrange all elements to communicate information and ideas, clarify function, illustrate relationships, and indicate relative importance.	Apply appropriate format and layout features to some elements, but not others. Overuse features, causing minor distraction.	Apply format and layout that does not communicate information or ideas clearly. Do not use format and layout features to clarify function, illustrate relationships, or indicate relative importance. Use available features excessively, causing distraction.
4-Process	Use an organized approach that integrates planning, development, self-assessment, revision, and reflection.	Demonstrate an organized approach in some areas, but not others; or, use an insufficient process of organization throughout.	Do not use an organized approach to solve the problem.

Apply a combination of the 1A and 1B skills.

GO! Think	Project 1L Video Sales

Project Files

For Project 1L, you will need the following file:

New blank Excel workbook

You will save your workbook as:

Lastname_Firstname_1L_Video_Sales

Michelle Barry, President of Pro Fit Marietta, needs a worksheet that summarizes the following data regarding the first quarter sales of training videos. Michelle would like the worksheet to include a calculation of the total sales for each type of video and a total of the sales of all of the videos. She would also like to know each type of video's percentage of total sales.

	Number Sold	Price
Pilates	156	29.99
Step	392	14.99
Weight Training	147	54.99
Kickboxing	282	29.99
Yoga	165	34.99

Create a worksheet that provides Michelle with the information needed. Include appropriate worksheet, column, and row titles. Using the formatting skills that you practiced in this chapter, format the worksheet in a manner that is professional and easy to read and understand. Insert a footer with the file name and add appropriate document properties. Save the file as **Lastname_Firstname_1L_Video_Sales** and print or submit as directed by your instructor.

You have completed Project 1L	END

GO! Think	Project 1M Planner	IRC

You and GO!	Project 1N Personal Resume	IRC

GO! Collaborative Group Project	Project 1O Bell Orchid Hotels	IRC

Introduction to Microsoft Access 2019

ACCESS 2019

Mego studio/Shutterstock

Access 2019: Introduction Introduction to Access

Microsoft Access 2019 provides a convenient way to organize data that makes it easy for you to utilize and present information. Access uses tables to store the data; like Excel spreadsheets, data is stored in rows and columns in a table. So why use a database rather than an Excel spreadsheet? By using a database, you can manipulate and work with data in a more robust manner. For example, if you have thousands of records about patients in a hospital, you can easily find all of the records that pertain to the patients who received a specific type of medicine on a particular day. Information from one table can be used to retrieve information from another table.

For example, by knowing a patient's ID number, you can view immunization records or view insurance information or view hospitalization records. Having information stored in an Access database enables you to make bulk changes to data at one time even when it is stored in different tables.

It's easy to get started with Access by using one of the many prebuilt database templates. For example, a nonprofit organization can track events, donors, members, and donations for a nonprofit organization. A small business can use a prebuilt database to track inventory, create invoices, monitor projects, manage pricing, track competitors, and manage quotes.

Getting Started with Microsoft Access 2019

1

ACCESS 2019

PROJECT 1A

Outcomes
Create a new database.

Objectives

1. Identify Good Database Design
2. Create a Table and Define Fields in a Blank Desktop Database
3. Change the Structure of Tables and Add a Second Table
4. Create a Query, Form, and Report
5. Close a Database and Close Access

PROJECT 1B

Outcomes
Create a database from a template.

Objectives

6. Use a Template to Create a Database
7. Organize Objects in the Navigation Pane
8. Create a New Table in a Database Created with a Template
9. View a Report

Rawpixel.com/Shutterstock

In This Chapter

GO! To Work
with Access

In this chapter, you will use Microsoft Access 2019 to organize a collection of related information. You will create new databases, create tables, and enter data into the tables. You will create a query, a form, and a report—all of which are Access objects that make a database useful for locating and analyzing information. You will also create a complete database from a template that is provided, or that you can modify to meet your needs. In this chapter, you will also learn how to apply good database design principles to your Access database and to define the structure of a database.

The projects in this chapter relate to **Texas Lakes Community College**, which is located in the Austin, Texas area. Its four campuses serve over 30,000 students and offer more than 140 certificate programs and degrees. The college has a highly acclaimed Distance Education program and an extensive Workforce Development program. The college makes positive contributions to the community through cultural and athletic programs and has significant partnerships with businesses and nonprofit organizations. Popular fields of study include nursing and health care, solar technology, computer technology, and graphic design.

Student Advising Database with Two Tables

MyLab IT
Project 1A Grader for Instruction
Project 1A Simulation for Training and Review

Project Activities

In Activities 1.01 through 1.17, you will assist Dr. Daniel Martinez, Vice President of Student Services at Texas Lakes Community College, in creating a new database for tracking students and their faculty advisors. Your completed Navigation Pane will look similar to Figure 1.1.

Project Files for **MyLab IT Grader**

1. In your storage location, create a folder named **Access Chapter 1**.
2. In your **MyLab IT** course, locate and click **Access 1A Advising**, Download Materials, and then Download All Files.
3. Extract the zipped folder to your Access Chapter 1 folder. Close the Grader download screens.
4. Take a moment to open the downloaded **Access_1A_Advising_Instructions**; note any recent updates to the book.

Project Results

GO! Project 1A
Where We're Going

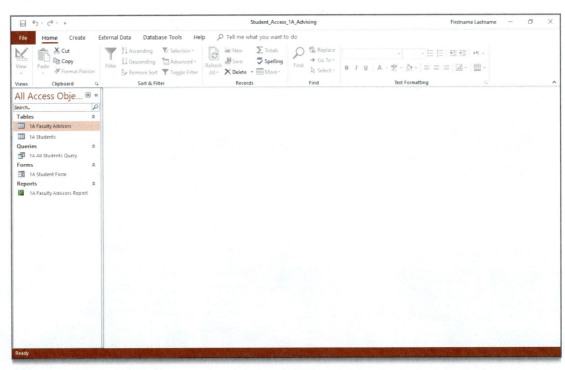

Figure 1.1 Project 1A Advising

For Non-MyLab Submissions	**Start with a new blank Access database**
For Project 1A, you will need the following files:	In your storage location, create a folder named **Access Chapter 1**
Blank database	In your Access Chapter 1 folder, save your database as:
a01A_Students (Excel workbook)	**Lastname_Firstname_1A_Advising**
a01A_Faculty_Advisors (Excel workbook)	
After you have named and saved your workbook, on the next page begin by comparing your screen with Figure 1.4 in Step 3.	

NOTE **If You Are Using a Touch Screen**

Tap an item to click it.

Press and hold for a few seconds to right-click; release when the information or commands display.

Touch the screen with two or more fingers and then pinch together to zoom out or stretch your fingers apart to zoom in.

Slide your finger on the screen to scroll—slide left to scroll right and slide right to scroll left.

Slide to rearrange—similar to dragging with a mouse.

Swipe to select—slide an item a short distance with a quick movement—to select an item and bring up commands, if any.

Objective 1 **Identify Good Database Design**

ALERT Because Office 365 is a cloud-based subscription service that receives continuous updates, you may encounter some variations in what appears on your screen and what is shown in this instruction. Microsoft Office 365 is fully installed on your PC or Mac; no internet access is necessary to create or edit documents. When you *are* connected to the internet, you will receive monthly upgrades and new features, so you always have the latest versions of Office apps as soon as they are available. Your subscription gives you continuous free access to the latest innovations and refinements.

GO! Learn How
Video A1-1

A *database* is an organized collection of *data*—facts about people, events, things, or ideas—related to a specific topic or purpose. *Information* is data that is accurate, timely, and organized in a useful manner. Your contact list is a type of database, because it is a collection of data about one topic—the people with whom you communicate. A simple database of this type is called a *flat database* because it is not related or linked to any other collection of data. Another example of a simple database is your music collection. You do not keep information about your music collection in your contact list because the data is not related to the people in your contact list.

A more sophisticated type of database is a *relational database*, because multiple collections of data in the database are related to one another—for example, data about the students, the courses, and the faculty members at a college. Microsoft Access 2019 is a relational *database management system*—also referred to as a *DBMS*—which is software that controls how related collections of data are stored, organized, retrieved, and secured.

Activity 1.01 | Using Good Design Techniques to Plan a Database

Before creating a new database, the first step is to determine the information you want to keep track of by asking yourself, *What questions should this database be able to answer?* The purpose of a database is to store the data in a manner that makes it easy to find the information you need by asking questions. For example, in a student database for Texas Lakes Community College, the questions to be answered might include:

- How many students are enrolled at the college?
- How many students have not yet been assigned a faculty advisor?
- Which students live in Austin, Texas?
- Which students owe money for tuition?
- Which students are majoring in Information Systems Technology?

Tables are the foundation of an Access database because all of the data is stored in one or more tables. A table is similar in structure to an Excel worksheet because data is organized into rows and columns. Each table row is a *record*—all of the categories of data pertaining to one person, place, event, thing, or idea. Each table column is a *field*—a single piece of information for every record. For example, in a table storing student contact information, each row forms a record for only one student. Each column forms a field for every record—for example, the student ID number or the student last name.

When organizing the fields of information in your table, break each piece of information into its smallest, most useful part. For example, create three fields for the name of a student—one field for the last name, one field for the first name, and one field for the middle name or initial.

The *first principle of good database design* is to organize data in the tables so that *redundant*—duplicate—data does not occur. For example, record the student contact information in only *one* table, so that if a student's address changes, you can change the information in just one place. This conserves space, reduces the likelihood of errors when inputting new data, and does not require remembering all of the places where a student's address is stored.

The *second principle of good database design* is to use techniques that ensure the accuracy and consistency of data as it is entered into the table. Proofreading data is critical to maintaining accuracy in a database. Typically, many different people enter data into a database—think of all the people who enter data about students at your college. When entering a state in a student contacts table, one person might enter the state as *Texas*, while another might enter the state as *TX*. Use design techniques to help those who enter data into a database to enter the data more accurately and consistently.

Normalization is the process of applying design rules and principles to ensure that your database performs as expected. Taking the time to plan and create a database that is well designed will ensure that you can retrieve meaningful information from the database.

The tables of information in a relational database are linked or joined to one another by a *common field*—a field in two or more tables that stores the same data. For example, a Students table includes the Student ID, name, and full address of every student. The Student Activities table includes the club name and the Student ID of members, but not the name or address, of each student in the club. Because the two tables share a common field—Student ID—you can use the data together to create a list of names and addresses of all of the students in a particular club. The names and addresses are stored in the Students table, and the Student IDs of the club members are stored in the Student Activities table.

Objective 2   Create a Table and Define Fields in a Blank Desktop Database

GO! Learn How
Video A1-2

Three methods are used to create a new Access database. One method is to create a new database using a *database template*—a preformatted database designed for a specific purpose. A second method is to create a new database from a *blank desktop database*. A blank desktop database is stored on your computer or other storage device. Initially, it has no data and has no database tools; you create the data and the tools as you need them. A third method is to create a *custom web app* database from scratch or by using a template that you can publish and share with others over the Internet.

Regardless of the method you use, you must name and save the database before you can create any *objects* in it. Objects are the basic parts of a database; you create objects to store your data, to work with your data, and to display your data. The most common database objects are tables, queries, forms, and reports. Think of an Access database as a container for the objects that you create.

Activity 1.02 | Starting with a Blank Database

1 Start Microsoft Access 2019. Take a moment to compare your screen with Figure 1.2 and study the parts of the Microsoft Access opening screen described in the table in Figure 1.3.

From this Access opening screen, you can open an existing database, create a blank database, or create a new database from a template.

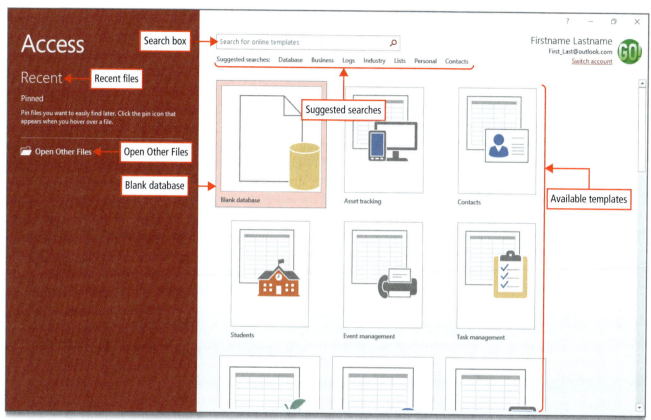

Figure 1.2

Screen Element	Description
Available templates	Starts a database for a specific purpose that includes built-in objects and tools ready for use.
Blank database	Starts a blank database that is stored on your computer or on a portable storage device.
Open Other Files	Enables you to open a database file from your computer, a shared location, or other location that you have designated.
Recent files	Displays a list of database files that have been recently opened.
Search box	Enables you to search the Microsoft Office website for templates.
Suggested searches	Enables you to click on a category to start an online search for a template.

Figure 1.3   Microsoft Access Opening Screen Elements

2 Navigate to your **Access Chapter 1 folder**, and then double-click the Access file that you downloaded from **MyLab IT** that displays your name—**Student_Access_1A_Advising**. In your blank database, if necessary, click **Enable Content** at the top.

3 Click the **Create tab**. In the **Tables group**, click **Table**. Compare your screen with Figure 1.4, and then take a moment to study the screen elements described in the table in Figure 1.5.

Recall that a table is an Access object that stores data in columns and rows, similar to the format of an Excel worksheet. Table objects are the foundation of a database because tables store data that is used by other database objects.

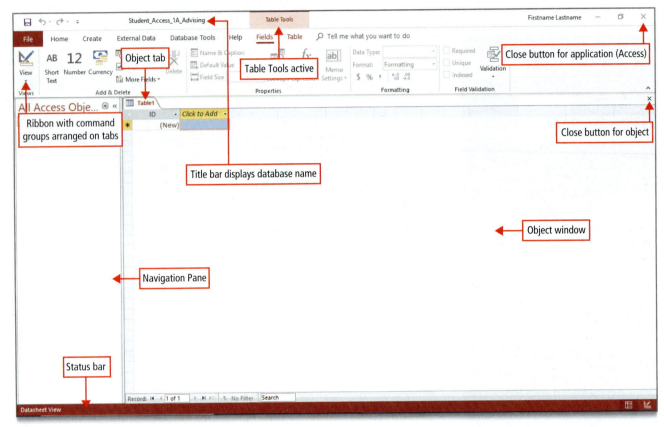

Figure 1.4

Access Window Element	Description
Navigation Pane	Displays the database objects that can be opened in the object window.
Object tab	Identifies the open object.
Object window	Displays the active or open object(s), including tables, queries, or other objects.
Close button for object	Closes the active object.
Ribbon	Displays commands grouped by related tasks and stored on different tabs.
Status bar	Indicates the active view and the status of action occurring within the database on the left; provides buttons on the right to switch between Datasheet view and Design view.
Table Tools	Provides tools on two tabs for working with the active table object, these are contextual tabs—only available when a table object is active.
Close button for application (Access)	Closes the active database and Access.

Figure 1.5   Microsoft Access Database Window Elements

Activity 1.03 | Assigning the Data Type and Name to Fields

2.4.1, 2.4.5

After you have named and saved your database, the next step is to consult your database design plan and then create the tables for your data. Limit the data in each table to *one* subject. For example, in this project, your database will have two tables—one for student information and one for faculty advisor information.

Recall that each column in a table is a field; field names display at the top of each column of the table. Recall also that each row in a table is a record—all of the data pertaining to one person, place, thing, event, or idea. Each record is broken up into its smallest usable parts—the fields. Use meaningful names for fields; for example, *Last Name*.

> **1** Notice the new blank table that displays in Datasheet view, and then take a moment to study the elements of the table's object window. Compare your screen with Figure 1.6.

The table displays in ***Datasheet view***, which displays the data in columns and rows similar to the format of an Excel worksheet. Another way to view a table is in ***Design view***, which displays the underlying design—the ***structure***—of the table's fields. The ***object window*** displays the open object—in this instance, the table object.

In a new blank database, there is only one object—a new blank table. Because you have not yet named this table, the ***object tab*** displays a default name of *Table1*. Access creates the first field and names it *ID*. In the ID field, Access assigns a unique sequential number—each number incremented by one—to each record as it is entered into the table.

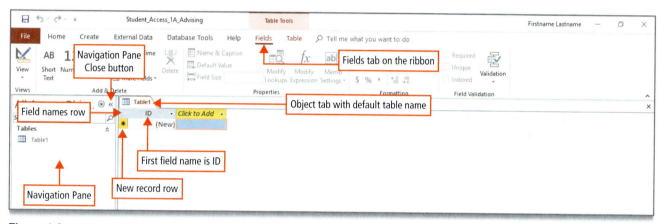

Figure 1.6

> **2** In the **Navigation Pane**, click **Shutter Bar Open/Close** « to collapse the **Navigation Pane** to a narrow bar on the left.

The ***Navigation Pane*** displays and organizes the names of the objects in a database. From the Navigation Pane, you can open objects. Collapse or close the Navigation Pane to display more of the object—in this case, the table.

 ANOTHER WAY   Press F11 to close or open the Navigation Pane.

3 ▶ In the field names row, click anywhere in the text *Click to Add* to display a list of data types. Compare your screen with Figure 1.7.

> A **data type** classifies the kind of data that you can store in a field, such as numbers, text, or dates. A field in a table can have only one data type. The data type of each field should be included in your database design. After selecting the data type, you can name the field.

🔄 **ANOTHER WAY**   To the right of *Click to Add*, click the arrow.

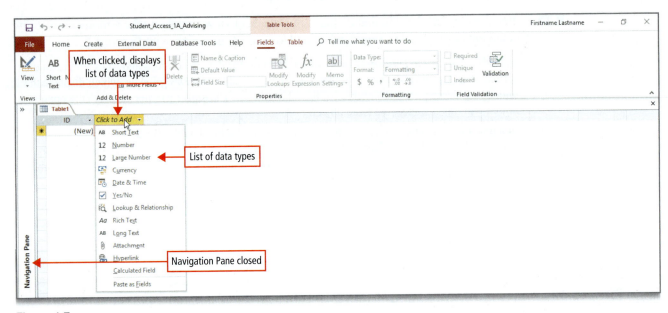

Figure 1.7

4 ▶ In the list of data types, click **Short Text**, and notice that in the second column, *Click to Add* changes to *Field1*, which is selected. Type **Last Name** and then press ⏎.

> The second column displays *Last Name* as the field name, and, in the third column, the data types list displays. The **Short Text data type** describes text, a combination of text and numbers, or numbers that do not represent a quantity or are not used in calculations, such as the Postal Code. This data type enables you to enter up to 255 characters in the field.

🔄 **ANOTHER WAY**   With the list of data types displayed, type the character that is underscored to select the data type. For example, type *t* to select Short Text or type *u* to select Currency.

5 ▶ In the third field name box, type **t** to select *Short Text*, type **First Name** and then press ⏎.

6 ▶ In the fourth field name box, click **Short Text**, type **Middle Initial** and then press ⏎.

7 ▶ Create the remaining fields from the table below by first selecting the data type, typing the field name, and then pressing ⏎. The field names in the table will display on one line–do not be concerned if the field names do not completely display in the column; you will adjust the column widths later.

Data Type		Short Text	Short Text	Short Text	Short Text	Short Text	Short Text	Short Text	Short Text	Short Text	Short Text	Currency
Field Name	ID	Last Name	First Name	Middle Initial	**Address**	**City**	**State**	**Postal Code**	**Phone**	**Email**	**Faculty Advisor ID**	**Amount Owed**

The Postal Code and Phone fields are assigned a data type of Short Text because the numbers are never used in calculations. The Amount Owed field is assigned the *Currency data type*, which describes monetary values and numeric data that can be used in calculations and that have one to four decimal places. A U.S. dollar sign ($) and two decimal places are automatically included for all of the numbers in a field with the Currency data type.

8 If necessary, scroll to bring the first column—ID—into view, and then compare your screen with Figure 1.8.

Access automatically created the ID field, and you created 11 additional fields in the table.

Figure 1.8

MORE KNOWLEDGE | **Create Fields by Entering Data**

You can create a new field in Datasheet view by typing the data in a new column. Access automatically assigns a data type based on the data you enter. For example, if you enter a date, Access assigns the Date & Time data type. If you enter a monetary amount, Access assigns the Currency data type. If Access cannot determine the data type based on the data entered, the Short Text data type is assigned. You can always change the data type if an incorrect data type is assigned. If you use this method to create fields, you must check the assigned data types to be sure they are correct. You must also rename the fields because Access assigns the names as *Field1*, *Field2*, and so on.

Activity 1.04 | Renaming Fields, Changing Data Types, and Setting Field Size in a Table

2.4.3, 2.4.4, 2.4.5

Once a table has been created, the field structure can be edited in Datasheet view. As you change data types and field sizes, you need to be sure that any existing data meets the new restrictions. In this Activity, you will modify the default ID field that displayed when you created the new table.

1 In the first column, click anywhere in the text *ID*. On the ribbon, under **Table Tools**, on the **Fields tab**, in the **Properties group**, click **Name & Caption**. In the **Enter Field Properties** dialog box, in the **Name** box, change *ID* to **Student ID**

The field name *Student ID* is a more precise description of the data contained in this field. In the Enter Field Properties dialog box, you have the option to use the *Caption* property to display a name for a field different from the one that displays in the Name box. Many database designers do not use spaces in field names; instead, they might name a field *LastName* or *LName* and then create a caption for the field so it displays as *Last Name* in tables, forms, or reports. In the Enter Field Properties dialog box, you can also provide a description for the field.

ANOTHER WAY Right-click the field name to display the shortcut menu, and then click Rename Field; or, double-click the field name to select the existing text, and then type the new field name.

---

2 Click **OK** to close the **Enter Field Properties** dialog box. On the ribbon, in the **Formatting group**, notice that the **Data Type** for the **Student ID** field is *AutoNumber*. Click the **Data Type arrow**, and then click **Short Text**.

In the new record row, the Student ID field is selected. By default, Access creates an ID field for all new tables and sets the data type for the field to AutoNumber. The *AutoNumber data type* describes a unique sequential or random number assigned by Access as each record is entered. Changing the data type of this field to Short Text enables you to enter a custom student ID number.

When records in a database have *no* unique value, such as a book ISBN or a license plate number, the AutoNumber data type is a useful way to automatically create a unique number. In this manner, you are sure that every record is different from the others.

3 On the ribbon, in the **Properties group**, click in the **Field Size** box to select the text *255*, and then type **7** Press Enter, and then compare your screen with Figure 1.9.

This action limits the size of the Student ID field to no more than seven characters. The default field size for a Short Text field is 255. Limiting the Field Size property to seven ensures that no more than 7 characters can be entered for each Student ID. However, this does not prevent someone from entering seven characters that are incorrect or entering fewer than seven characters. Setting the proper data type for the field and limiting the field size are two ways to help reduce errors during data entry.

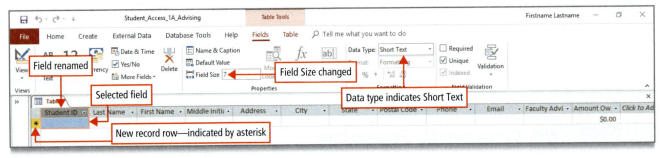

Figure 1.9

Activity 1.05 | Adding a Record to a Table

1.1.2

A new contact list is not useful until you fill it with names and phone numbers. Likewise, a new database is not useful until you *populate* it by filling one or more tables with data. You can populate a table with records by typing data directly into the table.

1 In the new record row, click in the **Student ID** field to display the insertion point, type **1023045** and then press Enter. Compare your screen with Figure 1.10.

The pencil icon 🖉 in the *record selector box* indicates that a record is being entered or edited. The record selector box is the small box at the left of a record in Datasheet view. When clicked, the entire record is selected.

ANOTHER WAY Press Tab to move the insertion point to the next field.

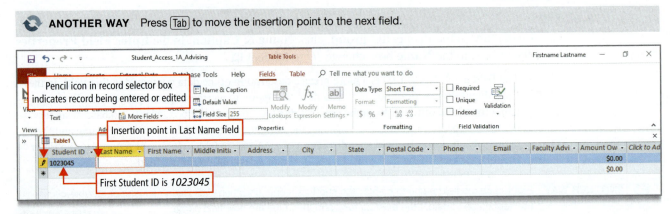

Figure 1.10

2 With the insertion point positioned in the **Last Name** field, type **Fresch** and then press Tab.

Pressing Enter or Tab will move the insertion point from field to field in the record.

3 In the **First Name** field, type **Jenna** and then press Enter.

4 In the **Middle Initial** field, type **A** and then press Enter.

5 In the **Address** field, type **7550 Douglas Ln** and then press Enter.

Do not be concerned if the data does not completely display in the column. As you progress in your study of Access, you will adjust column widths so that you can view all of the data.

6 Continue entering data in the fields as indicated in the table below, pressing Enter to move to the next field.

City	State	Postal Code	Phone	Email	Faculty Advisor ID
Austin	**TX**	**78749**	**(512) 555-7550**	**jfresch@tlcc.edu**	**FAC-2289**

7 In the **Amount Owed** field, type **250** and then press Enter. Compare your screen with Figure 1.11.

Pressing Enter or Tab in the last field moves the insertion point to the next row to begin a new record. Access automatically saves the record as soon as you move to the next row; you do not have to take any specific action to save a record.

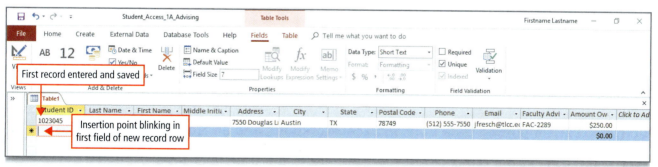

Figure 1.11

8 To give your table a meaningful name, click the **File tab**, and, on the left, click **Save As**. Under *Save As*, double-click **Save Object** As In the **Save As** dialog box, in the **Table Name** box, replace the selected text by typing **1A Students**

Save each database object with a name that identifies the data that it contains. When you save objects within a database, it is not necessary to use underscores in place of the spaces between words. Notice that the object tab—located directly above the *Student ID* field name—displays the table name.

MORE KNOWLEDGE **Renaming or Deleting a Table**

To change the name of a table, close the table, display the Navigation Pane, right-click the table name, and then click Rename. Type the new name or edit as you would any selected text. To delete a table, close the table, display the Navigation Pane, right-click the table name, and then click Delete.

Activity 1.06 | Adding Additional Records to a Table

1 In the new record row, click in the **Student ID** field, and then enter the data for two additional students as shown in the table below. Press Enter or Tab to move from field to field. The data in each field will display on one line in the table.

Student ID	Last Name	First Name	Middle Initial	Address	City	State	Postal Code	Phone	Email	Faculty Advisor ID	Amount Owed
2345677	Ingram	Joseph	S	621 Hilltop Dr	Leander	TX	78646	(512) 555-0717	jingram@tlcc.edu	FAC-2377	378.5
3456689	Snyder	Amanda	J	4786 Bluff St	Buda	TX	78610	(512) 555-9120	asnyder@tlcc.edu	FAC-9005	0

2 Press Enter, and compare your screen with Figure 1.12.

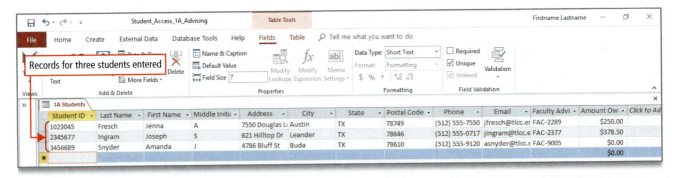

Figure 1.12

Activity 1.07 | Importing Data from an Excel Workbook into an Existing Access Table

2.1.1

You can type records directly into a table. You can also *import* data from a variety of sources. Importing is the process of copying data from one source or application to another application. For example, you can import data from a Word table or an Excel spreadsheet into an Access database because the data is arranged in columns and rows, similar to a table in Datasheet view.

In this Activity, you will *append*—add on—data from an Excel spreadsheet to your *1A Students* table. To append data, the table must already be created, and it should be closed.

1 In the upper right corner of the table, below the ribbon, click **Object Close** ⊠ to close your **1A Students** table. Notice that no objects are open.

2 On the ribbon, click the **External Data tab**. In the **Import & Link group**, click the **New Data Source** arrow, point to **From File**, and then click **Excel**. In the **Get External Data – Excel Spreadsheet** dialog box, click **Browse**.

3 In the **File Open** dialog box, navigate to your student files, double-click the Excel file **a01A_Students**, and then compare your screen with Figure 1.13.

The path to the *source file*—the file being imported—displays in the File name box. There are three options for importing data from an Excel spreadsheet: import the data into a *new* table in the current database, append a copy of the records to an existing table, or link the data from the spreadsheet to a linked table in the database. A *link* is a connection to data in another file. When linking, Access creates a table that maintains a link to the source data, so that changes to the data in one file are automatically made in the other—linked—file.

ANOTHER WAY   Click the file name, and then in the File Open dialog box, click Open.

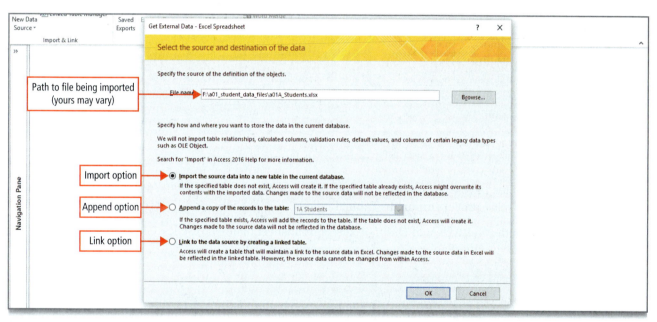

Figure 1.13

4 Click the **Append a copy of the records to the table** option button, and then, in the box to the right, click the **arrow**.

Currently, your database has only one table, so no other tables display on the list. However, when a database has multiple tables, click the arrow to select the table to which you want to append records. The table into which you import or append data is referred to as the *destination table*.

5 Press [Esc] to cancel the list, and in the dialog box, click **OK**. Compare your screen with Figure 1.14.

The first screen of the Import Spreadsheet Wizard displays. A *wizard* is a feature in a Microsoft Office program that walks you step by step through a process. The presence of scroll bars in the window indicates that records and fields are out of view. To append records from an Excel workbook to an existing database table, the column headings in the Excel worksheet or spreadsheet must be identical to the field names in the table. The wizard identified the first row of the spreadsheet as column headings, which are equivalent to field names.

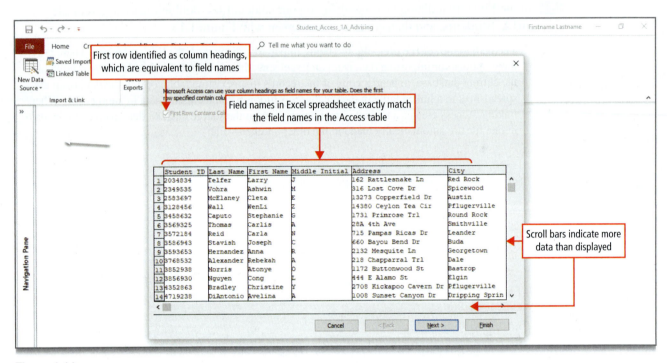

Figure 1.14

6 In the lower right corner of the wizard, click **Next**. Notice that the name of your table displays under **Import to Table**. In the lower right corner of the wizard, click **Finish**.

7 In the **Get External Data – Excel Spreadsheet** dialog box, click **Close**. **Open** [»] the **Navigation Pane**, and then compare your screen with Figure 1.15.

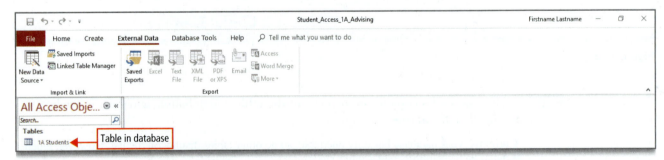

Figure 1.15

8 In the **Navigation Pane**, double-click your **1A Students** table to open the table in Datasheet view, and then **Close** [«] the **Navigation Pane**.

ANOTHER WAY To open an object from the Navigation Pane, right-click the object name, and then click Open.

---

9 In the lower left corner of your screen, locate the navigation area, and notice that there are a total of **25** records in the table—you entered three records and imported 22 additional records. Compare your screen with Figure 1.16.

The records that you entered and the records you imported from the Excel spreadsheet display in your table; the first record in the table is selected. The ***navigation area*** indicates the number of records in the table and has controls in the form of arrows that you click to move through the records.

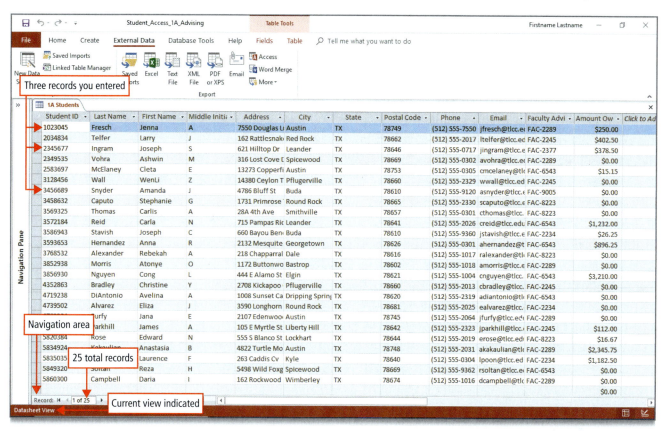

Figure 1.16

Objective 3 **Change the Structure of Tables and Add a Second Table**

GO! Learn How

Video A1-3

Recall that the structure of a table is the underlying design of the table and includes field names and data types. You can create or modify a table in Datasheet view. To define and modify fields, many database experts prefer to work in Design view, where you have more options for defining fields in a table.

Activity 1.08 | Deleting a Table Field in Design View

2.4.1

In a recent meeting, the Student Services department has decided that the Students table does not need to include a field for the middle initial. In this Activity, you will delete the *Middle Initial* field from the table.

1 Click the **Home tab**, and then in the **Views group**, click the **View arrow** to display a list of views.

There are two views for tables: Datasheet view and Design view. Other objects have different views. On the list, Design view is represented by a picture of a pencil, a ruler, and an angle. Datasheet view is represented by a picture of a table arranged in columns and rows. In the Views group, if the top of the View button displays the pencil, ruler, and angle, clicking View will switch your view to Design view. Likewise, clicking the top of the View button that displays as a datasheet will switch your view to Datasheet view.

2 ▶ On the list, click **Design View**, and then compare your screen with Figure 1.17.

Design view displays the underlying design—the structure—of the table and its fields. In Design view, the records in the table do not display. You can only view the information about each field's attributes. Each field name is listed, along with its data type. You can add explanatory information about a field in the Description column, but it is not required.

You can decide how each field should look and behave in the Field Properties area. For example, you can set a specific field size in the Field Properties area. In the lower right corner, information displays about the active selection—in this case, the Field Name.

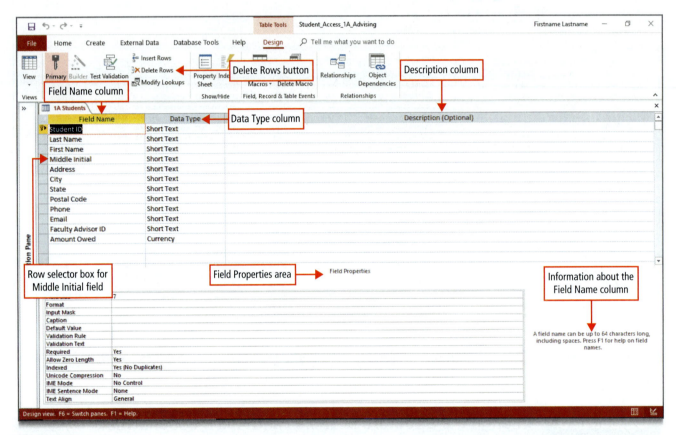

Figure 1.17

3 ▶ In the **Field Name** column, to the left of **Middle Initial**, point to the row selector box to display the ➡ pointer, and then click one time to select the entire row.

4 ▶ On the **Design tab**, in the **Tools group**, click **Delete Rows**. Read the warning in the message box, and then click **Yes**.

Deleting a field deletes both the field and its data. After you save the changes, you cannot undo this action, so Access prompts you to be sure you want to proceed. If you change your mind after deleting a field and saving the changes, you must add the field back into the table and then reenter the data for that field for every record.

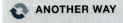 **ANOTHER WAY** In Design view, right-click the selected row, and then click Delete Rows; or, in Datasheet view, select the field—column—and on the Home tab, in the Records group, click Delete.

Activity 1.09 | Adding Field Descriptions and Changing Field Size

2.2.3, 2.4.4

Typically, many different individuals have the ability to enter data into a table. For example, at your college, many Registration Assistants enter and modify student and course information daily. Two ways to help reduce errors are to restrict what can be typed in a field and to add descriptive information to help the individuals when entering the data.

1 ▸ With your table still displayed in **Design** view, in the **Field Name** column, click anywhere in the **Student ID** field name.

2 ▸ In the **Student ID** row, click in the **Description** box, type **Seven-digit Student ID number** and then press Enter. Compare your screen with Figure 1.18.

> Descriptions for fields in a table are optional. Include a description if the field name does not provide an obvious explanation of the type of data to be entered. If a description is provided for a field, when data is being entered in that field in Datasheet view, the text in the Description displays on the left side of the status bar to provide additional information for the individuals who are entering the data.
>
> When you enter a description for a field, a Property Update Options button displays below the text you typed, which enables you to copy the description for the field to all other database objects that use this table as an underlying source.

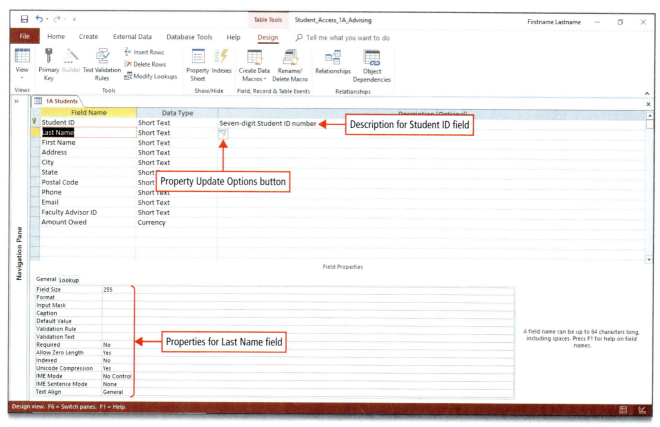

Figure 1.18

3 Click in the **State** field name box. In the lower area of the screen, under **Field Properties**, click in the **Field Size** box to select the text **255**, and type **2** Click in the **Description** box for this field, type **Two-character state abbreviation** and then press Enter.

Recall changing the size of a field limits the number of characters that the field will accept. *Field properties* control how the field displays and how data can be entered into the field. You can define properties for each field in the Field Properties area by first clicking on the field name to display the properties for that specific data type.

4 Click in the **Faculty Advisor ID** field name box. In the **Field Properties** area, change the **Field Size** to **8** and in the **Description** box for this field, type **Eight-character ID of the instructor assigned as advisor** and then press Enter.

MORE KNOWLEDGE **Add a Table Description**

You can create a description to provide more information to users regarding the entire table. With the table displayed in Design view, click the Design tab. In the Show/Hide group, click Property Sheet. Click in the Description box, type the table description, and then press Enter. Close the Property Sheet.

---

5 On the Quick Access Toolbar, click **Save** 🖫 to save the design changes to your table, and then notice the message.

The message indicates that the field size property of one or more fields has changed to a shorter size. If more characters are currently present in the State, or Faculty Advisor ID fields than you have allowed, the data will be *truncated*—cut off or shortened—because the fields were not previously restricted to these specific number of characters.

6 In the message box, click **Yes**.

Activity 1.10 | Viewing the Primary Key in Design View

Primary key refers to the required field in the table that uniquely identifies a record. For example, in a college registration database, your Student ID number identifies you as a unique individual—every student has a student number and no other student at the college has your exact student number. In the 1A Students table, the Student ID uniquely identifies each student.

When you create a table using the blank database template, Access designates the first field as the primary key field and names the field ID. It is good database design practice to establish a primary key for every table, because doing so ensures that you do not enter the same record more than once. You can imagine the confusion if another student at your college had the same Student ID number as you do.

1 ▶ With your table still displayed in **Design** view, in the **Field Name** column, click in the **Student ID** box. To the left of the box, notice the small icon of a key, as shown in Figure 1.19.

Access automatically designates the first field as the primary key field, but you can set any field as the primary key by clicking the field name, and then in the Tools group, clicking Primary Key.

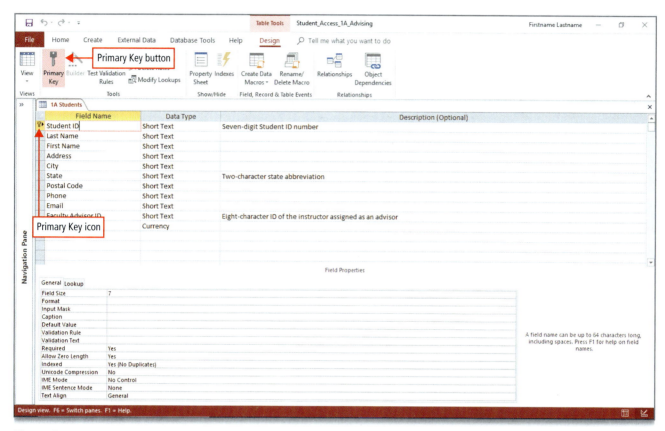

Figure 1.19

2 ▶ On the **Design tab**, in the **Views group**, notice that the View button displays a picture of a datasheet, indicating that clicking View will switch the view to Datasheet view. Click the top of the **View** button.

If you make design changes to a table and switch views without first saving the table, Access will prompt you to save the table before changing views.

Activity 1.11 │ Adding a Second Table to a Database by Importing an Excel Spreadsheet

1.1.1

Many Microsoft Office users track data in an Excel spreadsheet. The sorting and filtering capabilities of Excel are useful for a simple database where all of the information resides in one large Excel spreadsheet. However, Excel is limited as a database management tool because it cannot *relate* the information in multiple spreadsheets in a way that you can ask a question and get a meaningful result. Because data in an Excel spreadsheet is arranged in columns and rows, the spreadsheet can easily convert to an Access table by importing the spreadsheet.

1 ▶ On the ribbon, click the **External Data tab**. In the **Import & Link group**, click the **New Data Source** arrow, point to **From File**, and then click **Excel**. In the **Get External Data – Excel Spreadsheet** dialog box, to the right of the **File name** box, click **Browse**.

2 In the **File Open** dialog box, navigate to the location where your student data files are stored, and then double-click **a01A_Faculty_Advisors**. Compare your screen with Figure 1.20.

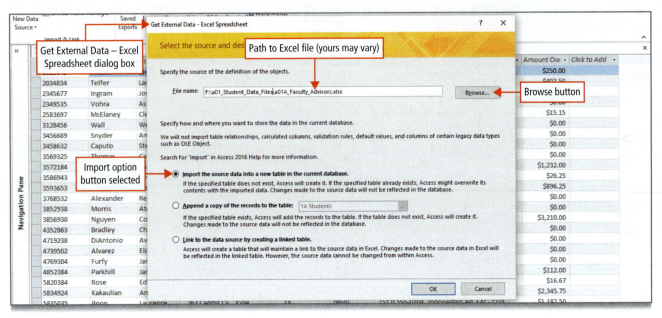

Figure 1.20

3 Be sure that the **Import the source data into a new table in the current database** option button is selected, and then click **OK**.

The Import Spreadsheet Wizard displays the spreadsheet data.

4 In the upper left corner of the wizard, select the **First Row Contains Column Headings** check box.

The Excel data is framed, indicating that the first row of Excel column titles will become the Access table field names, and the remaining rows will become the individual records in the new Access table.

5 Click **Next**. Notice that the first column—*Faculty ID*—is selected, and in the upper area of the wizard, the **Field Name** and the **Data Type** display. Compare your screen with Figure 1.21.

In this step, under Field Options, you can review and change the name or the data type of each selected field. You can also identify fields in the spreadsheet that you do not want to import into the Access table by selecting the Do not import field (Skip) check box.

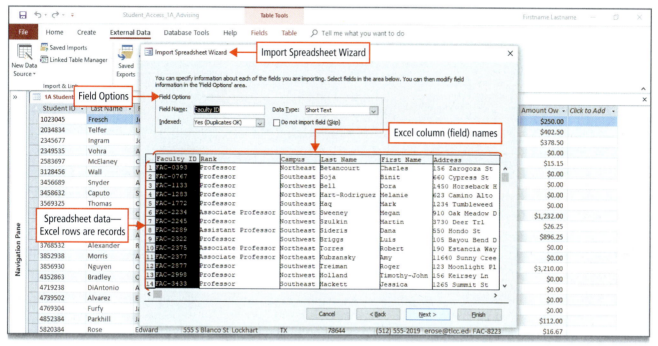

Figure 1.21

6 Click **Next**. In the upper area of the wizard, click the **Choose my own primary key** option button, and then verify that **Faculty ID** displays.

In the new table, Faculty ID will be the primary key. Every faculty member has a Faculty ID and no two faculty members have the same Faculty ID. By default, Access selects the first field as the primary key, but you can click the arrow and select a different field.

7 Click **Next**. In the **Import to Table** box, type **1A Faculty Advisors** and then click **Finish**.

8 In the **Get External Data – Excel Spreadsheet** dialog box, click **Close**. Open ⧉ the **Navigation Pane**.

9 In the **Navigation Pane**, double-click your **1A Faculty Advisors** table to open it in Datasheet view, and then **Close** ⧉ the **Navigation Pane**.

Two tables that are identified by their object tabs are open in the object window. Your 1A Faculty Advisors table is the active table and displays the 29 records that you imported from the Excel spreadsheet.

10 ▸ In your **1A Faculty Advisors** table, click in the **Postal Code** field in the first record. On the ribbon, under **Table Tools**, click the **Fields tab**. In the **Formatting group**, click the **Data Type arrow**, and then click **Short Text**. Compare your screen with Figure 1.22.

> When you import data from an Excel spreadsheet, check the data types of all fields to ensure they are correct. Recall that if a field, such as the Postal Code, contains numbers that do not represent a quantity or are not used in calculations, the data type should be set to Short Text. To change the data type of a field, click in the field in any record.

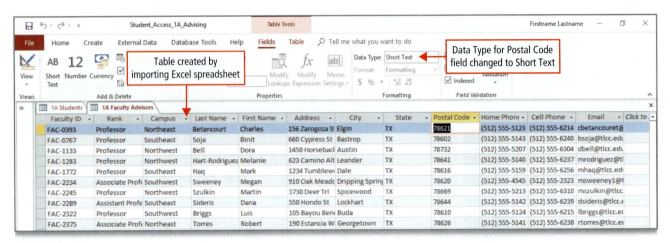

Figure 1.22

Activity 1.12 | Adjusting Column Widths and Viewing a Table in Print Preview

> You can adjust the column widths in a table displayed in Datasheet view by using techniques similar to those you use for Excel spreadsheets.

1 ▸ In the object window, click the **object tab** for your **1A Students** table to make it the active object and to display it in the object window.

> Clicking an object tab along the top of the object window enables you to display the open object and make it active so that you can work with it. All of the columns in the datasheet are the same width, regardless of the length of the data in the field, the length of the field name, or the field size that was set. If you print the table as currently displayed, some of the data or field names will not print completely, so you will want to adjust the column widths.

2 ▸ In the field names row, point to the right edge of the **Address** field to display the ⊞ pointer, and then compare your screen with Figure 1.23.

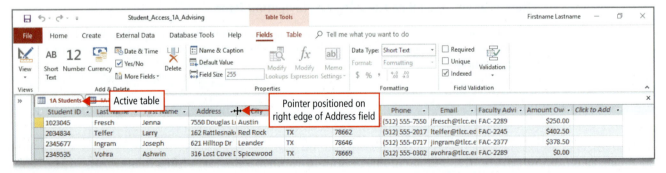

Figure 1.23

3 With the ⊞ pointer positioned as shown in Figure 1.23, double-click the right edge of the **Address** field.

The column width of the Address field widens to display the longest entry in the field fully. In this manner, the width of a column can be increased or decreased to fit its contents in the same manner as a column in an Excel spreadsheet. In Access, adjusting the column width to fit the contents is referred to as *Best Fit*.

4 Point to the **City** field name to display the ↓ pointer, right-click to select the entire column and display the shortcut menu. Click **Field Width**, and then in the **Column Width** dialog box, click **Best Fit**.

This is a second way to adjust column widths.

5 If necessary, scroll to the right to view the last three fields. Point to the **Email** field name to display the ↓ pointer, hold down the left mouse button, and then drag to the right to select this column, the **Faculty Advisor ID** column, and the **Amount Owed** column. Point to the right edge of any of the selected columns to display the ⊞ pointer, and then double-click to apply **Best Fit** to all three columns.

You can select multiple columns and adjust the widths of all of them at one time by using this technique or by right-clicking any of the selected columns, clicking Field Width, and clicking Best Fit in the Column Width dialog box.

6 If necessary, scroll to the left to view the **Student ID** field. To the left of the **Student ID** field name, click **Select All** ☐. Notice that all of the fields are selected.

7 On the ribbon, click the **Home tab**. In the **Records group**, click **More**, and then click **Field Width**. In the **Column Width** dialog box, click **Best Fit**. Click anywhere in the **Student ID** field, and then compare your screen with Figure 1.24.

Using the More command is a third way to adjust column widths. By using Select All, you can adjust the widths of all of the columns at one time. Adjusting the width of columns does not change the data in the table's records; it only changes the *display* of the data.

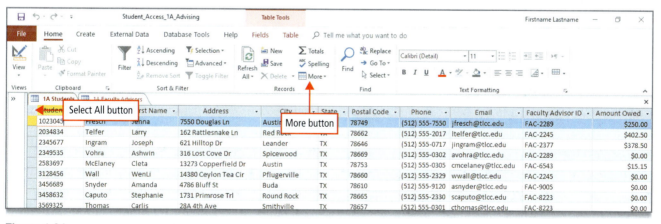

Figure 1.24

NOTE   Adjusting Column Widths

After adjusting column widths, scroll horizontally and vertically to be sure that all of the data displays in all of the fields. Access adjusts column widths to fit the screen size based on the displayed data. If data is not displayed on the screen when you adjust column widths—even if you use Select All—the column width may not be adjusted adequately to display all of the data in the field. After adjusting column widths, click in any field to remove the selection of the column or columns, and then save the table before performing other tasks.

8 On the Quick Access Toolbar, click **Save** 🔲 to save the table design changes—changing the column widths.

> If you do not save the table after making design changes, Access prompts you to save it when you close the table.

Activity 1.13 | Viewing a Table in Print Preview

There are times when you will want to print a table, even though a report may look more professional. For example, you may need a quick reference, or you may want to proofread the data that has been entered. In Access, it is best to preview a table before printing to make any necessary layout changes.

1 On the ribbon, click the **File tab**, click **Print**, and then click **Print Preview**. Compare your screen with Figure 1.25.

> The table displays in Print Preview with the default zoom setting of One Page, a view that enables you to see how your table will print on the page. It is a good idea to view any object in Print Preview before printing so that you can make changes to the object if needed before actually printing it. In the navigation area, the Next Page button is darker (available), an indication that more than one page will print.

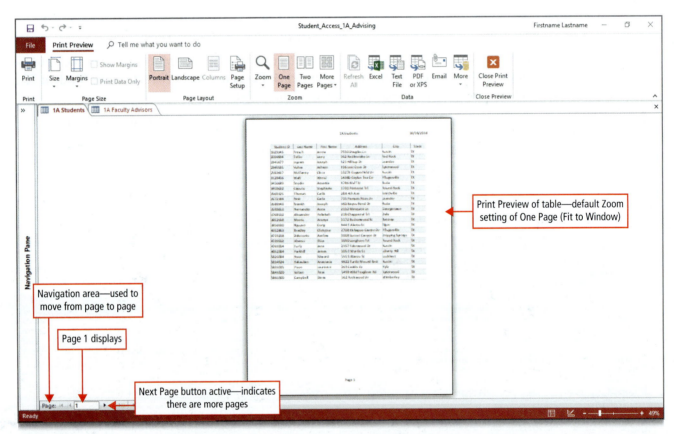

Figure 1.25

NOTE   Headers and Footers in Access Objects

The headers and footers in Access tables and queries are controlled by default settings; you cannot enter additional information or edit the information. The object name displays in the center of the header area, and the current date displays on the right. Adding your name to the object name is helpful in identifying your paper printouts or electronic results. The page number displays in the center of the footer area. The headers and footers in Access forms and reports are more flexible; you can add to and edit the information.

---

2 In the navigation area, click **Next Page** ▶ to display Page 2. Point to the top of the page to display the 🔍 pointer, click one time to zoom in, and then compare your screen with Figure 1.26.

> The Print Preview display enlarges, and the Zoom Out pointer displays. The second page of the table displays the last five fields. The Next Page button is dimmed, indicating that the button is unavailable because there are no more pages after Page 2. The Previous Page button is available, indicating that a page exists before this page.

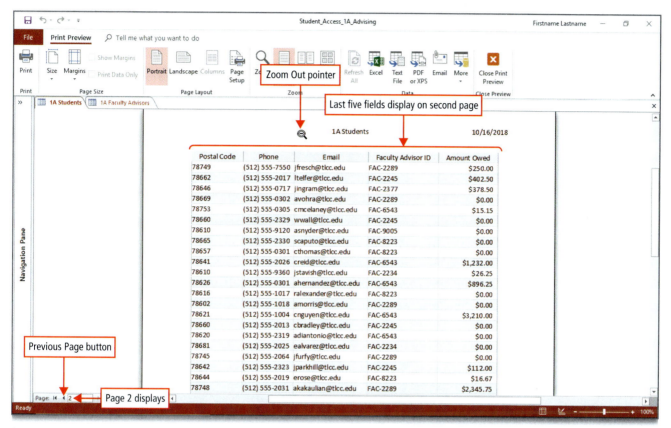

Figure 1.26

3 On the ribbon, on the **Print Preview tab**, in the **Zoom group**, click **Zoom** to change the zoom setting back to the default setting of One Page.

🔄 **ANOTHER WAY**   With the 🔍 pointer displayed on the page, click to zoom back to the One Page setting.

4 In the **Page Layout group**, click **Landscape**, and notice that there are only three fields on Page 2. In the navigation area, click **Previous Page** ◂ to display Page 1, and then compare your screen with Figure 1.27.

The orientation of the page to be printed changes. The header on the page includes the table name and current date, and the footer displays the page number. The change in orientation from portrait to landscape is not saved with the table. Each time you print, you must check the page orientation, the margins, and any other print parameters so that the object prints as you intend.

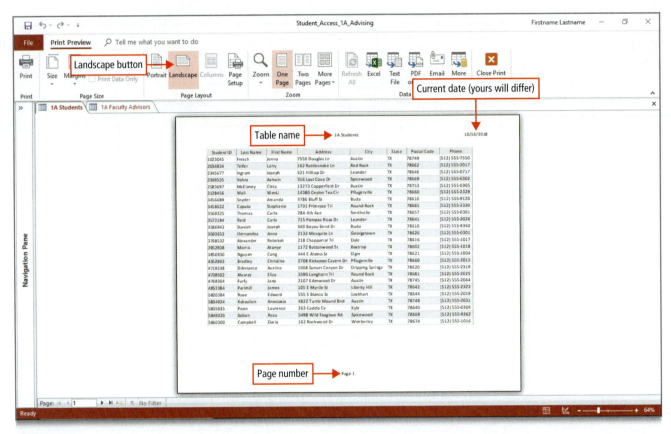

Figure 1.27

NOTE   **Creating a PDF Electronic Image of Your Database Object That Looks Like a Printed Document**

Display the object (table, query, form, report, and so on) in Print Preview and adjust margins and orientation as needed. On the Print Preview tab, in the Data group, click PDF or XPS. In the Publish as PDF or XPS dialog box, navigate to your chapter folder. Use the default file name, or follow your instructor's directions to name the object. If you wish to view the PDF file, in the dialog box, select the Open file after publishing check box. In the Publish as PDF or XPS dialog box, click Publish. If necessary, close any windows that try to display your PDF—Adobe Reader, Adobe Acrobat, or the Microsoft Edge browser, and then close the Export – PDF dialog box. On the ribbon, click Close Print Preview; your electronic image is saved. Close the Save Export Steps dialog box.

---

5 On the ribbon, in the **Close Preview group**, click **Close Print Preview**. In the upper right corner of the object window, click **Close Object** ☒ to close your **1A Students** table. Notice that the **1A Faculty Advisors** table is the active object in the object window.

ANOTHER WAY   In the object window, right-click the 1A Students object tab, and then click Close.

6 In your **1A Faculty Advisors** table, to the left of the **Faculty ID** field name, click **Select All** ☐ to select all of the columns. On the **Home tab**, in the **Records group**, click **More**, and then click **Field Width**. In the **Column Width** dialog box, click **Best Fit** to adjust the widths of all of the columns so that all of the data displays. Click in any field in the table to cancel the selection. Scroll horizontally and vertically to be sure that all of the data displays in each field; if necessary, use the techniques you practiced to apply Best Fit to individual columns. **Save** 🖫 the changes you made to the table's column widths, and then click in any record to cancel the selection, if necessary.

7 On the ribbon, click the **File tab**, click **Print**, and then click **Print Preview**. On the **Print Preview tab**, in the **Page Layout group**, click **Landscape**. Notice that the table will print on more than one page. In the **Page Size group**, click **Margins**, click **Normal**, and then notice that one more column moved to the first page—your results may differ depending upon your printer's capabilities.

> In addition to changing the page orientation to Landscape, you can change the margins to Normal to see if all of the fields will print on one page. In this instance, there are still too many fields to print on one page, although the Postal Code field moved from Page 2 to Page 1.

8 On the ribbon, in the **Close Preview group**, click **Close Print Preview**. In the object window, **Close** ☒ your **1A Faculty Advisors** table, saving changes if necessary.

> All of your database objects—your *1A Students* table and your *1A Faculty Advisors* table—are closed; the object window is empty.

Objective 4 | Create a Query, Form, and Report

GO! Learn How

Video A1-4

Recall that tables are the foundation of an Access database because all of the data is stored in one or more tables. You can use the data stored in tables in other database objects such as queries, forms, and reports.

Activity 1.14 | Creating a Query by Using the Simple Query Wizard

3.1.7

A *query* is a database object that retrieves specific data from one or more database objects—either tables or other queries—and then, in a single datasheet, displays only the data that you specify when you design the query. Because the word *query* means *to ask a question*, think of a query as a question formed in a manner that Access can answer.

A *select query* is one type of Access query. A select query, also called a *simple select query*, retrieves (selects) data from one or more tables or queries and then displays the selected data in a datasheet. A select query creates a subset of the data to answer specific questions; for example, *Which students live in Austin, TX?*

The objects from which a query selects the data are referred to as the query's *data source*. In this Activity, you will create a simple query using a wizard that walks you step by step through the process. The process involves selecting the data source and indicating the fields that you want to include in the query results. The query—the question you want to ask—is *What is the name, email address, phone number, and Student ID of every student?*

1 ▶ On the ribbon, click the **Create tab**, and then in then in the **Queries group**, click **Query Wizard**. In the **New Query** dialog box, be sure **Simple Query Wizard** is selected, and then click **OK**. Compare your screen with Figure 1.28.

In the wizard, the displayed table or query name is the object that was last selected on the Navigation Pane. The last object you worked with was your 1A Faculty Advisors table, so that object name displayed in the wizard.

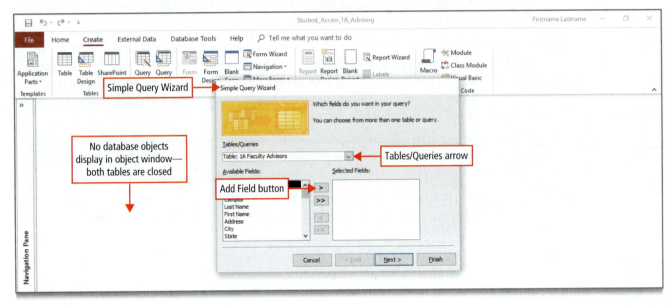

Figure 1.28

2 ▶ In the wizard, click the **Tables/Queries arrow**, and then click your **Table: 1A Students**.

To create a query, first select the data source—the object from which the query is to select the data. The information you need to answer the question is stored in your 1A Students table, so this table is your data source.

3 ▶ Under **Available Fields**, click **Last Name**, and then click **Add Field** [>] to move the field to the **Selected Fields** list on the right. Double-click the **First Name** field to add the field to the **Selected Fields** list.

Use either method to add fields to the Selected Fields list—you can add fields in any order.

4 ▶ By using **Add Field** [>] or by double-clicking the field name, add the following fields to the **Selected Fields** list in the order specified: **Email**, **Phone**, and **Student ID**. Compare your screen with Figure 1.29.

Selecting these five fields will answer the question, *What is the name, email address, phone number, and Student ID of every student?*

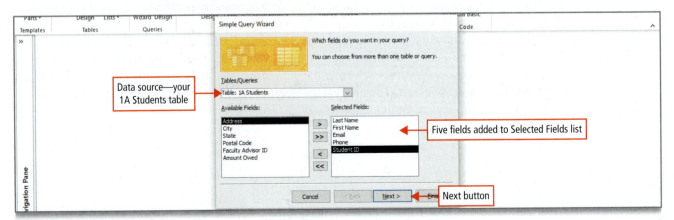

Figure 1.29

5 In the wizard, click **Next**. Click in the **What title do you want for your query?** box. Edit as necessary so that the query name is **1A All Students Query** and then compare your screen with Figure 1.30.

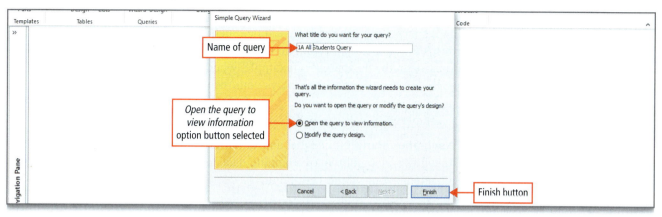

Figure 1.30

6 In the wizard, click **Finish**. Select all of the columns, apply **Best Fit**, and then **Save** 🔲 the query. In the first record, click in the **Last Name** field to cancel the selection. Compare your screen with Figure 1.31.

Access **runs** the query—performs the actions indicated in your query design—by searching the records in the specified data source, and then finds the records that match specified criteria. The records that match the criteria display in a datasheet. A select query *selects*—pulls out and displays—*only* the information from the data source that you request, including the specified fields. In the object window, Access displays every student from your 1A Students table—the data source—but displays *only* the five fields that you moved to the Selected Fields list in the Simple Query Wizard.

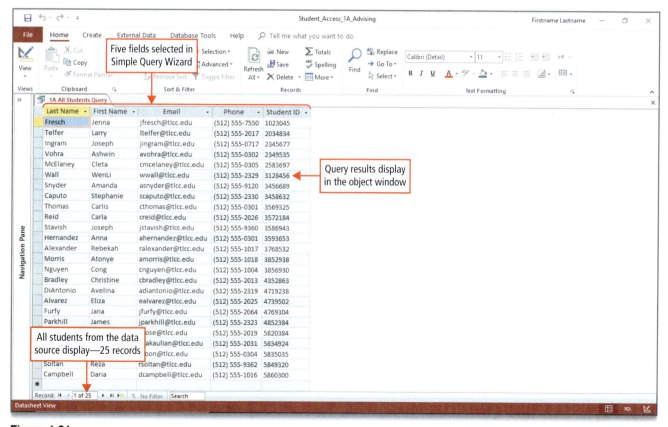

Figure 1.31

7 In the object window, **Close** ⊠ the query.

Activity 1.15 | Creating a Form

1.3.1, 4.1.1

A *form* is an Access object with which you can enter data, edit data, or display data from a table or query. In a form, the fields are laid out in an attractive format on the screen, which makes working with the database easier for those who must enter and look up data.

One type of form displays only one record at a time. Such a form is useful not only to the individual who performs the data entry—typing in the records—but also to anyone who has the job of viewing information in the database. For example, when you visit the Records office at your college to obtain a transcript, someone displays your record on the screen. For the viewer, it is much easier to look at one record at a time using a form than to look at all of the student records in the database table.

1 ▶ **Open** » the **Navigation Pane**. Notice that a table name displays with a datasheet icon, and a query name displays an icon of two overlapping datasheets. Right-click your **1A Students** table, and then compare your screen with Figure 1.32.

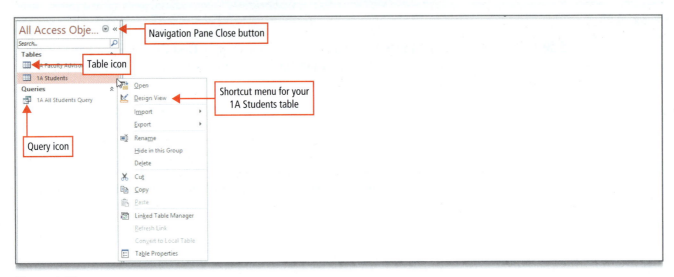

Figure 1.32

2 ▶ On the shortcut menu, click **Open** to display the table in the object window, and then **Close** « the **Navigation Pane** to maximize your object window space.

 ANOTHER WAY   In the Navigation Pane, double-click the object name to open it.

---

3 Notice that there are 11 fields in the table. On the **Create tab**, in the **Forms group**, click **Form**. Compare your screen with Figure 1.33.

The Form tool creates a form based on the currently selected object—your 1A Students table. The form displays all of the fields from the underlying data source—one record at a time—in a simple top-to-bottom format with all 11 fields in a single column. You can use this form as it displays, or you can modify it. Records that you create or edit in a form are automatically added to or updated in the underlying table or data source.

The new form displays in *Layout view*—the Access view in which you can make changes to elements of an object while it is open and displaying the data from the data source. Each field in the form displayed in Figure 1.33 displays the data for the first student record—*Jenna Fresch*—in your 1A Students table.

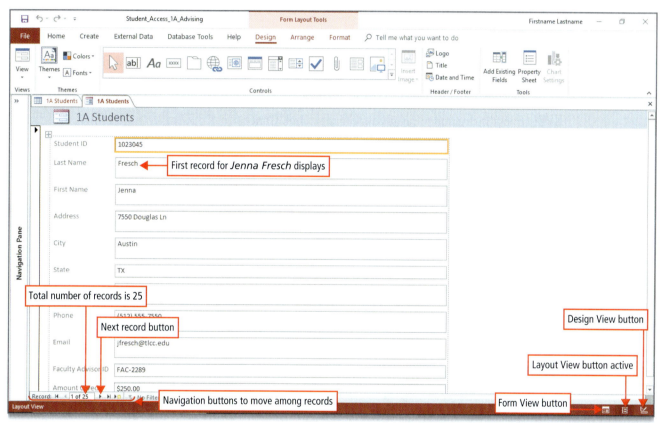

Figure 1.33

NOTE   **The Property Sheet Displays**

If the Property sheet was displayed the last time you were viewing a form in Access, it will display by default with the new form.

---

4 At the right side of the status bar, notice the three buttons. Point to each button to display its ScreenTip, and notice that **Layout View** ▤ is active, indicating that the form is displayed in Layout view.

5 In the status bar, click **Form View** ▤.

In *Form view*, you can view the records, create a new record, edit a record, and delete a record. You cannot change the layout or design of the form. Form view is useful for individuals who *access records* in your database. Layout view is useful for individuals who *design* the form.

🔄 **ANOTHER WAY**   On the Design tab, or on the Home tab, in the Views group, click View when the button displays an icon of a form.

---

6 In the navigation area, click **Next record** ▶ two times to display the third record—the record for *Joseph Ingram*.

> Use the navigation buttons to scroll among the records and to display any single record.

7 Save 🖫 the form as **1A Student Form**

8 On the ribbon, click the **File tab**, click **Print**, and then on the right, click **Print**—do *not* click Print Preview because you are going to print a *single* record—not all of the records.

9 In the **Print** dialog box, under **Print Range**, click the **Selected Record(s)** option button, and then click **Setup**.

10 In the **Page Setup** dialog box, click the **Columns tab**. Under **Column Size**, double-click in the **Width** box, type **7.5** and then click **OK**.

> Forms are usually not printed, so the default width for a form created with the Form command is larger than most printers can handle to print on one page. If you do not change the width, the form will print on two pages because the column flows over the margins allowed by the printer. If, after changing the Width to 7.5, your form still prints on two pages, try entering a different value for Width; for example, 7 or 6.5.

11 Unless instructed to print your objects, click Cancel.

> After printing, along the left edge of the record, the narrow bar—the *record selector bar*—displays in black, indicating that the record is selected.

NOTE   Printing a Single Form in PDF

On the File tab, click Print, and then on the right, click Print. In the Print dialog box, click Setup. In the Page Setup dialog box, click the Columns tab. Under Column Size, double-click in the Width box, type **7.5** and then click OK. In the Print dialog box, click Cancel. On the left edge of the form, click the record selector bar so that it is black—selected.

On the ribbon, click the External Data tab. In the Export group, click PDF or XPS. In the Publish as PDF or XPS dialog box, navigate to your chapter folder, and at the lower right corner of the dialog box, click Options. In the Options dialog box, under Range, click the Selected records option button, and then click OK. In the Publish as PDF or XPS dialog box, click Publish. If necessary, close Adobe Reader, Adobe Acrobat, or the Microsoft Edge browser.

---

12 Close ⊠ the form object; leave your **1A Students** table open.

Activity 1.16 | Creating and Modifying a Report

5.1.1, 5.1.2, 5.2.3

A *report* is a database object that displays the fields and records from a table or query in an easy-to-read format suitable for printing. Create professional-looking reports to summarize database information.

1 Open ⟫ the **Navigation Pane**, and then open your **1A Faculty Advisors** table by double-clicking the table name or by right-clicking the table name and clicking Open. **Close** ⟪ the **Navigation Pane**.

2 On the **Create tab**, in the **Reports group**, click **Report**.

> The Report tool creates a report in Layout view and includes all of the fields and all of the records in the data source—your 1A Faculty Advisors table. Dotted lines indicate how the report would break across pages if you print it now. In Layout view, you can make quick changes to the report layout while viewing the data from the table.

3 ▶ Click the **Faculty ID** field name, and then on the ribbon, under **Report Layout Tools**, click the **Arrange tab**. In the **Rows & Columns group**, click **Select Column**, and then press Del. Using the same technique, delete the **Rank** field.

> The Faculty ID and Rank fields, along with the data, are deleted from the report. The fields readjust by moving to the left. Deleting the fields from the report does *not* delete the fields and data from the data source—your 1A Faculty Advisors table.

ANOTHER WAY   Right-click the field name, click Select Entire Column, and then press Del.

4 ▶ Click the **Address** field name, and then by using the scroll bar at the bottom of the screen, scroll to the right to display the **Cell Phone** field; be careful not to click in the report.

5 ▶ Hold down Shift, and then click the **Cell Phone** field name to select all of the fields from *Address* through *Cell Phone*. With the field names selected—surrounded by a colored border—in the **Rows & Columns group**, click **Select Column**, and then press Del.

> Use this method to select and delete multiple columns in Layout view.

6 ▶ Scroll to the left and notice that the four remaining fields display within the dotted lines— they are within the margins of the report. Click the **Campus** field name. Hold down Shift, and then click the **First Name** field name to select the first three fields. In the **Rows & Columns group**, click **Select Column** to select all three fields.

7 ▶ On the ribbon, click the **Design tab**, and then in the **Tools group**, click **Property Sheet**.

> The *Property Sheet* for the selected columns displays on the right side of the screen. Every object and every item in an object has an associated Property Sheet where you can make precise changes to the properties—characteristics—of selected items.

8 ▶ In the **Property Sheet**, if necessary, click the **Format tab**. Click **Width**, type **1.5** and then press Enter. Compare your screen with Figure 1.34.

> The width of the three selected fields changes to 1.5", and the fields readjust by moving to the left. You can change the Width property if you need to move columns within the margins of a report. In this report, the fields already displayed within the margins, but some reports may need this minor adjustment to print on one page.

ANOTHER WAY   Select the column, and then drag the right edge of the column to the left to decrease the width of the field, or, drag to the right to increase the width of the field.

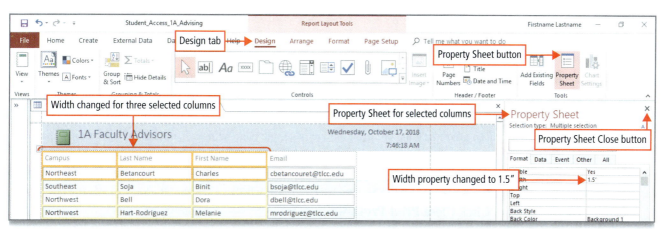

Figure 1.34

9 ▶ **Close** ⊠ the **Property Sheet**. Click the **Last Name** field name. On the ribbon, click the **Home tab**, and then in the **Sort & Filter group**, click **Ascending**.

Access sorts the report in ascending alphabetical order by the Last Name field. By default, tables are sorted in ascending order by the primary key field—in this instance, the Faculty ID field. Changing the sort order in the report does *not* change the sort order in the underlying table.

10 ▶ At the top of the report, to the right of the green report icon, click anywhere in the title of the report to select the title. On the **Home tab**, in the **Text Formatting group**, click the **Font Size arrow**, and then click **14**. **Save** 🖫 the report. In the **Save As** dialog box, in the **Report Name** box, add **Report** to the end of *1A Faculty Advisors*, and then click **OK**.

11 ▶ On the **File tab**, click **Print**, and then click **Print Preview**. On the **Print Preview tab**, in the **Zoom group**, click **Two Pages**, and then compare your screen with Figure 1.35

As currently formatted, the report will print on two pages, because the page number at the bottom of the report is positioned beyond the right margin of the report.

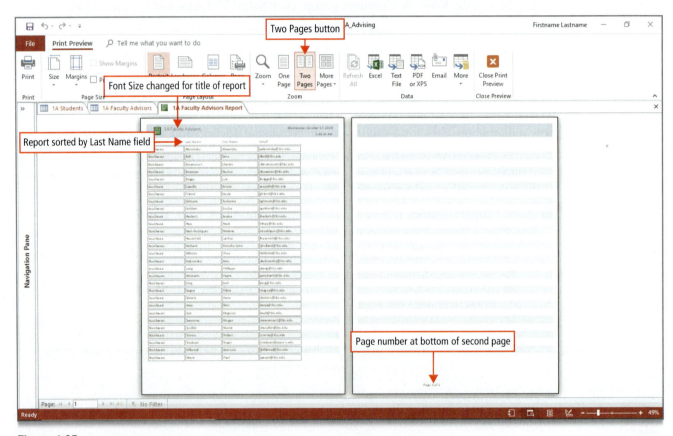

Figure 1.35

12 ▶ In the **Close Preview group**, click **Close Print Preview**. Scroll down to display the bottom of the report, and then, if necessary, scroll right to display the page number. Click the page number—**Page 1 of 1**—and then press ⌗Del⌗.

Because all of the data will print on one page, the page number is not necessary for this report. If you want the page number to display, you can drag it within the margins of the report.

13 ▶ Display the report in **Print Preview**, and notice that the report will now print on one page. In the **Zoom group**, click **One Page**. Click **Save** 🖫 to save the changes to the design of the report. Click **Close Print Preview**.

When you create a report by using the Report tool, the default margins are 0.25 inch. Some printers require a greater margin, so your printed report may result in two pages. As you progress in your study of Access, you will practice making these adjustments. Also, if a printer is not installed on your system, the electronic PDF printout might result in a two-page report.

14 ▸ In the object window, right-click any **object tab**, and then click **Close All** to close all of the open objects. Notice that the object window is empty.

Objective 5 | Close a Database and Close Access

GO! Learn How
Video A1-5

When you close a table, any changes made to the records are saved automatically. If you made changes to the structure or adjusted column widths, you will be prompted to save the table when you close the table or when you switch views. Likewise, you will be prompted to save queries, forms, and reports if you make changes to the layout or design. If the Navigation Pane is open when you close Access, it will display when you reopen the database. When you are finished using your database, close the database, and then close Access.

Activity 1.17 | Closing a Database and Closing Access

1 ▸ **Open** ⟩⟩ the **Navigation Pane**. Notice that your report object displays with a green report icon. Compare your screen with Figure 1.36.

Figure 1.36

2 ▸ On the **File tab**, click **Close** to close the database but leave Access open. This action enables you to continue working in Access with another database if you want to do so. In the Access opening screen, in the upper right corner, click **Close** ⟨×⟩ to close Access.

For Non-MyLab Submissions   **Determine What Your Instructor Requires for Submission**
As directed by your instructor, submit your completed database file.

3 ▸ In **MyLab IT**, locate and click the Grader Project **Access 1A Advising**. In **step 3**, under **Upload Completed Assignment**, click **Choose File**. In the **Open** dialog box, navigate to your **Access Chapter 1 folder**, and then click your **Student_Access_1A_Advising** file one time to select it. In the lower right corner of the **Open** dialog box, click **Open**.

The name of your selected file displays above the Upload button.

4 ▸ To submit your file to **MyLab IT** for grading, click **Upload**, wait a moment for a green **Success!** message, and then in **step 4**, click the blue **Submit for Grading** button. Click **Close Assignment** to return to your list of **Course Materials**.

You have completed Project 1A **END**

»»» GO! With Google

Objective	Export an Access Table to an Excel Spreadsheet, Open as a Google Sheet, Edit a Record, and Save to Your Computer

Access web apps are designed to work with Microsoft's **SharePoint**, a service for setting up websites to share and manage documents. Your college may not have SharePoint installed, so you will use other tools to share objects from your database so that you can work collaboratively with others. Recall that Google Drive is Google's free, web-based word processor, spreadsheet, slide show, form, and data storage and sharing service. For Access, you can *export* a database object to an Excel worksheet, a PDF file, or a text file, and then save the file to Google Drive.

ALERT   **Working with Web-Based Applications and Services**

Computer programs and services on the web receive continuous updates and improvements. Therefore, the steps to complete this web-based Activity may differ from the ones shown. You can often look at the screens and the information presented to determine how to complete the Activity.

   If you do not already have a Google account, you will need to create one before you begin this Activity. Go to **http://google.com** and in the upper right corner, click **Sign In**. On the Sign In screen, click **Create Account**. On the Create your Google Account page, complete the form, read and agree to the Terms of Service and Privacy Policy, and then click **Next step**. On the Welcome screen, click **Get Started**.

Activity | Exporting an Access Table to an Excel Spreadsheet, Saving the Spreadsheet to Google Drive, Editing a Record in Google Drive, and Saving to Your Computer

In this Activity, you will export your 1A Faculty Advisors table to an Excel spreadsheet, upload your Excel file to Google Drive as a Google Sheet, edit a record in the Google Sheet, and then download a copy of the edited spreadsheet to your computer.

1 Start Access, navigate to your **Access Chapter 1** folder, and then **Open** your **1A_Advising** database file. If necessary, on the Message Bar, click Enable Content. In the **Navigation Pane**, click your **1A Faculty Advisors** table to select it—do not open it.

2 On the ribbon, click the **External Data tab**, and then in the **Export group**, click **Excel**. In the **Export – Excel Spreadsheet** dialog box, click **Browse**, and then navigate to your **Access Chapter 1** folder. In the **File Save** dialog box, click in the **File name** box, type **Lastname_Firstname_a1A_Web** and then click **Save**.

3 In the **Export – Excel Spreadsheet** dialog box, under **Specify export options**, select the first two check boxes—**Export data with formatting and layout** and **Open the destination file after the export operation is complete**—and then click **OK**. Take a moment to examine the data in the file, and then **Close** Excel. In the **Export – Excel Spreadsheet** dialog box, click **Close**, and then **Close** Access.

4 Open your browser, navigate to **http://drive.google.com**, and sign in to your Google account; if necessary,

create a new Google account and then sign in. On the right side of the screen, click **Settings** ⚙, and then click **Settings**. In the **Settings** dialog box, to the right of *Convert uploads*, if necessary, select the **Convert uploaded files to Google Docs editor format** check box. In the upper right, click **Done**

> It is necessary to select this setting; otherwise, your document will upload as a pdf file and cannot be edited without further action.

5 Open your **GO! Web Projects** folder—or create and then open this folder by clicking **New** and then **Folder**. On the left, click **New**, and then click **File upload**. In the **Open** dialog box, navigate to your **Access Chapter 1** folder, and then double-click your **a1A_Web** Excel file to upload it to Google Drive. When the message *1 upload complete* displays, **Close** the message box.

6 Double-click your **Lastname_Firstname_a1A_Web** file to display the file, and then compare your screen with Figure A. The worksheet displays column letters, row numbers, and data.

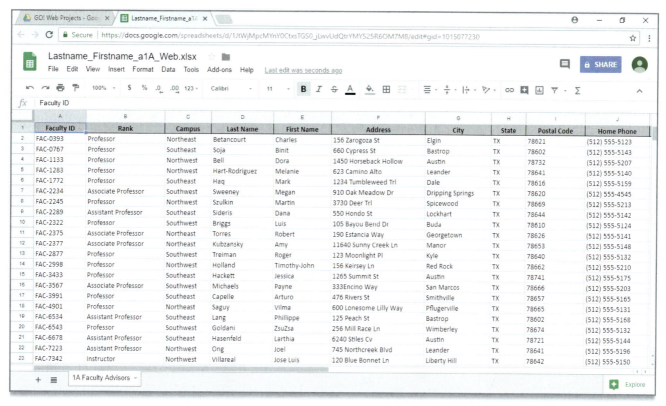

Figure A

7 Click in cell **C2** and replace the current Campus with **Southwest** Click in cell **D2** and replace Betancourt with your last name. Press Tab and then replace Charles with your first name.

8 Above row **1** and to the left of column **A**, click **Select All** [ ]. On the menu bar, click **Format**, and then click **Clear formatting** so that the default font is applied to all data; the cell borders are removed, and the formatting of the field names are removed.

9 In the column headings row, click **I** to select the entire column. On the menu bar, click **Format**, point to **Number**, and then click **Plain text** to format every number in the columns as text. Click in cell **A1** to deselect the column.

Recall that in Access, numbers that are not used in calculations should be formatted as Short Text. Because the formatting is cleared, you can enter new records into the spreadsheet in the same format as the existing records.

10 Click **File** to display the menu, point to **Download as**, and then click **Microsoft Excel (.xlsx)**. Click **Enable Content**. Click **File**, and then click **Save As**. In the **Save As** dialog box, navigate to your **Access Chapter 1** folder, click in the **File name** box, and type **Lastname_Firstname_a1A_Web_Download** and then click **Save**. **Close** the message box.

NOTE   Saving the Downloaded File to the Access Chapter 1 Folder

Depending on the browser you are using, you may need to open the file in Excel and then save the a1A_Web_Download worksheet to your Access Chapter 1 folder.

---

11 In Google Drive, at the top right corner of your screen, click your user name, and then click **Sign out**. **Close** your browser window.

12 Start Excel. In the Excel opening screen, click **Open Other Workbooks**, and then click **Browse**. Navigate to your **Access Chapter 1** folder, and then double-click your **a1A_Web** Excel file. Notice that this file is the original file—the record is not edited. If you are required to print your documents, use one of the methods in the following Note. **Close** your Excel file; and, if prompted, save the changes to your worksheet. Then **Open** and print your **a1A_Web_Download** Excel file using one of the methods in the following Note. **Close** Excel; and, if prompted, save the changes to your worksheet. As directed by your instructor, submit your two workbooks and the two paper printouts or PDF electronic images that are the results of this project.

NOTE **Adding the File Name to the Footer and Printing or Creating an PDF Electronic Image of an Excel Spreadsheet on One Page**

Click the File tab, click Print, and then click Page Setup. In the Page Setup dialog box, on the Page tab, under Orientation, click Landscape. Under Scaling, click the Fit to option button. In the Page Setup dialog box, click the Header/Footer tab, and then click Custom Footer. With the insertion point blinking in the Left section box, click the Insert File Name button, and then click OK. In the Page Setup dialog box, click OK.

To print on paper, click Print. To create an electronic file of your printout, on the left side of your screen, click Export. Under Export, be sure Create PDF/XPS Document is selected, and then click Create PDF/XPS. Navigate to your Access Chapter 1 folder, and then click Publish to save the file with the default name and an extension of pdf.

Student Workshops Database

Project Activities

In Activities 1.18 through 1.24, you will assist Dr. Miriam Yong, Director of Student Activities, in creating a database to store information about student workshops held at Texas Lakes Community College campuses. You will use a database template that tracks event information, add workshop information to the database, and then print the results. Your completed Navigation Pane will look similar to Figure 1.37.

Project Files for MyLab IT Grader

1. In your **MyLab IT** course, locate and click **Access 1B Student Workshops**, Download Materials, and then Download All Files. Close the Grader download screens.
2. Extract the zipped folder to your Access Chapter 1 folder.
3. Take a moment to open the downloaded **Access_1B_Student_Workshops_Instructions**; note any recent updates to the book.

Project Results

GO! Project 1B
Where We're Going

Figure 1.37

Project 1B Student Workshops

For Non-MyLab Submissions
For Project 1B, you will need this following files:
a01B_Event_Template
a01B_Workshops (Excel workbook)

Start with an Access Data File
In your Access Chapter 1 folder, save your workbook as:
Lastname_Firstname_1B_Student_Workshops

After you have saved your database, open it to launch Access. On the next page, begin with Activity 1.19.

GO! Learn How

Video A1-6

A database template contains prebuilt tables, queries, forms, and reports that perform a specific task, such as tracking events. For example, your college may hold events such as athletic contests, plays, lectures, concerts, and club meetings. Using a predefined template, your college's Activities Director can quickly create a database to manage these events. The advantage of using a template to start a new database is that you do not have to create the objects—all you need to do is enter the data and modify the prebuilt objects to suit your needs.

The purpose of the database in this project is to track the student workshops that are held by Texas Lakes Community College. The questions to be answered might include:

- What workshops will be offered and when will they be offered?
- In what rooms and on what campuses will the workshops be held?
- Which workshop locations have a computer projector for PowerPoint presentations?

Activity 1.18 | Using a Template to Create a Database

ALERT Because Office 365 is a cloud-based subscription service that receives continuous updates, you may encounter some variations in what appears on your screen and what is shown in this instruction. Microsoft Office 365 is fully installed on your PC or Mac; no internet access is necessary to create or edit documents. When you *are* connected to the internet, you will receive monthly upgrades and new features, so you always have the latest versions of Office apps as soon as they are available. Your subscription gives you continuous free access to the latest innovations and refinements.

These templates can be used to create databases that will be stored on your desktop. Because the templates available change so often, in this activity, you will use a previously saved template to create your database.

1 Start Access. In the Access opening screen, scroll down to display an **Inventory** template and a **Nutrition tracking** template. Compare your screen with Figure 1.38.

These templates are included with the Access program. To create a database to manage inventory on your desktop, select the *Inventory* template; to manage what you eat, select the *Nutrition tracking* template.

You can search the Microsoft Office website for more templates. You can also click on a category under the search box, where templates will be suggested.

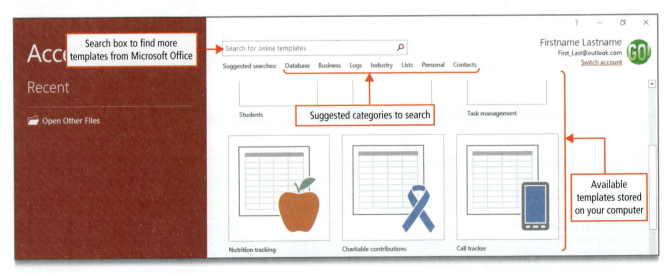

Figure 1.38

2 On the left, click **Open Other Files**, and then click **Browse**. Navigate to your **Access Chapter 1 folder**, and then double-click the Access file that you downloaded from **MyLab IT** that displays your name—**Student_Access_1B_Student_Workshops**. If necessary, at the top click **Enable Content**.

Activity 1.19 | Building a Table by Entering Records in a Multiple-Items Form and a Single-Record Form

2.3.1

One purpose of a form is to simplify the entry of data into a table—either for you or for others who enter data. In Project 1A, you created a simple form that enabled you to display or enter records in a table one record at a time. The Desktop Event management template creates a *multiple-items form* that enables you to display or enter *multiple* records in a table, but with an easier and simplified layout rather than typing directly into the table itself. The form opens when the database opens.

1 In the new record row, click in the **Title** field. Type **Your Online Reputation** and then press Tab. In the **Start Time** field, type **3/9/23 7p** and then press Tab.

Access formats the date and time. As you enter dates and times, a small calendar displays to the right of the field. You can use the calendar to select a date instead of typing it.

2 In the **End Time** field, type **3/9/23 9p** and then press Tab. In the **Description** field, type **Internet Safety** and then press Tab. In the **Location** field, type **Northeast Campus** and then press Tab three times to move to the **Title** field in the new record row. Compare your screen with Figure 1.39.

Because the workshops have no unique value, Access uses the AutoNumber data type in the ID field to assign a unique, sequential number to each record.

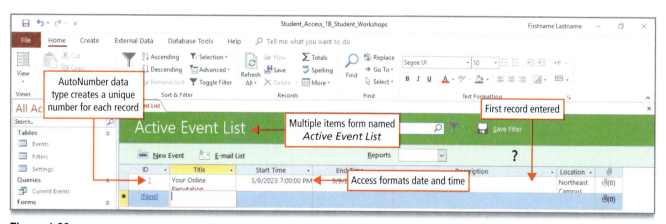

Figure 1.39

3 ▶ In the form, directly above the field names row, click **New Event**.

A *single-record form* with the name *Event Details* displays, similar to the simple form you created in Project 1A. A single-record form enables you to display or enter one record at a time into a table.

4 ▶ Using [Tab] to move from field to field, enter the following record in the **Event Details** form—press [Tab] two times to move from the **Title** field to the **Description** field, and then click the **Location** field. Then compare your screen with Figure 1.40.

Title	Description	Location	Start Time	End Time
Writing a Research Paper	Computer Skills	Southwest Campus	3/10/23 4p	3/10/23 6p

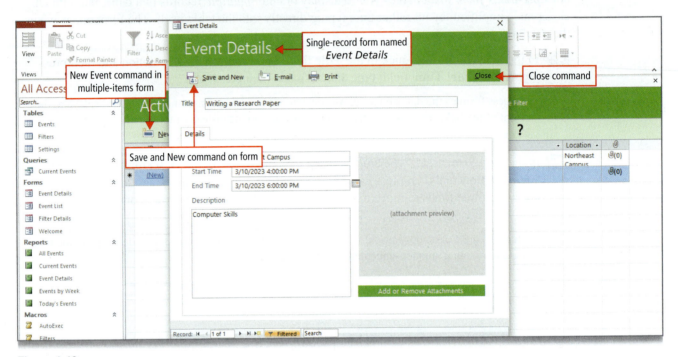

Figure 1.40

5 ▶ In the **Event Details** single-record form, in the Menu bar, click **Close**, and notice that the new record displays in the multiple-items form—*Event List*.

6 Enter the following records by using either the **Event List** form—the multiple-items form—or the **Event Details** form—the single-record form that is accessed by clicking the *New Event* command on the Event List form. Be sure the multiple-items form displays, and then compare your screen with Figure 1.41.

ID	Title	Start Time	End Time	Description	Location
3	**Resume Writing**	**3/18/23 2p**	**3/18/23 4p**	**Job Skills**	**Northwest Campus**
4	**Careers in the Legal Profession**	**3/19/23 2p**	**3/19/23 4p**	**Careers**	**Southeast Campus**

ALERT   Does a single-record form—*Event Details*—open?

In the multiple-items form, pressing [Enter] three times at the end of the row to begin a new record will display the single-record form—*Event Details*. If you prefer to use the multiple-items form—Event List—close the single-record form and continue entering records, using the [Tab] key to move from field to field.

Active Event List

Search [   ] Save Filter

Four records entered   E-mail List   Reports [   ]   ?

ID	Title	Start Time	End Time	Description	Location
1	Your Online Reputation	3/9/2023 7:00:00 PM	3/9/2023 9:00:00 PM	Internet Safety	Northeast Campus
2	Writing a Research Paper	3/10/2023 4:00:00 PM	3/10/2023 6:00:00 PM	Computer Skills	Southwest Campus
3	Resume Writing	3/18/2023 2:00:00 PM	3/18/2023 4:00:00 PM	Job Skills	Northwest Campus
4	Careers in the Legal Profession	3/19/2023 2:00:00 PM	3/19/2023 4:00:00 PM	Careers	Southeast Campus

Figure 1.41

7 In the object window, click **Close** [×] to close the **Event List** form.

Activity 1.20 | Appending Records by Importing from an Excel Spreadsheet

MOS
2.1.1

In this Activity, you will append records to the table storing the data that displays in the Events List form. You will import the records from an Excel spreadsheet.

1 On the ribbon, click the **External Data tab**. In the **Import & Link group**, click **New Data Source**, point to **From File**, and then click **Excel**.

2 In the **Get External Data – Excel Spreadsheet** dialog box, click **Browse**. Navigate to the location where your student data files are stored, and then double-click **a01B_Workshops**.

3 Click the second option button—**Append a copy of the records to the table:**—and then click **OK**.

> The table that stores the data is named *Events*. Recall that other objects, such as forms, queries, and reports, display data from tables; so the Event Details form displays data that is stored in the Events table.

4 In the **Import Spreadsheet Wizard**, click **Next**, and then click **Finish**. In the **Get External Data – Excel Spreadsheet** dialog box, click **Close**.

5 ▶ Double-click **Event List** to open the form that displays data from the Events table, and then **Close** ❮❮ the **Navigation Pane**. Compare your screen with Figure 1.42.

A total of 12 records display; you entered four records, and you appended eight records from the a01B_Workshops Excel workbook. The data displays truncated in several fields because the columns are not wide enough to display all of the data.

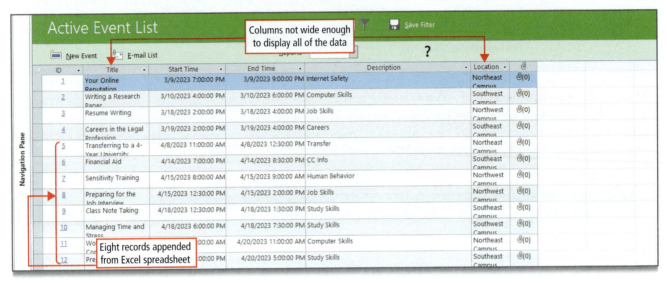

Figure 1.42

6 ▶ To the left of the **ID** field name, click **Select All** ☐ to select all of the columns and rows.

7 ▶ In the field names row, point to the right edge of any of the selected columns to display the ➕ pointer, and then double-click to apply Best Fit to all of the columns. Click in any field to cancel the selection, and then **Save** 💾 the form.

Objective 7 | **Organize Objects in the Navigation Pane**

GO! Learn How
Video A1-7

Use the Navigation Pane to open objects, organize database objects, and perform common tasks, such as renaming an object or deleting an object.

Activity 1.21 | **Grouping Database Objects in the Navigation Pane**

1.1.3

The Navigation Pane groups and displays your database objects and can do so in predefined arrangements. In this Activity, you will group your database objects using the ***Tables and Related Views*** category, which groups objects by the table to which the objects are related. This grouping is useful because you can determine easily the table that is the data source of queries, forms, and reports.

1 ▶ Open ⟫ the **Navigation Pane**. At the top of the **Navigation Pane**, click **More** ⊚. On the list, under **Navigate To Category**, click **Tables and Related Views**. Compare your screen with Figure 1.43.

In the Navigation Pane, you can see the number of objects that are included in the Desktop Events Management template, including the table named *Events*. Other objects in the database that display data from the Events table include one query, two forms, and five reports. In the Navigation Pane, the Event List form is selected because it is open in the object window and is the active object.

Other objects might display on the Navigation Pane; for example, Filters and Unrelated Objects. These filters are objects created for use by the Desktop Event management template.

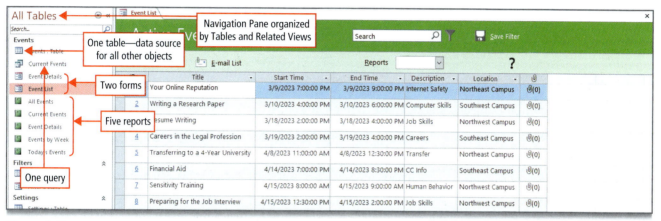

Figure 1.43

2 ▶ In the **Navigation Pane**, point to **Events: Table**, right-click, and then click **Open** to display the records in the underlying table.

The Events table is the active object in the object window. Use the Navigation Pane to open objects for use. The 12 records that display in the Event List multiple-items form are stored in this table. Recall that tables are the foundation of your database because your data must be stored in a table. You can enter records directly into a table or you can use a form to enter records.

↻ ANOTHER WAY Double-click the table name to open it in the object window.

3 ▶ In the object window, click the **Event List tab** to display the form as the active object in the object window.

Recall that a form presents a more user-friendly screen for entering records into a table.

4 In the **Navigation Pane**, double-click the **Current Events** *report* (green icon) to open the report. Compare your screen with Figure 1.44.

> An advantage of using a template to create a database is that many objects, such as reports, are already designed for you.

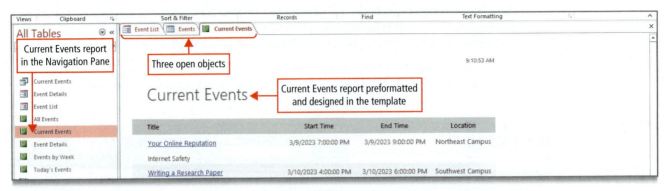

Figure 1.44

5 In the object window, **Close** ⊠ the **Current Events** report.

6 By double-clicking or right-clicking, from the **Navigation Pane**, open the **Events by Week** report.

> In this predesigned report, the events are displayed by week. After entering records in the form or table, the preformatted reports are updated with the records from the table.

7 In the object window, right-click any one of the **object tabs**, and then click **Close All** to close all of the objects. **Close** ⊠ the **Navigation Pane**.

Objective 8 | Create a New Table in a Database Created with a Template

GO! Learn How
Video A1-8

The Desktop Event management template included only one table—the *Events* table. It is easy to start a database with a template, and then you can add additional objects as needed.

Activity 1.22 | Using the Table Tool to Create a New Table

2.4.1, 2.4.5

Dr. Yong has information about the various locations where workshops are held. For example, on the Northeast Campus, she has information about the room, seating arrangements, number of seats, and multimedia equipment. In the Events table, workshops are scheduled in rooms at each of the four campuses. It would not make sense to store information about the campus rooms multiple times in the same table. It is *not* considered good database design to have duplicate information in a table.

When data becomes redundant, it is usually an indication that you need a new table to contain that information. In this Activity, you will create a table to track the workshop locations, the equipment, and the seating arrangements in each location.

1 On the ribbon, click the **Create tab**, and then in the **Tables group**, click **Table**.

2 In the field names row, click **Click to Add**, click **Short Text**, type **Campus/Location** and then press Enter.

3 In the third column, click **Short Text**, type **Room** and then press Enter. In the fourth column, click **Number**, type **Seats** and then press Enter.

> The *Number data type* describes numbers that represent a quantity and may be used in calculations. For the Seats field, you may need to determine how many seats remain after reservations are booked for a room. In the new record row, a *0* displays in the field.

4 In the fifth column, type **t** to select *Short Text*, type **Room Arrangement** and then press Enter. In the sixth column, type **t** and then type **Equipment** On your keyboard, press ↓.

With the data type list displayed, you can select the data type by either clicking it or typing the letter that is underscored for the data type.

This table has six fields. Access automatically creates the first field in the table—the ID field—to ensure that every record has a unique value. Before naming each field, you must define the data type for the field.

5 Right-click the **ID** field name, and then click **Rename Field**. Type **Room ID** and then press Enter. On the **Fields tab**, in the **Formatting group**, click the **Data Type arrow**, and then click **Short Text**. On the ribbon, in the **Field Validation group**, notice that **Unique** is selected.

Recall that, by default, Access creates the ID field with the AutoNumber data type so that the field can be used as the primary key. Here, this field will store a unique room ID that is a combination of letters, symbols, and numbers; therefore, it is appropriate to change the data type to Short Text. In Datasheet view, the primary key field is identified by the selection of the Unique check box.

> **MORE KNOWLEDGE** **Create a Table from a Template with Application Parts**
>
> To create a table using the Application parts gallery, click the Create tab, and in the Templates group, click Application Parts. Under Quick Start, click Comments. In the Create Relationships dialog box, specify a relationship between the Comments table and an associated table, click Next to choose the lookup column, and then click Create to create the table. If you choose No relationship, click Create to create the table. The Comments table displays in the Navigation Pane.

Activity 1.23 | Entering Records Into a New Table

1 In the new record row, click in the **Room ID** field. Enter the following record, pressing Enter or Tab to move from one field to the next. Do not be concerned that all of your text does not display; you will adjust the column widths later. After entering the record, compare your screen with Figure 1.45.

Recall that Access saves a record when you move to another row within the table. You can press either Enter or Tab to move between fields in a table.

Room ID	Campus/Location	Room	Seats	Room Arrangement	Equipment
NE-01	Northeast Campus	H265	150	Theater	Computer Projector, Surround Sound, Microphone

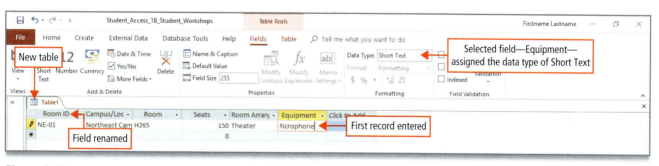

Figure 1.45

2 In the **Views group**, click the top of the **View** button to switch to **Design** view. In the **Save As** dialog box, in the **Table Name** box, using your own name, type **1B Workshop Locations** and then click **OK**.

Recall that when you switch views or when you close a table, Access prompts you to save the table if you have not previously saved it.

ANOTHER WAY On the right side of the status bar, click Design View to switch to Design view.

3 In the **Field Name** column, to the left of **Room ID**, notice the key icon.

In Design view, the key icon indicates that the field—Room ID—is the primary key field.

4 In the **Views group**, click the top of the **View** button to switch back to **Datasheet** view.

ANOTHER WAY On the right side of the status bar, click Datasheet View to switch to Datasheet view.

5 In the new record row, click in the **Room ID** field. Enter the following records, pressing Enter or Tab to move from one field to the next.

Room ID	Campus/Location	Room	Seats	Room Arrangement	Equipment
SW-01	Southwest Campus	A15	35	Lecture Classroom	Computer Projector
NW-01	Northwest Campus	C202	50	Lecture Classroom	Smart Board
SE-01	Southeast Campus	D148	20	U-shaped	White Board
NE-02	Northeast Campus	B105	25	U-shaped	25 Computers, Projector

6 To the left of the **Room ID** field name, click **Select All** to select all of the columns and rows in the table. On the **Home tab**, in the **Records group,** click **More**, and then click **Field Width**. In the **Column Width** dialog box, click **Best Fit** to display all of the data in each column. Click in any field to cancel the selection, and then **Save** the changes to the table. In the object window, **Close** your **1B Workshop Locations** table.

7 **Open** the **Navigation Pane** and notice that your new table displays in its own group. Point to the right edge of the **Navigation Pane** to display the pointer. Drag to the right to increase the width of the **Navigation Pane** so that your entire table name displays. Compare your screen with Figure 1.46.

Recall that organizing the Navigation Pane by Tables and Related Views groups the objects by each table and displays the related objects under each table name.

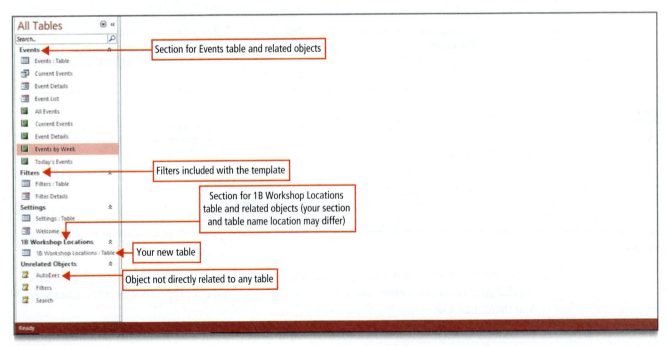

Figure 1.46

GO! Learn How
Video A1-9

Recall that one advantage to starting a new database with a template, instead of from a blank database, is that many report objects are already created for you.

Activity 1.24 | Viewing a Report

MOS
5.1.3

1 In the **Navigation Pane**, double-click the report (not the form) name **Event Details** to open it in the object window.

> This prebuilt Event Details report displays in an attractively arranged format.

2 Close ⊠ the **Event Details** report. Open the **All Events** report, and then **Close** « the **Navigation Pane**. On the **Home** tab, in the **Views group**, click the top of the **View** button to switch to **Layout** view.

> Recall that Layout view enables you to make changes to an object while viewing the data in the fields. Each prebuilt report displays the records in the table in different useful formats.

ANOTHER WAY On the right side of the status bar, click Layout View ▤ to switch to Layout view.

3 At the top of the report, click the title—*All Events*—to display a colored border around the title. Click to the left of the letter *A* to place the insertion point there. Type **1B** and then press Spacebar. Press Enter, and then **Save** 🖫 the report.

4 Close ⊠ your **1B All Events** report. For the convenience of the next individual opening the database, **Open** » the **Navigation Pane**.

> Notice the report name *All Events* did not change in the Navigation Pane. You changed the title of the report as it would print.

5 On the right side of the title bar, click **Close** ⊠ to close the database and to close Access.

For Non-MyLab Submissions   **Determine What Your Instructor Requires for Submission**
As directed by your instructor, submit your completed database file.

---

6 In **MyLab IT**, locate and click the Grader Project **Access 1B Student Workshops**. In **step 3**, under **Upload Completed Assignment**, click **Choose File**. In the **Open** dialog box, navigate to your **Access Chapter 1 folder**, and then click your **Student_Access_1B_Student_Workshops** file one time to select it. In the lower right corner of the **Open** dialog box, click **Open**.

> The name of your selected file displays above the Upload button.

7 To submit your file to **MyLab IT** for grading, click **Upload**, wait a moment for a green **Success!** message, and then in **step 4**, click the blue **Submit for Grading** button. Click **Close Assignment** to return to your list of **Course Materials**.

You have completed Project 1B   **END**

»» GO! With Google

Access web apps are designed to work with Microsoft's SharePoint, a service for setting up websites to share and manage documents. Your college may not have SharePoint installed, so you will use other tools to share objects from your database so that you can work collaboratively with others. Recall that Google Drive is Google's free, web-based word processor, spreadsheet, slide show, form, and data storage and sharing service. For Access, you can export a database object to an Excel worksheet, a PDF file, or a text file, and then save the file to Google Drive.

> **ALERT   Working with Web-Based Applications and Services**
>
> Computer programs and services on the web receive continuous updates and improvements. Therefore, the steps to complete this web-based Activity may differ from the ones shown. You can often look at the screens and the information presented to determine how to complete the Activity.

Activity | Exporting an Access Table to a Word Document, Saving the Document to Google Drive, Adding a Record in Google Drive, and Saving to Your Computer

In this activity, you will export your 1B Workshop Locations table to a Word document, upload your Word file to Google Drive as a Google Doc, add a record in Google Drive, and then download a copy of the edited document to your computer.

1 Start Access, navigate to your **Access Chapter 1** folder, and then **Open** your **1B_Student_Workshops** database file. If necessary, on the Message Bar, click Enable Content, and then **Close** the **Event List** form. In the **Navigation Pane**, click your **1B Workshop Locations** table to select it—do not open it.

2 On the ribbon, click the **External Data tab**. In the **Export group**, click **More**, and then click **Word**. In the **Export – RTF File** dialog box, click **Browse**, and then navigate to your **Access Chapter 1** folder. In the **File Save** dialog box, click in the **File name** box, using your own name, type **Lastname_Firstname_a1B_Web** and then click **Save**.

3 In the **Export – RTF File** dialog box, under **Specify export options**, select the second check box—**Open the destination file after the export operation is complete**—and then click **OK**. Take a moment to examine the data in the file.

Notice that the table is too wide to display fully with Portrait orientation.

4 **Close** Word. In the **Export – RTF File** dialog box, click **Close**, and then **Close** Access.

5 Open your browser, navigate to **http://drive.google .com**, and sign in to your Google account; if necessary, create a new Google account and then sign in. On the right side of the screen, click **Settings** [⚙], and then click **Settings**. In the **Settings** dialog box, to the right of *Convert uploads*, if necessary, select the **Convert uploaded files to Google Docs editor format** check box. In the upper right, click **Done**

It is necessary to select this setting; otherwise, your document will upload as a pdf file and cannot be edited without further action.

6 Open your **GO! Web Projects** folder—or create and then open this folder by clicking **New** and then clicking **New folder**. On the left, click **New**, and then click **File upload**. In the **Choose File to Upload** dialog box, navigate to your **Access Chapter 1** folder, and then double-click your **a1B_Web** Word file to upload it to Google Drive. When the title bar of the message box indicates *1 upload complete*, **Close** the message box.

7 Double-click your **a1B_Web** file to open the file in Google Docs. Notice that the table is not fully displayed on the page, and compare your screen with Figure A.

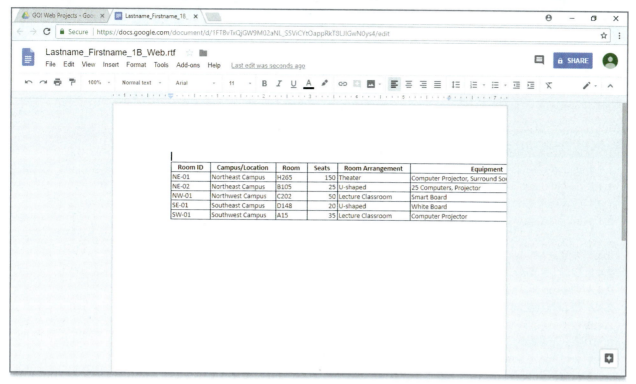

Figure A

8 Click **File** to display a menu, and then click **Page setup**. In the **Page setup** dialog box, under **Orientation**, click **Landscape**. Click **OK**.

The table displays fully with Landscape orientation.

Field	Room ID	Campus/Location	Room	Seats	Room Arrangement	Equipment
	SE-02	**Southeast Campus**	**D120**	**20**	**Testing Lab**	**20 Computers**

9 Click in the last cell in the table, and press ⟨Tab⟩. Add the following record.

10 On the menu, click **File**, point to **Download as**, and then click **Microsoft Word (.docx)**. In the message box—usually displays at the bottom of your screen—click the **Save arrow**, and then click **Save as**. In the **Save As** dialog box, navigate to your **Access Chapter 1** folder, click in the **File name** box, and type **Lastname_Firstname_a1B_Web_Download** and then click **Save**. If necessary, click OK to upgrade to the newest file format.

11 In Google Drive, at the top right corner of your screen, click your user name, and then click **Sign out**. **Close** your browser window.

12 Start Word. In the Word opening screen, click **Open**. Under **Open**, click **Browse**. Navigate to your **Access Chapter 1** folder, and then double-click your **a1B_Web** Word file. Notice that this file is the original file—the new record is not entered. If you are required to print your documents, use one of the methods in following Note. **Close** your Word file; and, if prompted, save the changes to your document. Then **Open** and print your **a1B_Web_Download** Word file using one of the methods in the following Note. **Close** Word; and, if prompted, save the changes to your document. As directed by your instructor, submit your two documents and the two paper printouts or PDF electronic images that are the results of this project.

NOTE **Adding the File Name to the Footer and Printing or Creating a PDF Electronic Image**

Click the Insert tab. In the Header & Footer group, click Footer, and then click Blank. With Type here selected, in the Insert group, click Document Info, and then click File Name. Close the Footer window. Click the Layout tab. In the Page Setup group, click Orientation, and then click Landscape.

To print on paper, click File, and then click Print. To create a pdf electronic image of your printout, click File, and then click Export. Under Export, be sure Create PDF/XPS Document is selected, and then click Create PDF/XPS. Navigate to your Access Chapter 1 folder, and then click Publish to save the file with the default name and an extension of pdf.

»»» GO! To Work

wavebreakmedia/Shutterstock, Monkey Business Images/Fotolia, Ivanko80/Shutterstock, Monkey Business Images/Shutterstock

Microsoft Office Specialist (MOS) Skills in This Chapter

Project 1A	Project 1B
1.1.1 Import objects or data from other sources	**1.1.3** Hide and display objects in the Navigation Pane
1.1.2 Delete database objects	**2.1.1** Import data into tables
1.3.1 Configure print options for records, forms, and reports	**5.1.3** Add and modify labels on reports
2.1.1 Import data into tables	
2.2.3 Add table descriptions	
2.4.1 Add or remove fields	
2.4.3 Change field captions	
2.4.4 Change field sizes	
2.4.5 Change field data types	
2.4.6 Configure fields to auto-increment	
3.1.7 Run queries	
4.1.1 Add, move and remove form controls	
5.1.2 Add report controls	
5.1.3 Add and modify labels on reports	
5.2.3 Format report elements	

Build Your E-Portfolio

An E-Portfolio is a collection of evidence, stored electronically, that showcases what you have accomplished while completing your education. Collecting and then sharing your work products with potential employers reflects your academic and career goals. Your completed documents from the following projects are good examples to show what you have learned: 1G, 1K, and 1L.

GO! For Job Success

Video: Customer Service

Your instructor may assign this video to your class, and then ask you to think about, or discuss with your classmates, these questions:

g-stockstudio/Shutterstock

How did Lee's responses demonstrate both good and bad customer service skills?

How well did Christine, the supervisor, handle Karen's situation? Provide specific examples.

Based on this call, what can SunTel Systems do to provide a better customer service experience? Provide two examples.

End of Chapter

Summary

Principles of good database design, also known as normalization, help ensure that the data in your database is accurate and organized in a way that you can retrieve information that is useful.

You can create databases from scratch by using the blank desktop database template or a custom web app or by using a template that contains prebuilt tables, queries, forms, reports, and other objects.

Tables are the foundation of a database, but before entering records in a table, you must define the data type and name the field. Common data types are Short Text, Number, Currency, and Date/Time.

Use forms to enter data into a table or view the data in a table. Use queries to retrieve information from tables. Reports display information from tables in a professional-looking format.

GO! Learn It Online

Review the concepts and key terms in this chapter by completing these online challenges, which you can find at **MyLab IT**.

Chapter Quiz: Answer matching and multiple-choice questions to test what you learned in this chapter.

Crossword Puzzle: Spell out the words that match the numbered cues, and then put them in the puzzle squares.

Answer questions to review the MOS skills that you practiced in this chapter.

GO! Collaborative Team Project (Available in Instructor Resource Center)

If your instructor assigns this project to your class, you can expect to work with one or more of your classmates—either in person or by using Internet tools—to create work products similar to those that you created in this chapter. A team is a group of workers who work together to solve a problem, make a decision, or create a work product. Collaboration is when you work together with others as a team in an intellectual endeavor to complete a shared task or achieve a shared goal.

Monkey Business Images/ Fotolia

Project Guide for Access Chapter 1

Your instructor will assign Projects from this list to ensure your learning and assess your knowledge.

		Review and Assessment Guide for Access Chapter 1		
Project	**Apply Skills from These Chapter Objectives**	**Project Type**		**Project Location**
1A **MyLab IT**	Objectives 1–5 from Project 1A	**1A Instructional Project (Grader Project)** A guided review of the skills from Project 1A.	Instruction	In **MyLab IT** and in text
1B **MyLab IT**	Objectives 6–9 from Project 1B	**1B Instructional Project (Grader Project)** A guided review of the skills from Project 1B.	Instruction	In **MyLab IT** and in text
1C	Objectives 1–5 from Project 1A	**1C Chapter Review (Scorecard Grading)** A guided review of the skills from Project 1A.	Review	In text
1D	Objectives 6–9 from Project 1B	**1D Chapter Review (Scorecard Grading** A guided review of the skills from Project 1B.	Review	In text
1E **MyLab IT**	Objectives 1–5 from Project 1A	**1E Mastery (Grader Project)** A demonstration of your mastery of the skills in Project 1A with extensive decision-making.	Mastery and Transfer of Learning	In **MyLab IT** and in text
1F **MyLab IT**	Objectives 6–9 from Project 1B	**1F Mastery (Grader Project)** A demonstration of your mastery of the skills in Project 1B with extensive decision-making.	Mastery and Transfer of Learning	In **MyLab IT** and in text
1G **MyLab IT**	Combination of Objectives from Projects 1A and 1B	**1G Mastery (Grader Project)** A demonstration of your mastery of the skills in Projects 1A and 1B with extensive decision-making.	Mastery and Transfer of Learning	In **MyLab IT** and in text
1H	Combination of Objectives from Projects 1A and 1B	**1H GO! Fix It (Scorecard Grading)** A demonstration of your mastery of the skills in Projects 1A and 1B by creating a correct result from a document that contains errors you must find.	Critical Thinking	IRC
1I	Combination of Objectives from Projects 1A and 1B	**1I GO! Make It (Scorecard Grading)** A demonstration of your mastery of the skills in Projects 1A and 1B by creating a result from a supplied picture.	Critical Thinking	IRC
1J	Combination of Objectives from Projects 1A and 1B	**1J GO! Solve It (Rubric Grading)** A demonstration of your mastery of the skills in Projects 1A and 1B, your decision-making skills, and your critical thinking skills. A task-specific rubric helps you self-assess your result.	Critical Thinking	IRC
1K	Combination of Objectives from Projects 1A and 1B	**1K GO! Solve It (Rubric Grading)** A demonstration of your mastery of the skills in Projects 1A and 1B, your decision-making skills, and your critical thinking skills. A task-specific rubric helps you self-assess your result.	Critical Thinking	In text
1L	Combination of Objectives from Projects 1A and 1B	**1L GO! Think (Rubric Grading)** A demonstration of your understanding of the Chapter concepts applied in a manner that you would outside of college. An analytic rubric helps you and your instructor grade the quality of your work by comparing it to the work an expert in the discipline would create.	Critical Thinking	In text
1M	Combination of Objectives from Projects 1A and 1B	**1M GO! Think (Rubric Grading)** A demonstration of your understanding of the Chapter concepts applied in a manner that you would outside of college. An analytic rubric helps you and your instructor grade the quality of your work by comparing it to the work an expert in the discipline would create.	Critical Thinking	IRC
1N	Combination of Objectives from Projects 1A and 1B	**1N You and GO! (Rubric Grading)** A demonstration of your understanding of the Chapter concepts applied in a manner that you would in a personal situation. An analytic rubric helps you and your instructor grade the quality of your work.	Critical Thinking	IRC
1O	Combination of Objectives from Projects 1A and 1B	**1O Cumulative Team Project for Access Chapter 1** A demonstration of your understanding of concepts and your ability to work collaboratively in a group role-playing assessment, requiring both collaboration and self-management.		IRC

Glossary

Glossary of Chapter Key Terms

Append To add on to the end of an object; for example, to add records to the end of an existing table.

AutoNumber data type A data type that describes a unique sequential or random number assigned by Access as each record is entered and that is useful for data that has no distinct field that can be considered unique.

Best Fit An Access command that adjusts the width of a column to accommodate the column's longest entry.

Blank desktop database A database that has no data and has no database tools—you must create the data and tools as you need them; the database is stored on your computer or other storage device.

Caption A property setting that displays a name for a field in a table, query, form, or report different from the one listed as the field name.

Common field A field included in two or more tables that stores the same data.

Currency data type An Access data type that describes monetary values and numeric data that can be used in mathematical calculations involving values with one to four decimal places.

Custom web app A database that you can publish and share with others over the Internet.

Data Facts about people, events, things, or ideas.

Data source The table or tables from which a query, form, or reports gathers its data.

Data type Classification identifying the kind of data that can be stored in a field, such as numbers, text, or dates.

Database An organized collection of facts about people, events, things, or ideas related to a specific topic or purpose.

Database management system (DBMS) Database software that controls how related collections of data are stored, organized, retrieved, and secured; also known as a DBMS.

Database template A preformatted database that contains prebuilt tables, queries, forms, and reports that perform a specific task, such as tracking events.

Datasheet view The Access view that displays data organized in columns and rows similar to an Excel worksheet.

DBMS An acronym for database management system.

Design view An Access view that displays the detailed structure of a table, query, form, or report. For forms and reports, may be the view in which some tasks must be performed, and only the controls, and not the data, display in this view.

Destination table The table to which you import or append data.

Export The process of copying data from one file into another file, such as an Access table into an Excel spreadsheet.

Field A single piece of information that is stored in every record; represented by a column in a database table.

Field properties Characteristics of a field that control how the field displays and how data can be entered in the field; vary for different data types.

First principle of good database design A principle of good database design stating that data is organized in tables so that there is no redundant data.

Flat database A simple database file that is not related or linked to any other collection of data.

Form An Access object you can use to enter new records into a table, edit or delete existing records in a table, or display existing records.

Form view The Access view in which you can view records, but you cannot change the layout or design of the form.

Import The process of copying data from another file, such as a Word table or an Excel workbook, into a separate file, such as an Access database.

Information Data that is accurate, timely, and organized in a useful manner.

Layout view The Access view in which you can make changes to a form or report while the data from the underlying data source displays.

Link A connection to data in another file.

Multiple-items form A form that enables you to display or enter multiple records in a table.

Navigation area An area at the bottom of the Access window that indicates the number of records in the table and contains controls in the form of arrows that you click to move among the records.

Navigation Pane An area of the Access window that displays and organizes the names of the objects in a database; from here, you open objects for use.

Normalization The process of applying design rules and principles to ensure that your database performs as expected.

Number data type An Access data type that represents a quantity, how much or how many, and may be used in calculations.

Object tab In the object window, a tab that identifies the object and which enables you to make an open object active.

Object window An area of the Access window that displays open objects, such as tables, queries, forms, or reports; by default, each object displays on its own tab.

Objects The basic parts of a database that you create to store your data and to work with your data; for example, tables, queries, forms, and reports.

Populate The action of filling a database table with records.

Primary key A required field that uniquely identifies a record in a table; for example, a Student ID number at a college.

Property Sheet A list of characteristics—properties—for fields or controls on a form or report in which you can make precise changes to each property associated with the field or control.

Query A database object that retrieves specific data from one or more database objects—either tables or other queries—and then, in a single datasheet, displays only the data you specify.

Record All of the categories of data pertaining to one person, place, event, thing, or idea; represented by a row in a database table.

Record selector bar The bar at the left edge of a record when it is displayed in a form, and which is used to select an entire record.

Record selector box The small box at the left of a record in Datasheet view that, when clicked, selects the entire record.

Redundant In a database, information that is duplicated in a manner that indicates poor database design.

Relational database A sophisticated type of database that has multiple collections of data within the file that are related to one another.

Report A database object that summarizes the fields and records from a table or query in an easy-to-read format suitable for printing.

Glossary

Run The process in which Access searches the records in the table(s) included in the query design, finds the records that match the specified criteria, and then displays the records in a datasheet; only the fields that have been included in the query design display.

Second principle of good database design A principle stating that appropriate database techniques are used to ensure the accuracy and consistency of data as it is entered into the table.

Select query A type of Access query that retrieves (selects) data from one or more tables or queries, displaying the selected data in a datasheet; also known as a simple select query.

SharePoint A Microsoft application used for setting up web sites to share and manage documents.

Short Text data type An Access data type that describes text, a combination of text and numbers, or numbers that are not used in calculations, such as the Postal Code.

Simple select query Another name for a select query.

Single-record form A form that enables you to display or enter one record at a time from a table.

Source file When importing a file, refers to the file being imported.

Structure In Access, the underlying design of a table, including field names, data types, descriptions, and field properties.

Table A format for information that organizes and presents text and data in columns and rows; the foundation of a database.

Tables and Related Views An arrangement in the Navigation Pane that groups objects by the table to which they are related.

Truncated Data that is cut off or shortened because the field or column is not wide enough to display all of the data or the field size is too small to contain all of the data.

Wizard A feature in Microsoft Office that walks you step by step through a process.

Chapter Review

Skills Review | Project 1C College Administrators

Apply 1A skills from these Objectives:

1. Identify Good Database Design
2. Create a Table and Define Fields in a Blank Desktop Database
3. Change the Structure of Tables and Add a Second Table
4. Create a Query, Form, and Report
5. Close a Database and Close Access

In the following Skills Review, you will create a database to store information about the administrators of Texas Lakes Community College and their departments. Your completed Navigation Pane will look similar to Figure 1.47.

Project Files

For Project 1C, you will need the following files:

Blank database
a01C_Administrators (Excel workbook)
a01C_Departments (Excel workbook)

You will save your database as:

Lastname_Firstname_1C_College_Administrators

Project Results

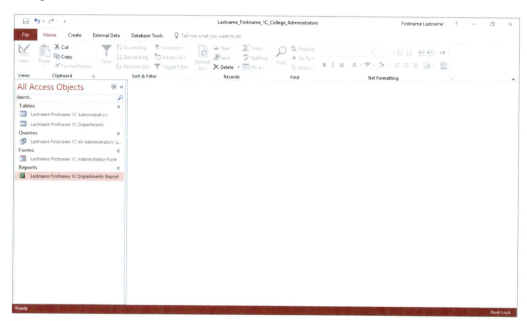

Figure 1.47

(continues on next page)

Chapter Review

1 ▶ Start Access. In the Access opening screen, click **Blank database**. In the **Blank database** dialog box, to the right of the **File Name** box, click **Browse**. In the **File New Database** dialog box, navigate to your **Access Chapter 1** folder. In the **File New Database** dialog box, click in the **File name** box, type **Lastname_Firstname_1C_College_Administrators** and then press Enter. In the **Blank database** dialog box, click **Create**.

a. **Close** the **Navigation Pane**. In the field names row, click in the text *Click to Add*, and then click **Short Text**. Type **Title** and then press Enter.

b. In the third field name box, click **Short Text**, type **Last Name** and then press Enter. In the fourth field name box, click **Short Text**, type **First Name** and then press Enter. Create the remaining fields shown in Table 1, pressing Enter after the last field name. All of the data is typed on one line.

Table 1

Data Type		Short Text	Short Text	Short Text	Short Text	Short Text	Short Text	Short Text	Short Text	Short Text	Short Text	Currency
Field Name	ID	Title	Last Name	First Name	**Middle Initial**	Address	City	State	Postal Code	Phone Number	Department ID	Salary

c. If necessary, scroll to bring the first column into view, and then click the **ID** field name. On the **Fields tab**, in the **Properties group**, click **Name & Caption**. In the **Name** box, change *ID* to **Employee ID** and then click **OK**. On the ribbon, in the **Formatting group**, click the **Data Type arrow**, and then click **Short Text**.

d. In the new record row, click in the **Employee ID** field, type, **ADM-9200** and press Enter. In the **Title** field, type **Vice President** and press Enter. Continue entering data in the fields shown in Table 2, pressing Enter or Tab to move to the next field and to the next row.

Table 2

Last Name	First Name	Middle Initial	Address	City	State	Postal Code	Phone Number	Department ID	Salary
Shaffer	**Lonnie**	**J**	**489 Ben Ave**	**Austin**	**TX**	**78734**	**(512) 555-6185**	**AS**	**123500**

e. On the Quick Access Toolbar, click **Save**. In the **Save As** dialog box, in the **Table Name** box, using your own name, replace the selected text by typing **Lastname Firstname 1C Administrators** and then click **OK**.

f. In the new record row, enter the data for two college administrators shown in Table 3, pressing Enter or Tab to move from field to field and to the next row.

Table 3

Employee ID	Title	Last Name	First Name	Middle Initial	Address	City	State	Postal Code	Phone Number	Department ID	Salary
ADM-9201	**Associate Vice President**	**Holtz**	**Diann**	**S**	**8416 Spencer Ln**	**George town**	**TX**	**78627**	**(512) 555-1069**	**AS**	**101524**
ADM-9202	**Director, Enrollment Services**	**Fitchette**	**Sean**	**H**	**3245 Deer Trl**	**Spice wood**	**TX**	**78669**	**(512) 555-9012**	**SS**	**45070**

g. **Close** your **1C Administrators** table. On the **External Data tab**, in the **Import & Link group**, click **New Data Source**, point to **From File**, and then click **Excel**. In the **Get External Data – Excel Spreadsheet** dialog box, click **Browse**. In the **File Open** dialog box, navigate to your student data files, and then double-click the **a01C_Administrators** Excel file.

h. Click the **Append a copy of the records to the table** option button, and then click **OK**. In the **Import Spreadsheet Wizard**, click **Next**, and then click **Finish**. In the **Get External Data – Excel Spreadsheet** dialog box, click **Close**.

(continues on next page)

Chapter Review

i. **Open** the **Navigation Pane**. Resize the Navigation Pane so that the entire table name displays. In the **Navigation Pane**, double-click your **1C Administrators** table to open it, and then **Close** the **Navigation Pane**—there are 30 records in this table.

2 ▶ Click the **Home tab**, and then in the **Views group**, click the top of the **View** button to switch to **Design** view. In the **Field Name** column, to the left of **Middle Initial**, click the row selector box to select the entire row. On the **Design tab**, in the **Tools group**, click **Delete Rows**. In the message box, click **Yes**.

a. Click in the **Employee ID** field name box. Under **Field Properties**, click **Field Size** to select the existing text. Type **8** and then in the **Employee ID** field row, click in the **Description** box. Type **Eight-character Employee ID** and then press Enter.

b. Click in the **State** field name box. In the **Field Properties** area, click **Field Size**, and then type **2** In the **State Description** box, type **Two-character state abbreviation** and then press Enter.

c. **Save** the design changes to your table, and in the message box, click **Yes**. On the **Design tab**, in the **Views group**, click the top of the **View** button to switch to **Datasheet** view.

d. On the ribbon, click the **External Data tab**, and then in the **Import & Link group**, click **New Data Source**, point to **From File**, and then click **Excel**. In the **Get External Data – Excel Spreadsheet** dialog box, to the right of the **File name** box, click **Browse**. In the **File Open** dialog box, navigate to your student data files, and then double-click **a01C_Departments**. Be sure that the **Import the source data into a new table in the current database** option button is selected, and then click **OK**.

e. In the upper left corner of the wizard, select the **First Row Contains Column Headings** check box, and then click **Next**. Click **Next** again. Click the **Choose my own primary key** option button, be sure that **Department ID** displays, and then click **Next**. In the **Import to Table** box, type **1C Departments** and then click **Finish**. In the **Get External Data – Excel Spreadsheet** dialog box, click **Close**.

f. **Open** the **Navigation Pane**, double-click your **1C Departments** table, and then **Close** the **Navigation Pane**. There are 12 records in your **1C Departments** table.

g. To the left of the **Department** field name, click **Select All**. On the ribbon, click the **Home tab**, and in the **Records group**, click **More**, and then click **Field Width**. In the **Column Width** dialog box, click **Best Fit**. Click in any field to cancel the selection, and then **Save** your table. In the object window, click the **object tab** for your **1C Administrators** table. Using the techniques you just practiced, apply **Best Fit** to the columns, cancel the selection, and then **Save** the table.

h. With your **1C Administrators** table displayed, on the ribbon, click the **File tab**, click **Print**, and then click **Print Preview**. On the **Print Preview tab**, in the **Page Layout group**, click **Landscape**. Click **Close Print Preview**, and then **Close** your **1C Administrators** table.

i. With your **1C Departments** table displayed, view the table in **Print Preview**. Change the orientation to **Landscape**, and then create a paper printout or PDF electronic image as directed by your instructor—one page results. Click **Close Print Preview**, and then **Close** your **1C Departments** table.

3 ▶ On the ribbon, click the **Create tab**, and then in the **Queries group**, click **Query Wizard**. In the **New Query** dialog box, be sure **Simple Query Wizard** is selected, and then click **OK**. In the wizard, click the **Tables/Queries arrow**, and then click your **Table: 1C Administrators**.

a. Under **Available Fields**, click **Last Name**, and then click **Add Field** to move the field to the **Selected Fields** list on the right. Double-click the **First Name** field to move it to the **Selected Fields** list. By using **Add Field** or by double-clicking the field name, add the following fields to the **Selected Fields** list in the order specified: **Title**, **Department ID**, and **Phone Number**. This query will answer the question, *What is the last name, first name, title, Department ID, and phone number of every administrator?*

b. In the wizard, click **Next**. Click in the **What title do you want for your query?** box. Using your own name, edit as necessary so that the query name is **1C All Administrators Query** and then click **Finish**. If necessary, apply Best Fit to the columns, and then Save the query. Display the query in **Print**. Click **Close Print Preview**, and then **Close** the query.

(continues on next page)

1
ACCESS

Chapter Review

c. **Open** the **Navigation Pane**, right-click your **1C Administrators** table, and then click **Open** to display the table in the object window. **Close** the **Navigation Pane**. Notice that the table has 11 fields. On the ribbon, click the **Create tab**, and in the **Forms group**, click **Form**. On the Quick Access Toolbar, click **Save**. In the **Save As** dialog box, click in the **Form Name** box, edit to name the form **Lastname Firstname 1C Administrator Form** and then click **OK**.

d. In the navigation area, click **Last record**, and then click **Previous record** two times to display the record for *Diann Holtz*. By using the instructions in Activity 1.15, print or create an PDF electronic image of only this record on one page. **Close** the form object, saving it if prompted. Your **1C Administrators** table object remains open.

e. **Open** the **Navigation Pane**, open your **1C Departments** table by double-clicking the table name or by right-clicking the table name and clicking Open. **Close** the **Navigation Pane**. On the **Create tab**, in the **Reports group**, click **Report**.

f. Click the **Department ID** field name, and then on the ribbon, under **Report Layout Tools**, click the **Arrange tab**. In the **Rows & Columns group**, click **Select Column**, and then press Del. Using the same technique, delete the **Department Email** field.

g. Click the **Department Phone** field name. Hold down Shift, and then click the **Suite Number** field name to select the last three field names. In the **Rows & Columns group**, click **Select Column**. On the ribbon, click the **Design tab**, and then in the **Tools group**, click **Property Sheet**. In the **Property Sheet**, on the **Format tab**, click **Width**, type **1.5** and then press Enter. **Close** the **Property Sheet**.

h. Click the **Department Name** field name. On the ribbon, click the **Home tab.** In the **Sort & Filter group**, click **Ascending** to sort the report in alphabetic order by *Department Name*. At the bottom of the report, on the right side, click **Page 1 of 1**, and then press Del.

i. **Save** the report as **Lastname Firstname 1C Departments Report** and then click **OK**. Display the report in **Print**. Click **Close Print Preview**. In the object window, right-click any **object tab**, and then click **Close All** to close all open objects, leaving the object window empty.

4 **Open** the **Navigation Pane**. If necessary, increase the width of the Navigation Pane so that all object names display fully. On the right side of the title bar, click **Close** to close the database and to close Access. As directed by your instructor, submit your database for grading.

You have completed Project 1C | **END**

Chapter Review

| Skills Review | Project 1D Certification Events |

In the following Skills Review, you will create a database to store information about certification test preparation events at Texas Lakes Community College. Your completed Navigation Pane will look similar to Figure 1.48.

Apply 1B skills from these Objectives:

6. Use a Template to Create a Database
7. Organize Objects in the Navigation Pane
8. Create a New Table in a Database Created with a Template
9. View a Report

Project Files

For Project 1D, you will need the following files:

a01D_Certification_Template
a01D_Certification_Events (Excel workbook)

You will save your database as:

Lastname_Firstname_1D_Certification_Events

Project Results

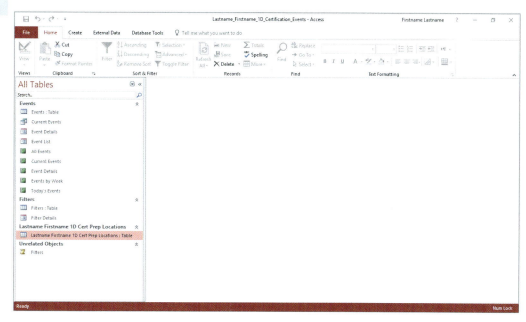

Figure 1.48

(continues on next page)

Chapter Review

1 Start Access. On the left, click **Open Other Files**, and then click **Browse**. Navigate to your student data for this chapter, and open the database named **a01D_Certification_Template**. On the ribbon, click the **File tab**, on the left, click **Save As**, and then, under *Save Database As*, click **Save As**. In the **Save As dialog box**, navigate to your **Access Chapter 1** folder, and then using your own name, type **Lastname_Firstname_1D_Certification_Events** and then click **Save**. Under the ribbon, on the **Message Bar**, click **Enable Content**.

a. In the first row, click in the **Title** field, type **Word 2019** and then press Tab. In the **Start Time** field, type **7/9/23 10a** and then press Tab. In the **End Time** field, type **7/9/23 4p** and then press Tab. In the **Description** field, type **Office 2019** and then press Tab. In the **Location** field, type **Southwest Campus** and then press Tab three times to move to the **Title** field in the new record row.

b. In the form, directly above the field names row, click **New Event** to open the **Event Details** single-record form. Using Tab to move from field to field, enter the record shown in **Table 1**. Press Tab three times to move from the **End Time** field to the **Description** field.

Table 1

Title	Location	Start Time	End Time	Description
Excel 2019	Northeast Campus	7/16/23 10a	7/16/23 4p	Office 2019

c. In the **Events Detail** form, click **Close**. Using either the **Event List** multiple-items form or the **Event Details** single-record form, enter the records shown in **Table 2**. If you use the Event Details form, be sure to close it after entering records to display the records in the Event List form.

Table 2

ID	Title	Start Time	End Time	Description	Location
3	Access 2019	7/23/23 12p	7/23/23 6p	Office 2019	Southeast Campus
4	PowerPoint 2019	7/30/23 9a	7/30/23 3p	Office 2019	Northwest Campus

d. **Close** the **Event List** form. On the ribbon, click the **External Data tab**, in the **Import & Link group**, click **New Data Source**, point to **From File**, and then click **Excel**. In the **Get External Data – Excel Spreadsheet** dialog box, click **Browse**. Navigate to your student data files, and then double-click **a01D_Certification_Events**. Click the second option button—**Append a copy of the records to the table: Events**—and then click **OK**.

e. In the **Import Spreadsheet Wizard**, click **Next**, and then click **Finish**. In the **Get External Data – Excel Spreadsheet** dialog box, click **Close**. Open the **Navigation Pane**, and then double-click **Event List** to open the form that displays data stored in the Events table—12 total records display. **Close** the **Navigation Pane**.

f. To the left of the **ID** field name, click **Select All**. In the field names row, point to the right edge of any of the selected columns to display the ⊹ pointer, and then double-click to apply **Best Fit** to all of the columns. Click in any field to cancel the selection, and then **Save** the form.

2 Open the **Navigation Pane**. At the top of the Navigation Pane, click **More**. On the list, under **Navigate To Category**, click **Tables and Related Views**.

a. In the **Navigation Pane**, point to **Events: Table**, right-click, and then click **Open** to display the records in the underlying table. In the **Navigation Pane**, double-click the **Current Events** *report* (green icon) to view this predesigned report. From the **Navigation Pane**, open the **Events by Week** report to view this predesigned report.

b. In the object window, right-click any of the **object tabs**, and then click **Close All**. **Close** the **Navigation Pane**.

3 On the ribbon, click the **Create tab**, and in the **Tables group**, click **Table**.

a. In the field names row, click **Click to Add**, click **Short Text**, type **Campus Location** and then press Enter. In the third column, click **Short Text**, type **Lab** and then press Enter. In the fourth column, click **Number**, type **# Computers** and then press Enter. In the fifth column, click **Short Text**, type **Additional Equipment** and then press ↓.

(continues on next page)

Chapter Review

Skills Review: Project 1D Certification Events (continued)

b. Right-click the **ID** field name, and then click **Rename Field**. Type **Lab ID** and then press Enter. On the **Fields tab**, in the **Formatting group**, click the **Data Type arrow**, and then click **Short Text**.

c. In the new record row, click in the **Lab ID** field, and then enter the records shown in **Table 3**, pressing Enter or Tab to move from one field to the next.

Table 3

Lab ID	Campus Location	Lab	# Computers	Additional Equipment
NW-L01	Northwest Campus	H202	35	3 printers, DVD player
SE-L01	Southeast Campus	E145	25	Projector, document camera, smart board
NE-L01	Northeast Campus	F32	40	4 printers, smart board, instructor touch screen
SW-L01	Southwest Campus	G332	30	Projector, 4 digital displays
SE-L02	Southeast Campus	A225	25	Projector, white board, instructor touch screen

d. In the **Views group**, click the upper portion of the **View** button to switch to **Design** view. In the **Save As** dialog box, in the **Table Name** box, using your own name, type **Lastname Firstname1D Cert Prep Locations** and then click **OK**. Notice that the **Lab ID** field is the **Primary Key**. On the **Design tab**, in the **Views group**, click the upper portion of the **View** button to switch to **Datasheet** view.

e. To the left of the **Lab ID** field name, click **Select All** to select all of the columns and rows in the table. On the **Home tab**, in the **Records group**, click **More**, and then click **Field Width**. In the **Column Width** dialog box, click **Best Fit**. Click in any field to cancel the selection, and then **Save** the changes to the table. **Close** the table, and then **Open** the **Navigation Pane**. Increase the width of the **Navigation Pane** so that your entire table name displays.

4 In the Navigation Pane, double-click the **All Events** report to open it in the object window. **Close** the **Navigation Pane**. On the **Home tab**, in the **Views group**, click the top of the **View** button to switch to **Layout** view. At the top of the report, click the title—*All Events*—to display a colored border around the title. Click to the left of the letter *A* to place the insertion point there. Using your name, type **Lastname Firstname 1D** and then press Spacebar. Press Enter, and then **Save** the report.

a. On the right side of the status bar, click **Print Preview**, and notice that the report will print on one page. Click **Close Print Preview**, and then **Close** the report.

b. **Open** the **Navigation Pane**, double-click your **1D Cert Prep Locations** table, and then **Close** the **Navigation Pane**. On the ribbon, click the **File tab**, click **Print**, and then click **Print Preview**. On the **Print Preview tab**, in the **Page Layout group**, click **Landscape**. **Close Print Preview**. Close your **1D Cert Prep Locations** table.

c. **Open** the **Navigation Pane**. On the right side of the title bar, click **Close** to close the database and to close Access. As directed by your instructor, submit your database for grading.

You have completed Project 1D   **END**

| MyLab IT Grader | Mastering Access | Project 1E Kiosk Inventory |

Apply 1A skills from these Objectives:

1. Identify Good Database Design
2. Create a Table and Define Fields in a Blank Desktop Database
3. Change the Structure of Tables and Add a Second Table
4. Create a Query, Form, and Report
5. Close a Database and Close Access

In the following Mastering Access project, you will create a database to track information about the inventory of items for sale in the kiosk located in the Snack Bar at the Southeast Campus of Texas Lakes Community College. Your completed Navigation Pane will look similar to Figure 1.49.

Project Files for MyLab IT Grader

1. In your **MyLab IT** course, locate and click **Access 1E Kiosk Inventory**, Download Materials, and then Download All Files. Close the Grader download screens.
2. Extract the zipped folder to your Access Chapter 1 folder.
3. Take a moment to open the downloaded **Access_1E_Kiosk_Inventory_Instructions**; note any recent updates to the book.

Project Results

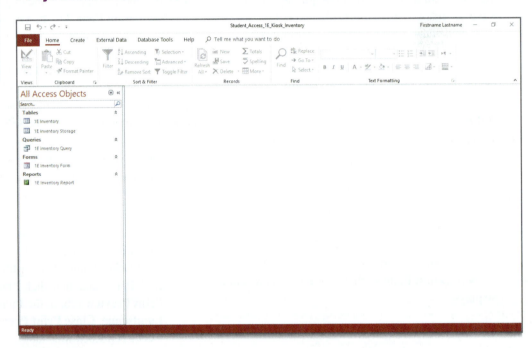

Figure 1.49

For Non-MyLab Submissions

For Project 1E, you will need these starting file:

Blank database

a01E_Inventory (Excel workbook)

a01E_Inventory_Storage (Excel workbook)

Start with a New Blank Access Database

In your Access Chapter 1 folder, save your database as:

Lastname_Firstname_1E_Kiosk_Inventory

After you have saved your database, open it to launch Access. On the next page, begin with Step 2.

After Step 11, submit your database as directed by your instructor.

(continues on next page)

Content-Based Assessments (Mastery and Transfer of Learning)

1 Start Access. Navigate to your **Access Chapter 1 folder**, and then double-click the downloaded file that displays your name—**Student_1E_Kiosk_Inventory**. If necessary, at the top, click Enable Content.

2 **Close** the **Navigation Pane**. Create a new table in Datasheet view, and create the fields shown in **Table 1**.

Table 1

Data Type		Short Text	Short Text	Short Text	Short Text	Currency	Number
Field Name	ID	Item	Category	Campus	Storage Location	Price	Quantity in Stock

3 For the **ID** field, change the **Data Type** to **Short Text**, rename the field to **Item ID** and then enter the records shown in **Table 2**.

Table 2

Item ID	Item	Category	Campus	Storage Location	Price	Quantity in Stock
C-1	Chocolate Bar	Candy	Southeast	SE100A	.89	250
C-2	Lollipop	Candy	Southeast	SE100A	.5	500
T-1	T-shirt	Clothing	Southeast	SE100B	17.5	100

4 **Save** the table as **1E Inventory** and **Close** the table. From your student data files, import and then **Append** the data in the Excel file **a01E_Inventory** to your **1E Inventory** table. After importing, open your **1E Inventory** table—17 records display.

5 In **Design** view, delete the **Campus** field, which is redundant data. For the **Category** field, change the **Field Size** to **25** and enter a **Description** of **Enter the category of the item** For the **Item ID** field, change the **Field Size** to **10** and then **Save** the changes to your table. Switch to **Datasheet** view, apply **Best Fit** to all of the fields in the table, and then **Save** your changes. Display the table in **Print Preview**, change the orientation to **Landscape**. **Close Print Preview**, and then **Close** the table.

6 From your student data files, import the **Excel** file **a01E_Inventory_Storage** into the database as a new table; designate the first row as column headings and the **Category** field as the primary key. In the wizard, name the table **1E Inventory Storage** and then open your **1E Inventory Storage** table—five records display. In **Design** view, for the **Location Detail** field, change the **Field Size** to **35** and enter a **Description** of **Room and bin number or alternate location of inventory item Save** the design changes, switch to **Datasheet** view, apply **Best Fit** to all of the fields, and then **Save** your changes. **Close** the table.

7 **Create** a **Simple Query**, by using the **Query Wizard**, based on your **1E Inventory** table. Include only the three fields that will answer the question, *For all items, what is the storage location and quantity in stock?* In the wizard, accept the default name for the query. Display the query in **Print Preview**, create a paper printout or PDF electronic image as directed, **Close Print Preview**, and then **Close** the query.

8 Open your **1E Inventory** table, and then **Create** a **Form** for this table. **Save** the form as **1E Inventory Form** and then view the records. **Close** the form object, saving changes if prompted.

9 With your **1E Inventory** table open, **Create** a **Report**. Delete the **Category** and **Price** fields, and then sort the **Item ID** field in **Ascending** order. Using the **Property Sheet**, for the **Item ID** field, change the **Width** to **0.75** and then for the **Storage Location** field, change the **Width** to **1.5** Scroll to display the bottom of the report, if necessary, and then delete the page number— **Page 1 of 1**. **Save** the report as **1E Inventory Report Close** the report.

10 **Close All** open objects. **Open** the **Navigation Pane** and be sure that all object names display fully.

11 **Close** the database, and then **Close** Access.

(continues on next page)

Content-Based Assessments (Mastery and Transfer of Learning)

12 In **MyLab IT**, locate and click the Grader Project **Access 1E Kiosk Inventory**. In **step 3**, under **Upload Completed Assignment**, click **Choose File**. In the **Open** dialog box, navigate to your **Access Chapter 1 folder**, and then click your **Student_Access_1E_Kiosk_Inventory** file one time to select it. In the lower right corner of the **Open** dialog box, click **Open.**

13 To submit your file to **MyLab IT** for grading, click Upload, wait a moment for a green **Success!** message, and then in **step 4**, click the blue **Submit for Grading** button. Click **Close Assignment** to return to your list of **Course Materials**.

You have completed Project 1E   **END**

Content-Based Assessments (Mastery and Transfer of Learning)

MyLab IT Grader

Mastering Access | **Project 1F Recruitment Events**

Apply 1B skills from these Objectives:

6. Use a Template to Create a Database
7. Organize Objects in the Navigation Pane
8. Create a New Table in a Database Created with a Template
9. View a Report

In the following Mastering Access project, you will create a database to store information about the recruiting events that are scheduled to attract new students to Texas Lakes Community College. Your completed Navigation Pane will look similar to Figure 1.50.

Project Files for MyLab IT Grader

1. In your **MyLab IT** course, locate and click **Access 1F Recruitment Events**, Download Materials, and then Download All Files. Close the Grader download screens.
2. Extract the zipped folder to your Access Chapter 1 folder.
3. Take a moment to open the downloaded **Access_1F_Recruitment_Events_Instructions**; note any recent updates to the book.

Project Results

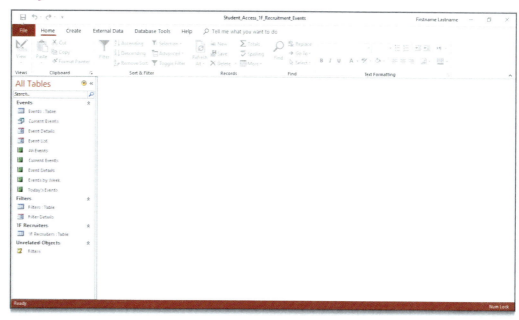

Figure 1.50

For Non-MyLab Submissions
For Project 1F, you will need these starting files:
a01F_Recruitment_Template
a01F_Recruiting_Events (Excel workbook)

Start with an Access Data File
In your Access Chapter 1 folder, save your database as:
Lastname_Firstname_1F_Recruitment_Events

After you have saved your database, open it to launch Access. On the next page, begin with Step 2.
After Step 9, submit your database as directed by your instructor.

(continues on next page)

Mastering Access: Project 1F Recruitment Events (continued)

1 Start Access. Navigate to your **Access Chapter 1 folder**, and then double-click the downloaded file that displays your name—**Student_1F_Recruitment_Events**. If necessary, at the top, click Enable Content.

2 In the **Event List** multiple-items form or the **Event Details** single-record form—open by clicking **New Event** on the Event List form—enter the records shown in **Table 1**.

Table 1

ID	Title	Start Time	End Time	Description	Location
1	Health Professions	6/1/23 8a	6/1/23 12p	Science Students	Hill Country High School
2	New Students	6/1/23 10a	6/1/23 3p	College Fair	Brazos Convention Center
3	Information Technology	6/2/23 9a	6/2/23 12p	Technical Students	Round Rock Technical Center
4	International Students	6/2/23 2p	6/2/23 5p	Open House	Southeast Campus

3 **Close** the **Event List** form. From your student data files, import and **Append** the data from the **Excel** file **a01F_Recruiting_Events** to the **Events** table. **Open** the **Navigation Pane**, organize the objects by **Tables and Related Views**, and then open the **Events** table to display 13 records. **Close** the table, and then **Close** the **Navigation Pane**.

4 **Create** a new **Table** defining the new fields shown in **Table 2**.

Table 2

Data Type		Short Text	Short Text	Short Text	Short Text	Short Text
Field Name	ID	Location	Last Name	First Name	Email Address	Business Phone

5 For the **ID** field, change the **Data Type** to **Short Text**, rename the field to **Recruiter ID** and then enter the records shown in **Table 3**.

Table 3

Recruiter ID	Location	Last Name	First Name	Email Address	Business Phone
R-01	Hill Country High School	Rostamo	Robyn	rrostamo@hillcohs.sch	(512) 555-3410
R-02	Brazos Convention Center	Hart	Roberto	rlhart@brazosconv.ctr	(512) 555-1938
R-03	Round Rock Technical Center	Sedlacek	Belinda	bsedlacek@rrocktech.sch	(512) 555-0471
R-04	Southeast Campus	Nguyen	Thao	tnguyen@tlcc.edu	(512) 555-2387

6 Apply **Best Fit** to all of the columns. **Save** the table as **1F Recruiters** and then **Close** the table.

7 From the **Navigation Pane**, open the **Event Details** *report* (green icon). Switch to **Layout** view. In the report, click in the title—*Event Details*—and then click to position the insertion point to the left of the word *Event*. **1F** and then press Spacebar and Enter. **Save** and **Close** the report.

8 From the **Navigation Pane**, open the **Events** table, select all of the columns, and then apply **Best Fit** to all of the columns by double-clicking the right edge of any of the selected columns. Cancel the selection, and then **Save** the table. Display the table in **Print Preview**, change the orientation to **Landscape**, change the **Margins** to **Normal**. **Save** and **Close** the table.

(continues on next page)

Mastering Access: Project 1F Recruitment Events (continued)

9 In the **Navigation Pane**, be sure that all object names display fully. **Close** the database and **Close** Access.

10 In In **MyLab IT**, locate and click the Grader Project **Access 1F Recruitment Events**. In **step 3**, under **Upload Completed Assignment**, click **Choose File**. In the **Open** dialog box, navigate to your **Access Chapter 1 folder**, and then click your **Student_Access_1F_Recruitment_Events** file one time to select it. In the lower right corner of the **Open** dialog box, click **Open**.

11 To submit your file to **MyLab IT** for grading, click **Upload**, wait a moment for a green **Success**! message, and then in **step 4**, click the blue **Submit for Grading** button. Click **Close Assignment** to return to your list of **Course Materials**.

You have completed Project 1F **END**

MyLab IT Grader

Mastering Access   Project 1G College Construction

Apply **1A** and **1B** skills from these Objectives:

1. Identify Good Database Design
2. Create a Table and Define Fields in a Blank Desktop Database
3. Change the Structure of Tables and Add a Second Table
4. Create a Query, Form, and Report
5. Close a Database and Close Access
6. Use a Template to Create a Database
7. Organize Objects in the Navigation Pane
8. Create a New Table in a Database Created with a Template
9. View a Report

In the following Mastering Access project, you will create one database to store information about construction projects for Texas Lakes Community College and a second database to store information about the public events related to the construction projects. Your completed Navigation Pane will look similar to Figure 1.51.

Project Files for **MyLab IT Grader**

1. In your **MyLab IT** course, locate and click **Access 1G College Construction** Download Materials, and then Download All Files. Close the Grader download screens.
2. Extract the zipped folder to your Access Chapter 1 folder.
3. Take a moment to open the downloaded **Access_1G_College_Construction_Instructions**; note any recent updates to the book.

Project Results

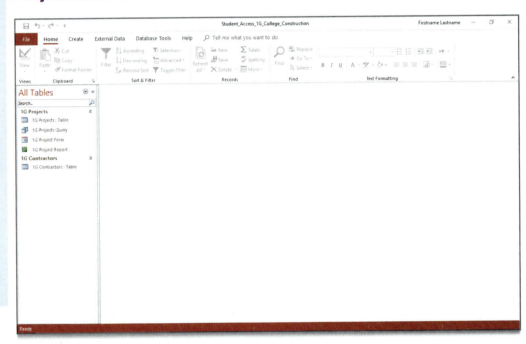

Figure 1.51

For Non-MyLab Submissions

For Project 1G, you will need these starting files:

a01G_College_Construction
a01G_Projects (Excel workbook)
a01G_Contractors (Excel workbook)

Start with an Access Data File

In your Access Chapter 1 folder, save your database as:

Lastname_Firstname_1G_College_Construction

After you have saved your database, open it to launch Access. On the next page, begin with Step 2.
After Step 13, submit your database as directed by your instructor.

(continues on next page)

Content-Based Assessments (Mastery and Transfer of Learning)

1 Navigate to your **Access Chapter 1 folder**, and then double-click the downloaded file that displays your name—**Student_Access_1G_College_Construction**. If necessary, at the top, click Enable Content.

2 **Close** the Navigation Pane. Create a new table with the fields shown in **Table 1**.

Table 1

Data Type		Short Text	Short Text	Short Text	Currency
Field Name	ID	Building Project	Site	Contractor	Budget Amount

3 For the **ID** field, change the **Data Type** to **Short Text**, rename the field to **Project ID** and change the **Field Size** to **5** Enter the three records shown in **Table 2**.

Table 2

Project ID	Building Project	Site	Contractor	Budget Amount
P-356	Student Center, 3-story	Northeast Campus	RR Construction	61450000
P-823	Student Center, 2-story	Southeast Campus	RR Construction	41960000
P-157	Health Professions Center	Northwest Campus	Marshall Ellis Construction	42630000

4 **Save** the table as **1G Projects** and **Close** the table. From your student data files, import and then **Append** the data in the **Excel** file **a01G_Projects** to your **1G Projects** table. After importing, open your **1G Projects** table—eight records display.

5 In **Design** view, for the **Project ID** field, enter a **Description** of **Enter the Project ID using the format P-###** For the **Site** field, change the field size to **25** and enter a **Description** of **Campus location** Save the changes to your table. Switch to **Datasheet** view, apply **Best Fit** to all of the fields in the table, and then **Save** your changes. Display the table in **Print Preview**, change the orientation to **Landscape. Close Print Preview**, and then **Close** the table.

6 From your student data files, import the **Excel** file **a01G_Contractors** into the database as a new table; designate the first row as column headings and the **CO ID** field as the primary key. In the wizard, name the table **1G Contractors** and then open your **1G Contractors** table—four records display. Apply **Best Fit** to all of the fields, and then **Save** your changes. Display the table in **Print Preview**, change the orientation to **Landscape. Close Print Preview**, and then **Close** the table.

7 **Create**, by using the **Query Wizard**, a **Simple Query** based on your **1G Projects** table. Include only the three fields that will answer the question, *For every site, what is the building project and the budget amount?* In the wizard, accept the default name for the query. **Close** the query.

8 Open your **1G Projects** table, and then **Create** a **Form** for this table. **Save** the form as **1G Project Form** and **Close** the form object.

9 With your **1G Projects** table open, **Create** a **Report**. Delete the **Budget Amount** field, and then sort the **Building Project** field in **Ascending** order. For the **Building Project**, **Site**, and **Contractor** fields, using the **Property Sheet**, change the **Width** of all three fields to **2** At the bottom of the report, delete the page number— **Page 1 of 1**. Change the **Report title** to **1G Project Report** Save the report as **1G Project Report**

10 Open the Navigation Pane, open the **Event List** form, and then close the Navigation Pane. In the Event List multiple-items form, enter the following two records (the Start Time and End Time data will reformat automatically):

Table 3

ID	Title	Start Time	End Time	Location	Description
1	Groundbreaking	6/13/22 10a	6/13/22 11a	Northeast Campus	Student Center groundbreaking
2	Dedication	8/26/22 12:30p	8/26/22 2p	Southwest Campus	Gymnasium building dedication

(continues on next page)

11 In the **Event List** form, click **New Event**, and in the **Event Details** single-record form, enter the following record (the Start Time and End Time data will reformat automatically):

Table 4

ID	Title	Start Time	End Time	Location	Description
3	Community Arts Expo	10/5/21 6p	10/5/22 9p	Southeast Campus	Book and Art Expo at Library Location

12 **Close All** open objects. **Open** the **Navigation Pane**, arrange the objects by **Tables and Related Views**, and be sure that all object names display fully.

13 In the **Navigation Pane**, be sure that all object names display fully. **Close** the database and **Close** Access.

14 In In **MyLab IT**, locate and click the Grader Project **Access 1G College Construction**. In **step 3**, unde **Upload Completed Assignment**, click **Choose File**. In the **Open** dialog box, navigate to your **Access Chapter 1 folder**, and then click your **Student_Access_1G_College_Construction** file one time to select it. In the lower right corner of the **Open** dialog box, click **Open**.

15 To submit your file to **MyLab IT** for grading, click **Upload**, wait a moment for a green **Success!** message, and then in **step 4**, click the blue **Submit for Grading** button. Click **Close Assignment** to return to your list of **Course Materials**.

You have completed Project 1G **END**

Content-Based Assessments (Critical Thinking)

Apply a combination of the **1A** and **1B** skills.

GO! Fix It	**Project 1H Scholarships**	IRC
GO! Make It	**Project 1I Theater Events**	IRC
GO! Solve It	**Project 1J Athletic Scholarships**	IRC
GO! Solve It	**Project 1K Student Activities**	

Project Files

For Project 1K, you will need the following files:

Event management template
a01K_Student_Activities (Word document)
You will save your database as:
Lastname_Firstname_1K_Student_Activities

Use the Event management template to create a database, and then save it in your Access Chapter 1 folder as **Lastname_Firstname_1K_Student_Activities** From your student data files, use the information in the Word document a01K_Student_Activities to enter data into the Event List multiple-items form. Each event begins at 7 p.m. and ends at 10 p.m.

After entering the records, close the form, and arrange the Navigation Pane by Tables and Related Views. Open the Event Details *report*, and then add your **Firstname Lastname 1K** to the beginning of the report title. Decrease the font size of the title so that it displays on one line. Create a paper printout or PDF electronic image as directed—two pages result. As directed, submit your database for grading.

		Performance Level		
		Exemplary	**Proficient**	**Developing**
Performance Criteria	**Create database using Event management template and enter data**	Database created using the correct template, named correctly, and all data entered correctly.	Database created using the correct template, named correctly, but not all data entered correctly.	Database created using the correct template, but numerous errors in database name and data.
	Modify report	Event Details report title includes name and project on one line.	Event Details report title includes name and project, but not on one line.	Event Details report title does not include name and project and does not display on one line.
	Create report printout	Event Details report printout is correct.	Event Details printout is incorrect.	Event Details report printout not created.

You have completed Project 1K | END

Outcomes-Based Assessments (Critical Thinking)

Rubric

The following outcomes-based assessments are *open-ended assessments*. That is, there is no specific correct result; your result will depend on your approach to the information provided. Make *Professional Quality* your goal. Use the following scoring rubric to guide you in how to approach the problem and then to evaluate how well your approach solves the problem.

The *criteria*—Software Mastery, Content, Format & Layout, and Process—represent the knowledge and skills you have gained that you can apply to solving the problem. The *levels of performance*—Professional Quality, Approaching Professional Quality, or Needs Quality Improvements—help you and your instructor evaluate your result.

	Your completed project is of Professional Quality if you:	Your completed project is Approaching Professional Quality if you:	Your completed project Needs Quality Improvements if you:
1-Software Mastery	Choose and apply the most appropriate skills, tools, and features and identify efficient methods to solve the problem.	Choose and apply some appropriate skills, tools, and features, but not in the most efficient manner.	Choose inappropriate skills, tools, or features, or are inefficient in solving the problem.
2-Content	Construct a solution that is clear and well organized, contains content that is accurate, appropriate to the audience and purpose, and is complete. Provide a solution that contains no errors of spelling, grammar, or style.	Construct a solution in which some components are unclear, poorly organized, inconsistent, or incomplete. Misjudge the needs of the audience. Have some errors in spelling, grammar, or style, but the errors do not detract from comprehension.	Construct a solution that is unclear, incomplete, or poorly organized, contains some inaccurate or inappropriate content, and contains many errors of spelling, grammar, or style. Do not solve the problem.
3-Format and Layout	Format and arrange all elements to communicate information and ideas, clarify function, illustrate relationships, and indicate relative importance.	Apply appropriate format and layout features to some elements, but not others. Overuse features, causing minor distraction.	Apply format and layout that does not communicate information or ideas clearly. Do not use format and layout features to clarify function, illustrate relationships, or indicate relative importance. Use available features excessively, causing distraction.
4-Process	Use an organized approach that integrates planning, development, self-assessment, revision, and reflection.	Demonstrate an organized approach in some areas, but not others; or, use an insufficient process of organization throughout.	Do not use an organized approach to solve the problem.

Apply a combination of the 1A and 1B skills.

GO! Think	Project 1L Student Clubs

Project Files

For Project 1L, you will need the following files:

Blank database
a01L_Clubs (Word document)
a01L_Student_Clubs (Excel workbook)
a01L_Club_Presidents (Excel workbook)
You will save your database as
Lastname_Firstname_1L_Student_Clubs

Dr. Daniel Martinez, Vice President of Student Services, needs a database that tracks information about student clubs. The database should contain two tables—one for club information and one for contact information for the club presidents.

Create a desktop database, and then save the database in your Access Chapter 1 folder as **Lastname_Firstname_1L_Student_Clubs** From your student data files, use the information in the Word document a01L_Clubs to create the first table and to enter two records. Name the table appropriately to include your name and 1L, and then append the 23 records from the Excel workbook a01L_Student_Clubs to your table. For the Club ID and President ID fields, add a description and change the field size.

Create a second table in the database by importing 25 records from the Excel workbook a01L_Club_Presidents, and then name the table appropriately to include your name and 1L. For the State and Postal Code fields, add a description and change the field size. Be sure that the field data types are correct—recall that numbers that are not used in calculations should have a data type of Short Text. Be sure all of the data and field names display in each table.

Create a simple query based on the Clubs table that answers the question, *What is the club name, meeting day, meeting time, campus, and Room ID for all of the clubs?* Create a form based on the Clubs table, saving it with an appropriate name that includes your name and 1L. Create a report based on the Presidents table, saving it with an appropriate name that includes your name and 1L, that displays the president's last name (in ascending order), the president's first name, and the phone number of every president. Change the width of the three fields so that there is less space between them, but being sure that each record prints on a single line.

Create paper printout or PDF electronic images of the two tables, the query, only Record 21 of the form, and the report as directed being sure that each object prints on one page. Organize the objects on the Navigation Pane by Tables and Related Views, and be sure that all object names display fully. As directed, submit your database for grading.

	You have completed Project 1L	END

GO! Think	Project 1M Faculty Training Online	IRC
You and GO!	Project 1N Personal Contacts Online	IRC
GO! Cumulative Group Project	Project 1O Bell Orchid Hotels Online	IRC

Introducing Microsoft PowerPoint 2019

Sunshine Studio/Shutterstock

PowerPoint 2019: Introduction **Introduction to PowerPoint**

Communication skills are critical to your success in many careers, and when it comes to communicating *your* ideas, presentation is everything! Whether you are planning to deliver your presentation in person or online—to a large audience or to a small group—Microsoft PowerPoint 2019 is a versatile business tool that will help you create presentations that make a lasting impression. Additionally, collaborating with others to develop a presentation is easy because you can share the slides you create by using your free Microsoft OneDrive cloud storage.

Microsoft PowerPoint 2019 includes a variety of themes that you can apply to a new presentation. Each theme includes several theme variants that coordinate colors, fonts, and effects. The benefit of this approach is that the variations evoke different moods and responses, yet the basic design remains the same. As a result, you can use a similar design within your company to brand your presentations, while still changing the colors to make the presentation appropriate to the audience and topic. You do not have to determine which colors work well together in the theme you choose, because professional designers have already done that for you. So you can concentrate on how best to communicate your message. Focus on creating dynamic, interesting presentations that keep your audience engaged!

Getting Started with Microsoft PowerPoint

1

POWERPOINT
2019

Bety X/Shuttestock

In This Chapter

GO! To Work
with PowerPoint

In this chapter, you will use Microsoft PowerPoint to study presentation skills, which are among the most important skills you will learn. Good presentation skills enhance your communications—written, electronic, and interpersonal. In this technology-enhanced world, communicating ideas clearly and concisely is a critical personal skill. Microsoft PowerPoint 2019 is presentation software with which you create electronic slide presentations. Use PowerPoint to present information to your audience effectively. You can start with a new, blank presentation and add content, pictures, and themes, or you can collaborate with colleagues by inserting slides that have been saved in other presentations.

The projects in this chapter relate to **Kodiak West Travel**, which is a travel agency with offices in Juneau, Anchorage, and Victoria. Kodiak West Travel works closely with local vendors to provide clients with specialized adventure travel itineraries. The company was established in 2001 in Juneau and built a loyal client base that led to the expansion into Anchorage and Victoria. As a full-service travel agency, Kodiak West Travel agents strive to provide their clients with travel opportunities that exceed their expectations. The company works with all major airlines, cruise lines, hotel chains, and vehicle rental companies as well as with small, specialized, boutique hotels.

Company Overview Presentation

Project Activities

In Activities 1.01 through 1.16, you will create the first five slides of a new presentation that Kodiak West Travel tour manager Ken Dakano is developing to introduce the tour services that the company offers. Your completed presentation will look similar to Figure 1.1.

Project Files for MyLab IT Grader

1. In your storage location, create a folder named **PowerPoint Chapter 1**.
2. In your **MyLab IT** course, locate and click **PowerPoint 1A KWT Overview**, Download Materials, and then Download All Files.
3. Extract the zipped folder to your PowerPoint Chapter 1 folder. Close the Grader download screens.
4. Take a moment to open the downloaded **PowerPoint_1A_KWT_Overview_Instructions**; note any recent updates to the book.

Project Results

GO! Project 1A
Where We're Going

Figure 1.1 Project 1A KWT Overview

For Non-MyLab Submissions

For Project 1A, you will need:
p01A_KWT_Overview
p01A_Bay
p01A_Glacier

In your storage location, create a folder named **PowerPoint Chapter 1**
In your PowerPoint Chapter 1 folder, save your presentation as:
Lastname_Firstname_1A_KWT_Overview

After you have named and saved your presentation, close the file and then, on the next page, begin with Step 1.

NOTE   If You Are Using a Touch Screen

Tap an item to click it.

Press and hold for a few seconds to right-click; release when the information or commands display.

Touch the screen with two or more fingers and then pinch together or stretch your fingers apart to zoom in and out.

Slide your finger on the screen to scroll—slide left to scroll right and slide right to scroll left.

Slide to rearrange—similar to dragging with a mouse.

Swipe to select—slide an item a short distance with a quick movement—to select an item and bring up commands, if any.

Objective 1   **Create a New Presentation**

ALERT   Because Office 365 is a cloud-based subscription service that receives continuous updates, you may encounter some variations in what appears on your screen and what is shown in this instruction. Microsoft Office 365 is fully installed on your PC or Mac; no internet access is necessary to create or edit documents. When you *are* connected to the internet, you will receive monthly upgrades and new features, so you always have the latest versions of Office apps as soon as they are available. Your subscription gives you continuous free access to the latest innovations and refinements.

GO! Learn How
Video P1-1

Microsoft PowerPoint 2019 is software you can use to present information to your audience effectively. You can edit and format a blank presentation by adding text, a presentation theme, and pictures. When you start PowerPoint, presentations you have recently opened, if any, display on the left. On the right you can select either a blank presentation or a *theme*—a set of unified design elements that provides a look for your presentation by applying colors, fonts, and effects. A presentation consists of one or more slides. Similar to a page in a document—a presentation *slide* can contain text, pictures, tables, charts, and other multimedia or graphic objects.

Activity 1.01 | **Identifying Parts of the PowerPoint Window**

In this Activity, you will start PowerPoint and identify the parts of the PowerPoint window.

1 ▷ Start PowerPoint. In the list of templates, click **Facet** to view a preview of the Facet theme and the color variations associated with this theme. If Facet is not visible, use the Search templates box to search for it. Below the theme preview, click either the left- or right-pointing **More Images** ◀ and ▶ arrows to view how various types of slides in this theme display. To the right of the preview, click each of the color variations. After you have viewed each color, click the original green color.

 MAC TIP   There is no color preview available in the Mac version of PowerPoint.

2 On either the left or right side of the preview window, notice the arrow, and then compare your screen with Figure 1.2. Click the right- or left-pointing arrow several times to view other available themes, and then return to the **Facet** theme.

You can use the arrows to the left and right of the preview window to scroll through the available themes.

MAC TIP Scroll down on the opening screen to view other themes.

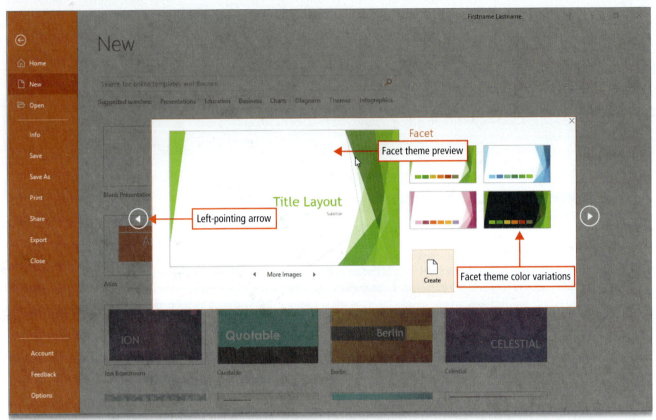

Figure 1.2

3 In the lower right area of the preview window, click **Create** to begin a new presentation using the **Facet** theme.

4 Compare your screen with Figure 1.3, and then take a moment to study the parts of the PowerPoint window described in the table in Figure 1.4.

The presentation displays in *normal view*, which is the primary editing view in PowerPoint where you write and design your presentations. On the left, a pane displays miniature images— *thumbnails*—of the slides in your presentation. On the right, the *Slide pane* displays a larger image of the active slide.

MAC TIP To display group names on the ribbon, display the menu, click PowerPoint, click Preferences, click View, select the Show group titles check box.

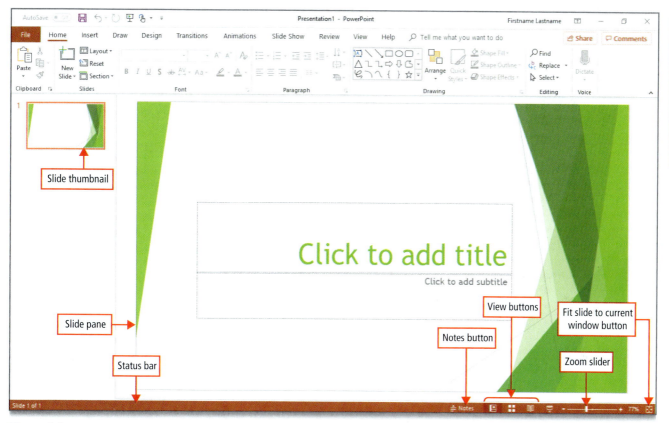

Figure 1.3

Microsoft PowerPoint Screen Elements	
Screen Element	**Description**
Slide pane	Displays a large image of the active slide.
Slide thumbnails	Miniature images of each slide in the presentation. Clicking a slide thumbnail displays the slide in the Slide pane.
Status bar	Displays, in a horizontal bar at the bottom of the presentation window, the current slide number, number of slides in a presentation, Notes button, View buttons, Zoom slider, and Fit slide to current window button; you can customize this area to include additional information.
View buttons	Control the look of the presentation window with a set of commands.
Zoom slider	Zooms the slide displayed in the Slide pane, in and out.
Fit slide to current window button	Fits the active slide to the maximum view in the Slide pane.

Figure 1.4

5 In the upper right corner of your screen, click **Close** ⊠ to close PowerPoint. Do not save your file. Navigate to your **PowerPoint Chapter 1 folder**, and then double-click the PowerPoint file you downloaded from MyLab IT that displays your name—**Student_PowerPoint_1A_KWT_Overview**. In your presentation, if necessary, at the top, click **Enable Editing**.

For Non-MyLab Submissions

Open your saved **Lastname_Firstname_1A_KWT_Overview** presentation.

Activity 1.02 | Entering Presentation Text

When you create a new presentation, PowerPoint displays a new blank presentation with a single slide—a title slide in Normal view. The *title slide* is usually the first slide in a presentation; it introduces the presentation topic.

1 In the **Slide pane**, click in the text *Click to add title*, which is the title placeholder.

A *placeholder* is a box on a slide with dotted or dashed borders that holds title and body text or other content such as charts, tables, and pictures. This slide contains two placeholders, one for the title and one for the subtitle.

2 Type **Kodiak West** and then click in the subtitle placeholder. Type **Your Travel** and then press Enter to create a new line in the subtitle placeholder. Type **Your Way** and then compare your screen with Figure 1.5.

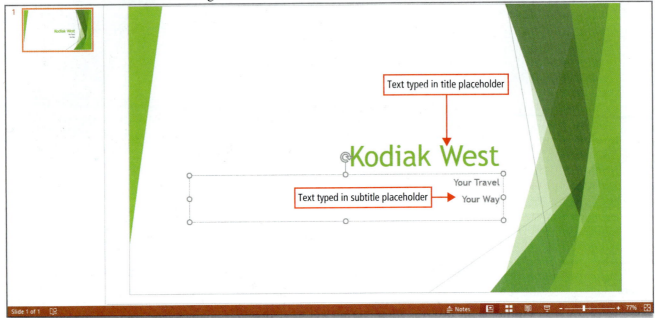

Figure 1.5

3 On the **Quick Access Toolbar**, click **Save** 🖫.

Activity 1.03 | Applying a Presentation Theme

A theme is a set of unified design elements that provides a look for your presentation by applying colors, fonts, and effects. After you create a presentation, you can change the look of your presentation by applying a different theme. Kodiak West Travel wants a theme that evokes a feeling of nature.

1 On the ribbon, click the **Design tab**. In the **Themes group**, click **More** 🔽 to display the **Themes** gallery. Compare your screen with Figure 1.6.

The themes displayed on your system may differ from Figure 1.6.

Figure 1.6

2 In the gallery, point to several of the themes and notice that a ScreenTip displays the name of each theme, and the Live Preview feature displays how each theme would look if applied to your presentation.

The first theme that displays is the Office Theme.

MAC TIP Live previews do not display in the Mac version of PowerPoint.

3 Use the ScreenTips to locate the **Organic** theme shown in Figure 1.7.

Figure 1.7

4 Click **Organic** to change the presentation theme and then **Save** 🔲 your presentation.

ALERT If your system does not have the Organic theme, use the theme file downloaded with your data files from **MyLab IT**. In the themes gallery, click Browse for Themes, navigate to your PowerPoint Chapter 1 folder, locate the Organic.thmx file and click Apply.

Objective 2   **Edit a Presentation in Normal View**

GO! Learn How
Video P1-2

Editing is the process of modifying a presentation by adding and deleting slides or by changing the contents of individual slides.

Activity 1.04 | **Inserting a New Slide**

2.1.3

Your presentation consists of a single slide. Most presentations consist of multiple slides. This presentation will highlight the company and consist of five slides when finished.

1 On the **Home tab**, in the **Slides group**, point to the **New Slide arrow**—the lower part of the New Slide button. Compare your screen with Figure 1.8.

The New Slide button is a *split button*—a type of button in which clicking the main part of the button performs a command and clicking the arrow opens a menu, list, or gallery. The upper, main part of the New Slide button, when clicked, inserts a slide without displaying any options. The lower part—the New Slide arrow—when clicked, displays a gallery of slide *layouts*— the arrangement of elements, such as title and subtitle text, lists, pictures, tables, charts, shapes, and movies, on a slide.

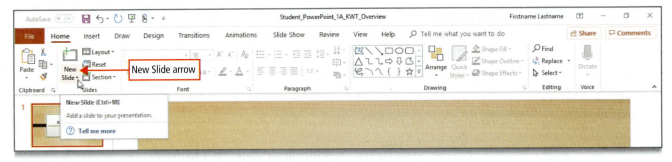

Figure 1.8

> **2** In the **Slides group**, click the lower portion of the **New Slide** button—the **New Slide arrow**—to display the gallery, and then compare your screen with Figure 1.9.

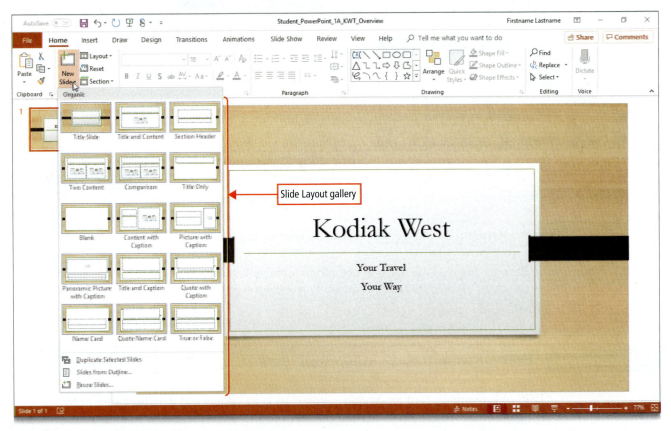

Figure 1.9

> **3** In the gallery, click the **Panoramic Picture with Caption** layout to insert a new slide. Notice that the new blank slide displays in the **Slide pane**, and a slide thumbnail displays at the left. Compare your screen with Figure 1.10.

🡒 **BY TOUCH**   In the gallery, tap the desired layout to insert a new slide.

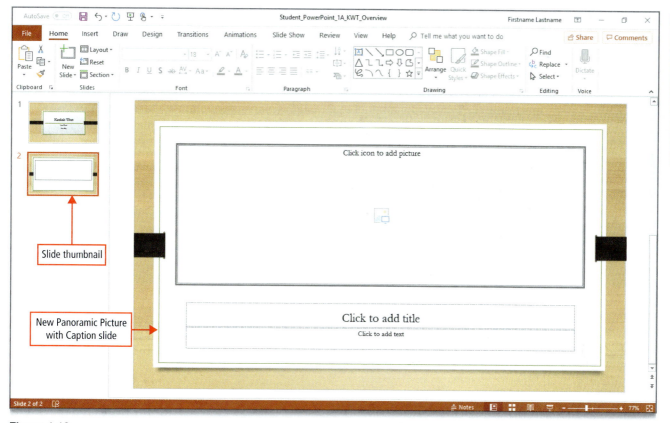

Figure 1.10

4 On the new slide, below the picture placeholder, click the text *Click to add title*, and then type **Your Dreams**

5 Below the title placeholder, click in the text placeholder. Type **Whether you want to trek on a glacier or spend your time in quiet solitude, Kodiak West Travel can make your dream a reality.** Compare your screen with Figure 1.11.

Figure 1.11

6 On the **Home tab**, in the **Slides group**, click the **New Slide arrow** to display the gallery, and then click **Title and Content**. In the title placeholder, type **Our Expertise** and then below the title placeholder, click in the content placeholder. Type **Over 20 years of experience in the travel industry**

7 **Save** 🔲 your presentation.

Activity 1.05 | Increasing and Decreasing List Levels

MOS
3.1.3

You can organize text in a PowerPoint presentation according to *list levels*. List levels, each represented by a bullet symbol, are similar to outline levels. On a slide, list levels are identified by the bullet style, indentation, and the size of the text. The first level on an individual slide is the title.

Increasing the list level of a bullet point increases its indent and results in a smaller text size. Decreasing the list level of a bullet point decreases its indent and results in a larger text size. Use list levels to organize information.

1 On **Slide 3**, if necessary, click at the end of the first bullet point after the word *industry*, and then press Enter to insert a new bullet point.

2 Press Tab, and then notice that the bullet is indented. Type **Certified Travel Associates**

By pressing Tab at the beginning of a bullet point, you can increase the list level and indent the bullet point.

3 Press Enter and notice that a new bullet point displays at the same level as the previous bullet point.

4 On the **Home tab**, in the **Paragraph group**, click **Decrease List Level** . Type **Specializing in land and sea travel** and then compare your screen with Figure 1.12.

The indent is removed and the size of the text increases.

Figure 1.12

5 Press Enter, and then on the **Home tab**, click **Increase List Level** . Type **Pacific Northwest including U.S. and Canada**

You can use the Increase List Level button to indent the bullet point.

6 Compare your screen with Figure 1.13, and then **Save** your presentation.

Figure 1.13

Activity 1.06 | Adding Speaker Notes to a Presentation

The *Notes pane* is an area of the Normal view window that displays below the Slide pane with space to type notes about the active slide. You can refer to these notes while making a presentation, reminding you of the important points that you want to discuss. This will be helpful when employees of Kodiak West give the presentation before new customers.

1 With **Slide 3** displayed, in the **Status bar**, click **Notes**, and then notice that below the Slide pane, the Notes pane displays. Click in the **Notes** pane, and then type **Kodiak West Travel has locations in Juneau, Anchorage, and Victoria.**

> The Notes button is a toggle button. Clicking once will display the Notes pane, clicking again will hide it.

2 **Save** your presentation, and then compare your screen with Figure 1.14.

Figure 1.14

Activity 1.07 | Displaying and Editing Slides in the Slide Pane

1 On the left side of the PowerPoint window, look at the slide thumbnails, and then notice that the presentation contains three slides. On the right side of the PowerPoint window, in the vertical scroll bar, point to the scroll box, and then hold down the left mouse button to display a ScreenTip indicating the slide number and title.

2 Drag the scroll box up until the ScreenTip displays *Slide: 2 of 3 Your Dreams*. Compare your slide with Figure 1.15, and then release the mouse button to display **Slide 2**.

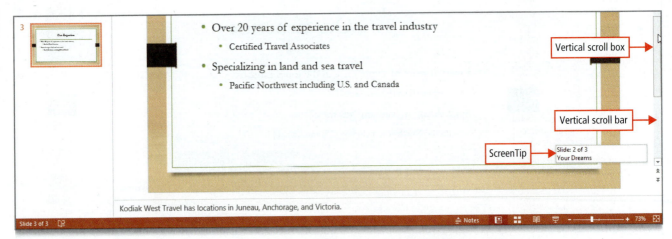

Figure 1.15

3 At the bottom of the slide, in the content placeholder, click at the end of the sentence, after the period. Press Spacebar, and then type **If you can dream it, we can help you get there.**

4 On the left side of the PowerPoint window, in the slide thumbnails, point to **Slide 3**, and then notice that a ScreenTip displays the slide title. Compare your screen with Figure 1.16.

Figure 1.16

5 Click **Slide 3** to display it in the Slide pane. On the **Home tab**, in the **Slides group**, click the **New Slide arrow** to display the **Slide Layout** gallery, and then click **Section Header**.

A *section header* is a type of slide layout that changes the look and flow of a presentation by providing text placeholders that do not contain bullet points.

6 Click in the title placeholder, and then type **About Our Company**

7 Click in the content placeholder below the title, and then type **Kodiak West Travel was established in May of 2001 by Ken Dakona and Mariam Dorner, two Alaska residents whose sense of adventure and commitment to ecotourism is an inherent aspect of their travel itineraries.** Compare your screen with Figure 1.17.

The placeholder text is resized to fit within the placeholder. The AutoFit Options button displays.

Figure 1.17

8 Click **AutoFit Options** ⊹, review the AutoFit options and then click outside the menu to close it.

The *AutoFit Text to Placeholder* option keeps the text contained within the placeholder by reducing the size of the text. The *Stop Fitting Text to This Placeholder* option turns off the AutoFit option so that the text can flow beyond the placeholder border; the text size remains unchanged. You can also choose to split the text between two slides, continue on a new slide, or divide the text into two columns.

 MAC TIP To adjust AutoFit, on the Shape Format tab, click More Formats to open the Format pane. On the Format pane, click Text Options, and click the Text Box tab.

9 In the slide thumbnails, click **Slide 1** to display it in the Slide pane, and then in the slide title, click at the end of the word *West*. Press [Spacebar], and then type **Travel**

Clicking a slide thumbnail is the most common method used to display a slide in the Slide pane.

10 **Save** 🔚 your presentation.

Objective 3 | Add Pictures to a Presentation

GO! Learn How
Video P1-3

Photographic images add impact to a presentation and help the audience visualize your message. Photos can be inserted from files or from online sources, and format and enhance the images using tools built into PowerPoint.

Activity 1.08 | Inserting a Picture from a File

Many slide layouts in PowerPoint accommodate digital picture files so that you can easily add pictures you have stored. The travel agency has a collection of photographs to be inserted in the presentation that highlights the beauty of the region.

1 Display **Slide 2**, and then compare your screen with Figure 1.18.

In the center of the picture placeholder, the *Pictures* button displays.

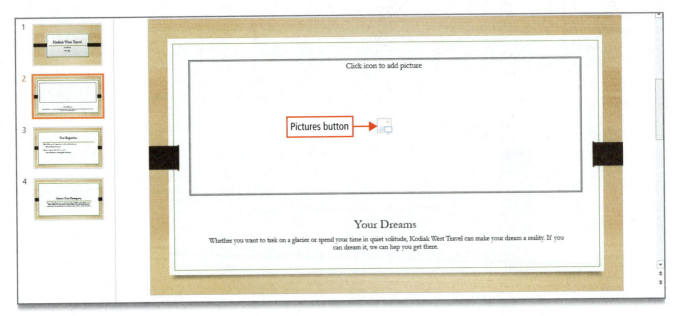

Figure 1.18

2 In the picture placeholder, click **Pictures** 🖼 to open the **Insert Picture** dialog box. Navigate to the data files downloaded with this project, click **p01A_Glacier**, and then click **Insert** to insert the picture in the placeholder. If necessary, close the Design Ideas pane. Compare your screen with Figure 1.19.

Small circles—*sizing handles*—surround the inserted picture and indicate that the picture is selected and can be modified or formatted. The *rotation handle*—a circular arrow above the picture—provides a way to rotate a selected image. The Picture Tools are added to the ribbon, providing picture formatting commands.

NOTE   Design Ideas Pane

The Design Ideas pane may open each time you insert a picture. The pane includes ideas for ways to format and lay out a slide. In this project you will not use these suggestions, so you can close the pane each time it opens.

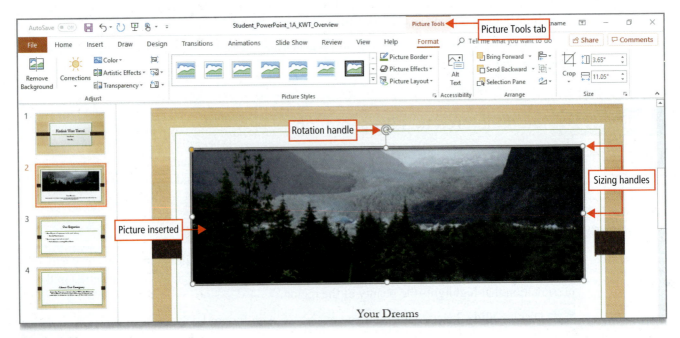

Figure 1.19

3 ▶ Display **Slide 3**. On the **Home tab**, in the **Slides group**, click the **New Slide arrow**, and then click **Title and Content**. In the title placeholder, type **Your Vacation**

4 ▶ In the content placeholder, click **Pictures** 🖼. Navigate to the data files for this project, and then click **p01A_Bay**. Click **Insert**, **Save** 💾 the presentation, and then compare your screen with Figure 1.20.

Figure 1.20

Activity 1.09 | Applying a Style to a Picture

3.3.2

When you select a picture, the Picture Tools display, adding the Format tab to the ribbon. The Format tab provides numerous styles that you can apply to your pictures. A *style* is a collection of formatting options that you can apply to a picture, text, or an object.

1 ▶ With **Slide 4** displayed, if necessary, click the picture to select it. On the ribbon, notice that the *Picture Tools* are active and the *Format* tab displays.

2 ▶ On the **Picture Tools Format tab**, in the **Picture Styles group**, click **More** ▾ to display the **Picture Styles** gallery, and then compare your screen with Figure 1.21.

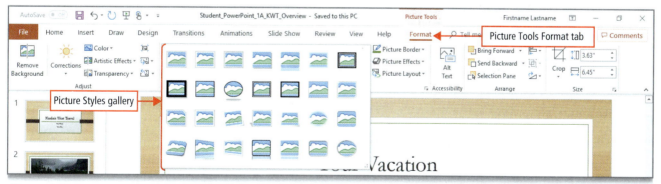

Figure 1.21

3 In the gallery, point to several of the picture styles to display the ScreenTips and to view the effect on your picture. Point to each style to display a ScreenTip, and then locate and click **Simple Frame, Black**. Click in a blank area of the slide, compare your screen with Figure 1.22, and then **Save** 🔲 the presentation.

Figure 1.22

Activity 1.10 | Applying and Removing Picture Artistic Effects

3.3.2

Artistic effects are formats applied to images that make pictures resemble sketches or paintings.

1 On **Slide 4**, click the picture to select it. On the **Picture Tools Format tab**, in the **Adjust group**, click **Artistic Effects** to display the **Artistic Effects** gallery. Compare your screen with Figure 1.23.

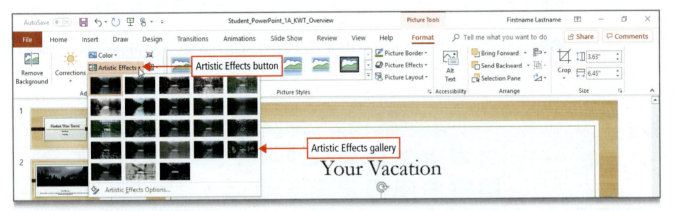

Figure 1.23

2 In the gallery, point to several of the artistic effects to display the ScreenTips and to have Live Preview display the effect on your picture. Then, locate and click the **Glow Diffused** effect.

3 With the picture still selected, on the **Format tab**, in the **Adjust group**, click **Artistic Effects** again to display the gallery. In the first row, click the first effect—**None**—to remove the effect from the picture and restore the previous formatting. **Save** 🔲 the presentation.

Objective 4 | Print and View a Presentation

There are several print options in PowerPoint. For example, you can print full page images of your slides, presentation handouts to provide your audience with copies of your slides, or Notes pages displaying speaker notes below an image of the slide.

GO! Learn How
Video P1-4

Activity 1.11 | Viewing a Slide Show

MOS
1.2.2

When you view a presentation as an electronic slide show, the entire slide fills the computer screen, and an audience can view your presentation if your computer is connected to a projection system.

1 On the ribbon, click the **Slide Show tab**. In the **Start Slide Show group**, click **From Beginning**. Compare your slide with Figure 1.24.

The first slide fills the screen, displaying the presentation as the audience would see it if your computer was connected to a projection system.

ANOTHER WAY Press F5 to start the slide show from the beginning. Or, display the first slide you want to show and click the Slide Show button on the lower right side of the status bar.

MAC TIP On the Slide Show tab click Play from Start.

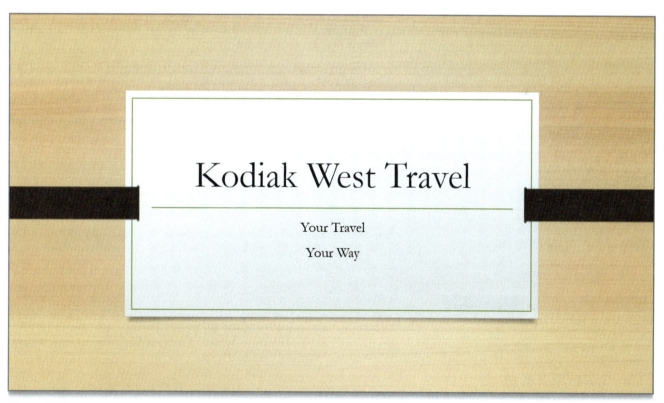

Figure 1.24

2 Click the left mouse button or press Spacebar to advance to the second slide.

3 Continue to click or press Spacebar until the last slide displays, and then click or press Spacebar one more time to display a *black slide*—a slide that displays after the last slide in a presentation indicating that the presentation is over.

4 With the black slide displayed, click the left mouse button to exit the slide show and return to the presentation.

> **↻ ANOTHER WAY** Press [Esc] to exit the slide show.

Activity 1.12 | Using Presenter View

1.4.5

Presenter View shows the full-screen slide show on one monitor or projection screen for the audience to see, while enabling the presenter to view a preview of the next slide, notes, and a timer on another monitor.

1 On the **Slide Show tab**, in the **Monitors** group, if necessary, select the Use Presenter View check box. Hold down [Alt] and press [F5]. Take a moment to study the parts of the PowerPoint Presenter View window described in the table in Figure 1.25.

If you do not have two monitors, you can practice using Presenter View by pressing [Alt] + [F5]. You will see only the presenter's view—not the audience's view—in this mode.

> **ALERT** **Alt + F5 does not open Presenter View**
> On a notebook computer, you may need to press the Fn or Function Lock key to override the preassigned function of the F5 key.

> **💻 MAC TIP** On the Slide Show tab, click Presenter View. Point to the current slide to display Presenter View tools.

Microsoft PowerPoint Presenter View Elements	
Screen Element	**Description**
 0:00:00 ‖ ↻	**Timer:** running time, pause timer, and reset timer options
✏	**Pen and laser pointer tools:** point to or annotate slides during a presentation
⊞	**See all slides:** displays all slides on the screen to easily navigate between them
🔍	**Zoom into the slide:** focus on a part of a slide while presenting
🖵	**Black or unblack slide show:** hide or unhide the presentation
⊙	**More slide show options:** including hide presenter view, help, pause, and end show
🔵 and ▶	**Navigation buttons:** move back and forth through the presentation
 SHOW TASKBAR DISPLAY SETTINGS ▾ END SLIDE SHOW	**Presenter View ribbon:** controls slide presentation display options
A˙	**Notes pane text size adjustment:** make notes text larger or smaller

Figure 1.25

2 Below the current slide, click the **Advance to the next animation or slide arrow** ▶ to display **Slide 2**.

> **☞ BY TOUCH** Advance to the next slide by swiping the current slide to the left.

3 In the upper right corner of the **Presenter View** window, point to the next slide—*Our Expertise*—and then click. Notice that the notes that you typed on **Slide 3** display. Compare your screen with Figure 1.26.

Clicking the image of the next slide advances the presentation.

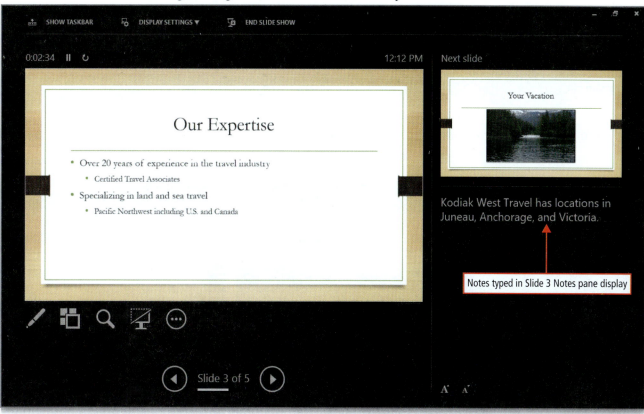

Figure 1.26

4 Below the notes, click **Make the text larger** $A^{^*}$ to increase the font size of the notes in Presenter view to make the notes easier to read.

5 Below the current slide, click the second button—**See all slides** 🔳. Compare your screen with Figure 1.27.

A thumbnail view of all of the slides in your presentation displays. Here you can quickly move to another slide, if for example, you want to review a concept or answer a question related to a slide other than the current slide.

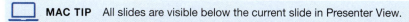

🖥 **MAC TIP** All slides are visible below the current slide in Presenter View.

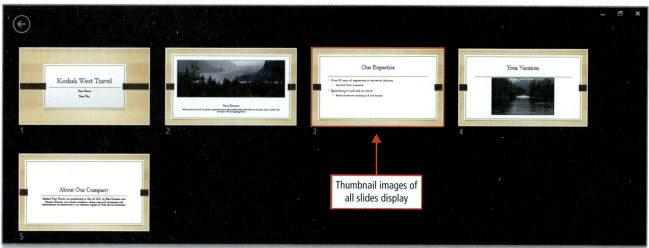

Figure 1.27

6 Click **Slide 4** to make Slide 4 the current slide in Presenter View. Below the current slide, click the third button—**Zoom into the slide** 🔍. Move the 🔍 pointer to the middle of the picture on the current slide, and then click to zoom in on the picture. Notice that the 🖑 pointer displays. Compare your slide with Figure 1.28.

With the 🖑 pointer displayed, you can move the zoomed image to draw close-up attention to a specific part of your slide.

BY TOUCH Touch the current slide with two fingers and then pinch together to zoom in or stretch your fingers apart to zoom out.

MAC TIP The Zoom into the slide feature is not available in the Mac version of PowerPoint.

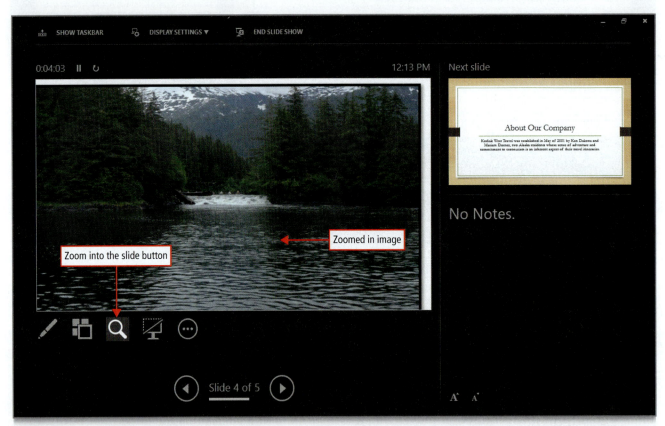

Figure 1.28

7 Below the current slide, click the **Advance to the next animation or slide arrow** 🔘 to display **Slide 5**. At the top of the **Presenter View** window, click **END SLIDE SHOW** to return to your presentation.

Activity 1.13 | Inserting Headers and Footers on Slide Handouts

A *header* is text that prints at the top of each sheet of *slide handouts* or *notes pages*. Slide handouts are printed images of slides on a sheet of paper. These can be given to customers to follow along and take notes during the presentation. Notes pages are printouts that contain the slide image on the top half of the page and notes that you have created in the Notes pane in the lower half of the page.

In addition to headers, you can insert *footers*—text that displays at the bottom of every slide or that prints at the bottom of a sheet of slide handouts or notes pages.

1 ▶ Click the **Insert tab**, in the **Text group**, click **Header & Footer** to display the **Header and Footer** dialog box.

2 ▶ In the **Header and Footer** dialog box, click the **Notes and Handouts tab**. Under **Include on page**, select the **Date and time** check box, and as you do so, watch the Preview box in the upper right corner of the Header and Footer dialog box.

> The two narrow rectangular boxes at the top of the Preview box are placeholders for the header text and date. When you select the Date and time check box, the placeholder in the upper right corner is outlined, indicating the location in which the date will display.

3 ▶ Be sure that the **Update automatically** option button is selected so that the current date prints on the notes and handouts each time the presentation is printed. If it is not selected, click the Update automatically option button.

4 ▶ Verify that the **Page number** check box is selected and select it if it is not. If necessary, clear the Header check box to omit this element. Notice that in the **Preview** box, the corresponding placeholder is not selected.

5 ▶ Select the **Footer** check box, and then click in the **Footer** box. Type **1A_KWT_Overview** so that the file name displays as a footer, and then compare your dialog box with Figure 1.29.

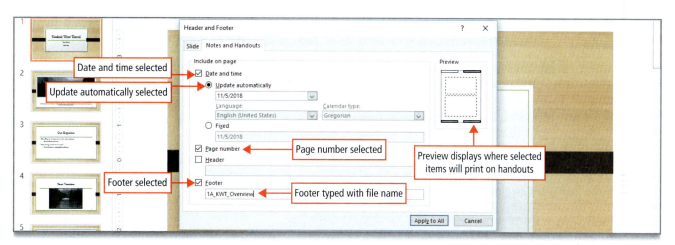

Figure 1.29

6 ▶ In the lower right corner of the dialog box, click **Apply to All**. Save 💾 your presentation.

Activity 1.14 | Inserting Slide Numbers on Slides

1.2.3,
2.2.3

In this Activity, you will insert the slide numbers on the presentation slides.

1 ▶ Display **Slide 1**. On the **Insert tab**, in the **Text group**, click **Header & Footer** to display the **Header and Footer** dialog box.

2 ▶ In the **Header and Footer** dialog box, if necessary, click the Slide tab. Under **Include on slide**, select the **Slide number** check box, and then select the **Don't show on title slide** check box. Verify that all other check boxes are cleared, and then compare your screen with Figure 1.30.

> Selecting the *Don't show on title slide* check box omits the slide number from the first slide in a presentation.

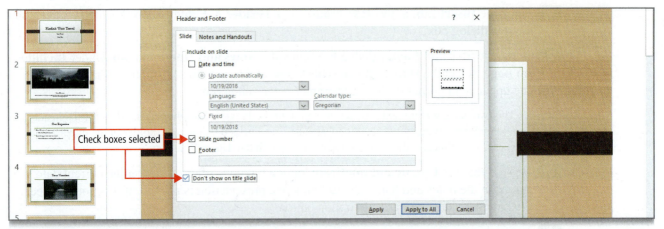

Figure 1.30

3 ▶ Click **Apply to All**, and then notice that on the first slide, the slide number does not display.

4 ▶ Display **Slide 2**, and then notice that the slide number displays in the lower right area of the slide. Display each slide in the presentation and notice the placement of the slide number.

The position of the slide number and other header and footer information is determined by the theme applied to the presentation.

5 ▶ Click **File** to redisplay **Backstage** view. On the Info tab, click **Show All Properties**. In the list of **Properties**, click to the right of **Tags**, and then type **company overview**

6 ▶ Click to the right of **Subject**, and then type your course name and section number. Under **Related People**, be sure that your name displays as the author, and edit if necessary.

 MAC TIP Click the File menu, click Properties, click the Summary tab, and instead of Tags, use the Keywords box.

7 ▶ Click **Save** 🖫. If you will not be completing the following optional Activity, on the right end of the title bar, click **Close** ⨯ to close the presentation and close PowerPoint.

For Non-MyLab Submissions Determine What Your Instructor Requires
As directed by your instructor, submit your completed PowerPoint file.

8 ▶ In **MyLab IT**, in your **Course Materials**, locate and click the Grader Project **PowerPoint 1A KWT Overview**. In **step 3**, under **Upload Completed Assignment**, click **Choose File**. In the **Open** dialog box, navigate to your **PowerPoint Chapter 1 folder**, and then click your **Student_PowerPoint_1A_KWT_Overview** file one time to select it. In the lower right corner of the **Open** dialog box, click **Open**.

The name of your selected file displays above the Upload button.

9 ▶ To submit your file to **MyLab IT** for grading, click **Upload**, wait a moment for a green **Success!** message, and then in **step 4**, click the blue **Submit for Grading** button. Click **Close Assignment** to return to your list of **Course Materials**.

Activity 1.15 | Printing Presentation Handouts

1.3.3

Use Backstage view to preview the arrangement of slides and to print your presentation.

1 If necessary, open your **Student_PowerPoint_1A_KWT_Overview** presentation. Display **Slide 1**. Click **File** to display **Backstage** view, and then click **Print**.

The Print tab displays the tools you need to select your settings and view a preview of your presentation. On the right, Print Preview displays your presentation exactly as it will print. If your system is not connected to a color printer, your slide may display in black and white.

2 Under **Settings**, click **Full Page Slides**, and then compare your screen with Figure 1.31.

The gallery displays either the default print setting—Full Page Slides—or the most recently selected print setting.

MAC TIP In the Print window, click Show Details. Under Layout, click Slides.

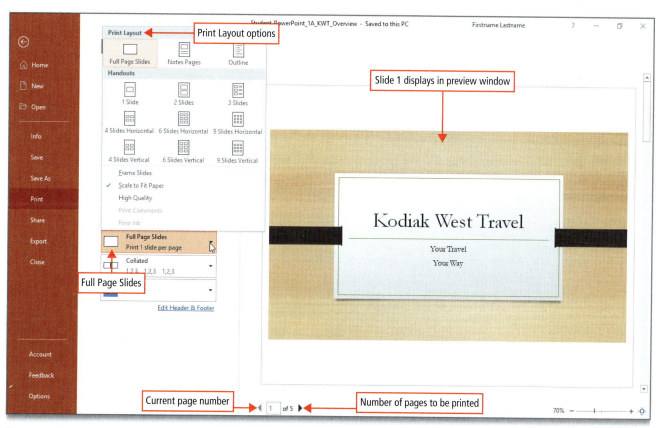

Figure 1.31

3 In the gallery, under **Handouts**, click **6 Slides Horizontal**. Notice that the **Print Preview** on the right displays the slide handout, and that the current date, file name, and page number display in the header and footer. Compare your screen with Figure 1.32.

In the Settings group, the Portrait Orientation option displays; here you can change the print orientation from Portrait to Landscape.

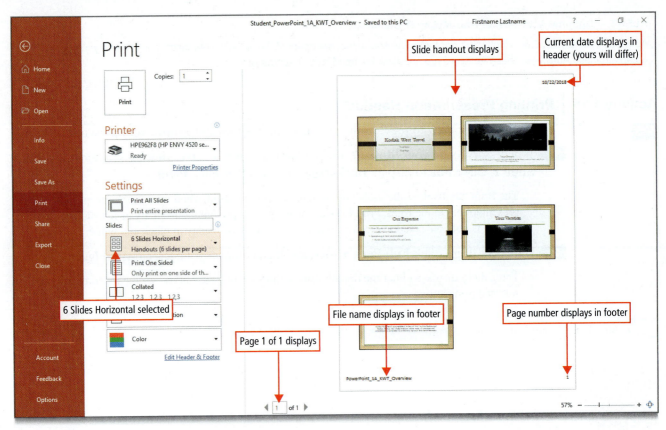

Figure 1.32

4 ▶ To create an electronic image of your handouts that looks like printed handouts, skip this step and continue to Step 5. To print your handout document on paper using the default printer on your system, in the upper left portion of the screen, click **Print**.

> The handout will print on your default printer—on a black and white printer, the colors will print in shades of gray. To save the cost of color ink, you can print in grayscale by clicking the Color button. Backstage view closes and your file redisplays in the PowerPoint window.

5 ▶ To create an electronic image of your presentation that looks like a printed document, on the left click **Export**. On the right, click the **Create PDF/XPS** button to display the **Publish as PDF or XPS** dialog box.

6 ▶ In the **Publish as PDF or XPS** dialog box, click **Options.** Under **Publish what**, click the **Slides arrow**, and then click **Handouts.** Be sure **Slides per page** is set to **6** and **Order** is set to **Horizontal.** Click **OK.**

> **MAC TIP**   In the Print window, click the PDF arrow, and then click Save as PDF.

7 ▶ Navigate to your **PowerPoint Chapter 1** folder, and then click **Publish**. If your Adobe Acrobat or Reader program displays your PDF, close the PDF file. If your PDF displays in Microsoft Edge, in the upper right corner click Close ⊠. Notice that your presentation redisplays in PowerPoint.

Activity 1.16 | Printing Speaker Notes

1.3.2

1 On the **Print tab**, under **Settings**, click **6 Slides Horizontal**, and then under **Print Layout**, click **Notes Pages** to view the presentation notes for **Slide 1**; recall that you created notes for **Slide 3**.

> Indicated below the Notes page are the current slide number and the number of pages that will print when Notes Pages is selected. You can use the Next Page and Previous Page arrows to display each Notes page in the presentation.

2 At the bottom of the **Print Preview**, click **Next Page** ▶ two times so that **Page 3** displays. Notice that the notes that you typed for Slide 3 display below the image of the slide. Compare your screen with Figure 1.33.

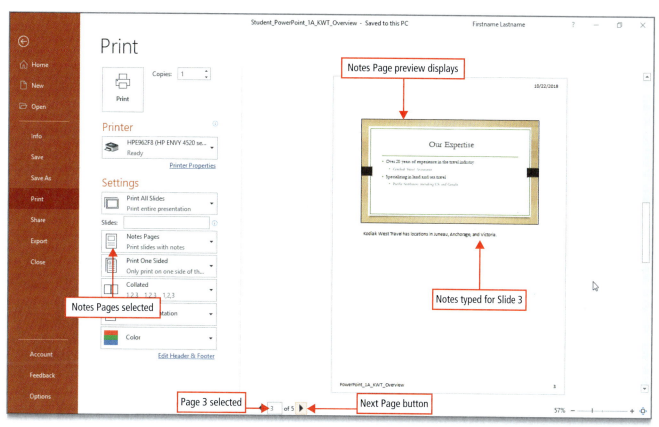

Figure 1.33

3 Under **Settings**, click in the **Slides box**. Type **3** and then click **Notes Pages**. In the lower section, click **Frame Slides**. Under **Printer**, click the printer arrow, click **Microsoft Print to PDF**, and then click **Print** to print your presentation to a PDF file.

> Microsoft Print to PDF is an automatically installed printer option in Windows 10, which enables you to create an image that looks like a printed document.

ALERT   No Microsoft Print to PDF Printer Option Available

If you are using Windows 7 or 8, select the Microsoft XPS Document Writer printer instead to print your presentation to the XPS format, a Microsoft file format that also creates an image of your document and that opens in the XPS viewer.

---

4 Navigate to the location where you store your files for this chapter, name the file **Lastname_Firstname_1A_KWT_Overview_Notes** and then click **Save** 🗄. **Close** PowerPoint.

You have completed Project 1A   **END**

»» GO! With Google Slides

Objective	Create a Company Overview Presentation in Google Slides

ALERT   **Working with Web-Based Applications and Services**

Computer programs and services on the web receive continuous updates and improvements, so the steps to complete this web-based activity may differ from the ones shown. You can often look at the screens and the information presented to determine how to complete the activity.

If you do not already have a Google account, you will need to create one before you begin this activity. Go to http://google.com and in the upper right corner, click Sign in. On the Sign In screen, click Use another account, click Create Account. On the Create your Google Account page, complete the form, read and agree to the Terms of Service and Privacy Policy, and then click Next step. On the Welcome screen, click Get Started.

Activity | Creating a Company Overview Presentation in Google Slides

In this Activity, you will use Google Slides to create a presentation similar to the one you created in Project 1A.

1 From the desktop, open your browser, navigate to **http://google.com**, and sign in to your Google account. Click **Google apps** and click Drive . Open your **GO! Web Projects** folder—or click New to create and then open this folder if necessary.

2 In the left pane, click **New**, and then click **Google Slides**. In the **Themes** pane, click **Tropic**. If this theme is not available, select another theme. **Close** the **Themes** pane.

3 At the top of the window, click **Untitled presentation** and then, using your own name, type **Lastname_Firstname_1A_Google_Slides** as the file name and then press Enter.

4 In the title placeholder, type **Kodiak West Travel** and then in the subtitle placeholder type **Your Travel - Your Way**

5 On the **toolbar**, click the **New slide with layout arrow** +, and then click **Caption**.

6 On the **toolbar**, click **Image** . Click **Upload from computer**. Navigate to your student data files, and then click **p01A_Glacier**. Click **Open**.

7 In the text placeholder, type **Your Dreams**

8 On the **toolbar**, click the **New slide with layout arrow** +, and then click **Title and body**. In the title placeholder, type **Our Expertise**

9 Click in the content placeholder. On the toolbar, if necessary, click More, and click **Bulleted list** . In the placeholder, type **Over 20 years of experience in the travel industry** and then press Enter. Press Tab. Type **Certified Travel Associates** and then press Enter. On toolbar, if necessary, click More, and then click **Decrease indent** . Type **Specializing in land and sea travel** and then press Enter. Press Tab and then type **Pacific Northwest including U.S. and Canada**

10 Below the slide, click in the **Notes** pane. Type **Kodiak West Travel has locations in Juneau, Anchorage, and Victoria.** Compare your screen to Figure A.

11 In the upper right, click the **Present button arrow**, click **Present from beginning**. Click the left mouse button to progress through the presentation. When the last slide displays, press Esc or click **Exit**.

12 Your presentation will be saved automatically. If you are instructed to submit your file, click the File menu, point to Download as, and then click Microsoft PowerPoint, PDF Document, or another format as directed by your instructor. The file will download to your default download folder as determined by your browser settings. Sign out of your Google account and close your browser.

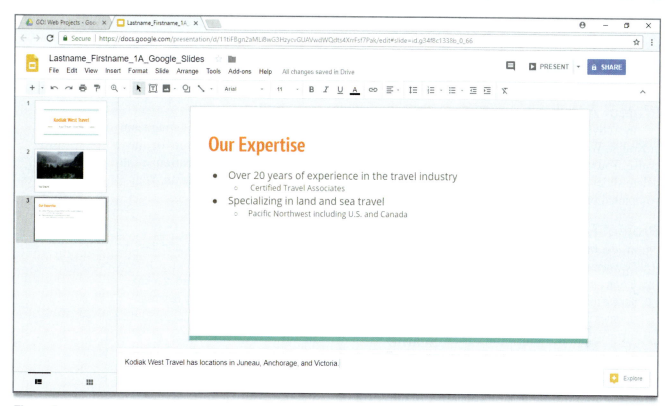

Figure A

PROJECT 1B Itinerary Presentation

Project Activities

In Activities 1.17 through 1.33, you will combine two presentations that the marketing team at Kodiak West Travel developed describing itinerary ideas when visiting Seattle before or after a cruise. You will insert slides from one presentation into another, and then you will rearrange and delete slides. You will also apply font formatting and slide transitions to the presentation. Your completed presentation will look similar to Figure 1.34.

Project Files for MyLab IT Grader

1. In your **MyLab IT** course, locate and click **PowerPoint 1B Seattle**, Download Materials, and then Download All Files.
2. Extract the zipped folder to your PowerPoint Chapter 1 folder. Close the Grader download screens.
3. Take a moment to open the downloaded **PowerPoint_1B_Seattle_Instructions**; note any recent updates to the book.

Project Results

GO! Project 1B
Where We're Going

Figure 1.34 Project 1B Seattle

For Non-MyLab Submissions

For Project 1B, you will need:
p01B_Seattle
p01B_Slides

In your PowerPoint Chapter 1 folder, save your presentation as:
Lastname_Firstname_1B_Seattle

After you have named and saved your presentation, on the next page, begin with Step 2.

Objective 5   Edit an Existing Presentation

ALERT   Because Office 365 is a cloud-based subscription service that receives continuous updates, you may encounter some variations in what appears on your screen and what is shown in this instruction. Microsoft Office 365 is fully installed on your PC or Mac; no internet access is necessary to create or edit documents. When you *are* connected to the internet, you will receive monthly upgrades and new features, so you always have the latest versions of Office apps as soon as they are available. Your subscription gives you continuous free access to the latest innovations and refinements.

GO! Learn How
Video P1-5

Recall that editing refers to the process of adding, deleting, and modifying presentation content. You can edit presentation content in either the Slide pane or in the presentation outline.

Activity 1.17 │ Changing Slide Size

1.2.1

Presentations created with one of the new themes in PowerPoint default to a widescreen format using a 16:9 *aspect ratio*—the ratio of the width of a display to the height of the display. This slide size is similar to most television and computer monitor screens. Previous versions of PowerPoint used a squarer format with a 4:3 aspect ratio.

1 ▶ Navigate to your **PowerPoint Chapter 1 folder**, and then double-click the downloaded PowerPoint file that displays your name—**Student_PowerPoint_1B_Seattle**. In your presentation, if necessary, at the top click **Enable Editing**.

2 ▶ Notice that **Slide 1** displays in a squarish format.

3 ▶ On the **Design tab**, in the **Customize group**, click **Slide Size**, and then click **Widescreen (16:9)**. Compare your screen with Figure 1.35 and notice that the slide fills the slide pane. **Save** 🔲 the presentation.

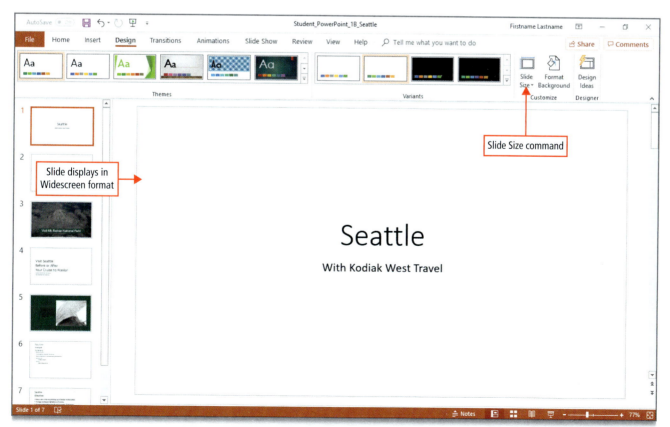

Figure 1.35

Activity 1.18 | Inserting Slides from an Existing Presentation

2.1.2

Presentation content is commonly shared among group members in an organization. Rather than re-creating slides, you can insert slides from an existing presentation into the current presentation. In this Activity, you will insert slides from an existing presentation into your 1B_Seattle presentation.

1 ▶ With **Slide 1** displayed, on the **Home tab**, in the **Slides group**, click the **New Slide arrow** to display the **Slide Layout** gallery and additional commands for inserting slides. Compare your screen with Figure 1.36.

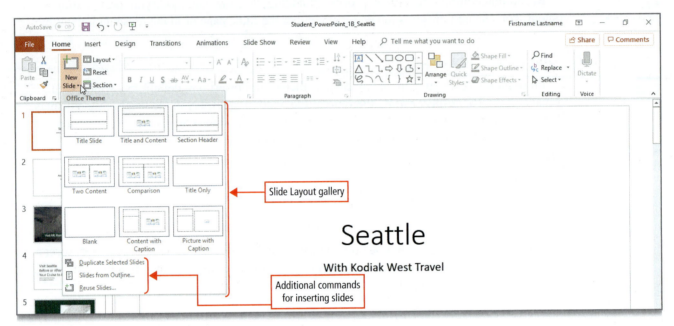

Figure 1.36

2 ▶ Below the gallery, click **Reuse Slides** to open the Reuse Slides pane on the right side of the PowerPoint window.

3 ▶ In the **Reuse Slides** pane, click **Browse**. In the **Browse** dialog box, navigate to the data files downloaded with this project, and then double-click **p01B_Slides** to display the slides from this presentation in the Reuse Slides pane.

4 ▶ At the bottom of the **Reuse Slides** pane, be sure that the **Keep source formatting** check box is *cleared*, and then compare your screen with Figure 1.37.

When the *Keep source formatting* check box is cleared, the theme formatting of the presentation into which the slides are inserted is applied. When the *Keep source formatting* check box is selected, you retain the formatting of the slides when inserted into the presentation.

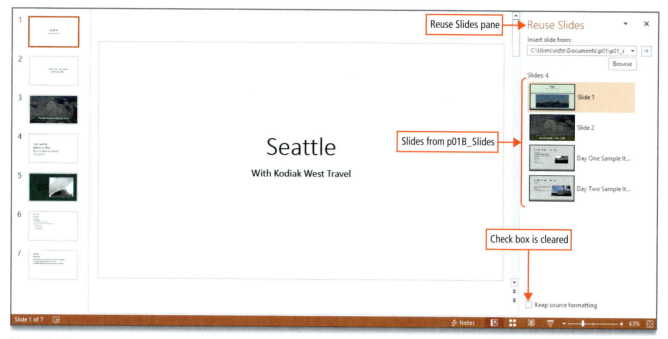

Figure 1.37

5 In the **Reuse Slides** pane, point to each slide to view a ScreenTip displaying the file name and the slide title.

6 In the **Reuse Slides** pane, click the first slide to insert the slide after **Slide 1** in your Seattle presentation. Notice that the inserted slide adopts the color of your Seattle presentation theme.

NOTE   **Inserting Slides**

You can insert slides into your presentation in any order; remember to display the slide that will come before the slide that you want to insert.

MAC TIP   Mac users can only insert all slides from an existing presentation. With Slide 1 selected, on the Home tab, click the New Slide arrow, click Reuse Slides, and navigate to the data files for this project. Double-click p01B_Slides to insert all four slides into your presentation after Slide 1. Select and press delete to delete Slide 3—*Visit Mt. Rainier National Park!* and Slide 4—*Day One Sample Itinerary*. Drag the new Slide 3—*Day Two Sample Itinerary* after the existing Slide 7. Skip to Step 9.

---

7 In your **1B_Seattle** presentation, in the slide thumbnails, click **Slide 7** to display it in the **Slide pane**.

8 In the **Reuse Slides** pane, click the fourth slide, *Day Two Sample Itinerary*, to insert it after **Slide 7**.

Your presentation contains nine slides. When a presentation contains a large number of slides, a scroll box displays to the right of the slide thumbnails so that you can scroll and then select the thumbnails.

9 Close ☒ the **Reuse Slides** pane, and then Save 🖫 the presentation.

MORE KNOWLEDGE   **Inserting All Slides**

You can insert all of the slides from an existing presentation into the current presentation at one time. In the Reuse Slides pane, right-click one of the slides that you want to insert, and then click Insert All Slides.

Activity 1.19 | Displaying and Editing the Presentation Outline

MOS
1.2.2

Outline View displays the presentation outline to the left of the Slide pane. You can use the outline to edit the presentation text. Changes that you make in the outline are immediately displayed in the Slide pane.

1 To the right of the slide thumbnails, if necessary, drag the scroll box up, and then click **Slide 1** to display it in the Slide pane. On the **View tab**, in the **Presentation Views group**, click **Outline View**. Compare your screen with Figure 1.38.

The outline displays at the left of the PowerPoint window in place of the slide thumbnails. Each slide in the outline displays the slide number, slide icon, and the slide title in bold. Slides that do not display a slide title in the outline use a slide layout that does not include a title, for example, the Blank layout.

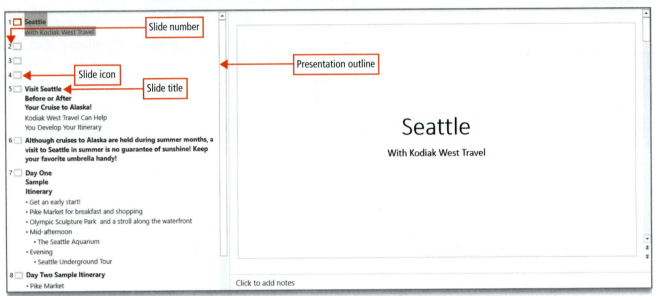

Figure 1.38

2 In the **Outline**, in **Slide 7**, drag to select the text of the second and third bullet points—*Pike Market for breakfast and shopping*, and *Olympic Sculpture Park and a stroll along the waterfront*. Compare your screen with Figure 1.39.

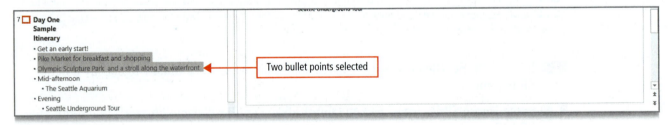

Figure 1.39

3 On the **Home tab**, in the **Paragraph group**, click **Increase List Level** one time to increase the list level of the selected bullet points.

When you type in the outline or change the list level, the changes also display in the Slide pane.

4 In the **Outline**, in **Slide 7**, click at the end of the last bullet point after the word *Tour*. Press Enter to create a new bullet point at the same list level as the previous bullet point. Type **Pike Place Market for dinner** and then compare your screen with Figure 1.40.

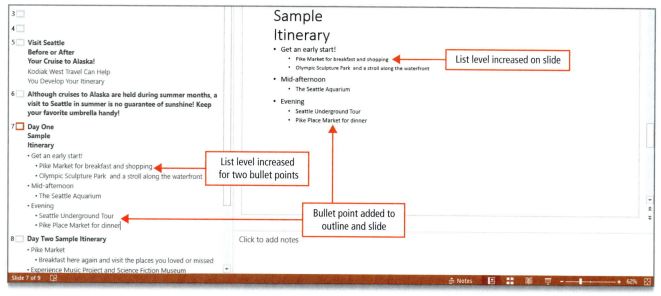

Figure 1.40

5 In the **Status bar**, click **Normal** to close Outline View and redisplay the slide thumbnails. **Save** the presentation.

You can type text in the Slide pane or in the Outline. Displaying the Outline enables you to view the entire flow of the presentation text.

Activity 1.20 | Deleting and Moving a Slide

MOS
2.3.2

1 To the right of the slide thumbnails, locate the vertical scroll bar and scroll box. If necessary, drag the scroll box down so that **Slide 9** displays in the slide thumbnails. Click **Slide 9** to display it in the Slide pane. Press Delete to delete the slide from the presentation.

Your presentation contains eight slides.

2 If necessary, scroll the slide thumbnails so that **Slide 4** displays. Point to **Slide 4**, hold down the left mouse button, and then drag down to position the **Slide 4** thumbnail below the **Slide 8** thumbnail. Release the mouse button, and then compare your screen with Figure 1.41. **Save** the presentation.

You can easily rearrange your slides by dragging a slide thumbnail to a new location in the presentation.

BY TOUCH Use your finger to drag the slide you want to move to a new location in the presentation.

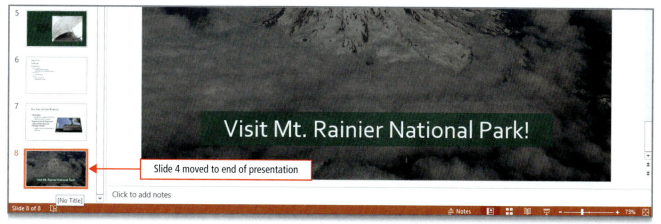

Figure 1.41

Activity 1.21 | Finding and Replacing Text

The Replace command enables you to locate all occurrences of specified text and replace it with alternative text.

1 ▶ Display **Slide 1**. On the **Home tab**, in the **Editing group**, click **Replace**. In the **Replace** dialog box, in the **Find what** box, type **Pike Market** and then in the **Replace with** box, type **Pike Place Market** Compare your screen with Figure 1.42.

 MAC TIP Find and Replace are in the Edit menu.

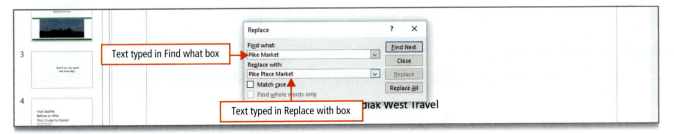

Figure 1.42

2 ▶ In the **Replace** dialog box, click **Replace All** to display a message box indicating that two replacements were made.

3 ▶ In the message box, click **OK**. **Close** ⊠ the **Replace** dialog box, and then click **Save** 🖫.

Objective 6 | Format a Presentation

GO! Learn How

Video P1-6

Formatting refers to changing the appearance of the text, layout, and design of a slide. Recall that a theme is a set of unified design elements that provides a look for your presentation by applying colors, fonts, and effects.

Activity 1.22 | Applying a Theme Variant

Each PowerPoint theme includes several *variants*—variations on the theme style and color. The themes and variants that are available on your system may vary.

1 ▶ On the **Design tab**, in the **Variants group**, notice that four variants of the current theme display and the second variant is applied.

2 ▶ Point to each of the variants to view the change to **Slide 1**.

If you do not see the same variants, refer to the figures for this activity.

3 ▶ With **Slide 1** displayed, in the **Variants group**, point to the **third variant**, and then right-click. Compare your screen with Figure 1.43.

The shortcut menu displays options for applying the variant.

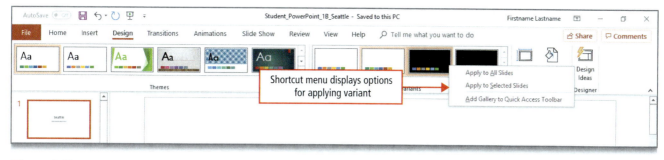

Figure 1.43

4 ▶ Click **Apply to Selected Slides** to apply the variant to **Slide 1** only. Compare your screen with Figure 1.44.

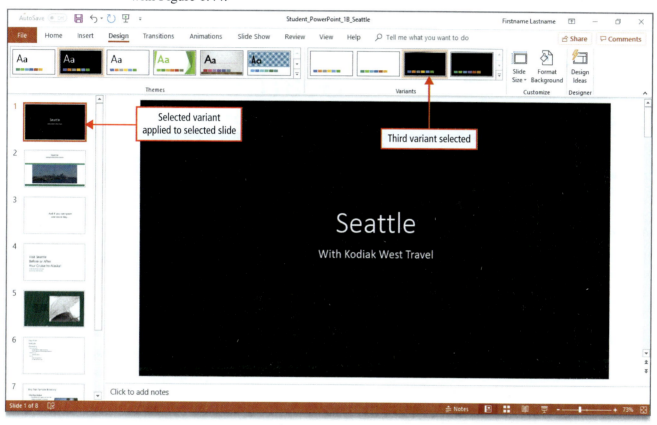

Figure 1.44

5 ▶ In the **Variants group**, right-click the **second variant**. On the shortcut menu, click **Apply to All Slides** so that the original variant color is applied to all of the slides in the presentation. **Save** 🖫 your presentation.

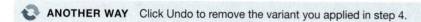
ANOTHER WAY Click Undo to remove the variant you applied in step 4.

Activity 1.23 │ Changing Fonts and Font Sizes

A font is a set of characters with the same design and shape and fonts are measured in points. Font styles include bold, italic, and underline, and you can apply any combination of these styles to presentation text. Font styles and font color are useful to provide emphasis and are a visual cue to draw the reader's eye to important text.

1 ▶ Display **Slide 2**. Select all of the text in the title placeholder, point to the mini toolbar, and then click the **Font arrow** to display the available fonts. Scroll the font list, and then click **Georgia**.

🔲 **MAC TIP** Use the formatting options on the Home tab.

2 Select the first line of the title—*Seattle*. On the mini toolbar, click the **Font Size arrow** and then click **80**.

3 Select the second line of the title—*Making the Most of Your First Port*. On the **Home tab**, in the **Font group**, click the **Font Size arrow**, and then click **36**. Click in a blank area of the slide to cancel your selection, and then compare your screen with Figure 1.45. **Save** 🖫 your presentation.

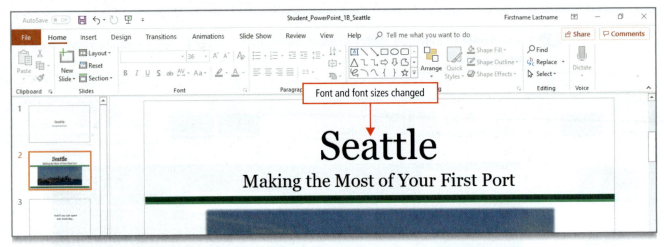

Figure 1.45

Activity 1.24 | Changing Font Styles and Font Colors

Font styles include bold, italic, and underline, and you can apply any combination of these styles to presentation text. Font styles and font color are useful to provide emphasis and are a visual cue to draw the reader's eye to important text.

1 Display **Slide 3**, and then select both lines of text. On the **Home tab**, in the **Font group**, click the **Font Color arrow** 🅰▾ and then compare your screen with Figure 1.46.

The colors in the top row of the color gallery are the colors associated with the presentation theme—*Frame*. The colors in the rows below the first row are light and dark variations of the theme colors.

Figure 1.46

2 ▶ Point to several of the colors and notice that a ScreenTip displays the color name and Live Preview displays the selected text in the color to which you are pointing.

3 ▶ Under Theme Colors, in the fifth column of colors, click the last color to change the font color. Notice that on the **Home tab**, the lower part of the **Font Color** button displays the most recently applied font color.

> When you click the Font Color button instead of the Font Color button arrow, the color displayed in the lower part of the Font Color button is applied to selected text without displaying the color gallery.

4 ▶ With the two lines of text still selected, right-click within the selected text to redisplay the mini toolbar, and then from the mini toolbar, apply **Bold** and **Italic**.

5 ▶ Display **Slide 4**, and then select the title—*Visit Seattle Before or After Your Cruise to Alaska!* On the mini toolbar, click **Font Color** [A] to apply the most recently applied font color to the selection. Select the subtitle—*Kodiak West Travel Can Help You Develop Your Itinerary*—and then change the **Font Color** to most recently applied color. Compare your screen with Figure 1.47. **Save** [💾] your presentation.

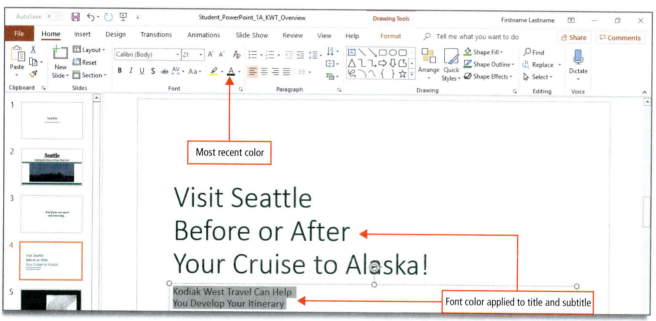

Figure 1.47

Activity 1.25 | Aligning Text

In PowerPoint, ***text alignment*** refers to the horizontal placement of text within a placeholder. You can align text left, centered, right, or justified.

1 ▶ Display **Slide 5**, and then select all of the text in the paragraph. Click the **Font Color arrow** [A] and change the font color to the first color in the first column.

2 ▶ On the **Home tab**, in the **Paragraph group**, click **Center** [≡] to center the text within the placeholder.

3 ▶ Display **Slide 4**, and then click anywhere in the slide title. Press Ctrl + E to use the keyboard shortcut to center the text.

4 On **Slide 4**, using one of the methods that you practiced, **Center** the subtitle. Click in a blank area of the slide. Compare your screen with Figure 1.48 and then **Save** 🔲 the presentation.

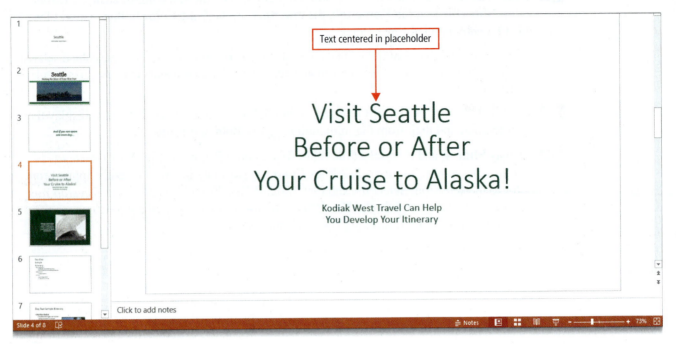

Figure 1.48

Activity 1.26 | Changing Line Spacing

1 Display **Slide 5**, and then click anywhere in the paragraph. On the **Home tab**, in the **Paragraph group**, click **Line Spacing** 📏. In the list, click **2.0** to change from single spacing to double spacing between lines of text. Compare your screen with Figure 1.49.

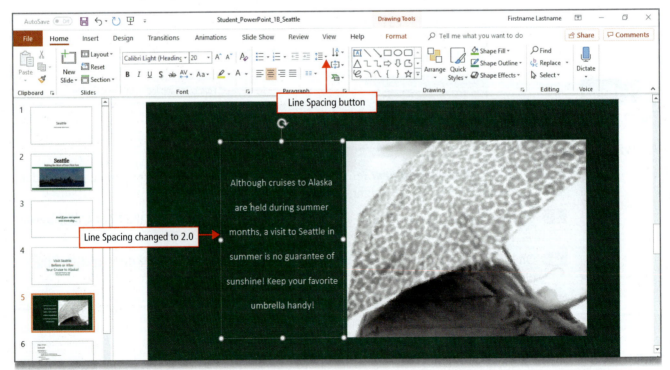

Figure 1.49

2 Save 🔲 your presentation.

Activity 1.27 | Changing the Slide Layout

The slide layout defines the placement of the content placeholders on a slide. PowerPoint includes predefined layouts that you can apply to your slide for arranging slide elements. For example, a Title Slide contains two placeholder elements—the title and the subtitle. When you design your slides, consider the content that you want to include, and then choose a layout with the elements that will display the message you want to convey in the best way.

1 Display **Slide 1**. On the **Home tab**, in the **Slides group**, click **Layout** to display the **Slide Layout** gallery. Notice that *Title Slide* is selected, indicating the layout of the current slide.

2 Click **Section Header** to change the slide layout. Compare your screen with Figure 1.50, and then **Save** 🖫 your presentation.

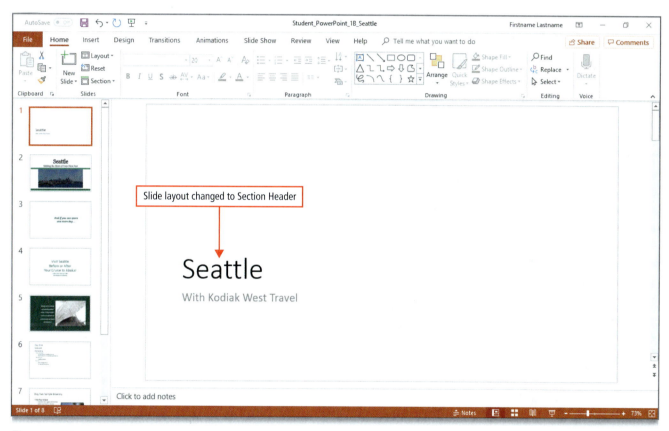

Figure 1.50

Objective 7 | Use Slide Sorter View

GO! Learn How

Video P1-7

Slide Sorter view displays thumbnails of all of the slides in a presentation. Use Slide Sorter view to rearrange and delete slides and to apply formatting to multiple slides.

Activity 1.28 | Deleting Slides in Slide Sorter View

1 In the lower right corner of the PowerPoint window, click **Slide Sorter** to display all of the slide thumbnails. Compare your screen with Figure 1.51.

Your slides may display larger or smaller than those shown in Figure 1.51.

ANOTHER WAY On the View tab, in the Presentation Views group, click Slide Sorter.

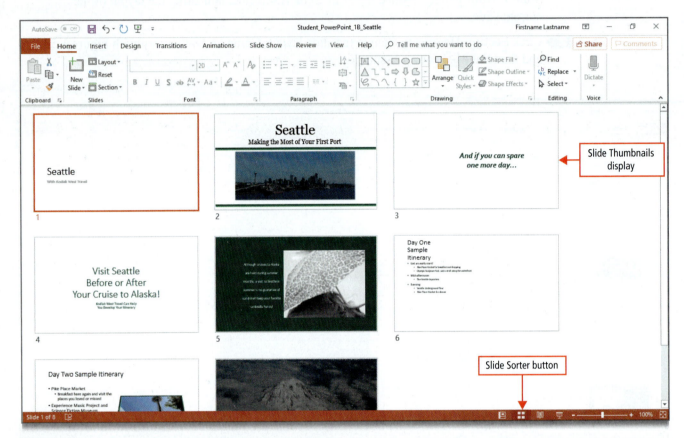

Figure 1.51

2 If necessary, click Slide 1, and notice that a thick outline surrounds the slide, indicating that it is selected. On your keyboard, press Delete to delete the slide. Click **Save**.

Activity 1.29 | Moving a Single Slide in Slide Sorter View

1 With the presentation displayed in Slide Sorter view, point to **Slide 2**. Hold down the left mouse button, and then drag to position the slide to the right of **Slide 6**, as shown in Figure 1.52.

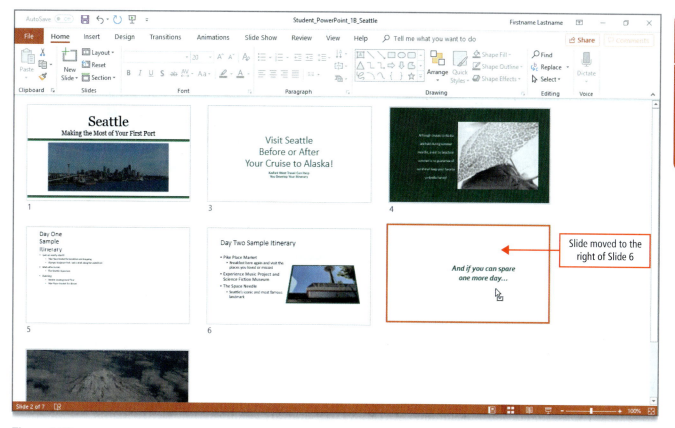

Figure 1.52

2 Release the mouse button to move the slide to the **Slide 6** position in the presentation. **Save**  your presentation.

Activity 1.30 | Selecting Contiguous and Noncontiguous Slides and Moving Multiple Slides

MOS
2.3.2

Contiguous slides are slides that are adjacent to each other in a presentation. *Noncontiguous slides* are slides that are not adjacent to each other in a presentation.

1 Click **Slide 2**, hold down Ctrl, click **Slide 4**, release Ctrl. Notice that both slides are selected.

The noncontiguous slides—Slides 2 and 4—are outlined, indicating that both are selected. By holding down Ctrl, you can select noncontiguous slides.

💻 **MAC TIP** Hold down command ⌘ + click.

2 Click **Slide 3**, so that only Slide 3 is selected. Hold down Shift, click **Slide 5**, and then release Shift. Compare your screen with Figure 1.53.

The contiguous slides—Slides 3, 4, and 5—are outlined, indicating that all three slides are selected. By holding down Shift, you can create a group of contiguous selected slides.

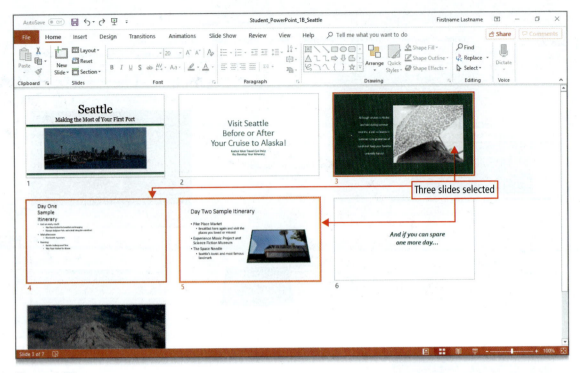

Figure 1.53

3 With **Slides 3, 4,** and **5** selected, hold down Ctrl, and then click **Slide 3**. Notice that only **Slides 4** and **5** are selected.

> With a group of selected slides, you can press Ctrl and then click a selected slide to *deselect* it.

4 Point to either of the selected slides, hold down the left mouse button, and then drag to position the two slides to the right of **Slide 2**. Compare your screen with Figure 1.54.

> The selected slides are dragged as a group, and the number 2 in the upper left area of the selected slides indicates the number of slides that you are moving.

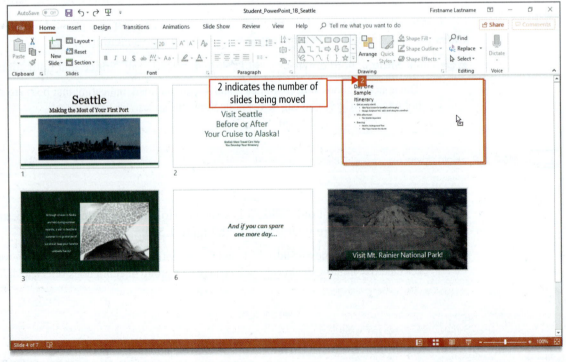

Figure 1.54

5 ▸ Release the mouse button to reposition the slides. On the View tab, click **Normal** to return to Normal view. **Save** 🖫 your presentation.

Objective 8 | Apply Slide Transitions

GO! Learn How
Video P1-8

Slide transitions are the motion effects that occur in Slide Show view when you move from one slide to the next during a presentation. You can choose from a variety of transitions, and you can control the speed and method with which the slides advance.

Activity 1.31 | Applying Slide Transitions to a Presentation

MOS
5.1.1, 5.1.2

In this Activity, you will apply a slide transition to all the slides in the presentation.

1 ▸ Display **Slide 1**. On the **Transitions tab**, in the **Transition to This Slide group**, click **More** ⯆ to display the **Transitions** gallery. Compare your screen with Figure 1.55.

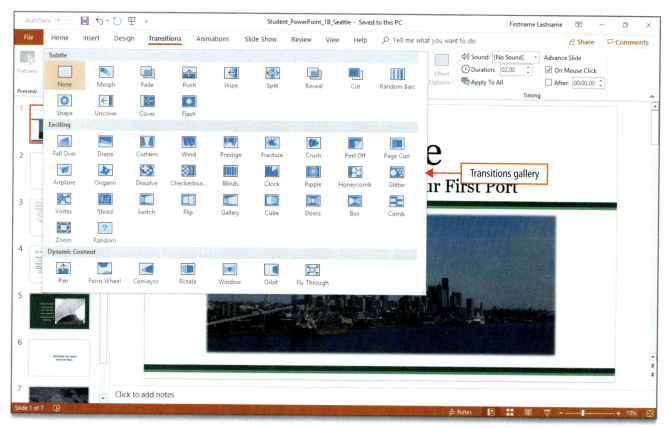

Figure 1.55

2 ▸ Under **Subtle**, click **Fade** to apply and view the transition. In the **Transition to This Slide group**, click **Effect Options** to display the way the slide enters the screen. Click **Smoothly**. In the **Timing group**, click **Apply To All** to apply the *Fade, Smoothly* transition to all of the slides in the presentation. **Save** 🖫 your presentation.

> The Effect Options vary depending on the selected transition. In the slide thumbnails, a star displays below the slide number providing a visual cue that a transition has been applied to the slide.

Activity 1.32 | Setting Slide Transition Timing Options

MOS
5.3.2

In this Activity, you will modify the duration of the transition—the amount of time it takes for the transition to complete.

1 In the **Timing group**, notice that the **Duration** box displays *00.70*, indicating that the transition lasts 0.70 seconds. Click the **Duration up spin arrow** several times until *01.75* displays. Under **Advance Slide**, verify that the **On Mouse Click** check box is selected. Compare your screen with Figure 1.56.

With On Mouse Click selected, the presenter controls when the current slide advances to the next slide by clicking the mouse button or by pressing Spacebar.

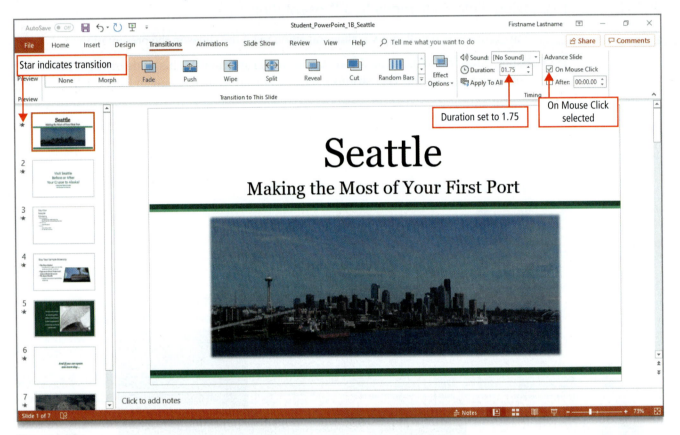

Figure 1.56

2 In the **Timing group**, click **Apply To All** so that the Duration of *1.75* seconds transition is applied to all of the slides in the presentation.

3 Click the **Slide Show tab**. In the **Start Slide Show group**, click **From Beginning**, and then view your presentation, clicking the mouse button to advance through the slides. When the black slide displays, click the mouse button one more time to display the presentation in Normal view. **Save** 🖫 your presentation.

MORE KNOWLEDGE **Applying Multiple Slide Transitions**

You can apply more than one type of transition in your presentation by displaying the slides one at a time, and then clicking the transition that you want to apply instead of clicking Apply To All.

Activity 1.33 | Displaying a Presentation in Reading View

1.2.2, 1.2.3

Organizations frequently conduct online meetings when participants are unable to meet in one location. The **_Reading view_** in PowerPoint displays a presentation in a manner similar to a slide show but the taskbar, title bar, and status bar remain available in the presentation window. Thus, a presenter can easily facilitate an online conference by switching to another window without closing the slide show. This is useful for Kodiak West Travel because employees are frequently on the road and attend online meetings.

1 In the lower right corner of the PowerPoint window, click **Reading View** 📖. Compare your screen with Figure 1.57.

> In Reading view, the status bar contains the Next and Previous buttons, which are used to navigate in the presentation, and the Menu button which is used to print, copy, and edit slides.

ANOTHER WAY On the View tab, in the Presentation Views group, click Reading View.

MAC TIP Reading view is not available in the Mac version of PowerPoint. Skip to Step 4.

Figure 1.57

2 Press Spacebar to display **Slide 2**. Click the left mouse button to display **Slide 3**. In the status bar, click **Previous** ◄ to display **Slide 2**.

3 In the status bar, click **Menu** 🗐 to display the Reading view menu, and then click **End Show** to return to Normal view.

4 On the **Insert tab**, in the **Text group**, click **Header & Footer**, and then click the **Notes and Handouts tab**. Under **Include on page**, select the **Date and time** check box, and if necessary, select Update automatically. If necessary, select the **Page number** check box and clear the **Header** check box. Select the **Footer** check box, in the **Footer** box, type **1B_Seattle** and then click **Apply to All**.

5 Display **Backstage** view. On the Info tab, on the right, at the bottom of the **Properties** list, click **Show All Properties**. On the list of properties, click to the right of **Tags**, and then type **Seattle** To the right of **Subject**, type your course name and section number. Under **Related People**, be sure that your name displays as the author; edit if necessary.

6 On the left, scroll up as necessary, and then click **Save** [save icon].

 For Non-MyLab Submissions Determine What Your Instructor Requires
As directed by your instructor, submit your completed PowerPoint presentation.

---

7 Close ⊠ PowerPoint.

8 In **MyLab IT**, in your **Course Materials**, locate and click the Grader Project **PowerPoint 1B Seattle**. In **step 3**, under **Upload Completed Assignment**, click **Choose File**. In the **Open** dialog box, navigate to your **PowerPoint Chapter 1 folder**, and then click your **Student_PowerPoint_1B_Seattle** file one time to select it. In the lower right corner of the **Open** dialog box, click **Open**.

The name of your selected file displays above the Upload button.

9 To submit your file to **MyLab IT** for grading, click **Upload**, wait a moment for a green **Success!** message, and then in **step 4**, click the blue **Submit for Grading** button. Click **Close Assignment** to return to your list of **Course Materials**.

You have completed Project 1B | **END**

ALERT   **Working with Web-Based Applications and Services**

Computer programs and services on the web receive continuous updates and improvements, so the steps to complete this web-based activity may differ from the ones shown. You can often look at the screens and the information presented to determine how to complete the activity.

If you do not already have a Google account, you will need to create one before you begin this activity.

Activity | Creating an Itinerary Presentation in Google Slides

In this Activity, you will use Google Slides to create a presentation similar to the one you created in Project 1B.

1 From the desktop, open your browser, navigate to **http://google.com**, and then sign in to your Google account. Click the **Google apps** icon ⊞ and then click **Drive** △.

Open your **GO! Web Projects** folder—or create and then open this folder, if necessary.

2 In the left pane, click **New**, and then click **File upload** 🖪. Navigate to your student data files, click **p01_1B_Web**, and then click **Open**.

3 Wait a moment for the upload to complete, point to the uploaded file **p01_1B_Google_Slides.pptx**, and then right-click. On the shortcut menu, click **Rename**. Delete the existing text, and then using your own last name and first name, type **Lastname_Firstname_1B_Google_Slides** Click **OK** to rename the file.

4 Right-click the file that you just renamed, point to **Open with**, and then click **Google Slides**.

5 On **Slide 1**, in the Title placeholder, drag to select the two lines of text. On the **toolbar**, click the **Font arrow** ▾, and then click **Georgia**.

6 Select the text *Making the Most of Your First Port*. On the **toolbar**, click the **Font Size arrow** 10, and then click **24**.

7 Click **Slide 2**. Click the **Edit menu**, and then click **Delete** to remove the slide from the presentation.

8 With **Slide 2**—*Seattle Weather*—displayed, press Delete to remove the slide from your presentation. Notice that the presentation contains seven slides.

9 Display **Slide 3**, and then click in the paragraph on the left side of the slide. Drag to select the text, and then on the **toolbar**, click **Text color** 🅰. Under **Theme**,

click the second color—**Theme Color white**. With the paragraph still selected, on the toolbar, click **Bold** 𝐁 and **Italic** 𝐼. Click **Align** ≡ ▾ and click **Center** ≡. Click anywhere in a blank area of the slide to cancel the selection and view your changes.

10 In the slide thumbnails, point to **Slide 4**, hold down the left mouse button, and then drag up slightly. Notice that a black bar displays above **Slide 4**. Continue to drag up until the black bar displays above **Slide 3**. Release the mouse button to move the slide.

11 Using the technique that you just practiced, move **Slide 5** to position it above **Slide 4**.

12 Display **Slide 6**. Select all three lines of text. Click **Align** ≡ ▾, and then click **Center** ≡. Click anywhere on the slide to cancel the selection. Click **Slide 1** and compare your screen with Figure A.

13 Display **Slide 1**. At the right end of the toolbar, click **Transition** to open the **Animations** pane. On the right, in the Animations pane, click **No transition button**, click **Slide from right**, and then click **Apply to all slides**.

14 To the right of the **menu bar**, click the **Present button arrow**, and then click **Present from beginning**. If necessary, click Allow. Click the left mouse button to progress through the presentation. When the last slide displays, press Esc or in the lower left corner, click **Exit**.

15 Your presentation will be saved automatically. Download as Microsoft PowerPoint, PDF Document, or another format, and submit as directed by your instructor. Sign out of your Google account and close your browser.

»» **GO!** With Google Slides continues on next page

»» GO! With Google Slides

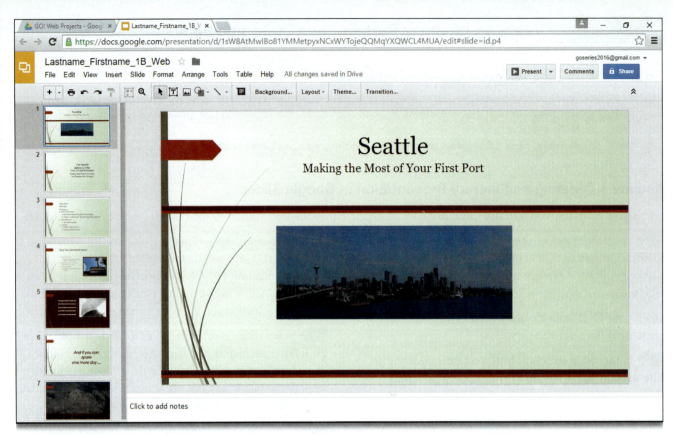

Figure A

wavebreakmedia/Shutterstock, Monkey Business Images/Fotolia, Ivanko80/Shutterstock, Monkey Business Images/Shutterstock

Microsoft Office Specialist (MOS) Skills in This Chapter	
Project 1A	**Project 1B**
1.2.2 Display presentations in different views	**1.2.1** Change slide size
1.2.3 Set basic file properties	**1.2.2** Display presentations in different views
1.3.2 Print notes pages	**1.2.3** Set basic file properties
1.3.3 Print handouts	**2.1.2** Insert slides from another presentation
1.4.5 Present slide shows by using Presenter View	**2.3.2** Modify slide order
2.1.3 Insert slides and select slide layouts	**5.1.1** Apply basic and 3D slide transitions
2.2.3 Insert slide headers, footers, and page numbers	**5.1.2** Configure transition effects
3.1.3 Create bulleted and numbered lists	**5.3.2** Configure transition start and finish options
3.3.2 Apply built-in styles and effects to images	

Build Your E-Portfolio

An E-Portfolio is a collection of evidence, stored electronically, that showcases what you have accomplished while completing your education. Collecting and then sharing your work products with potential employers reflects your academic and career goals. Your completed documents from the following projects are good examples to show what you have learned: 1G, 1K, and 1L.

 ## GO! for Job Success

Video: Personal Branding

Your instructor may assign this video to your class, and then ask you to think about, or discuss with your classmates, these questions:

g-stockstudio/Shutterstock

How do you suggest job seekers communicate their unique value—their personal brand—to potential employers online?

What are the best ways to network online and offline?

What are some of the biggest pitfalls in using social media to communicate a personal brand?

End of Chapter

Summary

In this chapter, you started a new presentation in PowerPoint. You inserted slides with various layouts, and you entered, edited, and formatted text. You also inserted text from another PowerPoint file.

Use a presentation theme to establish a unified presentation design. You can change the color of the presentation theme by applying one of the predefined variants that are supplied with each theme.

Presentations are often organized in a manner similar to outlines. List levels represent outline levels and are identified by the bullet style, indentation, and text size.

Slide layout defines the placement of content placeholders on a slide. Each presentation theme includes predefined layouts that you can apply to slides for the purpose of arranging slide elements.

GO! Learn It Online

Review the concepts, key terms, and MOS skills in this chapter by completing these online challenges, which you can find at **MyLab IT**.

Chapter Quiz: Answer matching and multiple choice questions to test what you learned in this chapter.

Lessons on the GO!: Learn how to use all the new apps and features as they are introduced by Microsoft.

MOS Prep Quiz: Answer questions to review the MOS skills that you practiced in this chapter.

GO! Collaborative Team Project (Available in Instructor Resource Center)

If your instructor assigns this project to your class, you can expect to work with one or more of your classmates—either in person or by using internet tools—to create work products similar to those that you created in this chapter. A team is a group of workers who work together to solve a problem, make a decision, or create a work product. Collaboration is when you work together with others as a team in an intellectual endeavor to complete a shared task or achieve a shared goal.

Monkey Business Images/Fotolia

Project Guide for PowerPoint Chapter 1

Your instructor will assign Projects from this list to ensure your learning and assess your knowledge.

Project	Apply Skills from These Chapter Objectives	Project Type		Project Location
1A **MyLab IT**	Objectives 1–4 from Project 1A	**1A Instructional Project (Grader Project)** Guided instruction to learn the skills in Project A.	**Instruction**	In **MyLab IT** and in text
1B **MyLab IT**	Objectives 5–8 from Project 1B	**1B Instructional Project (Grader Project)** Guided instruction to learn the skills in Project B.	**Instruction**	In **MyLab IT** and in text
1C	Objectives 1–4 from Project 1A	**1C Skills Review (Scorecard Grading)** A guided review of the skills from Project 1A.	**Review**	In text
1D	Objectives 5–8 from Project 1B	**1D Skills Review (Scorecard Grading)** A guided review of the skills from Project 1B.	**Review**	In text
1E **MyLab IT**	Objectives 1–4 from Project 1A	**1E Mastery (Grader Project)** A demonstration of your mastery of the skills in Project 1A with extensive decision making.	**Mastery and Transfer of Learning**	In **MyLab IT** and in text
1F **MyLab IT**	Objectives 5–8 from Project 1B	**1F Mastery (Grader Project)** A demonstration of your mastery of the skills in Project 1B with extensive decision making.	**Mastery and Transfer of Learning**	In **MyLab IT** and in text
1G **MyLab IT**	Objectives 1–8 from Projects 1A and 1B	**1G Mastery (Grader Project)** A demonstration of your mastery of the skills in Projects 1A and 1B with extensive decision making.	**Mastery and Transfer of Learning**	In **MyLab IT** and in text
1H	Combination of Objectives from Projects 1A and 1B	**1H GO! Fix It (Scorecard Grading)** A demonstration of your mastery of the skills in Projects 1A and 1B by creating a correct result from a document that contains errors you must find.	**Critical Thinking**	IRC
1I	Combination of Objectives from Projects 1A and 1B	**1I GO! Make It (Scorecard Grading)** A demonstration of your mastery of the skills in Projects 1A and 1B by creating a result from a supplied picture.	**Critical Thinking**	IRC
1J	Combination of Objectives from Projects 1A and 1B	**1J GO! Solve It (Rubric Grading)** A demonstration of your mastery of the skills in Projects 1A and 1B, your decision-making skills, and your critical thinking skills. A task-specific rubric helps you self-assess your result.	**Critical Thinking**	IRC
1K	Combination of Objectives from Projects 1A and 1B	**1K GO! Solve It (Rubric Grading)** A demonstration of your mastery of the skills in Projects 1A and 1B, your decision-making skills, and your critical thinking skills. A task-specific rubric helps you self-assess your result.	**Critical Thinking**	In text
1L	Combination of Objectives from Projects 1A and 1B	**1L GO! Think (Rubric Grading)** A demonstration of your understanding of the chapter concepts applied in a manner that you would outside of college. An analytic rubric helps you and your instructor grade the quality of your work by comparing it to the work an expert in the discipline would create.	**Critical Thinking**	In text
1M	Combination of Objectives from Projects 1A and 1B	**1M GO! Think (Rubric Grading)** A demonstration of your understanding of the chapter concepts applied in a manner that you would outside of college. An analytic rubric helps you and your instructor grade the quality of your work by comparing it to the work an expert in the discipline would create.	**Critical Thinking**	IRC
1N	Combination of Objectives from Projects 1A and 1B	**1N You and GO! (Rubric Grading)** A demonstration of your understanding of the chapter concepts applied in a manner that you would in a personal situation. An analytic rubric helps you and your instructor grade the quality of your work.	**Critical Thinking**	IRC
1O	Combination of Objectives from Projects 1A and 1B	**1O Collaborative Team Project for PowerPoint Chapter 1** A demonstration of your understanding of concepts and your ability to work collaboratively in a group role-playing assessment, requiring both collaboration and self-management.	**Critical Thinking**	IRC

Glossary

Glossary of Chapter Key Terms

Artistic effects Formats applied to images that make pictures resemble sketches or paintings.

Aspect ratio The ratio of the width of a display to the height of the display.

Black slide A slide that displays after the last slide in a presentation indicating that the presentation is over.

Contiguous slides Slides that are adjacent to each other in a presentation.

Editing The process of modifying a presentation by adding and deleting slides or by changing the contents of individual slides.

Footer Text that displays at the bottom of every slide or that prints at the bottom of a sheet of slide handouts or notes pages.

Formatting The process of changing the appearance of the text, layout, and design of a slide.

Header Text that prints at the top of each sheet of slide handouts or notes pages.

Layout The arrangement of elements, such as title and subtitle text, lists, pictures, tables, charts, shapes, and movies, on a slide.

List level An outline level in a presentation represented by a bullet symbol and identified in a slide by the indentation and the size of the text.

Noncontiguous slides Slides that are not adjacent to each other in a presentation.

Normal view The primary editing view in PowerPoint where you write and design your presentations.

Notes page A printout that contains the slide image on the top half of the page and notes that you have created on the Notes pane in the lower half of the page.

Notes pane An area of the Normal view window that displays below the Slide pane with space to type notes regarding the active slide.

Outline view A PowerPoint view that displays the presentation outline to the left of the Slide pane.

Placeholder A box on a slide with dotted or dashed borders that holds title and body text or other content such as charts, tables, and pictures.

Presenter view A view that shows the full-screen slide show on one monitor or projection screen while enabling the presenter to view a preview of the next slide, notes, and a timer on another monitor.

Reading view A view in PowerPoint that displays a presentation in a manner similar to a slide show but in which the taskbar, title bar, and status bar remain available in the presentation window.

Rotation handle A circular arrow that provides a way to rotate a selected image.

Section header A type of slide layout that changes the look and flow of a presentation by providing text placeholders that do not contain bullet points.

Sizing handles Small circles surrounding a picture that indicate that the picture is selected.

Slide A presentation page that can contain text, pictures, tables, charts, and other multimedia or graphic objects.

Slide handout Printed images of slides on a sheet of paper.

Slide pane A PowerPoint screen element that displays a large image of the active slide.

Slide Sorter view A presentation view that displays thumbnails of all of the slides in a presentation.

Slide transitions Motion effects that occur in Slide Show view when you move from one slide to the next during a presentation.

Split button A type of button in which clicking the main part of the button performs a command and clicking the arrow opens a menu, list, or gallery.

Style A collection of formatting options that you can apply to a picture, text, or an object.

Text alignment The horizontal placement of text within a placeholder.

Theme A set of unified design elements that provides a look for your presentation by applying colors, fonts, and effects.

Thumbnails Miniature images of presentation slides.

Title slide A slide layout—most commonly the first slide in a presentation—that provides an introduction to the presentation topic.

Variant A variation on the presentation theme style and color.

Chapter Review

Skills Review | **Project 1C Glaciers**

Apply **1A** skills from these Objectives:

1. Create a New Presentation
2. Edit a Presentation in Normal View
3. Add Pictures to a Presentation
4. Print and View a Presentation

In the following Skills Review, you will create a new presentation by inserting content and pictures, adding notes and footers, and applying a presentation theme. Your completed presentation will look similar to Figure 1.58.

Project Files

For Project 1C, you will need:

New blank PowerPoint presentation
p01C_Glacier_Bay
p01C_Ice
p01C_Ship

You will save your presentation as:

Lastname_Firstname_1C_Glaciers

Project Results

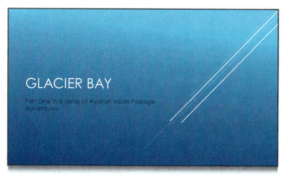

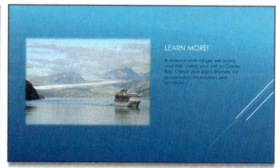

Figure 1.58 Project 1C Glaciers

(continues on next page)

Chapter Review

1 Start PowerPoint. On the right, if necessary, click Find More, click **Slice**, and then click **Create**. On the **Quick Access Toolbar**, click **Save** 🖫. Under **Save As**, click **Browse**. Navigate to your **PowerPoint Chapter 1** folder. In the **File name** box, using your own name, replace the existing text with **Lastname_Firstname_1C_ Glaciers** and then click **Save**. In the **Slide pane**, click in the text *Click to add title*. Type **Glacier Bay** and then click in the subtitle placeholder. Type **Part One in a Series of Alaskan Passage Adventures**

   a. On the **Home tab**, in the **Slides group**, click the **New Slide arrow**, and then in the gallery, click **Two Content**. Click the text *Click to add title*, and then type **About the Park**

2 On the left side of the slide, click in the content placeholder. Type **Located in the Southeast Alaskan Wilderness** and then press Enter. Press Tab. Type **3.3 million acres** and then press Enter. Type **A national park and preserve** and then press Enter.

   a. On the **Home tab**, in the **Paragraph group**, click **Decrease List Level**. Type **Visitor season** and then press Enter. On the **Home tab**, in the **Paragraph group**, click **Increase List Level**. Type **May to September**

   b. On the **Home tab**, in the **Slides group**, click the **New Slide arrow**, and then in the gallery, click **Panoramic Picture with Caption**. In the lower portion of the slide, click the text *Click to add title*, and then type **Prepare to be Amazed!**

   c. Click in the text placeholder. Type **Before you reach Glacier Bay, walk around your cruise ship to find the best viewing locations. Make sure your camera battery is charged!**

   d. On the **Home tab**, in the **Slides group**, click the **New Slide arrow**, and then in the gallery, click **Content with Caption**. In the title placeholder, type **Learn More!**

   e. Click in the text placeholder on the right, and then type **A national park ranger will board your ship during your visit to Glacier Bay. Check your ship's itinerary for presentation information and locations.**

3 With **Slide 4** displayed, in the **Status bar**, click **Notes**. Click in the **Notes pane**, and then type **Your cruise ship will spend between 6 and 8 hours in Glacier Bay.**

   a. On the left side of the PowerPoint window, in the slide thumbnails, click **Slide 1**. Click in the subtitle placeholder after the *n* in *Alaskan*. Press Spacebar, and then type **Inside**

   b. In the slide thumbnails, click **Slide 2**, and then click at the end of the last bullet point after the word *September*. Press Enter, and then type **Be prepared for rain**

4 With **Slide 2** displayed, in the placeholder on the right side of the slide, click **Pictures**. Navigate to your data files for this project, and then click **p01C_Glacier_Bay**. Click **Insert**. If necessary, close the Design Ideas pane.

   a. With the picture selected, on the **Format tab**, in the **Picture Styles group**, click **More** ⌄ to display the **Picture Styles** gallery. Point to several styles to display a ScreenTip, and then locate and click **Beveled Oval, Black**.

   b. Display **Slide 3**. In the Picture placeholder, click **Pictures**. Navigate to your student data files, and then click **p01C_Ice**. Click **Insert**.

   c. Display **Slide 4**. In the content placeholder on the left side of the slide, click **Pictures**. Navigate to the data files for this project, and then insert **p01C_ Ship**. On the **Format tab**, in the **Picture Styles group**, click **More** ⌄ to display the **Picture Styles** gallery. Point to each style to display a ScreenTip, and then locate and click **Soft Edge Rectangle**.

   d. With the picture still selected, on the **Format tab**, in the **Adjust group**, click **Artistic Effects** to display the gallery. Point to each effect to display a ScreenTip, and then locate and click **Crisscross Etching**.

5 On the **Slide Show tab,** in the **Start Slide Show group**, click **From Beginning**. (Mac users click Play from Start.)

   a. Click the left mouse button or press Spacebar to advance to the second slide. Continue to click or press Spacebar until the last slide displays, and then click or press Spacebar one more time to display a black slide.

   b. With the black slide displayed, click the left mouse button or press Spacebar to exit the slide show and return to the presentation.

(continues on next page)

Chapter Review

6 Click the **Insert tab**, and then in the **Text group**, click **Header & Footer** to display the **Header and Footer** dialog box.

a. In the **Header and Footer** dialog box, click the **Notes and Handouts tab**. Under **Include on page**, select the **Date and time** check box. If necessary, click the Update automatically option button so that the current date prints on the notes and handouts.

b. Select the **Page number** check box. If necessary, clear the Header check box to omit this element. Select the **Footer** check box. In the **Footer** box, type **1C_Glaciers** and then click **Apply to All**.

c. In the upper left corner of your screen, click the **File** tab to display **Backstage** view. On the right, at the bottom of the **Properties list**, click **Show All**

Properties. (Mac users, click the File menu, click Properties, click the Summary tab, and instead of Tags, use the Keywords box.)

d. On the list of Properties, click to the right of **Tags** to display an empty box, and then type **Glacier Bay** Click to the right of **Subject** to display an empty box, and then type your course name and section number. Under **Related People**, be sure that your name displays as the author; edit if necessary.

e. **Save** your presentation. As directed by your instructor, create and submit a paper printout or an electronic image of your presentation that looks like a printed document; or, submit your completed PowerPoint file. **Close** PowerPoint.

You have completed Project 1C | **END**

Chapter Review

In the following Skills Review, you will edit an existing presentation by inserting slides from another presentation, applying font and slide formatting, and applying slide transitions. Your completed presentation will look similar to Figure 1.59.

Project Files

For Project 1D, you will need:

p01D_Photography
p01D_Photography_Slides

You will save your presentation as:

Lastname_Firstname_1D_Photography

Project Results

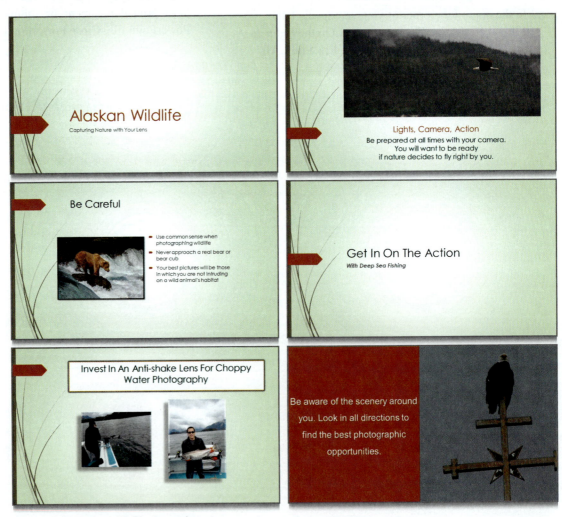

Figure 1.59 Project 1D Photography

(continues on next page)

Chapter Review

Skills Review: Project 1D Photography (continued)

1 From your student data files, double-click **p01D_Photography** to open it. On the **File tab**, click **Save As**, navigate to your **PowerPoint Chapter 1** folder, and then using your own name, save the file as **Lastname_Firstname_1D_Photography**

a. On the **Design tab**, in the **Customize group**, click **Slide Size**, and then click **Widescreen (16:9)**.

b. With **Slide 1** displayed, on the **Home tab**, in the **Slides group**, click the **New Slide arrow**, and then click **Reuse Slides**. In the **Reuse Slides** pane, click **Browse**. In the **Browse** dialog box, navigate to the data files for this project, and then double-click **p01D_Photography_Slides** to display the slides from this presentation in the **Reuse Slides** pane.

c. At the bottom of the **Reuse Slides** pane, be sure that the **Keep source formatting** check box is *cleared*. In the **Reuse Slides** pane, click the first slide—*Alaskan Wildlife*—to insert the slide after Slide 1.

d. At the left of your screen, in the slide thumbnails, click **Slide 6** to display it in the **Slide pane**. In the **Reuse Slides** pane, click the second slide—*Be Careful*—to insert it after **Slide 6**. **Close** the **Reuse Slides** pane. (Mac users click the New Slide arrow, click Reuse Slides, and navigate to the data files for this project. Double-click p01D_Photography_ Slides to insert all four slides into your presentation after Slide 1. Delete Slide 4—*Lights, Camera, Action*—and Slide 5— *Be aware of the scenery.* Drag the new Slide 3—*Be Careful*—after Slide 6.)

2 Display **Slide 1**. On the **View tab**, in the **Presentation Views group**, click **Outline View**.

a. In the **Outline**, in **Slide 7**, drag to select the second and third bullet points—beginning with *Never approach* and ending with *animal's home.*

b. On the **Home tab**, in the **Paragraph group**, click **Decrease List Level** one time.

c. In the **Outline**, in the same slide, click at the end of the first bullet point after the word *sense*. Press `Spacebar`, and then type **when photographing wildlife**

d. In the **Status bar**, click **Normal** to display the slide thumbnails.

3 Display **Slide 8**, and then press `Delete` to delete the slide from the presentation.

a. Display **Slide 1**. On the **Home tab**, in the **Editing group**, click **Replace**. In the **Replace** dialog box, in the **Find what** box, type **home** and then in the **Replace with** box, type **habitat**

b. In the **Replace** dialog box, click **Replace All** to display a message box indicating that one replacement was made. In the message box, click **OK**. **Close** the **Replace** dialog box. (Mac users, click the Edit menu, point to Find, and then click Replace.)

c. On the **Design tab**, in the **Variants group**, right-click the first variant. On the shortcut menu, click **Apply to All Slides** so that the variant color is applied to all of the slides in the presentation.

4 Display **Slide 5**. Select all of the text in the placeholder. On the **Home tab**, in the **Font group**, click the **Font arrow**, scroll the font list, and then click **Arial**. Click the **Font Size arrow**, and then click **32**. In the **Paragraph group**, click **Line Spacing**, and then click **1.5**.

a. Display **Slide 2**. On the **Home tab**, in the **Slides group**, click **Layout** to display the **Slide Layout** gallery. Click **Title Slide** to change the slide layout.

b. On **Slide 2**, select the title—*Alaskan Wildlife*. On the **Home tab**, in the **Font group**, click the **Font Color arrow**. In the fifth column, click the first color— **Dark Red, Accent 1**.

c. Display **Slide 3**, and then select the title—*Lights, Camera, Action*. On the mini toolbar, click **Font Color** to apply the font color **Dark Red, Accent 1**.

d. Display **Slide 4**, and then, click anywhere in the text. On the **Home tab**, in the **Paragraph group**, click **Center** to center the text within the placeholder.

e. Display **Slide 6**, and then select the subtitle. From the mini toolbar, apply **Bold** and **Italic**.

f. In the slide thumbnails, point to **Slide 7**, hold down the left mouse button, and then drag up to position the slide between **Slides 3** and **4**.

5 In the lower right corner of the PowerPoint window, click **Slide Sorter** to display all of the slide thumbnails. Click **Slide 1**, so that it is selected. On your keyboard, press `Delete` to delete the slide.

a. Click **Slide 4**, and then hold down `Ctrl` and click **Slide 5**. With both slides selected, point to either of the selected slides, hold down the left mouse button, and then drag to position the two slides to the right of **Slide 6**. Release the mouse button to move the two slides. In the status bar, click **Normal** to return to Normal view.

b. Display **Slide 1**. On the **Transitions tab**, in the **Transition to This Slide group**, click **More** to display the **Transitions** gallery.

(continues on next page)

Chapter Review

c. Under **Exciting**, click **Gallery** to apply and view the transition. In the **Transition to This Slide group**, click **Effect Options**, and then click **From Left**. In the **Timing group**, click **Apply To All** to apply the *Gallery, From Left* transition to all of the slides in the presentation.

d. In the **Timing group**, click the **Duration up spin arrow** so that *01.75* displays. Under **Advance Slide**, verify that the **On Mouse Click** check box is selected; select it if necessary. In the **Timing group**, click **Apply To All**.

e. Click the **Slide Show tab**. In the **Start Slide Show group**, click **From Beginning**, and then view your presentation, clicking the mouse button to advance through the slides. When the black slide displays, click the mouse button one more time to display the presentation in Normal view. (Mac users click Play from Start.)

6 On the **Insert tab**, in the **Text group**, click **Header & Footer** to display the **Header and Footer** dialog box.

a. In the **Header and Footer** dialog box, click the **Notes and Handouts tab**. Under **Include on page**, select the **Date and time** check box. If necessary, click the Update automatically option button so that the current date prints on the notes and handouts.

b. Select the **Page number** check box. If necessary, clear the Header check box to omit this element. Select the **Footer** check box. In the **Footer** box, type **1D_Photography** and then click **Apply to All**.

c. In the upper left corner of your screen, click the **File** tab to display **Backstage** view. On the right, at the bottom of the **Properties list**, click **Show All Properties**.

d. On the list of Properties, click to the right of **Tags**, and then type **photography** Click to the right of **Subject**, and then type your course name and section number. Under **Related People**, be sure that your name displays as the author. If necessary, right-click the author name, click Edit Property, type your name, and click OK. (Mac users, click the File menu, click Properties, click the Summary tab, and instead of tags, use the Keywords box.)

e. **Save** your presentation. As directed by your instructor, create and submit a paper printout or an electronic image of your presentation that looks like a printed document; or, submit your completed PowerPoint file. **Close** the presentation.

You have completed Project 1D | **END**

| MyLab IT Grader | **Mastering PowerPoint** | **Project 1E Juneau** |

In the following Mastering PowerPoint project, you will create a new presentation that Kodiak West Travel will use in their promotional materials to describe activities in the city of Juneau. Your completed presentation will look similar to Figure 1.60.

Apply 1A skills from these Objectives:

1. Create a New Presentation
2. Edit a Presentation in Normal View
3. Add Pictures to a Presentation
4. Print and View a Presentation

Project Files for MyLab IT Grader

1. In your **MyLab IT** course, locate and click **PowerPoint 1E Juneau**, Download Materials, and then Download All Files.
2. Extract the zipped folder to your PowerPoint Chapter 1 folder. Close the Grader download screens.
3. Take a moment to open the downloaded **PowerPoint_1E_Juneau_Instructions**; note any recent updates to the book.

Project Results

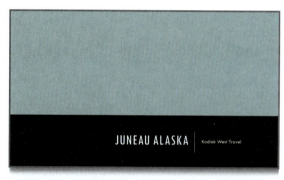

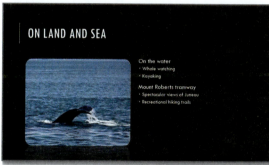

Figure 1.60 Project 1E Juneau

For Non-MyLab Submissions

For Project 1E, you will need:

p01E_Juneau
p01E_Glacier
p01E_Whale
p01E_Falls

In your PowerPoint Chapter 1 folder, save your presentation as:

Lastname_Firstname_1E_Juneau

After you have named and saved your presentation on the next page, begin with Step 2.

After Step 14, save and submit your file as directed by your instructor.

(continues on next page)

Mastering PowerPoint: Project 1E Juneau (continued)

1 Navigate to your **PowerPoint Chapter 1 folder** and then double-click the PowerPoint file you downloaded from **MyLab IT** that displays your name—**Student_PowerPoint_1E_Juneau**. If necessary, at the top, click **Enable Editing**.

2 As the title of this presentation, type **Juneau Alaska** and as the subtitle, type **Kodiak West Travel**

3 Insert a **New Slide** using the **Content with Caption** layout. In the title placeholder, type **The View from Above**

4 In the content placeholder on the right side of the slide, from the files downloaded with this project, insert the picture **p01E_Aerial_View**. Format the picture with the **Rotated, White** picture style.

5 In the text placeholder on the left, type **View a glacial ice field from above by plane or helicopter. If you are more adventurous, try glacier trekking in Juneau where you can land on a glacier and climb an ice wall.**

6 Insert a **New Slide** using the **Two Content** layout. In the title placeholder, type **On Land and Sea**

7 In the content placeholder on the right, type the following text, increasing and decreasing the list level as shown below. In this presentation theme, the first level bullet points do not include a bullet symbol.

> **On the water**
>> **Whale watching**
>> **Kayaking**
> **Mount Roberts tramway**
>> **Spectacular views of Juneau**
>> **Recreational hiking trails**

8 In the content placeholder on the right, from the files downloaded with this project, insert the picture **p01E_Whale**. Apply the **Reflected Rounded Rectangle** picture style.

9 Insert a new slide with the **Picture with Caption** layout. In the title placeholder, type **Mendenhall Glacier** and then in the picture placeholder, from the files downloaded with this project, insert the picture **p01E_Falls**.

10 In the text placeholder, type **Walk to Mendenhall Glacier from the Visitor Center to get a close-up view of Nugget Falls.**

11 In the **Notes pane**, type **Mendenhall Glacier is the most famous glacier in Juneau and in some years is visited by over 400,000 people.**

12 Insert a **Header & Footer** on the **Notes and Handouts**. Include the **Date and time** updated automatically, the **Page number**, and a **Footer** with the text **1E_Juneau** and apply to all the slides.

13 Display the **Document Properties**. As the **Tags** type **Juneau** As the **Subject** type your course and section number. Be sure your name is indicated as the Author. (Mac users use the Keywords box.)

14 **Save** your presentation, and then view the slide show from the beginning. **Close** the presentation and close PowerPoint.

15 In **MyLab IT**, in your **Course Materials**, locate and click the Grader Project **PowerPoint 1E Juneau**. In **step 3**, under **Upload Completed Assignment**, click **Choose File**. In the **Open** dialog box, navigate to your **PowerPoint Chapter 1 folder**, and then click your **Student_PowerPoint_1E_Juneau** file one time to select it. In the lower right corner of the **Open** dialog box, click **Open**.

The name of your selected file displays above the Upload button.

16 To submit your file to **MyLab IT** for grading, click **Upload**, wait a moment for a green **Success!** message, and then in **step 4**, click the blue **Submit for Grading** button. Click **Close Assignment** to return to your list of **Course Materials**.

You have completed Project 1E **END**

MyLab IT Grader

Mastering PowerPoint | **Project 1F Refuge**

Apply 1B skills from these Objectives:

5. Edit an Existing Presentation
6. Format a Presentation
7. Use Slide Sorter View
8. Apply Slide Transitions

In the following Mastering PowerPoint project, you will edit a presentation regarding a wildlife refuge where Kodiak West Travel conducts tours. Your completed presentation will look similar to Figure 1.61.

Project Files for **MyLab IT Grader**

1. In your **MyLab IT** course, locate and click **PowerPoint 1F Refuge**, Download Materials, and then Download All Files.
2. Extract the zipped folder to your PowerPoint Chapter 1 folder. Close the Grader download screens.
3. Take a moment to open the downloaded **PowerPoint_1F_Refuge_Instructions**; note any recent updates to the book.

Project Results

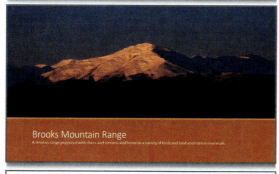

Figure 1.61 Project 1F Refuge

For Non-MyLab Submissions

For Project 1F, you will need:
p01F_Refuge
p01F_Excursions

In your PowerPoint Chapter 1 folder, save your workbook as:
Lastname_Firstname_1F_Refuge

After you have named and saved your presentation on the next page, begin with Step 2.
After Step 14, save and submit your file as directed by your instructor.

(continues on next page)

Content-Based Assessments (Mastery and Transfer of Learning)

1 Navigate to your **PowerPoint Chapter 1 folder** and then double-click the PowerPoint file you downloaded from **MyLab IT** that displays your name—**Student_PowerPoint_1F_Refuge**. If necessary, at the top, click **Enable Editing**.

2 Change the **Slide Size** to **Widescreen (16:9)**.

3 Display the presentation **Outline**. In the **Outline**, on **Slide 2**, increase the list level of the third and the fifth bullet points. Click at the end of the last bullet point after the word *roads*, and then type **or facilities**

4 Return the presentation to **Normal view**, and then display **Slide 4**. Display the **Reuse Slides** pane. Browse to open from the files downloaded with this project, **p01F_Excursions**. Make sure the **Keep source formatting** check box is *cleared*. With **Slide 4** in your presentation displayed, insert the last two slides from the **Reuse Slides** pane. (Mac users insert all slides and delete Slide 5—*Wildlife and Excursions*.)

5 Display **Slide 1**, and then change the layout to **Title Slide**.

6 Select the subtitle—*Experience Alaska with Kodiak West Travel*. Change the **Font** to **Arial**, and the **Font Size** to **28**. Change the **Font Color** to **Black, Text 1**. **Center** the title and the subtitle.

7 Display **Slide 5**, and then select the paragraph in the content placeholder. Apply **Bold** and **Italic**, and then change the **Font Size** to **16**.

8 **Center** the paragraph text, and then change the **Line Spacing** to **1.5**. **Center** the slide title.

9 In **Slide Sorter** view, delete **Slide 3**. Move **Slide 5** to position it after **Slide 2**.

10 Move **Slide 4** to the end of the presentation.

11 In **Normal** view, display **Slide 1**. Apply the **Split** transition and change the **Effect Options** to **Horizontal Out**. Change the **Duration** to **1.75** and apply the transition to all of the slides in the presentation. View the slide show from the beginning.

12 Insert a **Header & Footer** on the **Notes and Handouts**. Include the **Date and time** updated automatically, the **Page number**, and a **Footer** with the text **1F_Refuge**

13 Display the **Document Properties**. As the **Tags** type **refuge, tours** As the **Subject** type your course and section number. Be sure your name is indicated as the **Author**. (Mac users use the Keywords box.) **Save** your presentation.

14 In the upper right corner of your screen, click **Close** ☒ to close PowerPoint.

15 In **MyLab IT**, in your **Course Materials**, locate and click the Grader Project **PowerPoint 1F Refuge**. In **step 3**, under **Upload Completed Assignment**, click **Choose File**. In the **Open** dialog box, navigate to your **PowerPoint Chapter 1 folder**, and then click your **Student_PowerPoint_1F_Refuge** file one time to select it. In the lower right corner of the **Open** dialog box, click **Open**.

The name of your selected file displays above the Upload button.

16 To submit your file to **MyLab IT** for grading, click **Upload**, wait a moment for a green **Success!** message, and then in **step 4**, click the blue **Submit for Grading** button. Click **Close Assignment** to return to your list of **Course Materials**.

You have completed Project 1F | **END**

Content-Based Assessments (Mastery and Transfer of Learning)

MyLab IT Grader | **Mastering PowerPoint** | **Project 1G Northern Lights**

In the following Mastering PowerPoint project, you will edit an existing presentation that describes the Northern Lights and ideal viewing areas. Your completed presentation will look similar to Figure 1.62.

Project Files for **MyLab IT Grader**

1. In your **MyLab IT** course, locate and click **PowerPoint 1G Northern Lights**, Download Materials, and then Download All Files.
2. Extract the zipped folder to your PowerPoint Chapter 1 folder. Close the Grader download screens.
3. Take a moment to open the downloaded **PowerPoint_1G_Northern_Lights_Instructions**; note any recent updates to the book.

Project Results

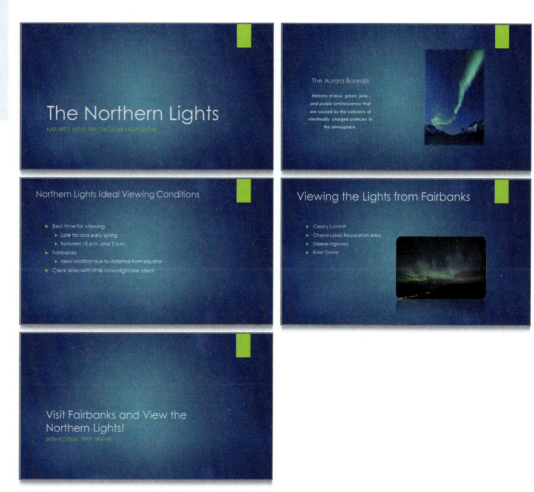

Figure 1.62 Project 1G Northern Lights

For Non-MyLab Submissions

For Project 1G, you will need:
p01G_Northern_Lights
p01G_Lights
p01G_Slides

In your PowerPoint Chapter 1 folder, save your presentation as:
Lastname_Firstname_1G_Northern_Lights

After you have named and saved your presentation on the next page, begin with Step 2.

After Step 17, save and submit your file as directed by your instructor.

1 Navigate to your **PowerPoint Chapter 1 folder,** and then double-click the PowerPoint file you downloaded from **MyLab IT** that displays your name—**Student_PowerPoint_1G_Northern_Lights**. If necessary, at the top, click **Enable Editing**.

2 Replace all occurrences of the text **North** with **Northern** and then change the layout of **Slide 1** to **Title Slide**.

3 Apply the **Ion** theme, with the second, blue variant option.

4 Change the **Slide Size** to **Widescreen (16:9)**.

5 Display **Slide 2**, open the **Reuse Slides** pane, and then from the files downloaded with this project, browse for and open the presentation **p01G_Slides**. If necessary, clear the Keep source formatting check box, and then insert the last two slides from the **p01G_Slides** file. (Mac users insert all slides and delete Slide 3—*Alaska Slides*.)

6 Display **Slide 2**. In either the slide pane or in the slide outline, click at the end of the first bullet point after the word *time*. Add the words **for viewing** and then in the same slide, increase the list level of the second and third bullet points.

7 With **Slide 2** still displayed, select the title and change the **Font Size** to **32**. In the **Notes pane**, type the following notes: **The lights reach their peak in September and March.**

8 Display **Slide 3**. Select the paragraph of text, and then change the **Font Color** to **Green, Accent 6, Lighter 60%**—in the last column, the third color**. Change the **Font Size** to **16**, and then apply **Bold**.

9 Change the paragraph **Line Spacing** to **1.5**, and then **Center** the paragraph and the slide title.

10 With **Slide 3** still displayed, format the picture with the **Soft Edge Rectangle** picture style and the **Marker** artistic effect.

11 Display **Slide 4**. In the content placeholder on the right, from your student data files, insert the picture **p01G_Lights**. Apply the **Reflected Rounded Rectangle** picture style.

12 Move **Slide 3** between **Slides 1** and **2**.

13 Display **Slide 4**. Insert a **New Slide** with the **Section Header** layout. In the title placeholder type **Visit Fairbanks and View the Northern Lights!** In the text placeholder, type **With Kodiak West Travel**

14 Apply the **Uncover** transition and change the **Effect Options** to **From Top**. Change the **Timing** by increasing the **Duration** to **01.25**. Apply the transition effect to all of the slides. View the slide show from the beginning.

15 Insert a **Header & Footer** on the **Notes and Handouts**. Include the **Date and time** updated automatically, the **Page number**, and a **Footer**, using your own name, with the text **1G_Northern_Lights**

16 Display the **Document Properties**. As the **Tags,** type **northern lights, Fairbanks** As the **Subject,** type your course and section number. Be sure your name is indicated as the Author. (Mac users use the Keywords box.) **Save** your presentation.

17 In the upper right corner of your screen, click **Close** to close PowerPoint.

18 In **MyLab IT**, in your **Course Materials**, locate and click the Grader Project **PowerPoint 1G Refuge**. In **step 3**, under **Upload Completed Assignment**, click **Choose File**. In the **Open** dialog box, navigate to your **PowerPoint Chapter 1 folder**, and then click your **Student_PowerPoint_1G_Refuge** file one time to select it. In the lower right corner of the **Open** dialog box, click **Open**.

The name of your selected file displays above the Upload button.

19 To submit your file to **MyLab IT** for grading, click **Upload**, wait a moment for a green **Success!** message, and then in **step 4**, click the blue **Submit for Grading** button. Click **Close Assignment** to return to your list of **Course Materials**.

You have completed Project 1G **END**

Content-Based Assessments (Critical Thinking)

Apply a combination of the **1A** and **1B** skills.	**GO! Fix It**	**Project 1H Rain Forest**	IRC
	GO! Make It	**Project 1I Eagles**	IRC
	GO! Solve It	**Project 1J Packrafting**	IRC
	GO! Solve It	**Project 1K Packing**	

Project Files

For Project 1K, you will need:

p01K_Packing

You will save your presentation as:

Lastname_Firstname_1K_Packing

Open the file p01K_Packing and save it as **Lastname_Firstname_1K_Packing** Complete the presentation by applying a theme and changing the variant. Format the presentation attractively by applying appropriate font formatting and by changing text alignment and line spacing. Change the layout of the last slide to an appropriate layout. On Slide 2, insert a picture that you have taken yourself, or use one of the pictures in your student data files that you inserted in other projects in this chapter. Apply a style to the picture. Apply slide transitions to all of the slides in the presentation, and then insert a header and footer that includes the date and time updated automatically, **1K_Packing** in the footer, and the page number. Add your name, your course name and section number, and the tags **packing, weather** to the properties. Save and print or submit as directed by your instructor.

		Performance Level		
		Exemplary	**Proficient**	**Developing**
Performance Criteria	**Apply a theme and a variant**	An appropriate theme and variant were applied to the presentation.	A theme was applied but the variant was not changed.	Neither a theme nor the variant theme were applied.
	Apply font and slide formatting	Font and slide formatting is attractive and appropriate.	Adequately formatted but difficult to read or unattractive.	Inadequate or no formatting.
	Use appropriate pictures and apply styles attractively	An appropriate picture was inserted and a style is applied attractively.	A picture was inserted but a style was not applied.	Picture was not inserted.
	Apply appropriate slide layout to Slide 4	An appropriate layout was applied to the last slide.	The slide layout was changed but is not appropriate for the type of slide.	The slide layout was not changed.

You have completed Project 1K | END

Outcomes-Based Assessments (Critical Thinking)

Rubric

The following outcomes-based assessments are open-ended assessments. That is, there is no specific correct result; your result will depend on your approach to the information provided. Make Professional Quality your goal. Use the following scoring rubric to guide you in how to approach the problem, and then to evaluate how well your approach solves the problem.

The *criteria*—Software Mastery, Content, Format and Layout, and Process—represent the knowledge and skills you have gained that you can apply to solving the problem. The *levels of performance*—Professional Quality, Approaching Professional Quality, or Needs Quality Improvements—help you and your instructor evaluate your result.

	Your completed project is of Professional Quality if you:	Your completed project is Approaching Professional Quality if you:	Your completed project Needs Quality Improvements if you:
1-Software Mastery	Choose and apply the most appropriate skills, tools, and features and identify efficient methods to solve the problem.	Choose and apply some appropriate skills, tools, and features, but not in the most efficient manner.	Choose inappropriate skills, tools, or features, or are inefficient in solving the problem.
2-Content	Construct a solution that is clear and well organized, contains content that is accurate, appropriate to the audience and purpose, and is complete. Provide a solution that contains no errors of spelling, grammar, or style.	Construct a solution in which some components are unclear, poorly organized, inconsistent, or incomplete. Misjudge the needs of the audience. Have some errors in spelling, grammar, or style, but the errors do not detract from comprehension.	Construct a solution that is unclear, incomplete, or poorly organized, contains some inaccurate or inappropriate content, and contains many errors of spelling, grammar, or style. Do not solve the problem.
3-Format and Layout	Format and arrange all elements to communicate information and ideas, clarify function, illustrate relationships, and indicate relative importance.	Apply appropriate format and layout features to some elements, but not others. Overuse features, causing minor distraction.	Apply format and layout that does not communicate information or ideas clearly. Do not use format and layout features to clarify function, illustrate relationships, or indicate relative importance. Use available features excessively, causing distraction.
4-Process	Use an organized approach that integrates planning, development, self-assessment, revision, and reflection.	Demonstrate an organized approach in some areas, but not others; or, use an insufficient process of organization throughout.	Do not use an organized approach to solve the problem.

Content-Based Assessments (Critical Thinking)

Apply a combination of the 1A and 1B skills.

GO! Think | **Project 1L Bears**

Project Files

For Project 1L, you will need:

New blank PowerPoint presentation
p01L_Bear
You will save your presentation as:
Lastname_Firstname_1L_Bears

Cindy Barrow, Tour Operations Manager for Kodiak West Travel, is developing a presentation describing brown bear viewing travel experiences that the company is developing. In the presentation, Cindy will be describing the brown bear habitat and viewing opportunities.

Kodiak bears are the largest known size of brown bears on record; they can weigh as much as 2,000 pounds and can get as large as polar bears. Kodiak bears are active during the day and are generally solitary creatures. The Kodiak Bear Travel Experience is a small, personalized travel adventure available to only eight participants at a time. It is an opportunity to peer into the life of these majestic mammals.

The adventure takes place on Kodiak Island near a lake with a high concentration of salmon, making it the perfect natural feeding ground for the Kodiak bears. Travelers can view the bears from boats, kayaks, and recently constructed viewing platforms, and guides are available.

This is a true wildlife experience as the area is home to deer, fox, and river otter. Accommodations are available at the Kodiak West Breakfast Inn from mid-June to the end of August. Peak season is early August, and reservations can be made up to one year in advance. The cost is $1,800 per person for one week, and includes all meals, use of watercraft, and guided tours.

Using the preceding information, create a presentation that Cindy can show at a travel fair. The presentation should include four to six slides describing the travel experience. Apply an appropriate theme and use slide layouts that will effectively present the content. Insert at least one picture and apply appropriate picture formatting. You may use your own image file, search for one online, or from your student data files, use the file p01L_Bear. Apply font formatting and slide transitions and modify text alignment and line spacing as necessary.

Save the file as **Lastname_Firstname_1L_Bears** and then insert a header and footer that include the date and time updated automatically, **1L_Bears** in the footer, and the page number. Add your name, your course name and section number, and the tags **bears, tours** to the properties. Save and print or submit as directed by your instructor.

You have completed Project 1L | **END**

Content-Based Assessments (Critical Thinking)

GO! Think	Project 1M Sitka	IRC
You and GO!	Project 1N Travel	IRC
GO! Cumulative Team Project	Project 1O Bell Orchid Hotels	IRC

Glossary

3D models A new kind of shape that you can insert from an online library of ready-to-use, three-dimensional graphics.

Absolute cell reference A cell reference that refers to cells by their fixed position in a worksheet; an absolute cell reference remains the same when the formula is copied.

Accounting Number Format The Excel number format that applies a thousand comma separator where appropriate, inserts a fixed U.S. dollar sign aligned at the left edge of the cell, applies two decimal places, and leaves a small amount of space at the right edge of the cell to accommodate a parenthesis for negative numbers.

Active cell The cell, surrounded by a black border, ready to receive data or be affected by the next Excel command.

Address bar In a File Explorer window, the area that displays your current location in the folder structure as a series of links separated by arrows.

Alignment The placement of paragraph text relative to the left and right margins.

Alignment guides Green lines that display when you move an object to assist in alignment.

Alt text Text added to a picture or object that helps people using a screen reader understand what the object is; also called *alternative text*.

Alternative text Text added to a picture or object that helps people using a screen reader understand what the object is; also called *alt text*.

Append To add on to the end of an object; for example, to add records to the end of an existing table.

Application A computer program that helps you perform a task for a specific purpose.

Arithmetic operators The symbols +, −, *, /, %, and ^ used to denote addition, subtraction (or negation), multiplication, division, percentage, and exponentiation in an Excel formula.

Artistic effects Formats applied to images that make pictures resemble sketches or paintings.

Aspect ratio The ratio of the width of a display to the height of the display.

Auto Fill An Excel feature that generates and extends values into adjacent cells based on the values of selected cells.

AutoCalculate A feature that displays three calculations in the status bar by default—Average, Count, and Sum—when you select a range of numerical data.

AutoComplete A feature that speeds your typing and lessens the likelihood of errors; if the first few characters you type in a cell match an existing entry in the column, Excel fills in the remaining characters for you.

AutoFit An Excel feature that adjusts the width of a column to fit the cell content of the widest cell in the column.

AutoNumber data type A data type that describes a unique sequential or random number assigned by Access as each record is entered and that is useful for data that has no distinct field that can be considered unique.

AutoSave An Office 365 feature that saves your document every few seconds—if saved on OneDrive, OneDrive for Business, or SharePoint Online—and enables you to share the document with others for real-time co-authoring.

AutoSum A button that provides quick access to the SUM function.

Backstage tabs The area along the left side of Backstage view with tabs to display screens with related groups of commands.

Backstage view A centralized space for file management tasks; for example, opening, saving, printing, publishing, or sharing a file.

Best Fit An Access command that adjusts the width of a column to accommodate the column's longest entry.

Bing Microsoft's search engine.

Black slide A slide that displays after the last slide in a presentation indicating that the presentation is over.

Blank desktop database A database that has no data and has no database tools—you must create the data and tools as you need them; the database is stored on your computer or another storage device.

Bookmark A command that marks a word, section, or place in a document so that you can jump to it quickly without scrolling.

Booting the computer The process of turning on the computer.

Bulleted list A list of items with each item introduced by a symbol such as a small circle or check mark, and which is useful when the items in the list can be displayed in any order; also referred to as unordered lists.

Bullets Text symbols such as small circles or check marks that precede each item in a bulleted list.

Caption A property setting that displays a name for a field in a table, query, form, or report different from the one listed as the field name.

Category axis The area along the bottom of a chart that identifies the categories of data; also referred to as the x-axis.

Category labels The labels that display along the bottom of a chart to identify the categories of data; Excel uses the row titles as the category names.

Cell The intersection of a column and a row.

Cell address Another name for a cell reference.

Cell content Anything typed into a cell.

Cell reference The identification of a specific cell by its intersecting column letter and row number.

Cell style A defined set of formatting characteristics, such as font, font size, font color, cell borders, and cell shading.

Center alignment The alignment of text or objects centered horizontally between the left and right margin.

Chart The graphic representation of data in a worksheet; data presented as a chart is usually easier to understand than a table of numbers.

Chart Elements button A button that enables you to add, remove, or change chart elements such as the title, legend, gridlines, and data labels.

Chart Filters button A button that displays options for changing the data displayed in a chart.

Chart layout The combination of chart elements that can be displayed in a chart such as a title, legend, labels for the columns, and the table of charted cells.

Chart style The overall visual look of a chart in terms of its graphic effects, colors, and backgrounds; for example, you can have flat or beveled columns, colors that are solid or transparent, and backgrounds that are dark or light.

Chart Styles button A button that displays options for setting the style and color scheme for a chart.

Chart Styles gallery A group of predesigned chart styles that you can apply to an Excel chart.

Chart types Various chart formats used in a way that is meaningful to the reader; common examples are column charts, pie charts, and line charts.

Check Accessibility A command that checks a document for content that people with disabilities might find difficult to read.

Check Compatibility A command that searches your document for features that may not be supported by older versions of Office.

Click The action of pressing the left button of the mouse pointing device.

Clipboard A temporary storage area that holds text or graphics that you select and then cut or copy.

Cloud computing Applications and services that are accessed over the internet.

Cloud storage Online storage of data so that you can access your data from different places and devices.

Collaboration The action of working together with others as a team in an intellectual endeavor to complete a shared task or achieve a shared goal.

Column A vertical group of cells in a worksheet.

Column chart A chart in which the data is arranged in columns and that is useful for showing data changes over a period of time or for illustrating comparisons among items.

Column heading The letter that displays at the top of a vertical group of cells in a worksheet; beginning with the first letter of the alphabet, a unique letter or combination of letters identifies each column.

Comma Style The Excel number format that inserts thousand comma separators where appropriate and applies two decimal places; Comma Style also leaves space at the right to accommodate a parenthesis when negative numbers are present.

Commands An instruction to a computer program that causes an action to be carried out.

Common field A field included in two or more tables that stores the same data.

Compressed files Files that have been reduced in size, take up less storage space, and can be transferred to other computers faster than uncompressed files.

Compressed Folder Tools Command available in File Explorer with which you can extract compressed files.

Constant value Numbers, text, dates, or times of day that you type into a cell.

Content pane In a File Explorer window, another name for the file list.

Context menus Menus that display commands and options relevant to the selected text or object; also called *shortcut menus*.

Context sensitive A command associated with the currently selected or active object; often activated by right-clicking a screen item.

Context-sensitive commands Commands that display on a shortcut menu that relate to the object or text that is selected.

Contextual tab A tab added to the ribbon automatically when a specific object is selected and that contains commands relevant to the selected object.

Contiguous slides Slides that are adjacent to each other in a presentation.

Copy A command that duplicates a selection and places it on the Clipboard.

Cortana Microsoft's intelligent personal assistant in Windows 10 and also available on other devices; named for the intelligent female character in the video game Halo.

Currency data type An Access data type that describes monetary values and numeric data that can be used in mathematical calculations involving values with one to four decimal places.

Custom web app A database that you can publish and share with others over the Internet.

Cut A command that removes a selection and places it on the Clipboard.

Dashboard The right side of the Start menu that is a one-screen view of links to information and programs that matter to you.

Data (Windows) The documents, worksheets, pictures, songs, and so on that you create and store during the day-to-day use of your computer.

Data (Access) Facts about people, events, things, or ideas.

Data (Excel) Text or numbers in a cell.

Data management The process of managing files and folders.

Data marker A column, bar, area, dot, pie slice, or other symbol in a chart that represents a single data point.

Data point A value that originates in a worksheet cell and that is represented in a chart by a data marker.

Data series Related data points represented by data markers; each data series has a unique color or pattern represented in the chart legend.

Data source (Access) The table or tables from which a form, query, or report retrieves its data.

Data type Classification identifying the kind of data that can be stored in a field, such as numbers, text, or dates.

Database An organized collection of facts about people, events, things, or ideas related to a specific topic or purpose.

Database management system (DBMS) Database software that controls how related collections of data are stored, organized, retrieved, and secured; also known as a DBMS.

Database template A preformatted database that contains prebuilt tables, queries, forms, and reports that perform a specific task, such as tracking events.

Datasheet view The Access view that displays data organized in columns and rows similar to an Excel worksheet.

DBMS An acronym for database management system.

Default The term that refers to the current selection or setting that is automatically used by a computer program unless you specify otherwise.

Deselect The action of canceling the selection of an object or block of text by clicking outside of the selection.

Design view An Access view that displays the detailed structure of a table, query, form, or report. For forms and reports, may be the view in which some tasks must be performed, and only the controls, and not the data, display in this view.

Desktop A simulation of a real desk that represents your work area; here you can arrange icons such as shortcuts to files, folders, and various types of documents in the same manner you would arrange physical objects on top of a desk.

Desktop app A computer program that is installed on your PC and requires a computer operating system such as Microsoft Windows to run; also known as a *desktop application*.

Desktop application A computer program that is installed on your PC and requires a computer operating system such as Microsoft Windows to run; also known as a *desktop app*.

Desktop shortcuts Desktop icons that can link to items accessible on your computer such as a program, file, folder, disk drive, printer, or another computer.

Destination table The table to which you import or append data.

Details pane When activated in a folder window, displays—on the right—the most common file properties associated with the selected file.

Details view A command that displays a list of files or folders and their most common properties.

Dialog box A small window that displays options for completing a task.

Dialog Box Launcher A small icon that displays to the right of some group names on the ribbon and that opens a related dialog box or pane providing additional options and commands related to that group.

Dictate A feature in Word, PowerPoint, Outlook, and OneNote for Windows 10; when you enable Dictate, you start talking and as you talk, text appears in your document or slide.

Displayed value The data that displays in a cell.

Document properties Details about a file that describe or identify it, including the title, author name, subject, and keywords that identify the document's topic or contents; also known as *metadata*.

Dot leader A series of dots preceding a tab that guides the eye across the line.

Double-click The action of pressing the left mouse button two times in rapid succession while holding the mouse still.

Download The action of transferring or copying a file from another location—such as a cloud storage location, your college's Learning Management System, or from an internet site—to your computer.

Drag The action of holding down the left mouse button while moving your mouse.

Drawing objects Graphic objects, such as shapes, diagrams, lines, or circles.

Drive An area of storage that is formatted with a file system compatible with your operating system and is identified by a drive letter.

Edit The process of making changes to text or graphics in an Office file.

Editing The process of modifying a presentation by adding and deleting slides or by changing the contents of individual slides.

Editor A digital writing assistant in Word and Outlook that displays misspellings, grammatical mistakes, and writing style issues.

Ellipsis A set of three dots indicating incompleteness; an ellipsis following a command name indicates that a dialog box will display if you click the command.

Enhanced ScreenTip A ScreenTip that displays useful descriptive information about the command.

Excel pointer An Excel window element with which you can display the location of the pointer.

Expand Formula Bar button An Excel window element with which you can increase the height of the Formula Bar to display lengthy cell content.

Expand horizontal scroll bar button An Excel window element with which you can increase the width of the horizontal scroll bar.

Export The process of copying data from one file into another file, such as an Access table into an Excel spreadsheet.

Extract To decompress, or pull out, files from a compressed form.

Field A single piece of information that is stored in every record; represented by a column in a database table.

Field properties Characteristics of a field that control how the field displays and how data can be entered in the field; vary for different data types.

File Information stored on a computer under a single name.

File Explorer The Windows program that displays the contents of locations, folders, and files on your computer.

File Explorer window A window that displays the contents of the current location and contains helpful parts so that you can navigate—explore within the file organizing structure of Windows.

File list In a File Explorer window, the area that displays the contents of the current location.

File name extension A set of characters at the end of a file name that helps Windows understand what kind of information is in a file and what program should open it.

File properties Information about a file, such as the author, the date the file was last changed, and any descriptive tags.

Fill The inside color of an object.

Fill handle The small black square in the lower right corner of a selected cell.

Filtered list A display of files that is limited based on specified criteria.

First principle of good database design A principle of good database design stating that data is organized in tables so that there is no redundant data.

Flat database A simple database file that is not related or linked to any other collection of data.

Floating object A graphic that can be moved independently of the surrounding text characters.

Folder A container in which you can store files.

Folder structure The hierarchy of folders.

Folder window A window that typically displays the File List for a folder.

Font A set of characters with the same design and shape.

Font styles Formatting emphasis such as bold, italic, and underline.

Footer (PowerPoint) Text that displays at the bottom of every slide or that prints at the bottom of a sheet of slide handouts or notes pages.

Footer (Word) A reserved area for text or graphics that displays at the bottom of each page in a document.

Form An Access object you can use to enter new records into a table, edit or delete existing records in a table, or display existing records.

Form view The Access view in which you can view, modify, delete, or add records in a table but you cannot change the layout or design of the form.

Format Changing the appearance of cells and worksheet elements to make a worksheet attractive and easy to read.

Format Painter The command to copy the formatting of specific text or to copy the formatting of a paragraph and then apply it in other locations in your document; when active, the pointer takes the shape of a paintbrush.

Formatting (PowerPoint) The process of changing the appearance of the text, layout, and design of a slide.

Formatting (Word) The process of applying Office commands to make your documents easy to read and to add visual touches and design elements to make your document inviting to the reader; establishes the overall appearance of text, graphics, and pages in an Office file—for example, in a Word document.

Formatting marks Characters that display on the screen, but do not print, indicating where the Enter key, the Spacebar, and the Tab key were pressed; also called *nonprinting characters*.

Formula An equation that performs mathematical calculations on values in a worksheet.

Formula Bar An element in the Excel window that displays the value or formula contained in the active cell; here you can also enter or edit values or formulas.

Free-form snip From the Snipping Tool, a command that draws an irregular line such as a circle around an area of the screen.

Full-screen snip From the Snipping Tool, a command that captures the entire screen.

Function A predefined formula—a formula that Excel has already built for you—that performs calculations by using specific values in a particular order or structure.

Gallery An Office feature that displays a list of potential results.

General format The default format that Excel applies to numbers; this format has no specific characteristics—whatever you type in the cell will display, with the exception that trailing zeros to the right of a decimal point will not display.

Gradient fill A fill effect in which one color fades into another.

Graphical user interface Graphics such as an image of a file folder or wastebasket that you click to activate the item represented.

Graphics Pictures, charts, or drawing objects.

Groups On the Office ribbon, the sets of related commands that you might need for a specific type of task.

GUI An abbreviation of the term graphical user interface.

Hamburger Another name for a hamburger menu.

Hamburger menu Another name for a menu icon, deriving from the three lines that bring to mind a hamburger on a bun.

Hard disk drive The primary storage device located inside your computer where some of your files and programs are typically stored, usually designated as drive C.

Header Text that prints at the top of each sheet of slide handouts or notes pages.

Hierarchy An arrangement where items are ranked and where each level is lower in rank than the item above it

Icons Small images that represent commands, files, applications, or other windows.

Import The process of copying data from another file, such as a Word table or an Excel workbook, into a separate file, such as an Access database.

Info tab The tab in Backstage view that displays information about the current file.

Information Data that is accurate, timely, and organized in a useful manner.

Inline object An object or graphic inserted in a document that acts like a character in a sentence.

Insertion point A blinking vertical line that indicates where text or graphics will be inserted.

Inspect Document A command that searches your document for hidden data of personal information that you might not want to share publicly.

JPEG An acronym that stands for *Joint Photographic Experts Group* and that is a common file type used by digital cameras and computers to store digital pictures.

Jump List A display of destinations and tasks from a program's taskbar icon when you right-click the icon.

Justified alignment An arrangement of text in which the text aligns evenly on both the left and right margins.

Keyboard shortcut A combination of two or more keyboard keys, used to perform a task that would otherwise require a mouse.

KeyTip The letter that displays on a command in the ribbon and that indicates the key you can press to activate the command when keyboard control of the ribbon is activated.

Keywords Custom file properties in the form of words that you associate with a document to give an indication of the document's content.

Label Another name for a text value; it usually provides information about number values.

Landscape orientation A page orientation in which the paper is wider than it is tall.

Layout The arrangement of elements, such as title and subtitle text, lists, pictures, tables, charts, shapes, and movies, on a slide.

Layout Options A button that displays when an object is selected and that has commands to choose how the object interacts with surrounding text.

Layout view The Access view in which you can make changes to a form or report while the data from the underlying data source displays.

Leader character Characters that form a solid, dotted, or dashed line that fills the space preceding a tab stop.

Left alignment (Excel) The cell format in which characters align at the left edge of the cell; this is the default for text entries and is an example of formatting information stored in a cell.

Left alignment (Word) An arrangement of text in which the text aligns at the left margin, leaving the right margin uneven.

Legend A chart element that identifies the patterns or colors that are assigned to the categories in the chart.

Lettered column headings The area along the top edge of a worksheet that identifies each column with a unique letter or combination of letters.

Line spacing The distance between lines of text in a paragraph.

Link A connection to data in another file.

List level An outline level in a presentation represented by a bullet symbol and identified in a slide by the indentation and the size of the text.

Live Layout A feature that reflows text as you move or size an object so that you can view the placement of surrounding text.

Live Preview A technology that shows the result of applying an editing or formatting change as you point to possible results—*before* you actually apply it.

Live tiles Tiles that are constantly updated with fresh information.

Location Any disk drive, folder, or other place in which you can store files and folders.

Lock screen A background that fills the computer screen when the computer boots up or wakes up from sleep mode.

Margins The space between the text and the top, bottom, left, and right edges of the paper.

Maximize A window control button that will enlarge the size of the window to fill the entire screen.

Menu A list of commands within a category.

Menu bar A group of menus at the top of a program window.

Menu icon A button consisting of three lines that, when clicked, expands a menu; often used in mobile applications because it is compact to use on smaller screens—also referred to a *hamburger menu*.

Merge & Center A command that joins selected cells in an Excel worksheet into one larger cell and centers the contents in the merged cell.

Metadata Details about a file that describe or identify it, including the title, author name, subject, and keywords that identify the document's topic or contents; also known as *document properties*.

Microsoft account A user account with which you can sign in to any Windows 10 computer on which you have, or create, an account.

Microsoft Store app A smaller app that you download from the Microsoft Store.

Middle Align An alignment command that centers text between the top and bottom of a cell.

Mini toolbar A small toolbar containing frequently used formatting commands that displays as a result of selecting text or objects.

Minimize A window control button that will keep a program open but will remove it from screen view.

Mouse pointer Any symbol that displays on the screen in response to moving the mouse.

Move In File Explorer, the action of removing a file or folder from its original location and storing it in a new location.

MRU Acronym for *most recently used*, which refers to the state of some commands that retain the characteristic most recently applied; for example, the Font Color button retains the most recently used color until a new color is chosen.

Multiple-items form A form that enables you to display or enter multiple records in a table.

Name Box An element of the Excel window that displays the name of the selected cell, table, chart, or object.

Navigate (Windows) A process for exploring within the file organizing structure of Windows.

Navigation area An area at the bottom of the Access window that indicates the number of records in the table and contains controls in the form of arrows that you click to move among the records.

Navigation pane The area on the left side of the File Explorer window to access your OneDrive, folders on your PC, devices and drives connected to your PC, and other PCs on your network.

Noncontiguous slides Slides that are not adjacent to each other in a presentation.

Nonprinting characters Characters that display on the screen, but do not print, indicating where the Enter key, the Spacebar, and the Tab key were pressed; also called *formatting marks*.

Normal view (Excel) A screen view that maximizes the number of cells visible on your screen and keeps the column letters and row numbers close to the columns and rows.

Normal view (PowerPoint) The primary editing view in PowerPoint where you write and design your presentations.

Normalization The process of applying design rules and principles to ensure that your database performs as expected.

Notepad A basic text-editing program included with Windows 10 that you can use to create simple documents.

Notes page A printout that contains the slide image on the top half of the page and notes that you have created on the Notes pane in the lower half of the page.

Notes pane An area of the Normal view window that displays below the Slide pane with space to type notes regarding the active slide.

Number data type An Access data type that represents a quantity, how much or how many, and that may be used in calculations.

Number format A specific way in which Excel displays numbers in a cell.

Number values Constant values consisting of only numbers.

Numbered list A list of items preceded by numbers, which indicate sequence or rank of the items. Sometimes called ordered lists.

Numbered row headings The area along the left edge of a worksheet that identifies each row with a unique number.

Object A text box, picture, table, or shape that you can select and then move and resize.

Objects (Access) The basic parts of a database that you create to store your data and to work with your data; for example, tables, queries, forms, and reports.

Object anchor The symbol that indicates to which paragraph an object is attached.

Object tab In the object window, a tab that identifies the object and enables you to make an open object active.

Object window An area of the Access window that displays open objects, such as tables, queries, forms, or reports; by default, each object displays on its own tab.

Office 365 A version of Microsoft Office to which you subscribe for an annual fee.

OneDrive Microsoft's free cloud storage for anyone with a free Microsoft account.

Operating system A specific type of computer program that manages the other programs on a computing device such as a desktop computer, a laptop computer, a smartphone, a tablet computer, or a game console.

Operators The symbols with which you can specify the type of calculation you want to perform in an Excel formula.

Option button In a dialog box, a round button that enables you to make one choice among two or more options.

Outline view A PowerPoint view that displays the presentation outline to the left of the Slide pane.

Page Width A command that zooms the document so that the width of the page matches the width of the window.

Paragraph symbol The symbol ¶ that represents the end of a paragraph.

Parent folder The location in which the folder you are viewing is saved.

Paste The action of placing cell contents that have been copied or moved to the Clipboard into another location.

Paste Options gallery A gallery of buttons that provides a Live Preview of all the Paste options available in the current context.

Path A sequence of folders that leads to a specific file or folder.

PDF The acronym for Portable Document Format, which is a file format that creates an image that preserves the look of your file, but that cannot be easily changed; a popular format for sending documents electronically, because the document will display on most computers.

Pen A pen-shaped stylus that you tap on a computer screen.

Personal folder The folder created on the hard drive for each Windows 10 user account on a computer; for each user account—even if there is only one user on the computer—Windows 10 creates a personal folder labeled with the account holder's name.

Picture effects Effects that enhance a picture, such as a shadow, glow, reflection, or 3-D rotation.

Picture element A point of light measured in dots per square inch on a screen; 64 pixels equals 8.43 characters, which is the average number of characters that will fit in a cell in an Excel worksheet using the default font.

Picture styles Frames, shapes, shadows, borders, and other special effects that can be added to an image to create an overall visual style for the image.

Pixel The abbreviated name for a picture element.

Placeholder A box on a slide with dotted or dashed borders that holds title and body text or other content such as charts, tables, and pictures.

Placeholder text Non-printing text that holds a place in a document where you can type.

.png file An image file type that can be transferred over the internet, an acronym for Portable Network Graphic.

Point-and-click The technique of constructing a formula by pointing to and then clicking cells; this method is convenient when the referenced cells are not adjacent to one another.

Point to The action of moving the mouse pointer over a specific area.

Pointer Any symbol that displays on your screen in response to moving your mouse.

Pointing device A mouse or touchpad used to control the pointer.

Points A measurement of the size of a font; there are 72 points in an inch.

Populate The action of filling a database table with records.

Portable Document Format A file format that creates an image that preserves the look of your file, but that cannot be easily changed; a popular format for sending documents electronically, because the document will display on most computers.

Portrait orientation A page orientation in which the paper is taller than it is wide.

Presenter view A view that shows the full-screen slide show on one monitor or projection screen while enabling the presenter to view a preview of the next slide, notes, and a timer on another monitor.

Primary key A required field that uniquely identifies a record in a table; for example, a Student ID number at a college.

Print Preview A view of a document as it will appear when you print it.

Program A set of instructions that a computer uses to accomplish a task.

Progress bar A bar that displays in a dialog box—and also on the taskbar button—that indicates visually the progress of a task such as a copy process, a download, or a file transfer.

Property Sheet A list of characteristics—properties—for fields or controls on a form or report in which you can make precise changes to each property associated with the field or control.

pt The abbreviation for *point* when referring to a font size.

Query A database object that retrieves specific data from one or more database objects—either tables or other queries—and then, in a single datasheet, displays only the data you specify.

Quick access In the navigation pane in a File Explorer window, a list of files you have been working on and folders you use often.

Quick Analysis Tool A tool that displays in the lower right corner of a selected range, with which you can analyze your data by using Excel tools such as charts, color-coding, and formulas.

Range Two or more selected cells on a worksheet that are adjacent or nonadjacent; because the range is treated as a single unit, you can make the same changes or combination of changes to more than one cell at a time.

Range finder An Excel feature that outlines cells in color to indicate which cells are used in a formula; useful for verifying which cells are referenced in a formula.

Reading view A view in PowerPoint that displays a presentation in a manner similar to a slide show but in which the taskbar, title bar, and status bar remain available in the presentation window.

Real-time co-authoring A process where two or more people work on the same file at the same time and see changes made by others in seconds.

Recommended Charts An Excel feature that displays a customized set of charts that, according to Excel's calculations, will best fit your data based on the range of data that you select.

Record All of the categories of data pertaining to one person, place, event, thing, or idea; represented by a row in a database table.

Record selector bar The bar at the left edge of a record when it is displayed in a form and that is used to select an entire record.

Record selector box The small box at the left of a record in Datasheet view that, when clicked, selects the entire record.

Rectangular snip From the Snipping Tool, a command that draws a precise box by dragging the mouse pointer around an area of the screen to form a rectangle.

Recycle Bin The area where deleted items are stored until you empty the bin; enables you to recover deleted items until the bin is emptied.

Redundant In a database, information that is duplicated in a manner that indicates poor database design.

Relational database A sophisticated type of database that has multiple collections of data within the file that are related to one another.

Relative cell reference In a formula, the address of a cell based on the relative positions of the cell that contains the formula and the cell referred to in the formula.

Removable storage device A device such as a USB flash drive used to transfer information from one computer to another.

Report A database object that summarizes the fields and records from a query or table in an easy-to-read format suitable for printing.

Resources The collection of the physical parts of your computer such as the central processing unit (CPU), memory, and any attached devices such as a printer.

Restore Down A command that resizes a window to its previous size.

Ribbon In Office applications, displays a group of task-oriented tabs that contain the commands, styles, and resources you need to work in an Office desktop app. In a File Explorer window, the area at the top that groups common tasks on tabs. such as copying and moving, creating new folders, emailing and zipping items, and changing view on related tabs.

Right alignment An arrangement of text in which the text aligns at the right margin, leaving the left margin uneven.

Right-click The action of clicking the right mouse button one time.

Rotation handle A symbol with which you can rotate a graphic to any angle; displays above the top center sizing handle.

Rounding A procedure in which you determine which digit at the right of the number will be the last digit displayed and then increase it by one if the next digit to its right is 5, 6, 7, 8, or 9.

Row A horizontal group of cells in a worksheet.

Row heading The numbers along the left side of an Excel worksheet that designate the row numbers.

Run The process in which Access looks at the records in the table(s) included in the query design, finds the records that match the specified criteria, and then displays the records in a datasheet; only the fields included in the query design display.

Sans serif font A font design with no lines or extensions on the ends of characters.

Scaling The process of shrinking the width and/or height of printed output to fit a maximum number of pages.

Screen reader Software that enables visually impaired users to read text on a computer screen to understand the content of pictures.

Screenshot An image of an active window on your computer that you can paste into a document.

ScreenTip A small box that that displays useful information when you perform various mouse actions such as pointing to screen elements or dragging.

Scroll arrow An arrow found at either end of a scroll bar that can be clicked to move within the window in small increments.

Scroll bar A vertical bar that displays when the contents of a window or pane are not completely visible; a scroll bar can be vertical, displayed at the side of the window, or horizontal, displayed at the bottom of a window.

Scroll box Within a scroll bar, a box that you can move to bring the contents of the window into view.

Second principle of good database design A principle stating that appropriate database techniques are used to ensure the accuracy and consistency of data as it is entered into the table.

Section header A type of slide layout that changes the look and flow of a presentation by providing text placeholders that do not contain bullet points.

Select To specify, by highlighting, a block of data or text on the screen with the intent of performing some action on the selection.

Select All box A box in the upper left corner of the worksheet grid that, when clicked, selects all the cells in a worksheet.

Select query A type of Access query that retrieves (selects) data from one or more tables or queries, displaying the selected data in a datasheet; also known as a simple select query.

Selecting Highlighting, by dragging with your mouse, areas of text or data or graphics, so that the selection can be edited, formatted, copied, or moved.

Series A group of things that come one after another in succession; for example, January, February, March, and so on.

Serif font A font design that includes small line extensions on the ends of the letters to guide the eye in reading from left to right.

Shape A line, arrow, star, banner, oval, rectangle, or other object with which you can illustrate an idea, a process, or a workflow.

SharePoint A Microsoft technology that enables employees in an organization to access information across organizational and geographic boundaries.

Sheet tab scrolling buttons Buttons to the left of the sheet tabs used to display Excel sheet tabs that are not in view; used when there are more sheet tabs than will display in the space provided.

Sheet tabs The labels along the lower border of the workbook window that identify each worksheet.

Short Text data type An Access data type that describes text, a combination of text and numbers, or numbers that are not used in calculations, such as the Postal Code.

Shortcut menu A menu that displays commands and options relevant to the selected text or object; also called a *context menu*.

Show Formulas A command that displays the formula in each cell instead of the resulting value.

Simple select query Another name for a select query.

Single-record form A form that enables you to display or enter one record at a time from a table.

Sizing handles Small circles surrounding a picture that indicate that the picture is selected.

Slide A presentation page that can contain text, pictures, tables, charts, and other multimedia or graphic objects.

Slide handout Printed images of slides on a sheet of paper.

Slide pane A PowerPoint screen element that displays a large image of the active slide.

Slide Sorter view A presentation view that displays thumbnails of all of the slides in a presentation.

Slide transitions Motion effects that occur in Slide Show view when you move from one slide to the next during a presentation.

SmartArt A designer-quality visual representation of your information that you can create by choosing from among many different layouts to effectively communicate your message or ideas.

Snap An action to arrange two or more open windows on your screen so that you can work with multiple screens at the same time.

Snip An image captured by the Snipping tool that can be annotated, saved, copied, or shared via email.

Snipping tool A Windows 10 program that captures an image of all or part of your computer's screen.

Source file When importing a file, refers to the file being imported.

Sparkline A tiny chart in the background of a cell that gives a visual trend summary alongside your data; makes a pattern more obvious.

Spin box A small box with an upward- and downward-pointing arrow that lets you move rapidly through a set of values by clicking.

Split button A button divided into two parts and in which clicking the main part of the button performs a command and clicking the arrow opens a menu with choices.

Spreadsheet Another name for a worksheet.

Start menu A Windows 10 menu that displays as a result of clicking the Start button and that displays a list of installed programs on the left and a customizable group of tiles on the right that can act as a user dashboard.

Status bar The area along the lower edge of the Excel window that displays, on the left side, the current cell mode, page number, and worksheet information; on the right side, when numerical data is selected, common calculations such as Sum and Average display.

Structure In Access, the underlying design of a table, including field names, data types, descriptions, and field properties.

Style A group of formatting commands, such as font, font size, font color, paragraph alignment, and line spacing that can be applied to a paragraph with one command.

Subfolder The term for a folder placed within another folder.

SUM function A predefined formula that adds all the numbers in a selected range of cells.

Switch Row/Column A charting command to swap the data over the axis—data being charted on the vertical axis will move to the horizontal axis and vice versa

Synchronization The process of updating computer files that are in two or more locations according to specific rules—also called *syncing*.

Syncing The process of updating computer files that are in two or more locations according to specific rules—also called *synchronization*.

System tray Another term for the notification area on the taskbar that displays notification icons and the system clock and calendar.

Tab stop A specific location on a line of text, marked on the Word ruler, to which you can move the insertion point by pressing the Tab key, and which is used to align and indent text.

Table (Access) A format for information that organizes and presents text and data in columns and rows; the foundation of a database.

Tables and Related Views An arrangement in the Navigation Pane that groups objects by the table to which they are related.

Tabs (ribbon) On the Office ribbon, the name of each activity area.

Tags Custom file properties in the form of words that you associate with a document to give an indication of the document's content; used to help find and organize files. Also called keywords.

Task View A taskbar button that displays your desktop background with small images of all open programs and apps and from which you can see and switch between open apps, including desktop apps.

Taskbar The bar at the bottom of your Windows screen that contains buttons to launch programs and buttons for all open apps.

Team A group of workers tasked with working together to solve a problem, make a decision, or create a work product.

Tell Me A search feature for Microsoft Office commands that you activate by typing what you are looking for in the Tell Me box.

Tell me more A prompt within a ScreenTip that opens the Office online Help system with explanations about how to perform the command referenced in the ScreenTip.

Template An existing document that you use as a starting point for a new document; it opens a copy of itself, unnamed, and then you use the structure—and possibly some content, such as headings—as the starting point for a new document.

Text alignment The horizontal placement of text within a placeholder.

Text box A movable resizable container for text or that you can position anywhere in an Office file.

Text effects Decorative formats, such as shadowed or mirrored text, text glow, 3-D effects, and colors that make text stand out.

Text pane A pane that displays to the left of a SmartArt graphic and is used to type text and edit text in a SmartArt graphic.

Text values Constant values consisting of only text, and which usually provide information about number values; also referred to as labels.

Text wrapping The manner in which text displays around an object.

Theme A predesigned combination of colors, fonts, and effects that look good together and that is applied to an entire document by a single selection.

Thumbnail A reduced image of a graphic.

Thumbnails (PowerPoint) Miniature images of presentation slides.

Tiles A group of square and rectangular boxes that display on the start menu.

Timeline A Windows 10 feature that when you click the Task view button, you can see activities you have worked on across your devices; for example, you can find a document, image, or video you worked on yesterday or a week ago.

Title bar The bar across the top of the window that displays the program, file, or app name.

Title slide A slide layout—most commonly the first slide in a presentation—that provides an introduction to the presentation topic.

Toggle button A button that can be turned on by clicking it once, and then turned off by clicking it again.

Toolbar A row, column, or block of buttons or icons that displays across the top of a window and that contains commands for tasks you perform with a single click.

Triple-click The action of clicking the left mouse button three times in rapid succession.

Truncated Data that is cut off or shortened because the field or column is not wide enough to display all of the data or the field size is too small to contain all of the data.

.txt file A simple file consisting of lines of text with no formatting that almost any computer can open and display.

Underlying formula The formula entered in a cell and visible only on the Formula Bar.

Underlying value The data that displays in the Formula Bar.

Undo On the Quick Access Toolbar, the command that reverses your last action.

Unzip The process of extracting files that have been compressed.

User account A user on a single computer.

Value Another name for a constant value.

Value axis A numerical scale on the left side of a chart that shows the range of numbers for the data points; also referred to as the Y-axis.

Variant A variation on the presentation theme style and color.

Wallpaper Another term for the Desktop background.

Window snip From the Snipping Tool, a command that captures the entire displayed window.

Windows 10 An operating system developed by Microsoft Corporation that works with mobile computing devices and also with traditional desktop and laptop PCs.

Wizard A feature in Microsoft Office that walks you step by step through a process.

Word wrap The feature that moves text from the right edge of a paragraph to the beginning of the next line as necessary to fit within the margins.

Workbook An Excel file that contains one or more worksheets.

Worksheet The primary document that you use in Excel to work with and store data, and which is formatted as a pattern of uniformly spaced horizontal and vertical lines.

Worksheet grid area A part of the Excel window that displays the columns and rows that intersect to form the worksheet's cells.

X-axis Another name for the horizontal (category) axis.

XML Paper Specification A Microsoft file format that creates an image of your document and that opens in the XPS viewer.

XPS The acronym for *XML Paper Specification*—a Microsoft file format that creates an image of your document and that opens in the XPS viewer.

Y-axis Another name for the vertical (value) axis.

Zip The process of compressing files.

Zoom The action of increasing or decreasing the size of the viewing area on the screen.

Index

creating folders, 87–88
Currency data type, 251
custom web app, 246
Customize Quick Access Toolbar, 20
cut, 32–36

D

dashboard, 51
data, 245
  defining, 46, 176
  displays of, 181
  entering by ranges, 206–207
  entering into worksheets, 176–182
  field creation by entering, 251
  importing from Excel workbooks, 254–257
data management, 47
data markers, 192
data points, 192
data series, 192
data source, 269
data types
  assigning to fields, 249–251
  AutoNumber, 252
  changing, 251–252
  Currency, 251
  defining, 250
  Number, 288
  Short Text, 250, 289
database management system (DBMS), 245
database template, 246
databases, 241, 245
  blank desktop, 246
  closing, 277
  creating from templates, 282–283
  design principles for, 246
  flat, 245
  planning, 245–246
  relational, 245
  starting with blank, 247–248
Datasheet view, 249
DBMS. See database management system
default, 12
deleting files, 87, 94
deselect, 18
Design Ideas pane, 334
Design view, 249
  deleting table fields in, 257–258
  viewing primary keys in, 260–261
desktop, 47, 52
desktop applications, 3
desktop apps, 3
  closing, 40–41
desktop backgrounds, 52, 53
desktop shortcuts, 82
destination tables, 255
Details pane, 76, 77
Details view, 87
Dialog Box Launcher, 34
dialog boxes, 6
  defining, 54, 80

elements of, 17, 81
  performing commands from, 15–17
Dictate feature, 44
Display settings, 48
displayed values, 181
Document Info, 37–38
document properties, 8, 37–38
  adding, 122–123
  for workbooks, 197
document settings, defaults, 106
documents
  activating Show/Hide in, 12
  blank, 5
  creating electronic images of, 41
  inspecting, 38
Documents folder, 82, 86, 87
dot leader, 142
double spacing, 130
double-click, 64
download
  defining, 10
  zipped files, 11–14, 65–66
drag, 13, 60
drawing objects, 108
drive, 54
Drop Shadow Rectangle style, 24

E

edit, 10
Edit Alt Text, 36
editing
  enabling, 11
  presentations, 327, 349–354
  slides, 331–333
  text, 11–14
Editor pane, 14–15
ellipsis, 16
Enable Editing, 11, 105
enhanced ScreenTips, 21
entering numbers, 181
entering text, 11–14
Error Checking, 210
Excel, 169
  pointer, 175
  starting, 173–176
  window parts, 174
  workbook window elements, 175
Expand Formula Bar button, 175
Expand horizontal scroll bar button, 174
exporting, tables to spreadsheets, 278–279
extract, 10
  with File Explorer, 73–74
  zipped files, 11–14, 65–66
Extract All, 11
Extract tab, 11

F

Facet theme, 323
Few, Stephen, 169
field properties, 260

fields, 246
  changing data types, 251–252
  changing size of, 259–260
  common, 246
  creating by entering data, 251
  data types and name assignment, 249–251
  deleting, 257–258
  ID, 251
  inserting in footers, 120–121
  renaming, 251
  setting size of, 251–252
  structure of, 249
File Explorer, 11, 52, 55
  copying and moving files by snapping windows in, 92–93
  copying files in, 89–90
  displaying locations, folders, and files with, 74–78
  extracting zipped files with, 73–74
  navigating with, 71–73
  OneDrive and, 54
  parts of window, 56–57
  searching, pinning, sorting, and filtering in, 84–85
  window parts, 73
  zipped folders in, 65
File Explorer window, 56
file list, 56, 58, 64, 73, 76, 87, 88
  All Files type in, 82
  quick access, 71
file name extension, 82s
file names, 64
  in footers, 37, 120–121
file properties, 76
File tab, 4, 6, 8
files, 6
  compressed, 10
  copying, 89–90
  copying and moving by snapping windows, 92–93
  copying from removable storage, 85–86
  creating and saving, 59–65
  creating folders for storing, 54–59
  defining, 54
  deleting, 87, 94
  displaying with File Explorer, 74–78
  moving, 90–91
  opening, 80–83
  renaming, 87–88
  saving after naming, 9
  selecting, 91
  zipped, 11–14
Fill Effects dialog box, 16
fill handles
  Auto Fill with, 178
  formula copying with, 184–185
Fill Series, 178
fills
  defining, 16
  gradient, 16
filtered lists, 85

text
  aligning, 177, 179–180, 357–358
  centering, 180
  color, 118
  copying, 32
  cutting, 32
  editing, 11–14
  entering, 11–14
  entering in worksheets, 176–177
  finding and replacing, 354
  formatting, 27–30
  formatting with Format Painter, 30–32
  formatting with text effects, 108
  indenting, 131–133
  inserting from another document, 107
  in list levels, 330
  presentation, 325–326
  typing in shapes, 117–118
  wrapping, in columns, 215–216
  wrapping around pictures, 110–111
text alignment, 357–358
text boxes, 116
  formatting, 119–120
  inserting, 118–119
  sizing and positioning, 119–120
text effects
  applying, 18–19
  formatting text with, 108
Text Effects and Typography gallery, 19
text values, 176
text wrapping, 22
  in columns, 215–216
  around pictures, 110–111
  settings for, 109
theme colors, 28
theme fonts, 28
themes
  applying to presentations, 326–327
  changing colors, 216–218
  colors, 28
  PowerPoint, 319
  presentations, 323
  variants, 354–355
  workbook, 188
This PC, 57, 71
3-D Models, 39
thumbnails, 68, 324
tiles, 56
  live, 51
Timeline, 69
Timing group, 362–363
title bars, 6, 66
title slides, 325
toggle buttons, 30, 137
toolbars, 9
touch screens
  accessing shortcut menus, 57
  accessing sign-in screen with, 50
  Snipping Tool and, 53–54
training videos, 44
transitions, 362
triple-click, 29

truncated, 260
.txt file, 82
typing errors, correcting, 253

U

underline, 29
underlying formulas, 183
underlying values, 181
undo, 18–19
unzip, 10
Up button, 57
USB flash drives, 54, 55, 58, 84
  deleting files and, 87
  searching and, 87
Use Alignment guides, 23
user accounts
  Office 365, 59
  signed-in, 6
  in Windows 10, 47–49

V

value axis, 191
values, 176
  displayed, 181
  editing in worksheets, 212–213
  underlying, 181
variants, 354–355
viewing reports, 291

W

wallpapers, 52
Weather app, 67, 68
web browsers, 11
window control buttons, 6
window snip, 62
windows, snapping, 92–93
Windows 10, 46
  Home version, 55
  lock screen, 50
  sign-in screen, 50–51
  user accounts in, 47–49
  variations in appearance, 49
  variations organization and
    functionality, 48
wizards, 256
  Import Spreadsheet Wizard, 256, 285
  Simple Query Wizard, 269–271
Word, 101
  opening files with, 80–83
Word documents
  aligning paragraphs, 128–130
  creating new, 105–106
  default document settings, 106
  indenting text, 131–133
  inserting, sizing, and positioning shapes,
    116–117
  inserting icons, 145–146
  inserting pictures, 109
  inserting SmartArt graphics in, 143–144

  inserting text from another, 107
  line spacing, 130–131
  lists, 134–139
  page borders, 115–116
  paragraph spacing, 133–134
  printing, 122–123
  setting margins, 127–128
Word files, opening, 80–83
word wrap, 106
WordPad Desktop app, 78
workbooks
  changing theme colors, 216–218
  defining, 173
  document properties for, 197
  importing data into Access tables from,
    254–257
  naming and saving, 173–176
  printing, 197
  themes, 188
  window elements for, 175
worksheets
  centering, 195–196
  defining, 173
  editing values in, 212–213
  entering data into, 176–182
  footers in, 195–196
  formatting, 214–218
  grid area, 174
  printing sections of, 198
  spellchecking, 204–206
wrapping text, 22
  in columns, 215–216
  around pictures, 110–111
  settings for, 109

X

x-axis, 191
XML Paper Specification, 41
XPS files, 41, 344

Y

y-axis, 191

Z

zip, 10
zipped files
  downloading and extracting, 11–14,
    65–66
  extracting with File Explorer, 73–74
zipped folders, 65
zoom, 25
zoom level
  changing, 25–26
  Page Width, 25–26
Zoom slider, 25–26